Postclassical Greek and Septuagint Lexicography

Septuagint and Cognate Studies

Martin Rösel, General Editor

Editorial Board:
Arie van der Kooij
Gideon R Kotze
Siegfried Kreuzer
Daniela Scialabba
Benjamin G. Wright III

Number 75

Postclassical Greek and Septuagint Lexicography

William A. Ross

 PRESS

Atlanta

Copyright © 2022 by William A. Ross

All rights reserved. No part of this work may be reproduced or transmitted in any form or by any means, electronic or mechanical, including photocopying and recording, or by means of any information storage or retrieval system, except as may be expressly permitted by the 1976 Copyright Act or in writing from the publisher. Requests for permission should be addressed in writing to the Rights and Permissions Office, SBL Press, 825 Houston Mill Road, Atlanta, GA 30329 USA.

Library of Congress Control Number: 2022934536

For Amos, Lucas, Samuel, and Phoebe
θαρσεῖτε

Contents

Acknowledgments ix
Abbreviations xi
Sigla xxiv
Tables and Figures xxv

1. Introduction 1

2. Septuagint Lexicography: Tracing the Hebrew-Priority
   Approach 17

3. "Who Shall Go Up First?" ΠΑΡΑΤΑΞΙΣ and ΠΑΡΑΤΑΣΣΩ 63

4. "For So the Young Men Used to Do": ΠΑΙΔΑΡΙΟΝ,
   ΠΑΙΔΙΟΝ, ΝΕΑΝΙΣΚΟΣ, and ΝΕΑΝΙΑΣ 113

5. "They Went up to Meet Them": ΑΠΑΝΤΑΩ,
   ΑΠΑΝΤΗΣΙΣ and ΣΥΝΑΝΤΑΩ, ΣΥΝΑΝΤΗΣΙΣ 163

6. General Conclusions 209

Appendix: Sample Lexical Entries 219

Bibliography 223
Ancient Sources Index 265
Modern Authors Index 271

Acknowledgments

This volume presents a slightly revised version of my doctoral thesis, completed between 2014 and 2018 at the University of Cambridge. As expected for such a task, I have benefited immensely from many forms of support and encouragement during that time, as well as in the intervening years.

I am immeasurably indebted to my supervisor, Dr. James (Jim) K. Aitken. Rarely have I known someone with such a level of mastery in his field who interacts with students with such charity and humor. Despite the serious personal challenges we each faced during the course of my studies, Jim nevertheless patiently shaped, challenged, and encouraged my thinking while always demonstrating rigorous scholarship to emulate. I am also deeply grateful to Dr. Peter (Pete) J. Williams for taking me on as temporary supervisor with such willingness and competence. Thank you both.

I also wish to express my gratitude to the Cambridge Trust for funding my doctoral research and, more importantly, for so willingly suspending (and then reinstating) it while I intermitted my studies to care for my family in late 2015. The Faculty of Divinity and Fitzwilliam College too have often granted funding to support my research in crucial ways, for which I am very appreciative. I would also like to thank Westminster Theological Seminary for the graduate fellowships granted consistently over six years, which have gone far in supporting my involvement in professional societies through travel and conferences. I am also appreciative to Reformed Theological Seminary for granting funding for the indexing of this volume, and to Ken McMullen for so capably completing the task.

Many colleagues also gave of their time and talent to help me along the way. John A. L. Lee, Trevor V. Evans, Patrick James, and Marieke Dhont rank among the most influential and generous. A similar note of thanks is due to the community at Tyndale House, not least of all to librarian Simon Sykes for his expertise and friendship. Even before my time at

Cambridge, James Mulroney, Fred Putnam, and Greg Beale did so much to enable and inspire me in academic work, for which I am immensely grateful. I also received much practical and theoretical assistance from both Srecko Koralija and Peter Montoro, to whom I am indebted. Thanks also go to my *viva* examiners as well as the anonymous reviewers for SBL Press's Septuagint and Cognate Studies series for their constructive comments.

This study, like so much else in life, has benefited from a wide array of friends and family members, too many to name. Of all these, none compare with my wife, Kelli. Your selflessness, joy, patience, and bravery underwrite everything I do as a husband, father, and scholar. If God is the rudder steering our life, then you must be the boat and I the blustering and sporadic wind. Onward, always together.

William A. Ross
αὐτῷ ἡ δόξα εἰς τοὺς αἰῶνας
Advent 2020

Abbreviations

AASF	Annales Academiae Scientiarum Fennicae
AII group	Subgroups KZgln(o)w and (d)ptv^2 (representative of Judg^{OG})
AB	Anchor Bible
AbrNSup	Abr-Nahrain Supplements
Ach.	Aristophanes, *Acharnenses*
Adul. amic.	Plutarch, *Quomodo adulator ab amico internoscatur*
Aeginet.	Isocrates, *Aegineticus* (Or. 7)
Aem.	Plutarch, *Aemilius Paullus*
Ag. Ap.	Joesphus, *Against Apion*
Ag. Cleom.	Plutarch, *Agis et Cleomenes*
Ages.	Plutarch, *Agesilaus*; Xenophon, *Agesilaus*
AJSL	American Journal of Semitic Languages and Literatures
Alex.	Plutarch, *Alexander*
Alex. fort.	Plutarch, *De Alexandri magni fortuna aut virtute*
An seni	Plutarch, *An seni respublica gerenda sit*
Anab.	Xenophon, *Anabasis*
AnBib	Analecta Biblica
Ann.	Tacitus, *Annales*
ANRW	Temporini, Hildegard, and Wolfgang Haase, eds. *Aufstieg und Niedergang der römischen Welt: Geschichte und Kultur Roms im Spiegel der neueren Forschung*. Part 2, *Principat*. Berlin: De Gruyter, 1972–.
Ant.	Josephus, *Jewish Antiquities*; Plutarch, *Antonius*
Ant. rom.	Dionysius of Halicarnassus, *Antiquitates romanae*
AP.F.B	Archiv für Papyrusforschung und verwandte Gebiete Beiheft
Arat.	Plutarch, *Aratus*
Archid.	Isocrates, *Archidamus* (Or. 6)
Arist.	Plutarch, *Aristedes*
Art.	Plutarch, *Artaxerxes*

Ath. pol.	Aristotle, *Athēnaīn politeia*
Att.	Cicero, *Epistulae ad Atticum*
BA	La Bible d'Alexandrie
BASP	*Bulletin of the American Society of Papyrologists*
BASPSup	*Bulletin of the American Society of Papyrologists Supplements*
BBR	*Bulletin for Biblical Research*
BCAW	Blackwell Companions to the Ancient World
BCH	*Bulletin de correspondance hellénique*
BECNT	Baker Exegetical Commentary on the New Testament
BETL	Bibliotheca Ephemeridum Theologicarum Lovaniensium
B group	Subgroups B(d)efjm(o)qsz and imrua$_2$ (representative of Judg^{Rv})
BGU	*Aegyptische Urkunden aus den Königlichen* [later *Staatlichen*] *Museen zu Berlin, Griechische Urkunden*. 15 vols. Berlin: Weidmann, 1895–1937.
BH	Biblical Hebrew
BHQ	Schenker, Adrian, et al., eds. *Biblia Hebraica Quinta*. Stuttgart: Deutsche Bibelgesellschaft, 2004–.
Bib	*Biblica*
BibInt	Biblical Interpretation Series
BIOSCS	*Bulletin of the International Organization for Septuagint and Cognate Studies*
BJGS	*Bulletin of Judeo-Greek Studies*
BNPSup	Brill's New Pauly Supplements
BSAH	Blackwell Sourcebooks in Ancient History
BT	*The Bible Translator*
BTS	Biblical Tools and Studies
Bus.	Isocrates, *Busiris* (*Or. 11*)
BZA	Beiträge zur Altertumskunde
BZAW	Beihefte zur Zeitschrift für die alttestamentliche Wissenschaft
BZNW	Beihefte zur Zeitschrift für die neutestamentliche Wissenschaft
Caes.	Plutarch, *Caesar*
Cam.	Plutarch, *Camillus*
Cat. Min.	Plutarch, *Cato Minor*
CATSS	Computer Assisted Tools for Septuagint Studies
Caus. plant.	Theophrastus, *De causiis plantarum*

CBET	Contributions to Biblical Exegesis and Theology
CCS	Cambridge Classical Studies
CDCH	Clines, David J. A., ed. *The Concise Dictionary of Classical Hebrew.* Sheffield: Sheffield Phoenix, 2009.
Chrest.Wilck.	Wilcken, Ulrich, ed. *Grundzüge und Chrestomathie der Papyruskunde.* 2 vols. in 4 parts. Leipzig: Teubner, 1912.
Cic.	Plutrach, *Cicero*
Cim.	Plutarch, *Cimon*
ClAnt	*Classical Antiquity*
ClR	*Classical Review*
CLR	Cognitive Linguistics Research
col.	column
Comp. Ages.	Plutarch, *Comparatio Agesilai et Pompeii*
Comp. Lys.	Plutarch, *Comparatio Lysius et Sullae*
Comp. Per.	Plutarch, *Comparatio Periclis et Fabii Maximi*
Cor.	Demosthenes, *De corona*
CPJ	Tcherikover, Victor A., and Alexander Fuks, eds. *Corpus Papyrorum Judaicarum.* 3 vols. Cambridge: Harvard University Press 1957–1964.
Crass.	Plutarch, *Crassus*
CrStHB	Critical Studies in the Hebrew Bible
CSL	Cambridge Studies in Linguistics
Ctes.	Aeschines, *In Ctesiphonem*
CTL	Cambridge Textbooks in Linguistics
CurBR	*Currents in Biblical Research*
Cyr.	Xenophon, *Cyropaedia*
DCH	Clines, David J. A., ed. *The Dictionary of Classical Hebrew.* 9 vols. Sheffield: Sheffield Phoenix, 1993–2014.
Deipn.	Athenaeus, *Deipnosophistae*
Dem.	Plutarch, *Demosthenes*
Demetr.	Plutarch, *Demetrius*
Demosth.	Dinarchus, *In Demosthenem*
Deo	Philo, *De Deo*
Det.	Philo, *Quod deterius potiori insidari soleat*
DGF	Chantraine, Pierre, and Louis Séchan, eds. *Dictionnaire Grec Français.* Rev. ed. Paris: Hachette, 1950.
Dion	Plutarch, *Dion*
DJD	Discoveries in the Judaean Desert
DSI	De Septuaginta Investigationes

EAGLL	Giannakis, Georgios K., ed. *Encyclopedia of Ancient Greek Language and Linguistics*. 3 vols. Leiden: Brill, 2014.
Ep. Her.	Epicurus, *Epistula ad Herodotum*
ETL	*Ephemerides Theologicae Lovanienses*
Eum.	Plutarch, *Eumenes*
ExpTim	*Expository Times*
Fab.	Plutarch, *Fabius Maximus*
FAT	Forschungen zum Alten Testament
Fayoum	Bernand, Étienne. *Recueil des inscriptions grecques du Fayoum*. 3 vols. Leiden: Brill, 1975–1981.
FF	Foundations and Facets
Flam.	Plutarch, *Titus Flamininus*
FNT	*Filología Neotestamentaria*
frag(s).	fragment(s)
Garr.	Plutarch, *De garrulitate*
GDI	Collitz, Hermann, and Friedrich Bechtel, eds. *Sammlung der griechischen Dialekt-Inschriften*. 4 vols. Göttingen: Vandenhoeck & Ruprecht, 1884–1915.
GELS	Muraoka, Takamitsu. *A Greek-English Lexicon of the Septuagint*. Leuven: Peeters, 2009.
Glor. Ath.	Plutarch, *De gloria Atheniensium*
GTS	Gettysburg Theological Studies
HALOT	Koehler, Ludwig, Walter Baumgartner, and Johann J. Stamm. *The Hebrew and Aramaic Lexicon of the Old Testament*. Translated and edited under the supervision of Mervyn E. J. Richardson. 4 vols. Leiden: Brill, 1994–1999.
HB	Hebrew Bible
HCS	Hellenistic Culture and Society
Hel. enc.	Isocrates, *Helenae encomium* (*Or.* 10)
Hell.	Xenophon, *Hellenica*
Hesperia	*Hesperia: The Journal of the American School of Classical Studies at Athens*
Hist.	*Historiae*
HRCS	Hatch, Edwin, and Henry A. Redpath. *Concordance to the Septuagint and Other Greek Versions of the Old Testament*. 2 vols. Oxford: Clarendon, 1897. 2nd ed. Grand Rapids: Baker, 1998.
HSK	Handbücher zur Sprach- und Kommunikationswissenschaft

HSM	Harvard Semitic Monographs
HTLS	Bons, Eberhard, ed. *Historical and Theological Lexicon of the Septuagint*. Tübingen: Mohr Siebeck, 2020–.
IAphMcCabe	McCabe, Donald F., ed. *Aphrodisias Inscriptions: Texts and Lists*. The Princeton Project on the Inscriptions of Anatolia, The Institute for Advanced Study, Princeton. Packard Humanities Institute CD 7, 1996.
Iasos	McCabe, Donald F., ed. *Iasos Inscriptions: Texts and List*. The Princeton Project on the Inscriptions of Anatolia, The Institute for Advanced Study, Princeton. Packard Humanities Institute CD 6, 1991.
IBubon	Schindler, Friedel, ed. *Die Inschriften von Bubon (Nordlykien)*. Österreichische Akademie der Wissenschaften. Philosophisch-historische Klasse. Sitzungsberichte 278.3. Vienna: Bohlaus, 1972.
ICC	International Critical Commentary
IDelos 6	Roussel, Pierre, and Marcel Launey, eds. *Inscriptions de Délos*. Vol. 6. Paris: Champion, 1937.
IEED	Leiden Indo-European Etymological Dictionary
IG 2	Kirchner, Johannes, ed. *Inscriptiones Atticae Euclidis anno posteriores*. 2nd ed. 4 vols. IG 2–3. Berlin: de Gruyter, 1913–1940.
IG 4.1	Gaertringen, Friedrich Hiller von, ed. *Inscriptiones Epidauri*. Fascicle 1 of *Inscriptiones Argolidis*. IG 4. 2nd ed. Berlin: de Gruyter, 1929.
IG 5.1	Kolbe, Walther, ed. *Inscriptiones Laconiae et Messeniae*. Fascicle 1 of *Inscriptiones Laconiae, Messeniae, Arcadiae*. IG 5. Berlin: Reimer, 1913.
IG 5.2	Gaertringen, Friedrich Hiller von, ed. *Inscriptiones Arcadiae*. Fascicle 2 of *Inscriptiones Laconiae, Messeniae, Arcadiae*. IG 5. Berlin: Reimer, 1913.
IG 7	Dittenberger, Wilhelm, ed. *Inscriptiones Megaridis, Oropiae, Boeotiae*. IG 7. Berlin: Reimer, 1892.
IG 9.1.1	Klaffenbach, Günther, ed. *Inscriptiones Aetoliae*. Fascicle 1 of *Inscriptiones Phocidis, Locridis, Aetoliae, Acarnaniae insularum Maris Ionii*. 2nd ed. Part 1 of *Inscriptiones Graeciae septentrionalis voluminibus VII et VIII non comprehensae*. IG 9. Berlin: de Gruyter, 1932.

IG 12.6	Hallof, Klaus, and Angelus P. Matthaiou, eds. *Inscriptiones Chii et Sami cum Corassiis Icariaque*. 2 parts. Fascicle 6 of Inscriptiones insularum maris Aegaei praeter Delum. IG 12. Berlin: de Gruyter, 2000–2003.
IG 12Sup	Gaertringen, Friedrich Hiller von, ed. *Supplementum*. Supplement to *Inscriptiones insularum maris Aegaei praeter Delum*. IG 12. Berlin: de Gruyter, 1939.
IIlon	Frisch, Peter, ed. *Die Inschriften von Ilion*. Inschriften griechischer Städte aus Kleinasien 3. Bonn: Habelt, 1975.
IMT Skam/ NebTäler	Barth, Matthias, and Josef Stauber, eds. *Inchriften Mysia und Troas*. Leopold Wenger Institut. Universität München. Version of 25.8.1993 (Ibycus). Packard Humanities Institute CD 7, 1996.
inf. cons.	infinitive construct
Inst. Lac.	Plutarch, *Instituta Laconica*
IOSCS	International Organization for Septuagint and Cognate Studies
IosPE 1	Latyshev, Basilius, ed. *Inscriptiones Tyriae, Olbiae, Chersonesi Tauricae*. Vol. 1 of *Inscriptiones antiquae orae septentrionalis Ponti Euxini graecae et latinae*. 2nd ed. St. Petersburg: Societatis Archaeologicae Imperii Russici, 1916.
IPergamon 1	Fränkel, Max, ed. *Bis zum Ende der Königszeit*. Vol. 1 of *Die Inschriften von Pergamon*. Altertümer von Pergamon 8.1. Berlin: Ulan, 1890.
IPriene	Gaertringen, Friedrich Hiller von, ed. *Inschriften von Priene*. Berlin: de Gruyter, 1906.
IPros.Pierre	Bernard, André, ed. *La Prose sur pierre dans l'Égypte hellénistique et romaine*. 2 vols. Paris: CNRS, 1992.
IScM 1	Pippidi, Dionisie M., ed. *Histria et vicinia*. Vol. 1 of *Inscriptiones Scythiae Minoris graecae et latinae*. Bucharest: Academiae Reipublicae Socialistae Romaniae, 1983.
IScM 2	Stoian, Iorgu, ed. *Tomis et territorium*. Vol. 2 of *Inscriptiones Scythiae Minoris graecae et latinae*. Bucharest: Academiae Reipublicae Socialistae Romaniae, 1987.
JBL	*Journal of Biblical Literature*
JHebS	*Journal of Hebrew Scriptures*
JJS	*Journal of Jewish Studies*
JNSL	*Journal of Northwest Semitic Languages*

JNSLSup	Journal of Northwest Semitic Languages Supplement Series
JRS	*Journal of Roman Studies*
JSCS	*Journal for Septuagint and Cognate Studies* (formerly *BIOSCS*)
JSJ	*Journal for the Study of Judaism*
JSJSup	Supplements to the Journal for the Study of Judaism
JSOT	*Journal for the Study of the Old Testament*
JSPSup	Journal for the Study of the Pseudepigrapha Supplement Series
JTS	*Journal of Theological Studies*
Judg	Hebrew text of Judges according to *BHQ*
Judg^A	Rahlfs-Hanhart A text of Greek Judges
Judg^B	Rahlfs-Hanhart B text of Greek Judges
Judg^{LXX}	Greek version of Judges in general or "Greek Judges"
Judg^{OG}	Reconstructed Old Greek translation of Judges (see AII group)
Judg^{Rv}	Revised text of Judg^{LXX} (See "B group")
J.W.	Josephus, *Jewish Wars*
LBW	Le Bas, Philippe, and William Henry Waddington, eds. *Inscriptions grecques et latines de la Syrie*. Paris: Didot, 1870. Repr. Hildesheim: Olms, 1972.
Leg.	Plato, *Leges*
LEH	Lust, Johann, Erik Eynikel, and Katrin Hauspie, eds. *Greek-English Lexicon of the Septuagint*. 3rd ed. Stuttgart: Deutsche Bibelgesellschaft, 2015.
Leoch.	Demosthenes, *Contra Leocharem*
Lex.	Photius, *Patriarchae Lexicon*
Lex. hom.	Apollonius, *Lexicon Homericum*
LHBOTS	Library of Hebrew Bible/Old Testament Studies
Life	Josephus, *The Life*
Lindos 2	Blinkenberg, Christian, ed. *Inscriptions*. Vol. 2 of *Lindos: Fouilles et recherches, 1902–1914*. 2 vols. Berlin: de Gruyter, 1941.
LLL	Longman Linguistics Library
LSJ	Liddell, Henry George, Robert Scott, and Henry Stuart Jones. *A Greek-English Lexicon*. 9th ed. with revised supplement. Oxford: Clarendon, 1996.
Luc.	Plutarch, *Lucullus*
Lyc.	Plutarch, *Lycurgus*

MAMA	Calder, W. M., et al., eds. *Monumenta Asiae Minoris Antiqua*. London: Manchester University Press; Longmans, Green, 1928–.
Mar.	Plutarch, *Marius*
Marc.	Plutarch, *Marcellus*
Meg.	Demosthenes, *Pro Megalopolitanis*
Metaph.	Aristotle, *Metaphysica*
MGS	Montanari, Franco. *The Brill Dictionary of Ancient Greek*. Edited by Madeleine Goh and Chad Schroeder. Leiden: Brill, 2015.
Mid.	Demosthenes, *In Midiam*
Migr.	Philo, *De migratione Abrahami*
MM	Moulton, James H., and George Milligan. *The Vocabulary of the Greek Testament Illustrated from the Papyri and Other Non-literary Sources*. London: Hodder & Stoughton, 1929.
Mor.	Plutarch, *Moralia*
MS(S)	manuscript(s)
MSU	Mitteilungen des Septuaginta-Unternehmens
MT	Masoretic Text
MtAthos	Duchesne, Louis, and Charles Bayet, eds. *Mémoire sur une mission au Mont Athos*. Paris: Thorin, 1876.
Mulier. virt.	Plutarch, *Mulierum virtutes*
NAC	New American Commentary
NETS	Pietersma, Albert, and Benjamin G. Wright, eds. *A New English Translation of the Septuagint*. 2nd ed. New York: Oxford University Press, 2009.
NewDocs	Horsley, G. H. R., et al., eds. *New Documents Illustrating Early Christianity*. North Ryde, NSW: The Ancient History Documentary Research Centre Macquarie University, 1981–.
NS	new series
NTOA	Novum Testamentum et Orbis Antiquus
NTS	*New Testament Studies*
Num.	Plutarch, *Numa*
OCT	Oxford Classical Texts
O.Did.	Cuvigny, Hélène, and Adam Bülow-Jacobsen, eds. *Les textes*. Vol. 2 of *Didymoi: Une garnison romaine dans le désert oriental d'Égypte*. Fouilles de l'IFAO 67. Cairo: Institut français d'archéologie orientale, 2012.

O.Krok. 1	Cuvigny, Hélène, ed. *La correspondance militaire et sa circulation: O. Krok 1–151.* Vol. 1 of *Ostraca de Krokodilô.* Cairo: Institut français d'archéologie orientale, 2005.
Od.	Homer, *Odyssey*
OG	Old Greek
OGIS	Dittenberger, Wilhelm, ed. *Orientis graeci inscriptiones selectae.* 2 vols. Leipzig: Hirzel, 1903–1905. Repr., Hildesheim: Olms, 1970.
Ol.	Pindar, *Olympionikai*
OL	Old Latin
Opif.	Philo, *De opificio mundi*
OTE	*Old Testament Essays*
Oth.	Plutarch, *Otho*
PAAJR	*Proceedings of the American Academy for Jewish Research*
P.Cair.Zen.	Edgar, Campbell Cowan, ed. *Zenon Papyri: Catalogue général des antiquités égyptiennes du Musée du Caire Nos.* 5 vols. Cairo: Institut français d'archéologie orientale, 1925–1940.
P.Col. 3	Westermann, William Linn, and Elisabeth Sayre Hasenoehrl, eds. *Zenon Papyri: Business Papers of the Third Century B.C. Dealing with Palestine and Egypt.* Vol. 1. Columbia Papyri Greek Series 3. New York: Columbia University Press, 1934.
P.Col. 4	Westermann, William Linn, C. W. Keyes, and H. Liebesny, eds. *Business Papers of the Third Century B.C. Dealing with Palestine and Egypt.* Vol. 1. Columbia Papyri Greek Series 4. New York: Columbia University Press, 1940.
P.Corn.	Westermann, William Linn, and Casper John Kraemer Jr., eds. *Greek Papyri in the Library of Cornell University Nos. 1–55.* New York: Columbia University Press, 1926.
P.Enteux.	Guéraud, Octave, ed. Εντευξεις: *Requêtes et plaintes adressées au Roi d'Égypte au IIIe siècle avant J.-C.* Cairo: Institut français d'archéologie orientale, 1931.
P.Giss.	Eger, Otto, Ernst Kornemann, and Paul M. Meyer, eds. *Griechische Papyri im Museum des oberhessischen Geschischtsvereins zu Giessen.* 3 parts. Leipzig: Teubner, 1910–1912.
P.Grenf. 1	Grenfell, Bernard P., ed. *An Alexandrian Erotic Fragment and Other Greek Papyri Chiefly Ptolemaic.* Oxford: Clarendon, 1896.

P.Hamb.	Meyer, Paul M., et al., eds. *Griechische Papyrusurkunden der Hamburger Staats- und Universitätsbibliothek*. 4 vols. Leipzig: Teubner, 1911–1998.
P.Heid. 6	Duttenhöffer, Ruth, ed. *Ptolemäische Urkunden aus der Heidelberger Papyrussammlung*. Vol. 6 of *Veröffentlichungen aus der Heidelberger Papyrussammlung*. Heidelberg: Winter, 1994.
P.Hib.	Grenfell, Bernard P., et al., eds. *The Hibeh Papyri*. 2 vols. London: Egypt Exploration Society, 1906–1955.
P.Iand.	Kalbfleisch, Karl, et al., eds. *Papyri Iandanae*. Leipzig: Teubner, 1912–1938.
P.Laur.	Pintaudi, Rosario, ed. *Dai Papiri della Biblioteca Medicea Laurenziana*. 4 vols. Firenze: Gonnelli, 1976–1983.
P.Leid.Inst.	Hoogendijk, Francisca A. J., and Peter van Minnen, eds. *Papyri, Ostraca, Parchments and Waxed Tablets in the Leiden Papyrological Institute*. Leiden, 1991.
P.Lille	Jouguet, Pierre, Paul Collart, Jean Lesquier, and Maurice Xoual, eds. *Papyrus grecs*. 2 vols. Lille: Institut Papyrologique de l'Université de Lille, 1907–1928.
P.Lond.	Kenyon, Frederic. G., et al., eds. *Greek Papyri in the British Museum*. 7 vols. London: British Museum, 1893–1974.
P.Mich. 1	Edgar, Campbell Cowan, ed. *Michigan Papyri: Zenon Papyri*. Ann Arbor: University of Michigan Press, 1931.
P.Mich. 18	Römer, Cornelia, and Traianos Gagos, eds. *Michigan Papyri: P.Michigan Koenen; Michigan Texts Published in Honor of Ludwig Koenen*. Amsterdam: Gieben, 1996.
P.Oxy.	Grenfell, Bernard P., et al., eds. *The Oxyrhynchus Papyri*. London: Egypt Exploration Fund, 1898–.
P.Petr.	Mahaffy, John P., and Josiah Gilbart Smyly, eds. *The Flinders Petrie Papyri*. 3 vols. Dublin: Academy House, 1891–1895.
P.Petr.Kleon	Beek, Bart van, ed. *The Archive of the Architektones Kleon and Theodoros (P. Petrie Kleon)*. Collectanea Hellenistica 7. Leuven: Peeters, 2017.
P.Polit.Iud.	Cowley, James M. S., and Klaus Maresch, eds. *Urkunden des Politeuma der Juden von Herakleopolis (144/3–133/2 v. Chr.) (P.Polit.Iud.)*. Papyrologica Coloniensia 29. Wiesbaden: Westdeutscher, 2001.
P.Princ. 3	Johnson, Allan Chester, and Sidney Pullman Goodrich, eds. *Papyri in the Princeton University Collections*. Princeton

University Studies in Papyrology 4. Princeton: Princeton University Press, 1942.

P.Ryl. Hunt, Arthur S., et al., eds. *Catalogue of the Greek and Latin Papyri in the John Rylands Library, Manchester.* 4 vols. Manchester: Manchester University Press, 1911–1952.

P.Sorb. 3 Clarysse, Willy, Hélène Cadell, and Kennokka Robic, eds. *Papyrus de la Sorbonne, nos. 70–144.* Papyrologica Parisina 1. Paris: Presses de l'Université Paris-Sorbonne, 2011.

P.Tarich Armoni, Charikleia, ed. *Das Archiv der Taricheuten Amenneus und Onnophris aus Tanis.* Leiden: Brill, 2013.

P.Tebt. Grenfell, Bernard P., et al., eds. *The Tebtunis Papyri.* London: Oxford University Press, 1902–.

P.Tor.Choach. Pestman, Pieter W., ed. *Il Processo di Hermias e altri documenti dell'archivio dei choachiti, papiri greci e demotici conservati a Torino e in altre collezioni d'Italia.* Catalogo del Museo Egizio di Torino 1.6. Turin: Ministero per i Beni Culturali e Ambientali, Soprintendenza al Museo delle Antichità Egizie, 1992.

P.Yale Oates, John F., et al., eds. *Yale Papyri in the Beinecke Rare Book and Manuscript Library.* 3 vols. New Haven: American Society of Papyrologists, 1967–2001.

P.Zen.Pestm. Pestman, Pieter W., ed. *Greek and Demotic Texts from the Zenon Archive.* Leiden: Brill, 1980.

Panath. Isocrates, *Panathenaicus* (*Or.* 12)
Paneg. Isocrates, *Panegyicus* (*Or.* 4)
Pel. Plutarch, *Pelopidas*
PFES Publications of the Finnish Exegetical Society
PGL Lampe, Geoffrey W. H., ed. *A Patristic Greek Lexicon.* Oxford: Clarendon, 1968.
Phil. Plutarch, *Philipoemen*
Philip. Demosthenes, *Philippica* (1–4)
Phoc. Plutarch, *Phocion*
Phis. Aristotle, *Physica*
Plat. Isocrates, *Plataicus* (*Or.* 14)
Pol. Aeneas Tacticus, *Poliorcetica*; Aristotle, *Politica*
Pomp. Plutarch, *Pompeius*
Post. Philo, *De posteritate Caini*
Praec. ger. Plutarch, *Praecepta gerendae rei publicae*
Praep. soph. Phrynichus, *Praeparatio sophistica*

prep.	preposition
PSI	Vitelli, Girolamo, et al., eds. *Papiri greci e latini*. Florence: Ariani, 1912–.
Pub.	Plutarch, *Publicola*
Pyrrh.	Plutarch, *Pyrrhus*
Quaest. conv.	Plutarch, *Questionum convivialum libri IX*
Quaest. rom.	Plutarch, *Quaestiones romanae et graecae* (*Aetia romana et graeca*)
REA	*Revue des études anciennes*
REG	*Revue des Études Grecques*
RelDis	*Religions and Discourse*
RevQ	*Revue de Qumran*
RFIC	*Rivista di Filologia e Istruzione Classica*
Rom.	Plutarch, *Romulus*
RSR	*Recherches de science religieuse*
SB	Preisigke, Friedrich, et al., eds. *Sammelbuch griechischer Urkunden aus Aegypten*. Wiesbaden: Harrassowitz, 1915–.
SBG	Studies in Biblical Greek
SCS	Septuagint and Cognate Studies
Se ipsum	Plutarch, *De se ipsum citra invidiam laudando*
Sef	*Sefarad*
SEG	Supplementum Epigraphicum Graecum
SIG	Dittengerger, Wilhelm, ed. *Sylloge inscriptionum graecarum*. 3rd ed. 4 vols. Leipzig: Hirzel, 1915–1924.
SNTS	Society for the Study of the New Testament
SNTSMS	Society for the Study of the New Testament Monograph Series
SNTW	Studies of the New Testament and Its World
Soll. an.	Plutarch, *De sollertia animalium*
Somn.	Philo, *De somniis*
Soph. elench.	Aristotle, *Sophistici elenchi* (*Top.* 9)
StHell	Studia Hellenistica
Sull.	Plutarch, *Sulla*
Superst.	Plutarch, *De superstitione*
SVTG	Septuaginta: Vetus Testamentum Graecum Auctoritate Academiae Scientiarum Gottingensis editum
TAM 2.1	Kalinka, Ernst, ed. *Pars Lyciae occidentalis cum Xantho oppido*. Fascicle 1 of *Tituli Lyciae linguis Graeca et Latina conscripti*. TAM 2. Vienna: Hoelder, 1920.

TAPA	*Transactions and Proceedings of the American Philological Association*
TBN	Themes in Biblical Narrative
TDNT	Kittel, Gerhard, and Gerhard Friedrich, eds. *Theological Dictionary of the New Testament*. Translated by Geoffrey W. Bromiley. 10 vols. Grand Rapids: Eerdmans, 1964–1976.
Text	*Textus*
Thes.	Plutarch, *Theseus*
Ti. C. Gracch.	Plutarch, *Tiberius et Caius Gracchus*
Tim.	Plutarch, *Timoleon*
TLG	*Thesaurus Linguae Graecae: A Digital Library of Greek Culture.* http://stephanus.tlg.uci.edu/.
TM	Trismegistos text number
Trag. frag.	Hunt, Arthur S. *Tragicorum graecorum fragmenta papyracea nuper reperta*. OCT. Oxford: Clarendon, 1912.
Tu. san.	Plutarch, *De tuenda sanitate praecepta*
UPZ	Wilcken, Ulrich, ed. *Urkunden der Ptolemäerzeit (ältere Funde)*. 2 vols. Berlin: de Gruyter, 1927–1957.
VT	*Vetus Testamentum*
VTSup	Supplements to Vetus Testamentum
WGRWSup	Writings of the Greco-Roman World Supplement Series
WUNT	Wissenschaftliche Untersuchungen zum Neuen Testament
YCS	Yale Classical Studies
ZAW	*Zeitschrift für die Alttestamentliche Wissenschaft*
ZPE	*Zeitschrift für Papyrologie und Epigraphik*
ZST	*Zeitschrift für systematische Theologie*

Sigla

—	epigraphical lacuna of uncertain length, may be enclosed with square brackets to combine with a partial word restoration
- ca.? -	traces illegible/vestiges of text
( )	modern editorial expansion of ancient abbreviation
(?)	indicates an uncertain translation
/ \	text written below the line in ancient text
:	separates variant readings in an ancient source
[ ]	modern editorial restoration of lacuna
[...]	uncertain reading
[[ ]]	characters deleted in antiquity
\ /	text written above the line in ancient text
|	line break in ancient text
< >	modern editorial emendation to ancient mistaken omission
vac.	space left empty in ancient source
αβγ	underdotted by modern editor to indicate characters ambiguous outside of context, damaged, illegible, or otherwise uncertain

Tables and Figures

Tables

1.1 Textual groups of Greek Judges	8
3.1. Judg^{LXX} *battle* vocabulary in Rahlfs-Hanhart	65
3.2. The underlying Hebrew *battle* vocabulary	65
3.3. The *battle* verbs in Judg^{LXX}	66
3.4. The *battle* nominals in Judg^{LXX}	70
3.5. Semantic distinction of ערך	72
3.6. ΠΑΡΑΤΑΣΣΩ and ΠΑΡΑΤΑΞΙΣ in current lexicons	74
3.7. Postclassical attestations of ΠΑΡΑΤΑΞΙΣ	84
4.1. Judg^{LXX} *young male* vocabulary in Rahlfs-Hanhart	115
4.2. The *young male* vocabulary in Judg^{LXX}	116
4.3. Select lexicon entries for *young male* vocabulary	123
4.4. Categories of *young male* vocabulary glosses	124
4.5. ΠΑΙΔΑΡΙΟΝ in Greek sources	127
4.6. ΝΕΑΝΙΣΚΟΣ in Greek sources	142
5.1. Judg^{LXX} *meeting* vocabulary in Rahlfs-Hanhart	165
5.2. The underlying Hebrew *meeting* vocabulary	166
5.3. The *meeting* vocabulary in Judg^{LXX}	167
5.4. Hebrew *meeting* vocabulary in Judges	175
5.5. Postclassical frequency of ΣΥΝΑΝΤΗΣΙΣ and ΣΥΝΑΝΤΑΩ	180
5.6. Postclassical frequency of ΑΠΑΝΤΗΣΙΣ and ΑΠΑΝΤΑΩ	187
5.7. *Meeting* vocabulary frequency	199

Figures

2.1. Entry for בֹּשֶׁם in Kircher's concordance	20
2.2. Entry for ζύμη in Aungier's concordance	27
2.3. Detail of entry for προφήτης from Tromm's concordance	29
2.4. Entry for ζεῦγος from Biel	31

2.5. Entry for ζεῦγος from Schleusner　　　　　　　　　31

1
Introduction

> It is well known to any one that ever perused the Septuagint, that they often translate word for word; though the phrase that results from it be against the genius of the Greek tongue.
> —Bentley, *A Dissertation upon the Epistles of Phalaris*

> To approach Koine Greek as a sort of debased Classical Greek is a serious mistake.
> —Lee, "The Vocabulary of the Septuagint and Documentary Evidence"

The language of the Septuagint has a mixed reputation. There are many reasons for this state of affairs. But in large measure it has arisen from the simple fact that the Septuagint is a diverse corpus of mostly translated texts, produced by many people in many places throughout the ancient Mediterranean world over an uncertain period of time. Differing scholarly assessments of the Greek found in the Septuagint understandably arise from perspectives that emphasize different aspects of the data and assess it against different standards.

As a result of this general state of affairs, the questions of first importance for evaluating the language of the Septuagint are: Which data and what standards? There is a long-standing tradition within biblical scholarship that views the degree of word-for-word correspondence to the source text as the data fundamental to evaluating the language of the Septuagint. This approach sets the Greek text constantly in relationship with its supposed Hebrew or Aramaic *Vorlage*—typically using MT—and examines the two together in terms of their grammatical alignment as a standard. Other scholars, however, frame the discussion in different terms, preferring instead to address the Septuagint first of all in light of its contemporary Greek linguistic milieu and only then to attempt to describe its language and style as a text.

The present study follows the second path. In so doing, I continue on in the routes trodden by many others, such as Adolf Deissmann, Henry St. John Thackeray, John A. L. Lee, Trevor V. Evans, and James K. Aitken. These scholars have repeatedly shown the importance of situating the language of the Septuagint within the broader history of Greek. From this perspective, the standard against which the language of the Septuagint is examined is found in the Greek linguistic milieu in which it was produced. Moreover, our knowledge of that milieu depends entirely upon the data offered by the surviving written sources from that era.

Yet as others have recognized and as is a central concern in this study, there are serious shortcomings in how the primary evidence for Greek has been handled in the reference works most commonly used among Septuagint scholars. Though the literary sources are themselves very relevant, of particular importance—and in regular neglect—is the nonliterary evidence for Greek found especially in the papyri and inscriptions. As difficult as they can be to navigate and decipher, these nonliterary sources preserve the variety of Greek closest to that most common throughout the Septuagint corpus. Because papyrology is such a vivacious discipline unto itself, more nonliterary sources are published each year. Yet, despite the widespread acknowledgement of its importance for Greek and Septuagint scholarship, the incorporation of this evidence into reference works has barely begun. It is true that the last decade has seen comparatively greater interest in Septuagint vocabulary, as is evident in new projects such as the ongoing *HTLS* and the publication of several related volumes.[1] But Septuagint lexicography as a whole remains remarkably underdeveloped, unsettled in method, and practically isolated from its broader postclassical Greek linguistic milieu.

The language of the Septuagint is the heart of this volume, specifically the interconnected challenges of lexical semantics and lexicography. This study sets out not only to draw attention to intramural debates and disciplinary shortcomings, but to contextualize them, to provide a constructive proposal for moving forward, and to demonstrate the validity and value of that proposal through textually based studies. To accomplish these tasks, I will focus on two key issues that bear certain conspicuous theoretical similarities. One key issue is the ongoing scholarly tendency to evaluate

---

1. Most significant here would be the volumes by Joosten and Bons (2011); Bons, Brucker, and Joosten (2014); and Bons, Joosten, and Hunziker-Rodewald (2015).

the language of the Septuagint from a lexical semantic perspective using the Hebrew Bible as a point of departure, a problematic approach that is deeply entangled with the history of biblical philology. Although in centuries past this approach was in some ways logistically justifiable, the burden of lexicographical research must now shift decisively in a Greek-oriented direction (as shown in ch. 2). Another key issue is to illustrate the benefits of analyzing stages in the textual development of the Septuagint in relation to broader language change in postclassical Greek. Similar to the tendency in lexical semantics just noted, Septuagint scholarship has typically evaluated Greek textual revisions primarily in terms of their relationship to the text of the Hebrew Bible. Although doing so is certainly appropriate, there is much to learn about the motivations for such revision and those who undertook it when the changes are also viewed as Greek linguistic phenomena (as shown in chs. 3–5). What connects these two issues—lexical semantics and textual revision—is the importance of handling the language of the Septuagint as part of the history of Greek at both practical and theoretical levels of lexicography.

The Textual History of Judges

The textual forum I have chosen for several case studies in Septuagint lexicography and postclassical Greek language change is the book of Judges. As explained in more detail below, because the book of Judges is a so-called double text in the textual history of the Septuagint, it offers a window into two distinct stages of the book. These two stages contain numerous instances of divergent vocabulary choices that reflect deliberateness in both original selection and subsequent change within the textual development of the book. The case studies in Greek Judges illustrate the practicalities and payoff of a Greek-oriented lexicographical method that situates the language of the Septuagint squarely within its contemporary historical and linguistic context.[2]

Though this study focuses almost exclusively upon Greek, it is important to highlight that that focus is possible in large measure thanks to the textual stability of the Hebrew tradition of Judges, to which we now turn our attention.

---

2. Evans (2010) provides an exemplar for this approach in the book of Tobit, one that first sparked my thinking for the present study.

Hebrew

The most up-to-date critical text of Judges in Hebrew is that of Natalio Fernández Marcos (2011) in the *BHQ* series, which will serve as the point of departure for all discussion in this study.[3] In terms of the textual history of the book in Hebrew, at a general level the MT of Judges appears on the basis of the available evidence to be very well-preserved, and therefore it "should be preferred over the variant readings of the versions or a good number of conjectures" (Fernández Marcos 2011, 5*). There is little variation between extant Hebrew textual witnesses, as is reflected in the *BHQ* apparatus, and the MT usually preserves "an acceptable/good/preferable text" (Tov 2012, 486). The Vulgate, Peshitta, and targum of Judges each appear to have had source texts very close to the MT, sometimes perhaps more so than that of the Greek version (Ausloos 2016, 277). The latter is a much more complicated case and is discussed below, but even so, many Greek variants appear to have arisen from haplography, parablepsis, assimilation, alternative vocalization, or explication (Fernández Marcos 2011, 8*).[4]

More significant than the versions for Hebrew textual history are the few but important witnesses discovered near the Dead Sea (see Lange 2016; Trebolle Barrera 2016a, 2016b). There are three fragments known from the Qumran site: 1QJudg (1Q6), 4QJudg^a (4Q49), and 4QJudg^b (4Q50).[5] There is broad agreement that 4Q50 and 1Q6 are very close to MT with only minor variants due mostly to haplography, orthography, and contextual assimilations (Fernández Marcos 2011, 6*; see also 2003). Scholars diverge more meaningfully in their evaluation of 4Q49 since it preserves the text of 6:2–13 with a minus at verses 7–10. As early as Julius Wellhausen, verses 7–10 had been viewed by some as a later editorial (Elohistic or Deuteronomistic) insertion purely on literary-critical grounds.

---

3. For a fairly recent survey of literature on the book of Judges in general, see Murphy (2017).

4. Satterthwaite (1991) also discusses theologically motivated variants.

5. A fourth manuscript known as XJudges also exists in seven privately owned fragments but is of unknown origin (see Fernández Marcos 2011, 5*–6*). It preserves just seventy-six complete or partial words, with no textual variants from MT (Lange 2016, 282–83). Later evidence for the Hebrew text of Judges from the Cairo Genizah was not collated in *BHQ* owing to its variants having been shown to postdate MT (Goshen-Gottstein 1976; Sanders 1999; Fernández Marcos 2006, 34).

So when 4Q49 was discovered in 1952 with precisely those verses missing, Julio Trebolle Barrera—who edited the fragment in the DJD series (1995)—argued that it preserves a shorter, earlier form of Judges (cf. 1989, esp. 239).[6] Since then others have followed suit (e.g., Tov 2002, 156; Ulrich 2008, 494; Rezetko 2013, 10–31; Ausloos 2014). Among those who have deemed 6:7–10 a plus, some have argued for a pre-Deuteronomistic monarchial setting for the insertion, while others favor a setting in the late Second Temple period.[7] On the contrary, many scholars argue instead that the variant in 4Q49 at 6:7–10 represents a minus, perhaps an instance of parablepsis (i.e., homoioarcton from -וי in 6:7 to -וי in 6:11) or abbreviation (see, e.g., Amit 1999; Block 1999; O'Connell 1996; Rofé 2011). Fernández Marcos (2003) has also argued that 4Q49 is too short a fragment to draw such a far-reaching conclusion about the literary development of the book of Judges (see also Hess 1997).

Whatever else might be said about the significance of 4Q49 for the textual history of Judges in Hebrew, it need not detain our attention here, as it does not in fact bear upon the present study in any major way. Even granting that Judg 6:7–10 represents an editorial insertion, it must have occurred early enough to have been present in the *Vorlage* of the Greek translator, who rendered it in his text just as one would expect on the basis of the reading in MT. In fact, Fernández Marcos (2011, 9*) finds that the original Greek translation (OG) was "a quite literal version of a text very similar, although not identical to MT."[8] Similarly, even granting that 4Q49 does represent a distinct literary version of Judges, that version was apparently either unknown to or of little concern among those who later revised the existing Greek version of Judges against a proto-MT text. In short,

---

6. Trebolle Barrera (2000, 455) also notes that six out of ten variant readings in 4Q49 do not align with either MT or LXX.

7. See Hendel and Joosten (2018, 57–58) for the former and Rezetko (2013) for the latter, both mounting arguments upon (theoretically opposed) historical linguistic grounds.

8. With this statement in view, Ausloos (2016, 278) suggests that more OG variants should therefore be "considered as witnesses to a different Hebrew *Vorlage*." However, Fernández Marcos (2011, 9*) immediately follows his statement by saying that the OG "was not as literal as it has been supposed by previous studies based on G^B [i.e., Judg^B], which has been corrected towards MT." On that note, it is important to recognize that, because a critical text of OG has not yet been produced, and thus no full studies of it undertaken, generalizing statements about the translation approach must be made (and/or read) with caution.

both the original translation of Judges into Greek and its later revision clearly worked with *Vorlagen* that were aligned with the otherwise stable and well-preserved tradition represented in MT (see Soggin 1981, 67–69; Fernández Marcos 2003, 15; Satterthwaite 2015, 102).[9]

Greek

The textual history of Greek Judges is far more complex. This complexity is itself striking in view of the apparent stability of the Hebrew textual tradition. But that stability is important insofar as it encourages the assumption of a (more or less) consistent source text behind the significant amount of divergence within the textual history of the Greek version.

Over the past two centuries, scholars have evaluated the divergence within the textual evidence for Greek Judges in various ways. Up through the end of the nineteenth century, most scholars presumed there was a single OG translation that was later revised (see Montalvo 1977, 7–10). This view seems to have influenced early scholarly editions of the Septuagint that appeared around the turn of the twentieth century, which printed either the text of the Alexandrinus (A) or Vaticanus (B) codices.[10] However, around that same period Paul de Lagarde (1891) postulated that these two texts actually derived from independent OG translations (see esp. 71–72; see also Moore 1895, 1912). Alfred Rahlfs also found the extensive difference between these codices in the text of Greek Judges difficult to reconcile, especially in chapter 5. Perhaps as a nod to his mentor Lagarde, when Rahlfs compiled his 1935 manual edition of the Septuagint he printed an eclectic text based on A in the upper part of the page (Judg^A) and one based on B in the lower part (Judg^B). Rahlfs's decision would prove influential for later scholarship, as A. V. Billen (1942), Paul Kahle (1959), and others continued to advance Lagarde's two-translation theory (see Ottley 1920, 22–23; Jellicoe 1968, 280–83; Fernández Marcos 2000, 94; Harlé 1995, 26).

---

9. Although opinion has fluctuated as to how the Greek tradition developed, as discussed below, no scholars have convincingly posited an alternative Hebrew version on that basis (Fernández Marcos 2003, 2). The exception to this rule may be Judg 5 (see Fernández Marcos 2011, 8*; Tov 2012, 487–88; Ausloos 2016, 278), which does not come under examination in this study, but see LaMontagne (2019).

10. Swete (1887) printed B, while Brooke and McLean (1897, 1917) printed A and, later, an eclectic text based on B.

A Single Old Greek Translation

While the issue was vigorously debated in the mid-twentieth century, scholars have now entirely abandoned Lagarde's view. Over the years, numerous studies have shown that the textual evidence for Greek Judges does not represent distinct translations, but rather a complex admixture of different stages and kinds of revision of a single OG text.[11] The first substantial defense of this view against the Lagardian double-translation thesis was Otto Pretzl (1926), who argued that it was impossible for the two text-types to represent independent translations in view of the high frequency with which they agree with one another against the Hebrew. Pretzl classified manuscript families into A and B types, the former of which having three groups (AI, AII, and AIII). Important refinements to these groups were then made by Ilmari Soisalon-Soininen (1951), who presented further evidence from syntax and vocabulary for a single OG translation. In addition to showing that there is Hexaplaric influence in all text groups, especially the A groups, Soisalon-Soininen demonstrated how the later revision to the (older) text(s) of Greek Judges tended to bring the text closer to a Hebrew exemplar very close or identical to MT (cf. Aejmelaeus 2020). A decade later, Dominique Barthélemy's landmark study of the Naḥal Ḥever scroll confirmed that the B text of Greek Judges reflects a Hebraizing revision and also took the critical step of connecting that revisional work to the kaige phenomenon (1963, esp. 34–5, 47).[12]

The work of Walter Bodine (1980) carried forward the conclusions of Soisalon-Soininen and Barthélemy and led to important developments. First of all, Bodine identified, on the one hand, how the B group does indeed clearly stand within the kaige revision. Yet Bodine—aware that kaige was a tradition or movement, rather than a singular phenomenon—also showed the "peculiarities" of the B group with respect to other kaige texts that made it distinct (67).[13] Second, and more central to the present

---

11. See the surveys in Harlé and Roqueplo (1999, 25–27); Satterthwaite (2015, 102–5); Dogniez (2016); and LaMontagne (2019, 15–20).

12. By this time, Schreiner (1957, 1961a, 1961b) considered Soisalon-Soininen's conclusions concerning the single OG translation theory to be fully established.

13. More recently, Karrer (2012, 605) has also classified the extant text of Greek Judges from Sinaiticus (S) as "a second main witness for the 'kaige'-text."

purposes, Bodine further refined the witnesses in the textual groups (and subgroups), which are given in table 1.1.[14]

Table 1.1. Textual groups of Greek Judges

AI	AGabckx
AII	KZgln(o)w + (d)ptv$_2$
AIII	MNhyb$_2$
B	B(d)efjm(o)qsz + imrua$_2$

The last few decades of scholarship has identified the AII group in particular (the so-called Antiochene/Lucianic text) as the best witness to the OG text of Judges, particularly when supported by the pre-Hexaplaric Old Latin version (Bodine 1980, 134–36; Lindars 1987; Dorival, Harl, and Munnich 1988, 175; Trebolle Barrera 1989, 1991, 2005; Fernández Marcos 2011, 7*). Still greater clarity concerning the textual history of Greek Judges has come from the studies published by José Manuel Cañas Reíllo as he has labored since 2013 to compile the Göttingen edition for the book. Having collated the evidence, including some new manuscripts, Cañas Reíllo (2020a, 546–47) has found enough "new data to corroborate the idea of a single original text" and to "dismantle" the notion of a double-translation. The most up-to-date refinements of the textual groups have now been published be Cañas Reíllo (2020b).

Before saying more about the revision to the OG text of Judges, it is worth addressing several doctoral dissertations that have advanced the two-translation theory of Greek Judges in some way.[15] Although their work remains unpublished, both John Ludlum (1957) and David Montalvo (1977) advance their arguments based on the divergent vocabulary of Greek Judges, which of course comes under close consideration in this study. Their basic argument is that, if lexical differences between the two

---

14. These manuscript sigla conform to those employed in the Cambridge larger Septuagint (see Brooke and Mclean 1906, v–vii) rather than the numerical sigla employed in Rahlfs and the Göttingen edition. On the latter, see Rahlfs (1914, 2004). For comparative tables, now slightly out of date, see Jellicoe (1968, 360–69). For the full list of manuscripts and editions currently being collated for the Göttingen edition of Judges, see Cañas Reíllo (2020b, 177).

15. Notably, Tov (2012, 484) also considers the evidence for the two-translation view "very strong," although he does not expand on this statement.

texts of Greek Judges exist without any discernable distinction in meaning between the readings, then they likely did not arise from revision—which necessarily implies improvement—but point toward distinct translations (see LaMontagne 2016, 50–51). But there are flaws in this approach. First, while improvement of some kind is of course inherent in the very notion of revision, it is problematic to assume that our notions of improvement match those of the revisers themselves or that their work was unidimensional in this respect. Second, the means by which Ludlum and Montalvo adjudicate distinction in meaning between words (and thus discern the possibility of "improvement") is far from satisfactory. Montalvo, for one, relies heavily upon *TDNT* and an earlier doctoral thesis by Charles Cooper (1941), who in his own lexical analysis relied entirely upon the ninth edition of LSJ (1940) and an edition of Hesychius's fifth-century CE lexicon by Mauricius Schmidt (1858–1868; see Montalvo 1977, 68–127). Taken together, these reference works omit any meaningful incorporation of the lexical evidence from the postclassical period of Greek that is most relevant to understanding Septuagint vocabulary, as discussed further in chapter 2. Moreover, as shown repeatedly throughout this study, it is evaluating the language of the Septuagint against precisely such evidence that facilitates discerning much finer linguistic subtleties, such as semantic change or distinctions in register, which in part motivated revisional efforts in Greek Judges, as we will see. Indeed, Septuagint lexicography that gives pride of place to contemporary literary and nonliterary sources—and is attentive to the social context—is able to provide enough detail about lexical use and meaning to explain the divergent vocabulary in Greek Judges as sensible and skilled revision of an earlier Greek text, rather than as representing separate translation efforts.[16]

---

16. Much more recently, LaMontagne (2016) advanced the argument that OG and the B group represent independent translations, evidently building upon his 2013 doctoral dissertation. However, the 2019 published version of LaMontagne's dissertation backs away significantly from this two-translation thesis, evidently owing to awareness at some level of Cañas Reíllo's work on the Göttingen edition. Compare, for example, the dissertation (2013, 30), where the study of Judg 5 is framed as diagnostic for the entire book, with the published version (2019, 21), where LaMontagne states that his aim is instead "to clarify the relationship between the texts [of Greek Judges] in light of the emerging agreement that the Song of Deborah demonstrates evidence of two translations, *even if it is believed that only one translation was made of the rest of Judges*" (emphasis added). Unfortunately, LaMontagne does not interact with the work of Cañas Reíllo at all, who in his own work has concluded that even Judg 5, with

An Intentional (Egyptian?) Revision to OG

Scholarship is now in a position to conclude that, despite its complexity, the manuscript evidence for Greek Judges attests two distinct stages in its textual history that may be realistically reconstructed and therefore studied. One stage is, of course, the OG text (Judg^{OG}) already discussed, as represented by the AII group of witnesses in table 1.1. The other stage is the revised version of Judg^{OG} as represented in the B group of witnesses (Judg^{Rv}). In this connection, Fernández Marcos (2012, 161) speaks in general terms of a double process in the textual transmission of the Historical Books in Greek: the initial production of the OG translation followed by a revision that shares tendencies with the kaige movement (cf. Fernández Marcos and Spottorno Díaz-Caro 2011, 13–15). This process is most visible, in Fernández Marcos's (2012, 163) estimation, in the textual history of Greek Judges, within which the B group "has been submitted to a conscious revision of the Old Greek in closer conformity with the Hebrew."

The basic characteristics of the B group include not only its relationship to the kaige movement but also peculiarities in vocabulary choice, a Hebrew source text closer to MT than that of non-B group witnesses, and the presence of doublets due to Hexaplaric influence (see Sáenz-Badillos 1973; Targarona Borrás 1983a). The most recent textual collation by Cañas Reíllo (2020b, 177–80) has subdivided the B group into two parts, one of which more clearly reflects a "compact group" that is very consistent in its distinctive vocabulary choice (B^1), while the other has some interference from other groups (B^2). As such, the B group as a whole should be understood as manifesting a "set of revisional processes" that likely began as an intentional effort that is perhaps better visible in the B^1 subgroup (Cañas Reíllo 2020a, 548; 2020b, 179).

Since no Göttingen edition of Greek Judges yet exists, the manuscript support for any given reading in either the OG or revised stage must be compiled on a case-by-case basis using the edition of Brooke and McLean (1917). In the chapters that follow, the texts of OG Judges that I provide are the product of my own text-critical reconstruction and, to avoid any ambiguity, are labeled accordingly. Two comments are necessary at this point. First, while in most cases the textual support is clear, some of my reconstructions

---

its additional complexity, does not stem from two independent translations (Cañas Reíllo 2020b, 177).

could be disputed and will most likely be clarified by further evidence once the Göttingen edition is complete. Second, while this study builds upon the text-critical scholarship described above, I make no systematic attempt here to refine text-critical scholarship in Greek Judges. As a final note, of very great importance to the present lexical study is the fact that *all* the textual data for the revised text of Greek Judges point to an Egyptian provenance. Those data include the Coptic and Old Latin versions, as well as the oldest direct witness to Greek Judges, a third-century CE papyrus (PSI 2.127 [TM 62071]) found at Oxyrhynchus (Cañas Reíllo 2016).[17]

Other Aspects of Greek Judges

Much else could be said about Greek Judges, but only a few comments are necessary here. First, scholarly discussion of translation technique in the book is often clouded by ambiguity over which text-historical stage is in view or the process by which it came about. Often the A or B codices—or Rahlfs's eclectic A or B texts—are discussed as if they represent a unified translation effort, one that is typically characterized as highly "literalistic" (e.g., Dogniez 2016, 296).[18] But any study of translation technique must be based on a critical reconstruction of an OG text (Satterthwaite 2015, 102; see, e.g., Trebolle Barrera 2008). Given the difficulty of this task for Greek Judges, scholarship has made only modest progress in this regard. In several studies conducted with these text-critical concerns in mind, Fernández Marcos (2003, 14–15) has characterized Judg^{OG} as an

> expansive text full of small additions (subjects, complements, pronouns) in order to clarify the meaning, with frequent doublets and some freedom in the word order and rearrangement of the verse, along with some light stylistic corrections.… In sum, the most ancient text attainable for the Greek translation of Judges is a relatively free translation compared with the text of *Vaticanus*.[19]

---

17. Also designated Rahlfs 968.
18. Sipilä (1999) purports to present a study of translation technique based on Judg^A. In his conclusion he states that his analysis "fits" the classification of Greek Judges by Thackeray (1909, 13) as a "literal or unintelligent" translation, when in fact Thackeray was referring to the B text (Sipilä 1999, 200). Similarly, Sollamo (1979, 286–87) categorizes Greek Judges as one of the "most slavish" translations but bases this evaluation upon analysis of Judg^A and Judg^B. See also Soisalon-Soininen (1951, 48).
19. Cf. Fernández Marcos (2006, 2010, 2012, 2014).

Others have described the characteristics of the OG translation as: "beaucoup moins littéraliste que A et B, une tendance à l'amplification par doublets allant parfois jusqu'à des développements d'allure targumique, et parfois une compréhension plus fine de la syntaxe hébraïque" (Harlé and Roqueplo 1999, 28). In this connection, it is necessary to recognize that the style and language of Judg^OG as a translation has not been studied in depth and thus is still not at all well understood.

Another important aspect of Greek Judges that scholars have noted takes pride of place in this study: its vocabulary. Numerous scholars have noticed the lexical differences between Judg^A and Judg^B, many of which are fairly consistent. For example, Judg^B tends to preserve ἐγώ εἰμι corresponding to אנכי (MT), ῥομφαία rather than μάχαιρα (Judg^A), Φυλιστιίμ rather than ἀλλόφυλλοι (Judg^A), βλέπω rather than ὁράω (Judg^A), θέλω rather than βούλομαι (Judg^A), ὄνος rather than ὑποζύγιον (Judg^A), and αὐλίζω corresponding to לין (MT) rather than καταλύω, ὑπνόω, or καταπαύω (Judg^A).[20] As mentioned, scholarship has recognized the similarity of many of these choices to the preferences apparent in other kaige-related texts. Yet many of the differences in vocabulary in the B group (Judg^Rv) compared to Judg^OG cannot be explained on the basis of a Hebraizing tendency. That is, the motivation for these changes seems to be stylistic in nature and thus intertwined with the development of the Greek language and the social context of those who produced and read the revised text (Fernández Marcos 2012, 169). In this sense, the complicated textual situation in Greek Judges is not a drawback, but an opportunity. Deissmann (1901, 73 n. 3) pointed out that "knowledge of the lexical conditions is itself a preliminary condition of textual criticism." To understand the phenomena of language change in Greek Judges that was not motivated by the underlying Hebrew exemplar, then, its vocabulary must be situated within the history of Greek as a language and its cultural environment.

Method, Tools, and Terms

The basic method of this study was established almost forty years ago by Lee (1983). By means of thorough examination of Hellenistic papyri, Lee demonstrated that the language of the Greek Pentateuch is essentially that

---

20. These, among others, are noted in Fernández Marcos (2012). See also Harlé and Roqueplo (1999, 53–69) and Cañas Reíllo (2020a, 2020b).

of its own time.[21] While his conclusions have been widely accepted, very little has occurred over the intervening years to carry forward his method (see Lee 2003b).[22] That is not to say, however, that the importance of nonliterary Greek sources for understanding the Septuagint has not been repeatedly confirmed. Nor has the near total absence of these sources from current lexicons been denied.[23] Both points are duly acknowledged and are addressed in more detail in the next chapter.[24] This study thus joins the more recent investigations of Septuagint vocabulary that reinforce Lee's conclusions, but with emphasis upon the theory and practice necessary to carry it forward for Septuagint lexicography.

The variety of Greek that appears in the Septuagint corpus is postclassical and largely nonliterary. Note, however, that nonliterary does not necessarily mean uneducated per se, but rather that the variety of language generally attested in the Septuagint differs functionally from that of Greek literature in register.[25] So while Greek literature from the Hellenistic and early Roman periods is often useful as a point of contrast, the nonliterary evidence found in papyri and inscriptions is of indispensable relevance to the Septuagint. In this study I refer to the language in and around the Septuagint corpus as postclassical Greek, by which I mean the historical phase of the Greek language that arose in the Hellenistic era and was used in a number of varieties beginning in the early third century and that endured and developed through the early Byzantine period (see Bubenik 2014). While more typical terms for this phase of the language are "Koine" or "Hellenistic" Greek, both have problems that are better avoided, as is the ambiguous phrase "Septuagint Greek" for related reasons.[26] In reality, the

---

21. See esp. 145. This was an important project since, in the 1960s, the notion of "Jewish Greek" was gaining in popularity, as discussed in ch. 2 below.

22. Evans (2010) has pointed to the promise of this line of research and developed Lee's approach for dating Septuagint texts based on external linguistic evidence. Elsewhere I (Ross 2016) have expanded on Lee's study of ὁράω and βλέπω and found his conclusions remain sound in light of new evidence. See also Lee (2018).

23. Lee (2016, 104) states that "a lexicon or extended treatment of the Koine Greek vocabulary is non-existent." See also Lee (2004b, 67).

24. Also see Horsley (1984, 1989), Lee (2003b, 2004b, 2016), Dines (2004, 114), Evans (2005), and Aitken (1999, 2014a, 2014b, 2014c, 2016).

25. "Register" defines a variety of language as a set of characteristics germane to the situational framework in which it is used. See Willi (2010) and Biber and Conrad (2009, 6–15).

26. "Hellenistic" Greek is inaccurate, since postclassical Greek was used all the

sources for postclassical Greek attest a wide variety of genres, registers, and styles that are best encapsulated by a broad and neutral term (Horrocks 2014, 88–123; Hanson 2015).

The fundamental assumption for Septuagint lexicography must therefore be the necessity of evaluating these diverse Greek sources afresh to understand word meaning (Aitken 2014b, 14). Only in so doing is it possible to obtain an accurate picture of how vocabulary was used according to the linguistic conventions contemporary to the production and revision of the Septuagint.[27] In this connection, owing to the general timeline within which scholars agree the Septuagint was likely produced, my lexical analysis is limited to sources dated to the third century BCE through the second century CE. A wealth of tools is available in both print and digital formats that, while not making lexical semantic analysis less challenging in itself, certainly facilitate access to and collection of the relevant data.[28] I have made constant use of these tools in my analyses and focused in my presentation of the data on the most reliable and illustrative sources.[29] The problems in citing nonliterary sources are well known, so I have used Trismegistos reference numbers wherever possible, which are enclosed in square brackets.[30]

---

way through the late Roman era. "Koine" Greek is sometimes considered uniformly vernacular or otherwise unsophisticated, which confuses the historical phase of a language with issues of register and language standards (cf. Dines 2004, 112–13). For example, Gibson and Campbell (2017, 2) incorrectly define what they call "Koine ('common') Greek" as "the language of the street." On the questionable value of the phrase "Biblical Greek," see Janse (2007, 647); on the related problem of "Septuagint Greek," see Ross (forthcoming).

27. By "linguistic conventions" or "conventional" use, I am referring to the norms of linguistic behavior in a particular linguistic community, including lexical forms, grammatical patterns, and discourse strategies (Evans 2007, 49–50; cf. Langacker 2013, 227). The term *conventional* provides a more linguistically informed and value-neutral way of talking about what others often call "normal" or "natural" or "standard" Greek.

28. The pertinent reference works and online databases are described by Van der Meer (2011, 65–69), Aitken (2014b, 7–11, 34–38), Pantelia (2014a), Ross (2016, 345 n. 13), Lee (2016, 103–5), and Reggiani (2017).

29. Frequency statistics from one research tool are not always reliable, so I have cross-referenced figures gleaned using different tools and often tallied occurrences myself, but my totals may differ slightly from those of others. I have excluded from my statistics and analyses most fragmentary literature, scholia, and Aesop. For nonliterary evidence I include only sources that are dated and in which the attestation of a word is unambiguous (i.e., not fragmentary).

30. On which see Aitken (2014b, 38) and Depauw and Gheldof (2014). I have

In dealing with this variety of sources, my approach to lexicography is rigorously evidence-based and thus focused on language in use, but with contemporary influences upon semantic analysis. My theoretical approach is informed by cognitive functional linguistics (see Taylor 2003; Cruse 2011; Geeraerts 2015; and Kroeger 2018). From this perspective, content words do not refer immediately to objects in the external world. Rather, words are associated with conceptual categories formed by embodied interaction with the external world. Words are of course *used* to refer to the external world, but the reason they are so used is because a given entity is being identified at the moment of the utterance as a member of a certain conceptual category. Throughout my lexical analysis I will identify these conceptual categories simply as "concepts" and use italic font to denote them. Where a word has more than one conceptual association, it is considered polysemous and for lexicographical purposes is attributed the corresponding number of senses in its entry. Those concepts/senses of the word each receive a definition as a description of their meaning, and that definition is also designated with italic font.[31] Finally, my approach to the practical aspects of lexicography—the details of actually collecting and reporting data—is fairly traditional with one significant exception. As already indicated, I use definitions to describe the senses of a given lexical item, in the tradition of the *Oxford English Dictionary*, rather than the gloss method that is described in chapter 2. To demonstrate the results of this approach I have created sample lexical entries for several of the words examined in this study, which are presented in the appendix.

The Plan of This Study

To address the ongoing problems and challenges in Septuagint lexicography as a discipline, it is necessary first to understand its place within the history of scholarship. Therefore, chapter 2 surveys the discipline and its surrounding discussion from the early seventeenth century to the present. This survey highlights how study of the language of the Septuagint has from its inception been almost totally severed from the study of Greek in general and points to the urgent need for change. The following

---

otherwise referred to papyri following Oates et al. (2001) and cite inscriptions as far as possible using Horsley and Lee (1994), supplemented with McLean (2002).

31. In general, I have used less technical language in speaking about linguistic meaning and have kept most theoretical discussion confined to footnotes.

three chapters then offer case studies from Greek Judges to illustrate a Greek-oriented method of lexical semantic analysis and its benefits. Each presents an examination of words used consistently in Judg[OG] that are in turn consistently replaced in Judg[Rv] with alternatives. The vocabulary in these case studies are content words that were selected for analysis on the basis of their relatively higher frequency in the book and the consistency with which they were at first used and later revised. Each chapter first explains the nature of the difference in vocabulary selection between the Judg[OG] and Judg[Rv] before moving on to lexical analysis of the relevant vocabulary in postclassical Greek sources. Each chapter also concludes by pointing to implications for Septuagint lexicography, the multifaceted motivations underlying the revision of Judg[OG], and the value of Septuagint vocabulary as evidence for Greek lexicography in general. Chapter 6 offers general conclusions.

This approach to studying the language of the Septuagint is innovative within the discipline as it currently exists, as stages in the transmission of a single book are evaluated here primarily as linguistically motivated and not merely text-critical. That is, this study gives virtually exclusive attention to evaluating the transmission of a Septuagint text as embedded within the broader context of postclassical Greek and its development, rather than to scrutinizing the correspondence of the constituents of that Greek text to a purported Hebrew source text. While there is certainly profit in the latter, the time has come—as the next chapter demonstrates—for far greater energy to be directed to the former. It is precisely because textual evidence encourages the assumption of a stable *Vorlage* for Judges that vocabulary change in the stages of the Septuagint version can be understood as part of the history of Greek, an attitude that must constitute the point of departure in all further lexicography for the corpus.

2

Septuagint Lexicography:
Tracing the Hebrew-Priority Approach

> Particularly for the Septuagint Lexicon the inscriptions and papyri are of the very greatest importance.
> —Deissmann, "The Philology of the Greek Bible: Its Present and Future"

> It is difficult to exaggerate how much outstanding work remains in the lexicography of the Septuagint.
> —Aitken, *No Stone Unturned*

The progress made in Septuagint lexicography over the past few decades is the culmination of a long, if sparse history. Although recent advances have been made, the discipline remains tangled among challenges and debates inherited from the philological practices and linguistic theories of centuries past. But understanding how those entanglements arose and how scholars have (or have not) addressed them helps identify the way forward. The heart of lexicography is evidence. Accordingly, this history will highlight changes in the kind and quantity of evidence for postclassical Greek, the methods with which it has been handled, and the shifting evaluations of the language of the Septuagint that have developed as a result. Doing so situates what I call a Greek-priority view within the history of scholarship and provides a rationale for the lexicographical method demonstrated in the case studies presented in the following chapters.

Septuagint Lexicography before the Twentieth Century

Septuagint lexicography prior to the twentieth century was severely flawed but has had lasting effects in both method and mindset. The main problems lie in how linguistic meaning was derived, expressed, documented, and transmitted in early reference works. As shown below, the foundations of Septuagint lexicography were laid upon the unstable terrain of early modern Bible concordances. The concordance is a natural stepping-stone toward a lexicon, since one needs to know not only which words to include, but also where to find all instances of a given word to document and express its meaning.[1] A Bible concordance, however, is only as useful for this task as its base texts are reliable. Still, early modern concordances conveniently offered later Septuagint lexicographers the practical benefit of one or two Latin translation equivalents—or glosses— of Greek words, and for centuries scholars were satisfied that these glosses sufficiently expressed lexical meaning. But viewed through the lens of linguistic theory, such an approach erroneously conflates lexical *correspondence* in translation with lexical *meaning* in different languages. Equally problematic in early philological reference works was the notion that the information that could be drawn from biblical texts and versions needed no external evidence to document (and thus support) the purported meaning of Greek words. This general approach persisted largely unscrutinized, and the glosses and references passed from one generation of scholars to the next. As that happened, early Septuagint lexicographers steadily accumulated data that was in fact textual—and problematically so—rather than linguistic in nature.

The Lost Concordance of Euthalius of Rhodes (ca. 1300)

The Dominican scholar Sixtus Senensis (1520–1569) referred to the work of a certain Basilian monk named Euthalius of Rhodes, who prepared a concordance of the Old and New Testaments in Greek around 1300 (see Le Long 1723, 1:456; Bindseil 1867, lii; Kraft and Tov 1998, xi). This concordance is the first such effort known, although the manuscript is now lost (Kraft and Tov 1998, xi n. 2).[2] It is uncertain what textual basis Euthalius might have used, as complete codices were rare in the medieval Christian

---

1. Medieval Greek scholarship also relied upon glossaries and wordlists, with the first known interlinear Bibles produced in ninth century Ireland (Herren 2015; Dionisotti 1988). See also Blair (2010) and Flanders (2020), whose discussions of developments in organizational systems is relevant to early philological practices.

2. See also Jones (1963, 527), Blair (2010, 24), and Mangenot (1912, col. 901).

East.³ Regardless, attestation of this concordance demonstrates an early interest in a reference work for Septuagint vocabulary.

The Foundational Concordance of Conrad Kircher (1607)

It is fair to say that all pre-twentieth-century Septuagint lexicography (and much in the twentieth century and beyond) stands in debt to Conrad Kircher. For that reason, his work is treated in more detail here than later scholars who depended on him. Kircher, a Lutheran theologian in Augsburg, labored for seven years to produce a concordance of the Greek Old Testament that was published in 1607. Printed in two volumes, this resource was the first of its kind and aimed at exhaustive treatment that included Hexaplaric readings and proper names.⁴

Importantly, rather than having entries based upon Greek headwords, Kircher chose a Hebrew-oriented structure for the concordance (see fig. 2.1). The Hebrew headwords were organized alphabetically by root, though not always correctly, as Henry Redpath (1896, 69–73) notes, among other idiosyncrasies (cf. Kraft and Tov 1998, xi). As shown in figure 2.1 (below), the Hebrew headword is followed by Latin glosses, which Kircher drew from Forster's 1556 lexicon with occasional reference to the 1529 thesaurus by Sanctus Pagninus. Each entry provides references for all instances of the headword, categorized into the Greek words (purportedly) used by Septuagint translators to translate the Hebrew headword. Each of those Greek words also has its own Latin gloss(es), under which are brief citations of the Greek text for each scripture reference (see also Dorival 2016, 272). Given this Hebrew-oriented layout, it is correct to say that Kircher's work is "really a Hebrew Concordance" (Redpath 1896, 70), and indeed that was how many perceived and used it (e.g., Chalmers 1815, 391; Horne 1839, 366).

---

3. Parpulov (2012, 321–22) reports of a complete Bible produced in the ninth century for one Abbot Basil.

4. The work nevertheless fell short in exhaustiveness and accuracy. For example, in his entry for רֹאֶה Kircher provides seven but omits nine texts where the word appears, seven of which are rendered by βλέπω (1 Sam 9:9 [2×], 11, 18, 19; 1 Chr 9:22; 29:29; Isa 28:7; 30:10). Moreover, the last four references he gives are in fact instances of the verb ראה rather than a nominal (N.B. Jer 52:22 should read 52:25). Similarly, his entry for בֹּשֶׂם, shown in fig. 2.1, omits Exod 35:28.

Although the Hebrew-oriented layout is significant, the sources from which Kircher drew his data are far more important because of the central role this concordance would play in the development of Septuagint lexicography. In his preface, Kircher mentions the inspiring work of Hugh of St. Cher and Rabbi Mordecai (Isaac) Nathan, who produced the first concordances of the Vulgate and Hebrew Bible, respectively.[5] It may have been by means of the latter that Kircher first located each instance of his headword. But, as stated in his preface, Kircher's chief textual source was the 1550 *Biblia Graeca et Latina*, printed in Basel by Nicholas Brylinger. For each Hebrew headword, it was from Brylinger's diglot that Kircher drew the Greek citations along with the corresponding Latin as a gloss for the Greek. The Septuagint text of Brylinger's 1550 diglot was drawn from the 1545 Basel edition that itself mostly reproduced the text of the 1518 Aldine Bible (Swete 1900, 174).[6] As for the Latin text, Brylinger reprinted the interlinear Latin translation of the Septuagint

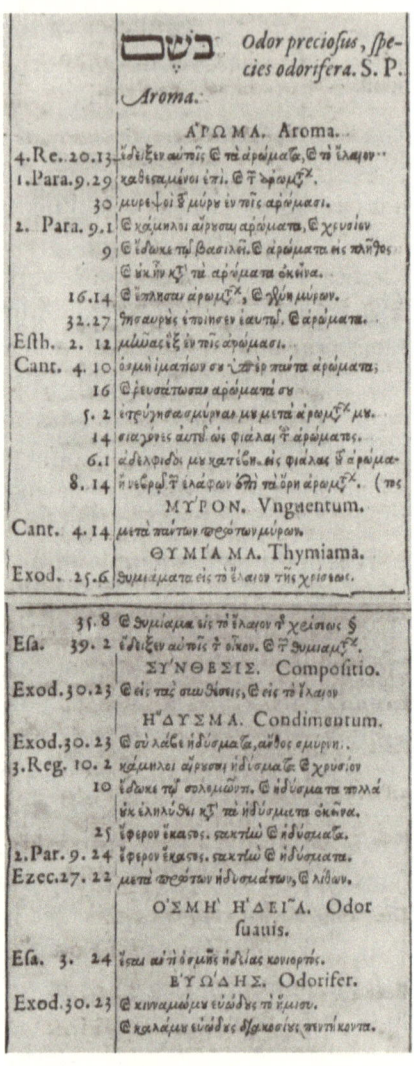

Figure 2.1. Entry for בֹּשֶׂם in Kircher's concordance (1607, 914–15). Image from the Hathi Trust Digital Library.

---

5. Hugh's work was produced ca. 1244 and printed first in 1479, forming the basis for many others, including that of Nathan, whose concordance was first published in 1523 (Jones 1963, 526).

6. Mandelbrote (2016, 98–99) attributes the use of the Aldine text of the Septuagint over that of the Complutensian in many sixteenth-century reprintings to the "slow and imperfect distribution" of the latter.

text of the Complutensian Polyglot (1514–1517).⁷ Since, as he states in his preface, one of the goals for Brylinger's diglot was to make the Greek more accessible to those of "moderate learning," wherever this Latin translation disagreed with his own Greek text, Brylinger appears to have emended the former toward the latter.

The upshot of this textual history is to point to problems for deriving Greek linguistic meaning that were entailed by Kircher's choice of the 1550 diglot as the base text for his concordance. First, the Septuagint text of the Aldine Bible—the ultimate source of Kircher's Greek vocabulary—was based on witnesses that were neither reliable nor ancient, and it is therefore of questionable character, especially in its relationship to the Hebrew Bible.⁸ Furthermore, the Latin text that furnished Kircher's glosses for Septuagint vocabulary offered what amounted only to the translation judgments of early modern editors. These judgments also entail a certain degree of semantic circularity since they were made in consultation with Hebrew and Vulgate texts and, moreover, have a dubious textual relationship to the Aldine Bible.⁹ There is no sure way to draw the thread of linguistic meaning in Greek from this textual Gordian knot. Indeed, it is correct to say that Kircher's concordance provided no direct linguistic evidence for the meaning of Greek vocabulary, but only what might be called circumstantial translation evidence derived from the morass of early modern manuscripts and editions of the Bible.

---

7. *Pace* Horne (1839, 43), who reports the Latin text was drawn from the Vulgate text of the Complutensian. The Latin translation of the Septuagint text was produced by the editors of the Polyglot (Hamilton 2016, 141; Mandelbrote 2016, 98) and had by Kircher's time already been independently printed, as in the 1526 Basel edition. I am indebted to the assistance of Dr. José Manuel Cañas Reíllo on these points.

8. Hall (1963, 57–58) reports that the Aldine text was established by Andreas Asolanus from manuscripts and late copies in the library of St. Mark in Venice (cf. Mandelbrote 2016, 99, esp. n. 67). Horne (1839, 43) states that Usher believed the Aldine text often followed Aquila. Redpath (1896, 71) also maintained that Kircher was "not based upon the best editions of the LXX," a judgment that Ziegler (1945) later proved correct when he showed that the Aldine reflects a late text that is heavily contaminated by Hexaplaric readings.

9. E.g., in producing their Latin interlinear translation of the Septuagint, the editors of the Complutensian Polyglot developed an exacting system of superscripted notations that cross-referenced the words of each version on the page. See Schenker (2008a, 289) and (Fernández Marcos 2016a, 8).

This problem in the derivation of linguistic meaning for Septuagint vocabulary points to a related problem in how it was purportedly expressed. Like so many others, Kircher equated the meaning of the Greek words with that of their corresponding translation equivalent. This attitude is clearest in his lengthy title, which reads in part:

> Concordantiae Veteris Testamenti graecae, Ebraeis vocibvs respondentes, πολύχρηστοι. Simul enim et Lexicon Ebraicolatinum, Ebraicograecum, Graecohebraicum: genuinam vocabulorum significationem, ex Septuaginta duorum, vt vulgo volunt, interpretum
> Greek Concordance of the Old Testament, Matching to the Hebrew Words, 'Very Useful.' In Fact, Also a Hebrew-Latin, Hebrew-Greek, Greek-Hebrew Lexicon: An Accurate Indication of Vocabulary, Sought From Translation of the Seventy-Two Interpreters, as Commonly Called

From Kircher's perspective, like that of so many of his contemporaries, to match up versions of the Bible word to word is to provide an "accurate indication" of the meaning of their respective vocabulary. This approach was only possible because of the word-for-word translation style typical of the Septuagint corpus, which facilitated understanding lexical correspondence as tantamount to lexical meaning. The same basic assumption underpins the gloss method of lexicography in general, which since the early modern period has provided the foundational data for, and approach to, virtually all Greek lexicography (Lee 2003a, 15–17, 120–21). Septuagint lexicography was no exception, as Kircher's concordance and its dependents show. Of course, the gloss method was at first somewhat unavoidable from a practical point of view. But under any circumstances it is problematic because it risks unintentional confusion from false cognates, as well as making imprecise or even incorrect statements of meaning owing to the different ways in which languages are used to categorize and refer to the world.[10] Most importantly, even as it takes these risks, the gloss method ultimately fails to provide an actual description of lexical meaning (Louw 1991, 140–41).

In short, Kircher produced a concordance that subordinated Greek to Hebrew structurally in terms of its layout. In addition, his method in

---

10. See Lee (2003a, 17–25), who traces several examples in New Testament vocabulary and notes that "renderings in the versions are simply taken and placed in the lexicons as the statement of meaning.... A gloss can pass easily from a translation into a lexicon, just as it can pass from a lexicon into a translation" (35).

producing it introduced practical and theoretical problems for the way that linguistic meaning was derived (owing to his choice of base text) and expressed (owing to the gloss method). Even though he saw no particular problems with the latter, Kircher was apparently aware of shortcomings in the former. After informing the reader of the source of his Latin glosses, he goes on to say that "though I would very often have liked to see [these] changed, I preferred nevertheless to leave it to the labors of others, rather than make the least emendation" (licet mutatam videre ſæpenumero exoptauerim: aliorum tamen laboribus parcere, quam velminimum emendare malui). In time, others would indeed take up this labor, though few would see it through to publication. But for better or worse, Kircher's concordance provided a body of Latin glosses as the explication of the meaning of Septuagint vocabulary that, as shown at the end of this section, would become the foundation for Septuagint lexicography up through the twentieth century.

Kircher's Dependents

Some records exist of independent efforts to create a concordance of the Septuagint. For example, one late seventeenth- or early eighteenth-century scholar, George Sugdures, is said to have compiled a concordance of the Greek Bible that apparently no longer exists.[11] But there is little reason to think these would have differed much in their working method from Kircher's own. Indeed, for the most part, effort was instead poured into adapting Kircher's concordance, though it was not fully replaced for over a century.

Concordances Unpublished and Unfinished

There were at least three attempts to improve upon Kircher in the first fifty years after his concordance appeared. Each of these scholars failed, like Sugdures, to see their work to press. Yet those failures are telling insofar as

---

11. Hobhouse (1813, 566) records that Sugdures is mentioned in a 1720 text written by Demetrius Procopius of "Moschopolis" (modern Moscopole, Albania) as a contemporary and one of ninety-nine Greeks worthy of commemoration as learned men (see 559–67). The entry reads: "83. Gregory Sugdures, of Ioannina, where he was chief schoolmaster; acquainted with Greek, Latin, and Italian; 'skilful in the Aristotelian philosophy, but more so in theology.' He wrote a Breviary of Logic, and a Concordance of the New and Old Testament."

the commonalities that appear among them identify what scholars wished to change about Kircher's concordance. One such consistent change was structural orientation toward Greek. But the problems involved in Kircher's Latin glosses for Septuagint vocabulary remained present as one scholar after another adopted Kircher's data as the foundation for their own work.

The earliest effort to improve upon Kircher was made by the English mathematician and classicist, Sir Henry Savile (1549–1622). This work has been enveloped by a cloud of uncertainty for some time, and not without reason. The manuscript is currently held in the Bodleian Library at Oxford (Auct. E 1.2, 3/Aleph system no. 013980457), having been acquired between 1634 and 1655 (see nos. 3046–3047 in Craster and Madan 1922, 576). But because there is no title page or other front matter, a long legacy of muddled attributions has developed, throwing into question the matters of timing, authorship, and motive. The finer details of this story have now been laid out elsewhere and need not be rehearsed here, beyond noting that authorship can indeed be confidently attributed to Savile (see Ross 2020b). More to the point, the curiosity of Savile's two-volume concordance was noted by Redpath (1896, 72), whose comment that it is "a mere work of scissors and paste" is not to be taken metaphorically.[12] For Savile literally cut out Kircher's entries, pasting them into new folios with Hebrew words added by hand where necessary. Whatever else may have motivated this tedious endeavor, Savile clearly desired a Greek-oriented concordance of the Septuagint.[13] Despite the lack of change in content per se, Savile's reorganized version of Kircher was considered for publication around 1690 (Doble 1889, 390) and again around 1718 (Ross 2020b, 892–93), but neither effort succeeded.

In the meantime, other scholars were busy with the same basic task. Another attempt to revise Kircher was made shortly after Savile's work by a Dutchman named Arnold de Boot (ca. 1600–1653). Although it was never published—and indeed never finished—de Boot put considerable effort into producing what appears to be a condensed version of Kircher's concordance around 1634.[14] The manuscript for his *Compendium concordantiarum Kircheri*

---

12. For an image of the manuscript, see Ross (2020b, 888).

13. For a history of Savile's method of compiling, see Considine (2015).

14. Le Long (1723, 456) and Bindseil (1867, lviii) refer to "Arnoldo Bootio" with no publication year or further comment. It seems that de Boot's other projects were better known—the concordance is not mentioned in Horne (1839), Gilbert (1886), or Redpath (1896). Even Kraft and Tov (1998, xii) only mention it in passing, citing

appears to have been produced in two stages. In the first, de Boot collated occurrences of each word of the Hebrew Bible in three handwritten volumes reaching over 1,200 pages (MSS Hébreu 136–138).[15] He may then have used these notes to check Kircher's work—albeit imperfectly—as he condensed it, primarily by omitting textual citations in his own concordance.[16] But de Boot also omitted something else: Latin glosses. Thus, his *Compendium* appears to have been motivated by something other than simply a desire for brevity. A suggestive note on the verso of folio 7 reads in part:

> Latina παερμηνευματα coepi adscribere inde a p. 283. | Kirch ad Lectore: Latina Graecarum vocum interpretation, ex Biblius | desumpta e[st] anno [- ca.? -] 1550 p[er] columnas, forma 8.ᵃ Basileae | graece[m] latineque excusis
>
> I began to record Latin "misinterpretations" from p. 283. Kircher *To the Reader*: "Latin interpretation of Greek words is drawn from the Bible, year 1550, in columns, in the eighth edition of Basel, printed in Greek and Latin"

This statement, in which Kircher's own preface is cited directly, makes it clear that de Boot perceived problems with Kircher's Latin glosses specifically related to the 1550 diglot. Exactly what de Boot might have considered παερμηνευματα and on what grounds are not certain, since the *Compendium* went unfinished. Regardless, de Boot's work demonstrates again a more widely felt desire for a Septuagint concordance ordered by Greek headwords. It also indicates an early awareness of shortcomings in Kircher's execution of an otherwise desirable tool.

A third revision of Kircher's concordance was completed in 1647 by Ambrose Aungier (1599–1654), chancellor of St. Patrick's Cathedral

---

Le Long. De Boot's concordance manuscript was originally referenced using "Bibl. Segueriana" and later "Bibl. Coisliniana" but is now kept in the archives of the Bibliothèque nationale de France (MSS Hébreu 136–139).

15. The manuscripts have a haphazard layout and are written in a difficult hand. Generally speaking, Hebrew words are written at the top of an entry, using pointing to disambiguate roots, a gloss provided to subdivide senses, with references listed in a column underneath, next to which is the clause where the word appears, occasionally with a Latin gloss or reading, Greek text, and various other notes.

16. His entry for רֹאֶה, for instance, is down to two lines from Kircher's eleven, and the references to Esth 1:14, Job 37:11, and Jer 52:22[25] have been removed, perhaps since de Boot recognized these as participle forms and not nouns. Still, de Boot apparently leans heavily on Kircher, as he misses the same nine occurrences of the headword in the Hebrew Bible.

in Dublin. It was a multistage project completed in two volumes.[17] One volume is entitled:

> Concordantiæ Hebraeo-Graecæ ex Opere Præstanti Conradi Kircheri Decerptæ
> Hebrew-Greek Concordance Drawn from the Work of the Excellent Conrad Kircher

Here Aungier took a very similar approach as that of de Boot. He retained the organization by Hebrew headword—with Latin glosses mostly identical to Kircher's—providing references categorized by the Greek words used to translate the headword, omitting most, though not all, citations. In this volume Aungier omitted all Latin glosses of Greek words. His second volume has two parts. The first is an alphabetical list of Greek words occurring in the New Testament or Septuagint with select references. The second is a Greek-oriented concordance of the Septuagint, entitled:

> Lexicon sacrum Graeco-Hebraeum liquido ostendens divinae, quae extat, Versionis Graecae analogiam cum Veritate Hebraea Veteris Testamenti: compositum ad pulcherimum exemplar Concordantiarum Hebraeo-Graecarum quas edidit vir p.m. Conradus Kercherus
> A Sacred Greek-Hebrew Lexicon Clearly Showing the Resemblance of the Divine Greek Version, What Remains, with the Truth of the Hebrew Old Testament: A Composition according to the Most Beautiful Example of the Hebrew-Greek Concordance that the Man Conrad Kircher, Foremost Teacher (?), Published

The entries are structured just as in the Hebrew-oriented volume, but inversely (see fig. 2.2). The Greek headword is followed by a Latin gloss drawn from Kircher, then organized using the Hebrew words it translates along with citations and references. Discussions took place to publish Aungier's work with the university press at Oxford (Mant 1840, 552–54), but owing to difficult financial circumstances in Ireland, it never happened. Aungier's efforts again demonstrate the broader desire for a published

---

17. Redpath (1896, 72) states the concordance was organized by Greek headword, which is only half true. But he never personally consulted the manuscript (see 72 n. 1), which is kept at Trinity College, Dublin (MS 170*).

2. Septuagint Lexicography

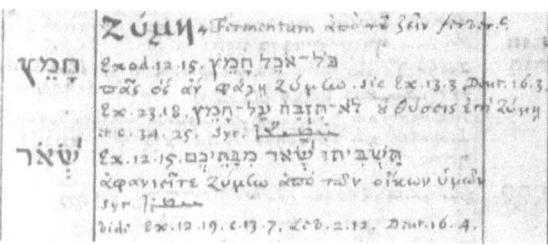

Figure 2.2. Entry for ζύμη in Aungier's concordance. Detail from MS 170* (139r). Image reproduced with permission from The Board of Trinity College Dublin.

improvement upon Kircher's work, but notably the sufficiency of the Latin glosses went either unquestioned or unresolved.[18]

The First Septuagint Lexicon by Zacharias Rosenbach (1634)

Amid the several unsuccessful attempts to revise and publish Kircher's work, the first self-described lexicon of the Septuagint emerged in 1634. It was compiled by Zacharias Rosenbach (1595–1638), a professor of medicine and oriental languages at Reformed Herborn Academy (Grün 1961).[19] This *Lexicon Breve* is just under two hundred pages, intended as a kind of elementary wordbook for students (Lee 2004a, 127). Terse though it is, it was groundbreaking in that Rosenbach finally provided a published reference work for Septuagint vocabulary in Greek alphabetical order. Yet he continued the tradition of providing Latin glosses, which he apparently drew from the 1572 Antwerp polyglot (*Biblia Regia*).[20] Of course, Rosenbach not only knew but also commended the work of his predecessor (5): "But if there is any doubt, consult after us the esteemed Kircher" (Quòd ſi alicui dubium ſit, conſulat à nobiſ laudatum Kircherum). With usually just one gloss per

---

18. Interestingly, de Boot also lived in Dublin from 1636 to 1644 and is likely to have interacted with Aungier. Another concordance that was based on Kircher is mentioned by both Le Long (1723, 456) and Bindseil (1867, lviii), dated to 1699 by Franciso Michaële Vogelio. This may have never been published either, as it is listed in Wiedemeyer (1699, 210) as *utilioresque futuræ*, "useful and forthcoming."

19. Tov (1999b, 97) mistakenly refers to this work as "Rosenarch (1624)."

20. As the Antwerp edition contains a revised Vulgate text drawn from the Complutensian Polyglot, as well as a Latin translation of the Septuagint (Schenker 2008b, 778–79), it is not entirely clear which of the two Rosenbach relied upon more.

Greek word—sometimes two or three—it is difficult either to confirm or deny Rosenbach's dependence upon Kircher. There is considerable overlap. In any case, Rosenbach's clear esteem for Kircher's work (which he assumes others share) as well as his perpetuation of Kircher's gloss method confirms the lack of awareness in this period of their respective problematic aspects.

Abraham Tromm's Updated Concordance (1718)

Kircher's concordance was finally superseded in 1718 when the Protestant minister Abraham Tromm of Groningen set out to rectify what he saw as its shortcomings. It took him sixteen years (Kraft and Tov 1998, xii). Chief among his aims was to organize his two-volume work with alphabetically ordered Greek headwords.[21] But just as heavily as Tromm critiqued Kircher did he also rely on him, stating that his own concordance (1718, sig. 4*v):

> could not have put on this form unless it [Kircher's concordance] had been cut apart page by page into the smallest possible parts, with amazing ingenuity and patience, and then put back together, page by page, piece by piece[22] (hanc formam induere non potuit, nisi mirabili artificio et patientia membratim in minutissimas partes discissus membratim rursus ac minutatim compingeretur).

Indeed, much of Tromm's work mirrors Kircher's in content, including citations of Aquila, Symmachus, and Theodotion, insertion of information from scholia, transliterated words, and omission of proper names (see fig. 2.3). The primary advance was that of providing an updated dataset that included a larger representation of texts from the Hexapla (Redpath 1896, 73–74; Kraft and Tov 1998, xii–xiii). Tromm provides Greek headwords alphabetically with a Latin gloss, under which are listed Hebrew equivalents that also have a gloss, along with textual references and citations. The concordance is still not fully accurate or exhaustive.[23] But Tromm's

---

21. See Redpath (1896, 72–75), who also mentions Tromm's critique of Kircher's flawed Hebrew alphabetization and problematic workflow that produced frequent incorrect citations.

22. Translation by Considine (2015, 495).

23. To continue comparison with prior treatment of רֹאָה, Tromm's glosses indicate he categorized רֹאֶה as a participle. He omits the incorrect references included in

προφήτης. Propheta, vates.

1. זָקֵן *senex.*
Thren. 4. 16. πρόσωπον ιερέων ουκ ελαβον, προφήτας ουκ ηλέησαν.
[πρεσβύτας alii.]

2. חֹזֶה part. *videns.*
2 Par. 19. 2. καὶ ἐξῆλθεν εἰς ἀπάντησιν αὐτοῦ Ιηοῦ. ὁ προφήτης.
29. 30. ἐν λόγοις δαβὶδ καὶ ἀσὰφ τοῦ προφήτου
35. 15. οἱ προφῆται τοῦ βασιλέως.

3. מַלְאָךְ *nuncius.*
2 Par. 36. 15. ἐν χειρὶ τῶν προφητῶν αὐτοῦ ὀρθρίζων

4. נָבִיא part. niph. *prophetans.*
1 Par. 25. 2. υἱοὶ ἀσὰφ. ἐχόμενοι ἀσὰφ τοῦ προφήτου.
Jere. 26. 18. μιχαίας. ἦν προφήτης ἐν ταῖς ἡμέραις ἐζεκίου. §.

Figure 2.3. Detail of entry for προφήτης from Tromm's concordance (1718, 2:376). Image from the Hathi Trust Digital Library.

work nevertheless made advances.[24] Aside from meeting the need for a Greek-oriented resource, Tromm also provided a Hebrew-Chaldee dictionary, a Greek dictionary to the Hexapla using Bernard de Montfaucon (1714) prepared by Lambert Bos (1670–1717), and Bos's comparison of the chapters and verses in the Frankfort and 1653 London editions (Jackson 1952, 207; Redpath 1896, 78).[25]

Moreover, Tromm paid significantly more attention to variant readings than his predecessors, perhaps since more editions were available to him. He states that the 1597 Frankfort edition, along with its scholia, was the primary text for the concordance, alongside the 1663 London, 1665 Cambridge, and 1683 Amsterdam editions.[26] Yet problems in Tromm's work

---

Kircher et al. (Esth 1:14; Job 34:26; 37:21; Jer 52:22[25]) but also omits Isa 30:10, where προφητής occurs. Further, although participle forms of βλέπω are used six times to render רֹאֶה (1 Sam 9:9 [2×], 11, 18; 1 Chr 9:22; 29:29), Tromm lists these instead under the verb רָאָה (omitting 1 Chr 9:22).

24. Dorival (2016, 273) points to its ongoing usefulness for locating words in manuscripts not used for HRCS.

25. Kircher used the chapter and verse divisions of the 1597 Frankfurt edition as well (Kraft and Tov 1998, xii).

26. In turn, the 1597 Frankfort followed the Complutensian, 1572 Antwerp, Strasbourg, and 1587 Sixtine editions (Horne 1839, 44). See Würthwein (1995, 76) and Swete (1902, 174–82) on the Sixtine.

remain, as Redpath (1896, 74) well describes.[27] For the present purposes, the primary problem was that, despite the plurality of his textual basis, Tromm in fact still relied heavily upon Kircher for his glosses, as illustrated below, passing on his foundational data even as it was supplemented.

The Lexicons of Johann Christian Biel (1779–1780) and Johann Friedrich Schleusner (1820–1821)

Aside from Rosenbach's concise work, it was not until the late eighteenth and early nineteenth century that a full lexicon of the Septuagint corpus appeared. The works of Johann Christian Biel (1687–1745) and Johann Friedrich Schleusner (1759–1831) are best discussed together, since they are closely related. Biel's three-volume lexicon was edited and published after his death by E. H. Mutzenbecher in 1779–1780 (von Liliencron 1875; Lust 1990, 256). In turn, Schleusner produced a five-volume lexicon that was published in 1820–1821.[28]

Biel's work, with its references and citations, is much closer than that of Rosenbach to the typical contents of modern lexicons, as shown in figure 2.4. Greek headwords are followed by one or more Latin glosses, followed by the Hebrew word(s) that the headword was used to translate in the Septuagint, each of which is followed by select references with Greek phrases or clauses—sometimes drawn from the New Testament—and the occasional Latin translation of that Greek reference. A Latin gloss of the Hebrew word is also given if it is considered relevant, and some citations from the Three and other versions are also provided.

Schleusner laid out his lexicon quite similarly to Biel, as shown in figure 2.5. In fact, it is right to call Biel and Schleusner "virtually identical in title, structure, and general content" (Kraft and Tov 1998, xiii).[29] Where

---

27. Tromm also used the 1663 London, 1665 Cambridge, and 1683 Amsterdam editions (folio six. 3*v–3*2r), which are linked by the fact that the London edition does not in fact follow the Sixtine edition as it claims. Rather, the editors aligned it with the Hebrew text and contemporary versions, interpolations that were then retained in the 1665 Cambridge and 1683 Amsterdam editions. See Horne (1839, 44).

28. Schleusner's original five-volume lexicon was also reprinted with corrections in Glasgow in 1822 in three volumes, correcting citations, references, and appending English translations of occasional German explanations of words. The third volume included an index of Hebrew words occurring in the lexicon.

29. Schleusner even reprints the preface E. H. Mutzenbecher contributed to Biel's work.

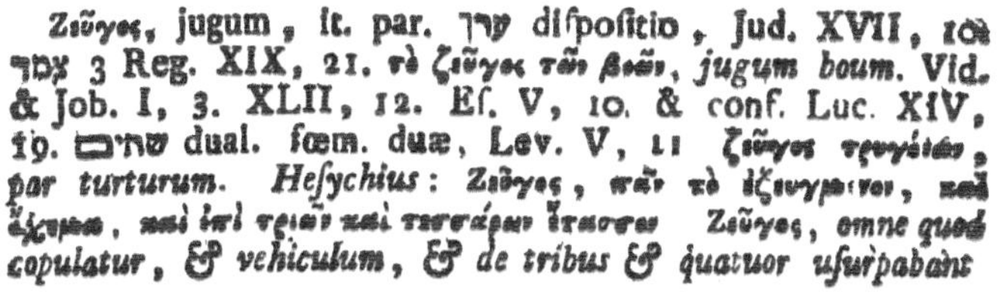

2. Septuagint Lexicography   31

> Ζεῦγος, jugum, It. par. צֶמֶד diſpoſitio, Jud. XVII, 10. צֶמֶד 3 Reg. XIX, 21. τὰ ζεύγη τῶν βοῶν, jugum boum. Vid. & Job. I, 3. XLII, 12. Eſ. V, 10. & conf. Luc. XIV, 19. שְׁנַיִם dual. fœm. duæ, Lev. V, 11 ζεῦγος τρυγόνων, par turturum. Heſychius: Ζεῦγος, πᾶν τὸ ἐζευγμένον, καὶ ὄχημα, καὶ ἐπὶ τριῶν καὶ τεσσάρων ἔτασσεν. Ζεῦγος, omne quod copulatur, & vehiculum, & de tribus & quatuor uſurpabant.

Figure 2.4. Entry for ζεῦγος from Biel (1779–1780, 2:2). Image from the Hathi Trust Digital Library.

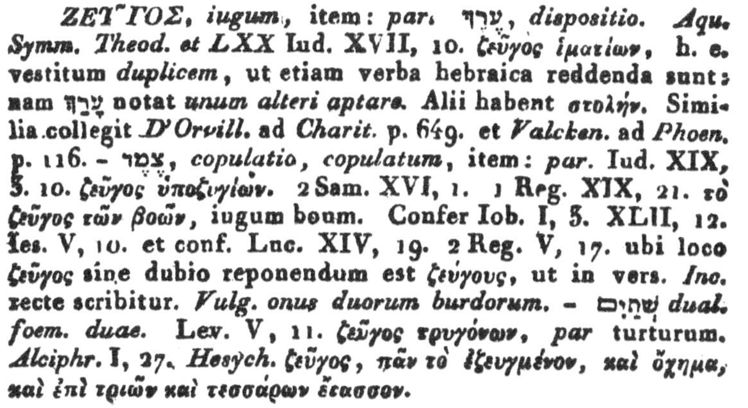

> ΖΕΥΓΟΣ, iugum, item: par, עֶרֶך, dispositio. Aqu. Symm. Theod. et LXX Iud. XVII, 10. ζεῦγος ἱματίων, h. e. vestitum duplicem, ut etiam verba hebraica reddenda sunt; nam עָרַך notat unum alteri aptare. Alii habent στολήν. Similia collegit D'Orvill. ad Charit. p. 649. et Valcken. ad Phoen. p. 116. – צֶמֶד, copulatio, copulatum, item: par. Iud. XIX, 3. 10. ζεῦγος ὑποζυγίων. 2 Sam. XVI, 1.) Reg. XIX, 21. τὸ ζεῦγος τῶν βοῶν, iugum boum. Confer Iob. I, 3. XLII, 12. Ies. V, 10. et conf. Luc. XIV, 19. 2 Reg. V, 17. ubi loco ζεῦγος sine dubio reponendum est ζεύγους, ut in vers. Ino. recte scribitur. Vulg. onus duorum burdorum. – שְׁנַיִם dual. foem. duae. Lev. V, 11. ζεῦγος τρυγόνων, par turturum. Alciphr. I, 27. Hesych. ζεῦγος, πᾶν τὸ ἐζευγμένον, καὶ ὄχημα, καὶ ἐπὶ τριῶν καὶ τεσσάρων ἔτασσεν.

Figure 2.5. Entry for ζεῦγος from Schleusner (1820–1821, 2:3). Image from the Hathi Trust Digital Library.

he did add information, Schleusner often marked it with an asterisk. Some of the information that is clearly an addition but is unmarked likely comes not from Biel, but from intermediary lexicographical work not often discussed. That material consisted of three supplementary works collecting overlooked data (*spicilegia*) in Biel.[30]

---

30. The first two were compiled by Schleusner in 1784 and 1786, which I have not been able to locate—though the first is listed as no. 2248 in the library catalogue of the French baron and philologist Antoine Isaac Silvestre de Sacy (1758–1838; 1841, 90). A third supplement was compiled by Bretschneider (1805). Jahn, Turner, and Whittingham (1827, 103) claim that Bretschneider supplemented Schleusner's lexicon again with two more volumes in 1822, but I have been unable to find further information about this work. That claim may be a mistaken reference to the reprint of Schleusner's lexicon. See Horne (1825, 706; 1833, 490–91).

More important for the present purposes than discussing the editions from which Biel and Schleusner worked is to demonstrate their dependence upon their predecessors.[31] To be sure, their work prompted some praise and much criticism (Lust 1990, 258–59). As for the latter, Deissmann (1907–1908, 511–12) went so far as to call Biel and Schleusner together a "rather insipid adaptation of Tromm's Concordance, useless at the present day except as a collection of material." Elsewhere Johan Lust (1990, 257) has clearly shown the lexicographical line of dependence back to Schleusner (see also Gosling 2000, 21). But the dependence goes even further than Lust indicates, indeed all the way to Kircher in 1607 and, ultimately, his 1550 diglot base text, as shown in the following.[32]

Brylinger (1550, 1:147, 382)
καὶ διεβοήθη ἡ φωνὴ εἰς τὸν οἶκον φαραὼ ‖ Et diuulgata eſt uox in domum Pharonis (Gen 45:16)
καὶ διαβοήσετε ἄφεσιν ἐπὶ τῆς γῆς ‖ & clamabitis remiſſionem in terra (Lev 25:10)

Kircher (1607, 2:1458, 2099)
קָרָא... ΔΙΑΒΟΑ′Ω. **Clamo. Leuit. 25.10** καὶ διαβοήσετε ἄφεσιν ἐπὶ τῆς γῆς
שָׁמַע... ΔΙΑΒΟΑ′Ω. **Diuulgo. Gen. 45:16** καὶ διεβοήθη ἡ φωνὴ εἰς τὸν οἶκον

Tromm (1718, 1:351)
Διαβοάω. Proclamo, **divulgo. 1.** נִשְׁמַע **niph. audior. Gen. 45.16.** καὶ διεβοήθη ἡ φωνὴ εἰς τὸν οἶκον Φαραὼ **2.** קָרָא **clamo. Lev. 25.10.** καὶ διαβήσετε ἄφεσιν ἐπὶ τῆς γῆς

Biel (1779–1780, 1:364)
Διαβοάω, *proclamo, divulgo.* נשמע niph. *audior*, Gen. XLV, 16. διεβοήθη ἡ φωνὴ εἰς τὸν οἶκον Φαραω, *rumor divulgabatur in domus Pharaonis.* קרא *clamo*, Lev. XXV, 10.

---

31. The supplementary materials and Schleusner were prompted in part by the edition of the Septuagint by Holmes and Parsons, published from 1795 to 1827 (Kraft and Tov 1998, xiv).

32. Boldfaced text indicates material drawn directly from the chronologically earlier work.

Schleusner (1820–1821, 2:81[33])
ΔΙΑΒΟΑ'Ω, *proclamo, divulgo*, celebro, rumorem dissemino. יִשָּׁמַע Niph. *audior.* Gen. XLV, 16. διεβοήθη ἡ φωνὴ εἰς τὸν οἶκον Φαραὼ, rumor *delatus est* ad Pharaonem, eiusque aulicos. *Hesych.* διεβοήθη, ἐνεφανίσθη, indicatum, annuntiatum est. – קָרָא, clamo. **Lev. XXV, 10.** διαβοήσετε ἄφεσιν ἐπὶ τῆς γῆς, omnibus terrae incolis libertatem indicate. Iudith. X, 18.

Compared to his predecessor, Schleusner adds two additional glosses (*celebro, rumorem dissemino*), a reading from Hesychius's lexicon and corresponding glosses, and a Latin citation of the Leviticus text cited by all. He also includes a reference to Jdt 10:18 from Bretschneider's *Spicilegia* (1805, 63). Of course, the collective efforts of Biel and Schleusner did make advances, specifically by collating more readings from the Three and thus identifying possible divergences in the *Vorlagen* (Kraft and Tov 1998, xiv). But what nevertheless remained were the fundamental problems latent within the gloss method, particularly as it was employed by Kircher, whose work so clearly underlies the whole pre-twentieth-century tradition of Septuagint lexicography.[34]

Evaluation of the Pre-Twentieth-Century Tradition

Despite the admirable efforts of these scholars, their labors produced a legacy of biblical reference works that had little to offer for understanding Greek lexical meaning. This result arose in large measure from the source from which Kircher derived foundational lexical data, which paired an unreliable Greek text with a borrowed and adjusted Latin translation. From that pair of texts in the 1550 diglot Kircher drew the first glosses for Septuagint vocabulary. While subsequent scholars added to Kircher's dataset, it remained fundamentally unchanged as it was transmitted and used as the basis for later lexicographical reference works, which thus became repositories of information that is more textual than linguis-

---

33. The entry is identical in the second edition (Schleusner 1822, 1:545).
34. Horne (1839, 215) notes a failed lexicon effort made by Fischer (1758) covering only A. Yet another work of note is Ewing (1827), whose Greek lexicon included limited Septuagint references. Another lexicon was begun by E. G. A. Böckel in 1820, who produced some forty pages on the letter Z but went no further. Böckel also critiques Kircher and Tromm, saying "imperfecta, minus accurata, male dispofita, imo confufa sunt" (v).

tic in nature. It would be centuries before a more principled distinction between translation equivalents and lexical semantics would develop. Still, the problems besetting Septuagint lexicography were not lost upon pre-twentieth-century scholarship. Gesenius's (1833, 9) withering critique cuts to the heart of the matter as he specifically addressed Kircher, Tromm, Biel, and Schleusner:

> The lexical helps yet extant for the *Septuagint* are in the highest degree imperfect. The authors of them, while they often give only an incomplete account of what the Greek translator meant ... merely write out from the concordance the Hebrew words for which each Greek word stands; busy themselves with conjectures;... and not unfrequently, in order to bring about a correspondence, force upon the Greek word the meaning of the Hebrew one, and *vice versa*. (see also Gesenius's n. 17)

This gloomy pronouncement against Septuagint lexicography went unanswered for nearly two centuries.[35]

Septuagint Lexicography in the Twentieth Century and Beyond

If any hope remains that pre-twentieth century Septuagint lexicography shed light upon the meaning of Greek, let it be vanquished. For among the flaws already discussed lurks yet another matter: the near total absence of any documented lexical evidence from sources outside the Greek Scriptures. This omission is partly symptomatic of a scholarly mindset that believed the language of the Greek Bible was in some way unique, as discussed below. But disregarding external evidence was not merely a result of wrongheaded views of language. The most relevant evidence was still literally buried underground. So even if Septuagint lexicographers had used sound method—which they did not—the state of the discipline would nevertheless have been rendered obsolete, except perhaps to serve as an index, with the discovery of the postclassical papyri and inscriptions (Lee 1983, 9). The discovery of this evidence marked the beginning of a new era in the study of Greek, since it provided attestation of nonliterary

---

35. Critique was also registered a few years earlier by Jebb (1828, 51), who warns against the "dangerous interpretation" in Schleusner and Bretschneider's lexical work (oddly, Biel is exempted), namely, the erroneous assumption that Greek words used in translation of Hebrew parallelism were synonymous. More recently, see Muraoka (1990c, 19; 2009, vii), Gosling (2000), Lust (1990, 256), and (Taylor 2009, xvii).

postclassical varieties of the language for the first time. In the absence of such evidence, Greek scholars had hotly debated the linguistic character of the New Testament and Septuagint for over two centuries.[36] The conditions that provoked the debate were complex, involving political history, religious conflict, and notions about linguistic propriety that are beyond the scope of the present inquiry.[37] But the contours of that debate went far in establishing mindsets that continue to shape the current state of Septuagint scholarship and its two prevailing views of what kind of Greek is found in the Septuagint.

Evaluations of Postclassical Greek through the Early Twentieth Century

There is no clear ancient or medieval recognition of a distinct Jewish Greek dialect, or even any extant remarks about a distinctive Jewish form of speech (de Lange 2007, 640). Yet, starting in the early modern period, a debate arose that would lead many scholars to characterize the language of the New Testament and Septuagint in precisely these terms from the sixteenth through the twentieth century, even after the discovery of the documentary evidence.

The debate appears to have begun with Henry Stephens, who wished to defend what he saw as the "Attic purity" of the language of the New Testament. Stephens's work, *De stilo, lectionibus, et interpunctionibus Novi Testamenti*, appeared in Theodore Beza's widely used 1576 edition of the New Testament, thus Stephens's view received considerable attention (Horne 1836, 195 n. 2).[38] His school of thought became known as the Pur-

---

36. The ancient debates over Greek language "correctness" (*Hellenismos*), also have many parallels to the early modern debates but will not be discussed here, though see Ross (forthcoming; see also Pagani 2015). Colvin (2009, 34) states, "The interpretation of linguistic variety as essence and variation (mostly conceived as corruption) which emerged in the complex sociolinguistic milieu of Hellenistic and Roman Greece was easily translated into a Latin context by Roman grammarians, and spread with equal ease into medieval and modern European thought."

37. See the numerous relevant articles in Christidis (2015a), who states that in "in the West, and mainly in Italy, the systematic study of Ancient Greek began in the fifteenth century and was associated with the mass exodus of scholars after the Fall of Constantinople" (2015b, 1221). On Greek scholarship prior to this period, see Dickey (2007), Novokhatko (2015), Montana (2015), Matthaios (2015), and Pontani (2015). For a survey of Greek lexicography overall, see Pantelia (2014b).

38. See the surveys of this debate in Winer (1882, 12–41) and Voelz (1984).

ists, later exemplified in the influential work of Sebastian Pfochen (1629). Purists maintained that New Testament Greek is free from all external linguistic influences, which they considered a corruption and thus a threat to the credibility of Scripture. Scholars such as Jacob Grosse (1640) and later J. J. Wettstein (1751–1752) therefore took pains to defend the language of Scripture against other views, even going so far as to call them heretical (Horne 1836, 195 n. 2).[39] Lying behind the Purist view is an idea that will resurface throughout this discussion: Attic Greek is "pure" Greek.[40] In their evaluation of New Testament Greek the Purists had no awareness of—or no interest in—either the historical development of the language or sociolinguistic factors such as class and register. They combined a prescriptivist linguistic mindset with classicizing bias and religiously motivated concepts of purity, setting trends that would persist for centuries.[41]

The opposing viewpoint held by the so-called Hebraists was equally problematic. Represented at first by Salomon Glassius (1623–1636) and J. Jung (1640) and later by Gottfried Olearius (1713), Gottlob Storr (1779), and others, this school of thought argued that New Testament Greek was influenced by Hebrew syntax and semantics. Their basic approach was to highlight linguistic features that could not be found in Classical Greek sources and on that basis categorize those features as Hebraic (Trollope 1842, 7; Horsley 2014, 280). Of course, this is an argument from silence in that it assumes that what is not attested in classical sources did not exist in the language and is therefore foreign. But it is more important to note that, while Purists and Hebraists vehemently disagreed over the nature of New Testament Greek, they did so from the same point of departure. Both sides agreed that Attic was the purest form of Greek and therefore the standard by which to evaluate the language of the New Testament.

As the debate unfolded, the prescriptivist and classicizing mindset persisted, mingling at points with classism. Unsurprisingly, the Purist

---

39. Voelz (1984, 897–900) and Trollope (1842, 7) list scholars who followed Pfochen.

40. Stuart and Robinson (1826, 85–86) suggest that the controversy arose from a mindset that attributed "perfection, in the absolute sense of the word, to every part and portion of the text.... If the New Testament was given from God in Greek, it must have been given in the best possible Greek, the pure, unadulterated Attic." Even recent scholars have noted ongoing classicizing bias against postclassical Greek within biblical scholarship, such as Swinn (1990, 56) and Taylor (2009, xvii–xviii).

41. Deissmann (1909b, 211) called their approach "a dogmatic philology" that "prevented the perception of the historical fact of the spread of a language to wider usage and of its consequent development." See Dines (2004, 112–13).

position proved untenable, and by the late eighteenth century some form of the Hebraist view became common (Voelz 1984, 900; Janse 2007, 647). As the latter solidified, it was informed by ongoing scholarly evaluation of postclassical Greek as a "mixed" and "impure" form of the language (so Ewing 1827, 135). Scholars in the early nineteenth century generally held that, following Alexander's conquest, the classical dialects had been thrown into "confusion," producing a "corrupted" and "degenerate progeny" (so Trollope 1842, 6; see also Horne 1836, 194–95; Ewing 1827, 135). It was diluted by the languages it replaced "as by pouring a great quantity of water to a little wine" (Bentley 1817, 316).[42] This idea was promulgated by Heinrich Ludwig Planck (1810), a well-respected scholar whose concise grammar became widely influential.[43]

Even within this pejorative and value-laden understanding of postclassical Greek the language of the New Testament and Septuagint was classified as unique. Planck held that postclassical Greek was represented by Hellenistic literature such as that of Plutarch, Polybius, and Diodorus Siculus. The language of the Scriptures he categorized as distinct altogether, a "Sacred Hellenism" (Trollope 1842, 6; see Stuart and Robinson 1826, 80–81). G. B. Winer (1822) also advanced this view. He noted the relationship of the language of the New Testament to contemporary literary sources, on the one hand, yet simultaneously regarded it as isolated and Hebraic.[44]

It was in this academic milieu that the notion of "Biblical Greek" arose (Porter 2016, 16–17). Winer's highly influential work had prompted scholars to reevaluate the language of the Septuagint as well (Gerber 2010, 7–8; Voelz 1984, 901–4). In his influential Grinfield Lectures on the Septuagint in 1888, Edwin Hatch proclaimed that it was "too obvious to require demonstration" that "Biblical Greek" was "a language which stands by itself"

---

42. Almost a century later, Conybeare and Stock (1995 [1905], 21) similarly stated that "Attic Greek was like a vintage of rare flavour which would only grow on a circumscribed soil. When Greek became a world-language, as it did after the conquests of Alexander, it had to surrender much of its delicacy."

43. "[Planck's grammar] has exerted a wider influence in the critical world than all the ponderous tomes produced during the centuries of the Attic Controversy" (Stuart and Robinson 1826, 106). Two English translations of Planck were produced soon after it appeared, in the Andover Biblical Repository and Edinburgh Biblical Cabinet (Horne 1839, 209).

44. Winer was followed by Thiersch (1841), Schilling (1886), Viteau (1893–1896), and Simcox (1889), among others.

(1889, 11; see also Simcox 1889, 16–19). Many agreed that the language of the Septuagint was largely an inferior style and part of a stand-alone Jewish Greek dialect (Ewing 1827, 139).[45] It was, after all, the language of "an alien race" (Hatch 1889, 9; cf. Wellhausen 1871, 10).[46] As a result, the supposed Jewish Greek dialect of the Septuagint was considered to have been "wholly unintelligible to a native Greek," owing in part to its Hebraic "lexicographical peculiarities" (Trollope 1842, 6).[47]

Hatch maintained that the philological value of the Septuagint relied upon its status as a translation. To him the meaning of the "great majority" of its vocabulary could be deduced directly from the Hebrew: "It is a true paradox that while, historically as well as philologically, the Greek is a translation of the Hebrew, philologically, though not historically, the Hebrew may be regarded as a translation of the Greek" (1889, 14). This statement is reminiscent of Kircher's title, and perhaps not coincidentally Hatch would later produce a concordance of the Septuagint that was finished by Redpath (1897, 1906, cf. 1998). Just like his predecessors, then, Hatch anchored lexical meaning in the Septuagint upon Hebrew, if for different reasons. Hatch's mistake lay in his belief that the language of the Septuagint was a unique Jewish dialect. Accordingly, to him it had a maximal semantic relationship with its Hebrew source text and a minimal semantic relationship to contemporary Greek sources. In the lexicographical enterprise, the Septuagint could safely be cordoned off from other Greek evidence.[48]

---

45. Ewing goes on to surmise that ancient Jews must have been "plain men, less anxious about style, and the reputation of elegance" (1827, 142).

46. According to Dorival (2016, 280), "Hatch privilégie la langue source au point qu'il la voit tout entière dans la langue cible."

47. Trollope (1842, 7) also maintained that New Testament authors sometimes found it "impossible to express themselves in genuine Greek." Stuart and Robinson (1826, 88–89) viewed the language of the New Testament as a "degenerate" form of the language.

48. Hatch (1889, 34) did believe "some" words in the Greek Bible could be understood in comparison with "contemporary secular Greek," particularly the "ordinary vernacular rather than the artificial literary Greek of the time." Certain scholars also began to take a similar lexicographical approach to the New Testament. Stuart and Robinson (1826, 92) claimed that "the circumstances of the nation to which the sacred writers belonged were such ... as to take the New Testament entirely out from the body of Grecian literature, and give to both the philology and interpretation of it a distinct and peculiar character, and render them a proper object of separate and particular investiga-

In the midst of these developments, an exasperated and prescient J. B. Lightfoot remarked in 1863, "if only we could get hold of a large number of private letters from individuals ... we would have a unique way of learning the meaning of Biblical Greek" (recorded by Moulton 1916, 11–12).[49] Of course, precisely such letters had already begun to be unearthed and even published in the mid-nineteenth century. These sources were soon to gain widespread attention and give new energy to the old debate.

Lexicographical Upheaval: The Discovery of the Documentary Evidence

It was customary in Hellenistic and Roman Egypt not to burn personal documents but to bury or use them for practical purposes (Moulton 1916, 12–13, 15–16). Thanks to this practice and the dry climate, many thousands of papyri were preserved in remarkable condition for millennia. In the eighteenth century these and many other kinds of sources started to be excavated, largely in conjunction with the military expeditions of Napoleon and the fascination with all things Egyptian (E. Turner 1980a, 18–24). Excavations expanded toward the end of the nineteenth century, facilitated by the British military occupation after nationalist conflicts following the death of Mohammad Ali (1769–1849; see Bowman et al. 2007; Keenan 2009).

The documentary sources began to arrive in Europe in the late nineteenth and early twentieth century and were published en masse.[50] They soon attracted attention from scholars such as Ulrich Wilcken and Frederic George Kenyon, whose names are now synonymous with papyrology.[51] Equally well known are the Oxford archaeologists Bernard Grenfell and Arthur Hunt and their remarkable discoveries at Oxyrhynchus (see Parsons 2007). Although there were periods of inactivity in the twentieth century, excavations in Egypt and elsewhere have continued to unearth documents written in postclassical Greek contemporary to the transla-

---

tion." See the description of this attitude in Deissmann (1901, 63–65), who rejects it as a transference of the notion of sacred canon to language (cf. Deissmann 1991, 41).

49. Lightfoot apparently understood the significance of the documentary evidence early on, which had only begun to appear in print.

50. On the overwhelming pace of publication, see Moulton (1901, 362).

51. The sources began to be published, for example, in the *Berliner Griechische Urkunden* (*BGU*) series in 1895, in which new volumes continue to emerge published by de Gruyter.

tion of the Septuagint and composition of the New Testament writings (Cuvigny 2009). Aside from the birth of papyrology as a new academic discipline, these discoveries were forever to alter the landscape of Greek scholarship (See E. Turner 1980a, 17–24; Worp 2014). Suddenly "vernacular" Greek "took form under our eyes, like a new planet swimming into our ken" (Moulton 1909, 464).[52] The documentary evidence thus prompted new categories of thought for evaluating postclassical Greek and the place of the language of the Septuagint within it (Porter 2016, 37; see also Evans and Obbink 2010, 1–3).

Developing Views of the Language of the Septuagint through the Mid-Twentieth Century

The documentary evidence had already begun to influence evaluations of Biblical Greek prior to the mid-twentieth century (e.g., Walch 1779; Jacob 1890; Gwynn 1920). But the flood of new evidence forced scholars to question the prevailing Jewish Greek paradigm. The most influential of these scholars was Deissmann, who in 1893 noticed on the desk of a colleague a new publication of Greek papyri called *Berliner Griechische Urkunden*. In examining these papyri, Deissmann noticed marked similarities with the language of the New Testament. He spent the rest of his influential career following this lead (Moulton 1916, 22–23; Gerber 2010, 24). Deissmann published a number of studies that drastically changed the course of Greek scholarship by bringing so-called Biblical Greek out of the isolation so consistently imposed on it (Lee 2016, 99).

In Deissmann's analysis, the documentary evidence demonstrated that postclassical Greek was a unified linguistic phenomenon throughout the Mediterranean world.[53] The pervasive idea of a Jewish dialect or Biblical Greek was therefore a result of flawed reasoning based on insufficient evidence and bad philology. He soon declared it "fanciful" (1909b, 212–13; 1991, 50). In his treatment of the Septuagint, Deissmann argued that the "real language" of the translators "was the Egyptian Greek of the period of the Ptolemies" found in the documentary evidence (1901,

---

52. By "vernacular" here, Moulton means postclassical Greek that is nonliterary in register.

53. Deissmann (1901, 66) speaks of an Alexandrian dialect at times but elsewhere cautions against "mechanistic differentiation of Hellenistic 'dialects'" and refers to "provincial differences" (48–49). Similar distinctions appear in Swete (1900, 291–92, 295).

70, a translation of 1895).⁵⁴ Thus, scholars began to recognize that the language of the Septuagint had thus far appeared unusual not because it is unique, but because it had been compared to the wrong varieties of Greek, namely, Attic or postclassical literature (Moulton 1909, 466).⁵⁵ The Septuagint however is largely written in the nonliterary variety of postclassical Greek. The Hebrew source texts certainly influenced the language of the Septuagint. Yet Deissmann (1908b, 65) maintained that "Semitisms do not place the Bible outside the scope of Greek philology; they are merely birthmarks."⁵⁶

The discoveries and ensuing shift in scholarly opinion had crucial implications for Septuagint lexicography since a massive amount of new and eminently relevant evidence became available (Deissmann 1909b, 211, 213). It did not take long for Deissmann (1901, 72–73; 1907–1908, 512) to point out the need for a new lexicon of the Septuagint taking documentary evidence into account. He was critical of the method used by Schleusner and his predecessors—which underpinned the entire history of Septuagint lexicography—deriding it as a "mechanical equating process." He argued that the "meaning of a Septuagint word cannot be deduced from the original which it translates or replaces but only from other remains of the Greek language, especially from those Egyptian sources that have lately flowed so abundantly" (1907–1908, 514–15).⁵⁷ Deissmann rejected the assumption that Septuagint vocabulary always represents the meaning of the Hebrew since there is inevitable semantic shift in translation and because there is sometimes intentional substitution instead of translation (1901, 73–74; 1991, 55).

---

54. Deissmann (1910, 140–42, a translation of 1909a), argued the same position for the New Testament (cf. Deissmann 1908a). Voelz (1984, 906–10) helpfully summarizes Deissmann's position.

55. Moulton (1908) carried Deissmann's ideas forward with reference to syntax rather than lexicon. Others included Abbott (1891), Kennedy (1895), Thumb (1901), and Robertson (1923). See Porter (2016, 20–23) and Voelz (1984, 910–19).

56. Deissmann (1908b, 55–56) railed against "qualitative judgments" against postclassical Greek as "uttered by doctrinaires" who are "enslaved to the prejudice that only the so-called classical Greek is beautiful" or "echoed from the grammarians who fancied themselves able by their authority to prevent the changes" in the language. "A good deal of their false judgments about late Greek is the simple consequence of their complete ignorance of it."

57. Deissmann (1901, 74) also argued the influence of the source text upon the syntax of the Septuagint was a result of the translation style.

Other important works appeared that continued the discussion about the position of the Septuagint within postclassical Greek.[58] Henry Barclay Swete's *Introduction to the Old Testament in Greek* (1900) retained some notion of Jewish Greek. Yet he believed further study would confirm Deissmann's position that Septuagint vocabulary "belonged to the language of business and conversation at Alexandria" (297).[59] At times both Swete and Deissmann appear to conflate nonliterary with uneducated categories of linguistic usage, though this is a mistake (Horsley 1984, 395; cf. Aitken 2014b, 27; Lee 2016, 99). Yet Swete (1900, 295) also acknowledges that, while nonliterary language was the "chief resource" of the Septuagint translators in Egypt, they occasionally employed more educated expressions of literary quality.

Another scholar to follow Deissmann was Thackeray, whose unfinished *Grammar of the Old Testament in Greek* (1909) remains important. Thackeray was utterly convinced that the documentary evidence proved the Septuagint corpus was made up of conventional nonliterary Greek. He went further in arguing that "the main function" of linguistic study of the Septuagint was to contribute to the "larger subject" of the grammar and "thesaurus of κοινή Greek" (16). Thackeray correctly viewed postclassical Greek—"the κοινή"—as a historical phase of Greek that contained both more- and less-educated varieties (17–19). Like Deissmann and to some extent Swete, Thackeray did not deny the influence of the source text on syntax in the Septuagint. Yet he too regarded the Septuagint as a corpus of the language of "the vernacular class" that nevertheless contains "some specimens of the literary κοινή" (1909, 17).[60]

Not all Septuagint scholars agreed. For example, in their short *Grammar of Septuagint Greek* (1995 [1905]), F. C. Conybeare and St. George Stock depart from Swete and Thackeray. They agreed that the documentary evidence showed Septuagint vocabulary was conventional postclassical

---

58. It was during this same period that Septuagint scholarship came into its own as a discipline, focusing largely on producing new editions. This was prompted mostly by Lagarde (1863), who drove scholars to recognize the mixed character of the main witnesses to the Septuagint and developed principles to produce critical texts.

59. Swete (1900, 229) points to the influence of translation style upon syntax, and goes on to say "the translators write Greek largely as they doubtless spoke it … they are almost indifferent to idiom, and seem to have no sense of rhythm."

60. Similar thoughts are expressed by Ottley (1920, 174–78). Other important works include those of Helbing (1907, 1928) and Abel (1927), discussed in Porter (2016, 24–25).

Greek. Yet Conybeare and Stock prioritize the role of syntax as constitutive of language. Construed in these terms, they considered the language of the Septuagint to represent a "very peculiar variety" of Greek that was "no fair specimen either of the colloquial or of the literary language of Alexandria" (21–22). It was "Hebrew in disguise" (21). Conybeare and Stock not only rejected outright the arguments of Deissmann, Swete, and Thackeray, but indeed they appear to have revived some of the concerns of the Purists. They lament that, as Septuagint translators strove "to give the very words of the Hebrew Bible to the Greek world," the "genius of the Greek language" was "entirely ignored … often such as to cause disgust to the classical student" (23).[61]

Most importantly, the views espoused by Conybeare and Stock entailed serious doubts about the very possibility of Septuagint lexicography. They state: "it is often doubtful whether the Greek *had* a meaning to those who wrote it. One often cannot be sure that they did not write down, without attaching any significance to them, the Greek words which seemed to be the nearest equivalents to the Hebrew before them" (23, emphasis original). In effect, the semantic errors that Gesenius had critiqued in Septuagint lexicons were attributed by Conybeare and Stock to the semantic intentions of the Septuagint translators.

The Mid-Twentieth-Century Revival of "Jewish Greek"

In the middle of the twentieth century, several scholars began to advocate once more the notion of a Jewish Greek dialect represented in the Septuagint and New Testament (see the surveys by Katz 1956; Jellicoe 1969b). Although this view is now thoroughly disproven, a seminal figure in this movement was Henry Gehman, whose publications on the topic coincided with his earliest—and ultimately unfinished—efforts toward a new lexicon of the Septuagint, discussed below. Gehman was aware not only of the inadequacies in the history of Septuagint lexigraphy, but also of the implications of the documentary evidence.[62] Yet at times he spoke of a "Hebraic character" or "cast" to the language of the Septuagint in both vocabulary and syntax. While dismissing, with Thackeray, the idea of a fully isolated "jargon," Gehman nevertheless felt the language of the Septuagint was not

---

61. Here also condescendingly comparing the translation of Numbers to a schoolboy's competency with Euripides.
62. Gehman (1974, 223–26) briefly rehearses the history from Kircher to Schleusner.

simply the result of the translation style. He argued it was "Jewish Greek" that reflected a "familiar *Denkart*" found in Jewish religious communities of Egypt (1951, 82, 87).⁶³ "If the LXX made sense to Hellenistic Jews, we may infer that there was a Jewish Greek which was understood apart from the Hebrew language" (1951, 90; see also 1953, 1954). Gehman's position soon elicited a response from Nigel Turner, who expanded it as he revived the old concept of Biblical Greek. Turner (1964, 45) argued in various publications through the 1950s and 1960s that the language of the Septuagint and New Testament was a "living dialect of Jewish Greek" that was distinct from postclassical Greek.⁶⁴ Other scholars followed, bringing more attention to this view and setting the stage for the two main positions currently advanced within Septuagint scholarship (e.g., Black 1965, 1970; Hill 1967).⁶⁵

The Formation of the International Organization for Septuagint and Cognate Studies and the Lexicographical "Scrum"

Modern Septuagint scholarship was born in Berkeley, California on 19 December 1968 when a group of scholars passed a motion to form the International Organization for Septuagint and Cognate Studies (IOSCS). Notably, one of the first items under discussion, aside from the need for a comprehensive bibliography for the discipline, was "the possibility of initiating a LXX lexicon project" (Fritsch 1969, 4).⁶⁶ In this section I survey efforts to do so in some detail with a view to providing a historical record

---

63. Around the same time, Bickerman (1959, 12–13) acknowledged that documentary evidence had demonstrated the Greek Pentateuch "basically agrees with the common speech of the contemporary Greeks," yet goes on to say "neverthless, the language of the Greek Torah is foreign and clumsy."

64. See also N. Turner (1954–1955; 1955; 1963, 2–9; 1964; 1965, 183; 1980b) and the discussion in Porter (2016, 27–28, esp. n. 56). John Lee was completing his doctoral research on the topic in the 1970s, discussed below, that would prove to be a milestone for the discipline (published 1983).

65. Porter (2016, 29–31) also draws attention to the work of Finnish scholars Ilmari Soisalon-Soininen and Raija Sollamo, among others, who tend to focus on Hebrew influence in the Septuagint translation. Useful surveys of the history of the debate as it stood up to this time can be found in Turner (1962) and (McKnight 1965).

66. In 1967 scholars had been polled for their opinion on the most pressing needs in reference works, and a Septuagint lexicon was the prevailing response (Gates 1972). See also Pietersma (1997, 177).

of these activities in the IOSCS and to outline the contemporary context for Septuagint lexicography.

At the inaugural meeting of the IOSCS, Sidney Jellicoe (1969b, 197) highlighted the importance of producing a specialized lexicon, pointing out that Septuagint scholars were dependent upon New Testament grammars and lexicons (cf. Fritsch 1969, 5). He clearly recognized the sea change brought about by the documentary evidence, stating that a Septuagint lexicon project must "take notice of the resources to hand since Schleusner." Yet Jellicoe (1969a, 15) knew this would be "a vast and detailed task, probably too great for any scholar to undertake and complete within a foreseeable period singlehanded." In light of this recognition, he began discussions for collaboration the following year at the 1969 seminar of the Society for New Testament Studies (SNTS).[67] Scholars were interested enough to immediately begin discussing the important—if more superficial—practical questions such as sponsorship, contributors, scope of literature covered, and the format of lexical entries.[68] Yet despite this show of interest, it would be almost thirty years before a Septuagint lexicon was finally published by the next generation of Septuagint scholars. Still, the intervening decades saw the appearance of important studies and considerable discussion over both practical and theoretical matters. Aside from the very real logistical challenges involved, it was precisely the extent of disagreement over practical and theoretical lexicographical issues that delayed any publication for so long.

Gehman made one of the first efforts. He had been approached to lead a Septuagint lexicon project as part of a larger series of theological dictionaries published by Westminster Press. After that project was abandoned, Gehman obtained a Guggenheim grant in 1953 and continued for at least five years with graduate assistance.[69] The underlying notion of a Jewish Greek dialect is clear in Gehman's intention to analyze all Septuagint

---

67. Kraft (1969–1970, esp. 392–95), who records Hill's comment that the New Testament and Septuagint contained "a special Greek with a pronounced Semitic cast … i.e. a 'Jewish Greek'" (387).

68. Discussions over funding began within a year with the Lutheran Missouri Synod, although it later fell through (Jellicoe 1970; Kraft and Tov 1981, 23). The 1970 meeting minutes record Howard's proposal that, owing to the link between textual criticism and lexicography, the IOSCS lexicon project begin with the prophetical books for which Göttingen editions had already emerged (Fritsch 1970b).

69. The result of this labor is stored in the archives of Princeton Theological Seminary.

vocabulary specifically in relation to its Hebrew or Aramaic equivalents. His method thus mirrors that of all Septuagint lexicons and concordances then existing, to which Gehman made "constant reference" (Kraft 1972c, 48–49). Although the pace of the work slowed drastically after Gehman's retirement in 1958, the project survived until at least 1969. By then only about half of the letter *alpha* had been catalogued. Charles Fritsch (1970a, 5) reported the first collision between theory and practice in modern Septuagint lexicography: Gehman's lexicon never materialized owing to a lack of personnel, funding, and, "above all, method."[70]

For better or worse, lexicographical efforts began afresh with the interest of scholars in the SNTS and the IOSCS (see Kraft 1972c, 16). At the meetings of the IOSCS in both 1970 and 1971, Walter Eisenbeis presented his ideas for meeting the "urgent need" for an updated Septuagint lexicon. He drew attention to the same challenges presented by "method, tools, and time" that had led to the demise of Gehman's project. Eisenbeis's proposals arose from his personal labors over the preceding two years preparing over ten thousand notecards (or "slips") by hand based on Rahlfs's edition. The notecards contained individual Greek words, references, citations, morphology, and relevant syntactical information, notations of treatment in other lexicons, and the Hebrew equivalent of transliterated proper names where appropriate (Jellicoe 1971a, 7; also see 1972, 6).[71] Based on his pace producing this material, Eisenbeis affirmed Jellicoe's opinion when he estimated it would take over one and a half million notecards and more than one hundred fifty years for one person to complete the project. His calls for collaboration to finish the project he had begun were not answered in the way Eisenbeis might have wished. But a working document for a new "Septuagint Lexicon Project" was soon drafted and approved by the IOSCS in collaboration with the Lutheran Missouri Synod (Jellicoe 1971b, 2; Fritsch 1971).[72]

---

70. In his reflections on his work, Gehman (1966, 126) states that in general, "transformation or extension of the Greek vocabulary [in the Septuagint] was not unreasonable and in many instances was developed under semantic principles." It was lexicographical method that was under examination around the same time in two important articles by Caird (1968, 1969), who discussed over one hundred entries in LSJ that neglected or mishandled Septuagint evidence. These were followed by a similar article by Lee (1969), which Pietersma (2015, 165) considers a turning point for Septuagint lexicography.

71. Cf. Kraft (1972b), which is a synthesis of Eisenbeis's papers.

72. At the 1971 SNTS seminar, F. F. Bruce and J. W. Doeve agreed to prepare lexi-

The attempts by Gehman and Eisenbeis, though unsuccessful, set the trajectory of the IOSCS lexicon project. The view of the language of the Septuagint underlying their method represented a Hebrew-priority position that was gaining momentum among their colleagues. Like Gehman, Eisenbeis considered the language of the Septuagint "translation Greek" that was a "specific dialect" (Kraft 1972b, 26–27). While he wished to give the vocabulary consideration first of all as Greek, this view entailed that the underlying Hebrew was "of decisive importance when the individual meanings of a given word are to be determined."[73] To produce a Septuagint lexicon, Eisenbeis argued, the MT would have to be "consulted constantly" (Kraft 1972b, 26). Robert Kraft also promoted this method and its underlying view at the 1970 SNTS seminar and the 1971 IOSCS meeting, based on his preliminary but detailed work producing entries for Greek interjections.[74] Indeed, Kraft played an instrumental role in the IOSCS Septuagint Lexicon Project not only in solidifying its theoretical orientation as a Hebrew-priority view. He also compiled an edited volume specifically intended to facilitate the ongoing discussions regarding the theoretical aspects of Septuagint lexicography (Kraft 1972e).

The Hebrew-priority view did not go unchallenged. Support for a Greek-priority view arose primarily from Sebastian Brock and John Lee, who also had different proposals for the practical matters of the lexicon project (see Brock and Lee 1972). For example, unlike Kraft, Eisenbeis, and Wevers, Brock and Lee wished to exclude the Septuagint recensions of Aquila, Symmachus, and Theodotion.[75] But Brock and Lee also argued for the importance of a unified theory to Septuagint lexical semantics for the lexicon project, without which "each contributor's work will differ

---

cographical sample entries for discussion the following year (Kraft 1970–1971, 490; 1972a, 31). An overview of the leadership structure and preliminary objectives of the project as they stood in 1970 is recorded by Kraft (1972c, 17).

73. Eisenbeis carried forward some of the problems well known in Kittel's *TDNT* insofar as he was sure that "no one will doubt that ... analyses must be made which will help to identify the edeational structures of Hebrew thought that underlie the various words in translational Greek" (Kraft 1972b, 27).

74. Kraft (1972b, 26–27) records his agreement with Eisenbeis (see also Kraft 1970–1971, 1972d).

75. Cf. Wevers (1972). They also argued for using HRCS as a basis for the project, while Eisenbeis supported using Rahlfs's edition, and Kraft and Wevers wanted to use the best critical texts as they became available (Kraft 1972c, 15–16; see also Kraft 1972a).

seriously from that of the others" (20). In this connection they correctly pointed out that one's view of the language of the Septuagint is "bound to affect one's approach to lexicography" (22–23). For that reason, Brock and Lee urged the project's editorial committee to decide on a distinct approach. To that end they warned against equating the "meaning of a Greek word with that of the Hebrew word it represents," and advocated for definitions rather than the problematic gloss method. Most significantly for lexicographical method, however, Brock and Lee maintained it was "axiomatic that before deciding the meaning of a word in the LXX it is necessary to investigate as fully as possible the usage of the word in non-biblical Greek of the same time" (22). Theirs was a Greek-priority view of Septuagint lexicography that understood the relationship of the language of the Septuagint to postclassical Greek in a manner informed by Deissmann, Moulton, and Thackeray. Nevertheless, the Greek-priority view remained a minority report for much of the next decade.[76]

In November 1973, a year after the passing of Jellicoe—who had been so instrumental in the initiative—the IOSCS approved Emanuel Tov as editor designate of the lexicon project.[77] Not long afterward, Tov published a detailed report from 1975 in which he states that "the exact shape of the lexicon project cannot be envisioned at this stage" (Tov 1976, reprinted 1999b).[78] Still, his lengthy report again highlighted the need for such a lexicon, discussed its possible target audience, and overviewed the theoretical issues involved: questions of scope, extant sources, entry content,

---

[76]. Lee had just dealt a death blow to the Jewish Greek hypothesis in his now highly influential doctoral dissertation, completed at Cambridge in 1970 but unpublished until 1983 (see Lee 2003b). Silva also made an important contribution in his 1980 *Biblica* article pointing out the imprecise terminology plaguing the long-standing debate over the nature of "Biblical Greek" and defending Deissmann's basic position. It is also notable that, almost twenty years after his retirement, Gehman (1974) had evidently changed his view, arguing in the midst of a discussion of the documentary evidence that "the Greek of the LXX represents the *koinē* of theird to the first century B.C." and that, although the "idiom" of the corpus is "Hebraic," that "does not justify us in calling without qualification the vernacular of the LXX a Jewish-Greek dialect" (226).

[77]. *Pace* Muraoka (1990a, vii–viii). See Pietersma (1974, 4) and Howard (1974, 5); Fritsch (1973, 5) reports "no change" in the lexicon project during the year cited by Muraoka. Cf. Taylor (2009, ix). Tov was to work with Frank Moore Cross, Moshe Goshen-Gottstein, Robert Hanhart, and John W. Wevers (chair) as a project committee.

[78]. For his reflection on his early work, see Tov (2010, 10).

and working method.[79] Tov also acknowledged the differing views of the language of the Septuagint. His own view recognized what he describes as an "Egyptian branch of Hellenistic Greek" and attributed the "special nature of the language of the LXX" to "its background as a translation." Notably, Tov is circumspect regarding any historical reality of a Jewish Greek dialect. He does, however, acknowledge what he calls a "Jewish Greek vocabulary" of technical terms that arose prior to the translation of the Pentateuch (1976, 22–23). Despite these finer points, like Eisenbeis and Kraft, Tov (1976, 25) characterized the language of the Septuagint in general as "translation Greek" and argued the lexicographer "must constantly pay attention to the *linguistic* background of the lexical equations of the Hebrew (Aramaic) and the Greek" (emphasis original). With Tov's appointment as editor and Kraft's ongoing involvement, soon to expand further, the IOSCS lexicon project proceeded according to the Hebrew-priority view.[80]

Three years later, after a period without any prospect of funding, a successful grant application for the project was made to the National Endowment for the Humanities from 1978 to 1979 (Pietersma 1977, 2; 1978, 3; 1979, 2; Muraoka 1990a, viii).[81] At the IOSCS session in 1978, Kraft presented a progress report on the lexicon project discussing the feasibility study conducted with the grant, based at the University of Pennsylvania under his direction. It was intended specifically "to determine the applicability of current computer technology to the proposed lexicon" and envisioned as an initial stage of a ten-year project (Kraft 1979, 14). Starting with a comprehensive database later distributed to project contributors, the project would then coordinate and edit results in multiple formats, including the lexicon as well as comprehensive concordances. Kraft goes

---

79. Oddly, although Tov was apparently well versed in the state of the question (see 1975, revised and enlarged in Tov 1983), he elsewhere states that "not much is known to me" about Gehman's work (1976, 20).

80. For Tov (1976, 41), relevant external evidence includes "all Greek texts, both literary and nonliterary, early and late. Hellenistic sources are of particular importance, especially those from Egypt." Yet he considered external and internal evidence to be of "equal importance," and included within his category of internal evidence both Septuagint usage and Hebrew translation equivalents (34).

81. Another grant was made for 1980–1981 (Kraft and Tov 1981, 23–24). In 1978, Silva responded to Tov's article by addressing more involved questions of lexical semantics, along with the prescient statement that "a lexicon that will truly meet the needs of biblical scholars for the next generation cannot be produced in less than 15 years" (25).

on to discuss "truly exciting possibilities" in computing that now appear as amusing relics, such as machine readable tapes, telephone line baud rates, Teletype line printers, and "mini-computers with video-screen components" (Kraft 1979, 15; cf. Kraft and Tov 1981, 25, 27).[82] The results of the study were encouraging, and plans were made to establish a project headquarters in order to take "a long step towards the fulfillment of this dream that has been nurtured by many for so long" (Kraft 1979, 16).

As foundational as such work was to contemporary Bible software, it nevertheless added a new layer of complexity to the lexicon project on top of the already contested discussions about practical and theoretical matters. Surely making any steps forward first required the proverbial step back. However, the development of computer-based tools for the lexicon project in fact turned attention in other directions. The redirection became evident within three years, when Kraft and Tov (1981) jointly published a detailed article discussing the lexicon project, tellingly entitled "Computer Assisted Tools for Septuagint Studies."[83] Tov spent the 1980–1981 academic year at the University of Pennsylvania working with Kraft and numerous students from there, Dropsie University, and the University of Toronto. Their aim was to create "a comprehensive and flexible computer 'data bank' available for efficient scholarly research on virtually all aspects of Septuagint studies—textcritical, lexical, grammatical, conceptual, translational, bibliographical" (1981, 28, 29; see also Tov 1983). In time, the result of this "preparatory stage" to the lexicon project became known as the CATSS database. Following this report, the IOSCS lexicon project fell silent for five years (1981, 33).[84]

At the 1986 Congress of the International Organization for Septuagint and Cognate Studies in Jerusalem, a new voice entered the discussion that would prove highly influential, that of Takamitsu Muraoka (Ulrich 1985, 6).[85] In his paper, Muraoka (1987, 255) points out that over twelve years

---

82. Another paper was given by Martin at the same IOSCS meeting about the promise of computer programming for biblical studies (Pietersma 1979, 1).

83. In the same year, yet another scholar instrumental in starting the lexicon project, Henry S. Gehman, passed away (Wevers 1981).

84. Samples of the project's results appeared in the same article (Kraft and Tov 1981, 34–40) and were published elsewhere (e.g., Abercrombie et al. 1986; Tov 1986, 1991; Marquis 1991). See also the abstract for a related paper by Martin (Ulrich 1981, 46). CATSS is currently available online: http://ccat.sas.upenn.edu/rak/catss.html.

85. Two years earlier Muraoka (1984, 441) had already discerned the contours of

had passed since the IOSCS lexicon project was launched and makes a pointed remark in regard to CATSS: "As we are all aware, a fundamental shift has taken place in the meantime in the direction of the project." While praising the work of the CATSS project, Muraoka (1987, 256) soberly points out that it amounted only to "an important and useful tool," while "the actual task of compiling a lexicon of the LXX has not yet even begun."[86] Muraoka also announced that he and Lee would collaborate on a lexicographical "pilot project" in the Minor Prophets, chosen for its manageable size and because Joseph Ziegler's Göttingen edition was available (1987, 257–58).[87] Most importantly, Muraoka and Lee agreed upon "the absolute necessity to pay due attention to the end product in Greek garb without allowing our judgment to be unduly influenced by the Hebrew *Vorlage* or what one conceives to be its meaning." Theirs was a Greek-priority view, which maintained that "one ought to allow the Greek to speak for itself" (Muraoka 1987, 261–62). Moreover, with the arguments made by Moisés Silva (1978) in mind, from the outset Muraoka and Lee aimed to provide word definitions rather than translation equivalents. In so doing they explicitly acknowledged and sought to avoid the problems inherent in the gloss method that had been part of Septuagint lexicography from its inception (Muraoka 1987, 263).[88]

So while the Hebrew-priority view of Septuagint lexicography had gained the upper hand among the leadership of the IOSCS lexicon project, the intervening sideline activity of the CATSS team allowed the Greek-priority view represented by Muraoka and Lee to be first out of the gate.[89] A year after announcing the pilot lexicon project, Muraoka held a sympo-

---

the growing divide in Septuagint scholarship between "translator-centred and reader-centred" views.

86. Years later, Tov (2010, 10) even states that some "will be surprised to find out" that the original purpose of CATSS was Septuagint lexicography.

87. Muraoka had approached Lee in 1984 to propose their collaboration and within a year was speaking of their "joint project," with drafts exchanged and research visits between Sydney and Melbourne following soon afterwards (Lee, pers. comm., 9 October 2017).

88. He illustrates the insufficiencies of the gloss method by citing Schleusner's supremely unhelpful entry for ἀνά: *praepositio. Respondet hebraico* בְּ *apud* Symm. *Zach. IV, 12*" (264).

89. By the early 1990s Tov had come to recognize, under the influence of Lee, the importance of the documentary evidence to Septuagint lexicography and his lack of ability to handle it as the IOSCS project editor (2010, 11).

sium at the University of Melbourne for which participants wrote lexical entries for vocabulary of their choice.⁹⁰ There a major question underlying the longstanding divide between Hebrew- and Greek-priority viewpoints came clearly to the surface: Is lexical semantics in a translated document framed primarily by the source language (Hebrew-priority) or the target language (Greek-priority)?⁹¹ Overall, the consensus that emerged from Melbourne was the latter: Septuagint lexicography ought to be framed in terms of the Greek target language and only refer to the Hebrew source text "if *the user of the lexicon* needs it in order to appreciate the translator's intention" (Lee 1990, 5, emphasis added).⁹² With this mindset, the usefulness of the long history of Septuagint concordances was finally but—from a linguistic perspective—appropriately reduced to the status of an index with which lexicographical investigation can only begin (see Muraoka 1990c, 32).

The results of these early efforts in the IOSCS to produce a lexicon were, if not an actual lexicon, the beginnings of one and the entrenchment of two broad views. Thanks to the work of scholars like Deissmann, Moulton, and Lee, by the late twentieth century all had rejected the notion of a standalone Jewish Greek dialect.⁹³ The documentary evidence had allowed crucial advances in understanding postclassical Greek. Moreover, all acknowledged that the language of the Septuagint is postclassical Greek. Yet, despite that consensus, opinions differed over the method with which to move forward. Aside from the practical disagreements over matters like the best base text and coverage of the lexicon, the conflict

---

90. The proceedings were later published (Muraoka 1990b). Not long after that event, Lust (1992, ii) could say that the IOSCS lexicon project "seems to be dormant." For an overview of the history of the IOSCS up through about this time, see Greenspoon (1995).

91. Muraoka (1990b, x) notes that as a result of interaction at the Melbourne symposium, Tov reconsidered his position and came essentially to adopt a Greek-priority view. Afterward, Tov (1990, 117) could say that the "rule of thumb we follow is that as long as possible we record the words of the LXX as if that text were a regular Greek text, explaining the words—conjecturally—in the way which a Greek reader would have taken them." Cf. Muraoka (1990c, 44–45).

92. Lee nevertheless warns the lexicographer to consult the Hebrew text in order to be aware of challenges such as "stereotyped rendering, or etymologizing, or where the Greek mirrors a Hebrew idiom strange to Greek." See Lee (2020) for his more recent articulation of how the language of the Septuagint should be compared with Hebrew.

93. Seminal studies here include those by Lee (1983) and Horsley (1984, 1989).

between the theoretical views was intractable. As Lee (2004a, 127) would later describe, the Greek- and Hebrew-priority positions had turned into "a kind of scrum" from which two players would ultimately emerge. Just as Muraoka and Lee's pilot project was beginning in the mid-1980s, another project began in Europe almost simultaneously, and these two would pursue different theoretical approaches to "the basic problem of Septuagint philology" (Evans 2005, 25).

The Contemporary Context: Two Views, Two Lexicons

The two views that currently prevail in Septuagint scholarship are not binary but rather exist along a spectrum and are often carefully nuanced. All recognize the difficulty involved in generalizing about the language of the entire Septuagint.[94] Still, a methodological divide exists that corresponds to the Greek- and Hebrew-priority views: Some prioritize the role of the target language in Septuagint lexicography and others that of the source language, respectively.[95] These diverging perspectives underlie the two contemporary lexicons of the Septuagint that emerged in the 1990s and early 2000s, that of Johan Lust, Erik Eynikel, and Katrin Hauspie (1992, 1996, 2003) and that of Muraoka (1993b, 2002, 2009).[96]

Before discussing these in more depth, it is worth noting other publications around the same period directed at Septuagint lexicography. The first is that of Friedrich Rehkopf (1989), who based his work on Rahlfs's edition. He lists Greek words alphabetically, with (usually one-word) German translation equivalents and the corresponding Hebrew for transliterations, along with references to Septuagint and New Testament use

---

94. See Aitken (1999, 24) and Ross (forthcoming). Evans (2001, 3) rightly warns that the Septuagint corpus "cannot usefully be treated as a single entity in terms of its linguistic content."

95. Porter (2016, 36) calls these views the "revived form of the Koine Greek hypothesis" and the "modified form of the Jewish Greek hypothesis." Dorival (2015, 227) states, "on peut répartir les lexicographes modernes de la Septante en deux catégories: ceux qui privilégient la lange source, l'amont, et ceux qui accordent la priorité à la langue cible, l'aval."

96. Lee's involvement in the pilot project that eventually led to the first iteration of Muraoka's lexicon—initially covering the Twelve Prophets as planned (1993a)—came to an end "well before the lexicon reached completion" (Lee 2004a, 127 n. 1). But see Muraoka (2009, xvi). For comparison of LEH with GELS, see Vervenne (1998) and Lust (1993b).

(see Hilhorst 1989, 256–57; Dorival 2016, 277). This publication was not intended to be anything other than a vocabulary handbook for theological students.[97] Another resource meant to facilitate reading the Septuagint was the analytical lexicon produced by Bernard Taylor (1994), again based on Rahlfs's edition (later expanded in 2009). Notably, this work arose from Taylor's involvement with the morphological tagging undertaking in the CATSS project under the guidance of Tov and Kraft (Taylor 2009, ix–xi).[98] A significant addition to the 2009 edition is the pairing of the CATSS morphological information with lexicographical information drawn from LEH.[99] Finally, there is the supplemental lexicon by Gary Chamberlain (2011), which is meant to complement Frederick Danker et al. (2000) by only covering Septuagint vocabulary not discussed in the latter. The primary resources for Chamberlain were LSJ and *PGL*; the final editions of LEH and *GELS* emerged during the course of Chamberlain's work (Chamberlain 2011, vii). For his part, Chamberlain aligns with the Greek-priority view, as he insists that the language of the Septuagint is "demonstrably normal Hellenistic Greek."[100]

---

97. Much the same could be said of Lanier and Ross (2019).

98. Though that analysis was finished in 1987 and released on CD-ROM, it underwent significant reanalysis before Taylor's first printing in 1994 and yet further corrections in the expanded 2009 edition.

99. Taylor is unclear as to whether his glosses come directly from LEH or were occasionally modified resulting from his own analysis. If the former, it appears that he has misconstrued the theoretical approach of LEH (see 2009, xix). Note also that a digital analytical lexicon based on Swete's edition is available from Logos (Hoogendyk et al. 2012).

100. Chamberlain (2011, xxvii–xxviii) states that "we err whenever we try to infer Hebrew meanings in Greek words apart from their Greek context." Accordingly, "words are generally taken to mean what they would have meant to a non-Jewish Hellenistic reader, regardless of the underlying Semitic base (if any)" (ix). Chamberlain states that his purpose is to systematically "acknowledge every word or use that conforms to ordinary expectations for fundamental/classical or Κοινή Greek," while also treating all cases were Septuagint vocabulary diverges from that usage with "attention to specific instances and contexts" (xii). According to Lust (2003, xiii), Chamberlain had initially joined the team working on LEH, but his involvement came to an end after the first volume was published (1992) due to his differing view. Note that, despite her work on LEH, Hauspie (2003) elsewhere defends a Greek-priority position, in part by appealing to cognitive semantics.

LEH and Hebrew Priority

On one side of the spectrum mentioned above is the Hebrew-priority view. At a very broad level, this position tends to emphasize the Semitic characteristics of the language of the Septuagint and to explain them as the result of the intention of the translators always to reproduce the meaning of their source text. On that basis, Septuagint lexical semantics may be framed in terms of the source text.

A primary proponent of this approach is Lust, who presented his theoretical approach to Septuagint lexicography at the Society of Biblical Literature Annual Meeting in 1991, one year prior to the publication of the first volume of LEH. Pointing to Lee's work in carrying forward Deissmann's conclusions, Lust (1993a, 109) acknowledges that the language of the Septuagint is not a Jewish Greek dialect or a holy language. Nevertheless, Lust (1993a, 110) ascribes to it a unique character owing to its close adherence to the syntax of the source text: "Septuagint Greek cannot simply be characterized as Koine Greek. It is first of all translation Greek."[101] Because the translators generally reproduced the word order of their source text, the Septuagint is characterized by "Hebraisms" or "translationisms," and is far from an "artistic Greek literary composition" (111, 112, 115). For Lust, this source text orientation not only affected the syntax but the vocabulary of the Septuagint as well, although it is "less blatant" (111, 119). As to the competency of the translators, Lust is ambivalent. On the one hand—note the number of qualifications—they "*appear* to have *most often* carefully selected Greek terms whose semantic range covered *more or less* that of the Hebrew equivalent" (111, 119, emphasis added). But, on the other hand, sometimes the translators "had problems finding an adequate equivalent" and so invented words, transliterated, and even resorted to "purely mechanical 'translations of embarrassment'" (111).[102] Accordingly, Lust reasons, if the object of Septuagint lexicography is to ascertain the meaning intended by the translators, then an approach that disregards or rarely consults the source text is untenable (115).

These same arguments are advanced in the introduction to LEH, a lexicon compiled by a team of scholars in Belgium and built upon Lust's theoretical assumptions about the language of the Septuagint (see Lust

---

101. Lust arrived at this position in part due to his examination of the parallel aligned texts produced by the CATSS project (1993a, n. 4).

102. Referring to the so-called *Verlegenheitsübersetzungen* of Flashar (1912).

2003, xvii–xxiv, largely a reproduction of 1993a). The project had begun independently of the Muraoka-Lee pilot project and made use of the CATSS database (Lust 2003, xii–xiii). The first installments of both LEH and *GELS* were published almost simultaneously (Lust, Eynikel, and Hauspie 1992; Muraoka 1993a). In the preface to the former, Lust (2003, xvi) reiterates the argument that

> LXX Greek is first of all translation Greek. A lexicon of the LXX, therefore, should refer to the Semitic original, at least in those cases where the deviations between a Greek word and its Semitic equivalent can be explained at the level of morphemes, but also when the Greek words are incomprehensible because they are transliterations or because they have adopted the meaning of the underlying Hebrew or Aramaic words.[103]

The final reason given in the quotation above is the most significant. Since Lust aims to represent the meaning intended by the translator and assumes the translator always "wished to render his *Vorlage* as faithfully as possible," then by this logic Septuagint words (and a Septuagint lexicon) should "adopt" the meaning of the underlying source text by default (Lust 2003, xix; cf. 1993a, 110).[104] Thus, Lust justifies framing Septuagint lexical semantics in terms of the source text when the two appear to agree. But by a different logic Lust also justifies the same approach when the two appear to disagree. On the one hand, Lust states that a Septuagint lexicographer should avoid the errors of Schleusner and "seek to render the meaning of the Greek words in their context, without direct reference to the Hebrew." Yet on the other hand, wherever the Greek "*appears* to differ from the Hebrew," direct reference to the source text is in fact justified (Lust 1993b, 97, emphasis added).[105] In effect, this approach begs the lexicographical question: one cannot know whether a given Greek word differs in meaning from the Hebrew except

---

103. Cf. Lust (2001, 396): "It is true that, where it is not influenced by the Hebrew, the Septuagint translation uses Koine language.... It is, however, not entirely correct when one proposes to study Septuagint Greek as a major source of knowledge of Koine Greek, forgetting that it is first of all translation Greek."

104. Lust's collaborator Eynikel (1999, 146) similarly argues that in the case of polysemous words, "il faut donner aux mots grecs dans le dictionnaire le sens le plus proche de l'hébreu, mais tout de même en accord avec le grec du temps de la Septante."

105. Again, the underlying logic being his assumption that the translators strove to render their source text "as faithfully as possible," including lexical semantics.

by relying on the very lexicons whose inadequacy for postclassical Greek provides the reason for compiling a Septuagint lexicon in the first place. This problem becomes explicit in the introduction to LEH, which states that "each occurrence of a word has been looked at in its immediate context … the work of Liddell-Scott-Jones has frequently served as our immediate guide" (Lust 2003, xvi).[106] Moreover, although Lust signals the importance of context in determining meaning, in practice LEH lists only up to five references—not citations—for a given word, which in fact provides the reader with no context at all (Lust 2003, xiv; see also Lee 2004b, 70; Aitken 2014b, 10).

Forms of the Hebrew-priority view are not limited to LEH in contemporary scholarship. In 1995, Abert Pietersma began to argue that the "fundamental nature" of the Septuagint as a translation is a "dependent and subservient *linguistic* relationship to its Semitic parent" (Pietersma and Wright 2009, xiv, emphasis original; cf. Pietersma 2001). He suggested the language of the Septuagint is "translationese" that is inherently unintelligible.[107] In a series of essays that situate him somewhere between the Hebrew- and Greek-priority views, Cameron Boyd-Taylor later applied Pietersma's theory to Septuagint lexicography. Because he is a disciple of Gideon Toury's descriptive translation studies, Boyd-Taylor (2005, 82) is concerned to deal with the Septuagint translation as a "product of and for the target culture." But central to his arguments is the categorical distinction between "a translation corpus" and compositional literature.[108] In his view, to whatever extent that the source text constrained the linguistic usage of the translators in ways somehow unconventional to the target

---

106. LSJ, as Lust knows, has received its fair share of criticism for the way Septuagint evidence was handled. See Aitken (2014b, 6–15). For broader historical context on LSJ, see the volume by Stray, Clarke, and Katz (2019).

107. See Pietersma and Wright (2009b, xiv–xv); cf. Pietersma (2000) and Boyd-Taylor (2011). For critique, see Mulroney (2016, 51–77) and Dorival (2016, 296–99). In discussing unintelligible renderings in the Septuagint, Boyd-Taylor (2008, 197) admits that such are statistically the exception but argues that "unintelligibility" is "a clue to its meaning as a translation" (200). The notion of "translationese" had appeared in Septuagint scholarship as early as the 1970s in the work of Soisalon-Soininen (1987, 175). Cf. "translation language" in Rabin (1968, 13) and "translation Greek" even earlier in Rife (1933), both of which focus on word order.

108. Boyd-Taylor (2001, 47), notably appealing to the arguments made by Hatch (1889) and relying on Tov's (1976) position prior to the Melbourne symposium. Tov (1990, 117) is cited but without recognition of his change of view.

language—a phenomenon called "negative transfer"—to that extent the Septuagint as a whole offers less than straightforward linguistic evidence for Greek (Boyd-Taylor 2001, 56, 62–63; 2004a, 58 n. 11).[109] From this perspective, the language of the Septuagint is not Greek but rather an "interlanguage" produced in translation (Boyd-Taylor 2004a, following Toury).[110] Boyd-Taylor's primary criterion at this point appears not to be whether Septuagint vocabulary is representative of its meaning in contemporary usage—he believes it generally is—but rather whether its usage differs quantitatively in frequency and distribution (Boyd-Taylor 2001, 52–53; 2004a, 57–58; 2004b, 151).[111] He therefore rules out Septuagint lexicography that is strictly corpus-based, because that corpus inevitably presents a skewed picture of linguistic usage—construed in such terms—for postclassical Greek.[112] The logic runs as follows: Septuagint translators typically adhere to the word order of their source text, which affects the frequency and distribution (and sometimes meaning) of linguistic features in the target text in ways not conventional to the target language, which produces an "interlanguage" that is not straightforward lexical evidence. Boyd-Taylor (2001, 53) thus finds the theoretical approaches of LEH and *GELS* problematic because they are corpus-based in different ways: LEH ascribes evidentiary value to the source text in terms of translation equivalence, while Muraoka ascribes evidentiary value to the target text in terms of word distribution.[113] Importantly, for Boyd-Taylor, when the meaning of

---

109. Boyd-Taylor uses "source-oriented" and "target-oriented" for LEH and *GELS*, respectively.

110. Elsewhere he states, "Quite simply, the evidentiary value of the Septuagint is categorically different from that of non-translation literature" (Boyd-Taylor 2004b, 150). Muraoka (2008, 233, 234) strongly objects to the "interlanguage" concept, stating that it "seems to carry unfavourable, if not downright derogatory, overtones" and even "verges on a form of cultural imperialism."

111. His argument closely follows that of Rabin (1968, 11–13), who speaks of "sublanguage" (13). Unconventional frequency and distribution of vocabulary itself is consistent, in Boyd-Taylor's (2001, 77; cf. 2004b, 150) analysis, with his view of the language of the Septuagint in general. Similarly, the translation manual for NETS stipulates frequency of translation equivalence as the determining factor for whether a word is given its conventional Greek meaning or the underlying Hebrew one (Pietersma 1996, 12–15).

112. Boyd-Taylor (2001, 56, 73), pointing to the cautions raised in the Brock-Lee (1972) memorandum and by Caird (1969, 1968).

113. Boyd-Taylor's (2001, 47) goal is a lexicon *"for* the Septuagint" rather than one *"of* the Septuagint" (emphasis original).

Septuagint vocabulary "is corroborated by the usage of non-translation literature, we may well have straightforward semantic evidence." But it must be demonstrated (Boyd-Taylor 2004a, 72).[114] If ambiguity remains owing to lack of corroboration from external evidence, however, the Hebrew is consulted to arbitrate the meaning of the Greek "interlanguage."[115]

GELS and Greek Priority

On the other side of the spectrum is the Greek-priority view. Again at a general level, this position tends to emphasize the conventional Greek character of the language of the Septuagint and therefore its value for Greek lexicography in general. The most significant work produced from this perspective is *GELS* by Muraoka.

In Muraoka's estimation, because the intention of the translator is "rather elusive" it is unsafe to assume the target text was always meant to represent the meaning of its source. Therefore, reference to the source text cannot eliminate semantic ambiguity and, even where there is no ambiguity, the meaning of the Greek does not always match the underlying Hebrew (Muraoka 2009, viii; see also 2004, 85–88). Even in cases of stereotyped equivalency Muraoka is reluctant to allow the source text to bear upon semantic description of the Greek precisely because our knowledge of Hebrew lexical semantics is itself imperfect (2008, 224–25).[116] He furthermore points out that lack of external attestation of a meaning or linguistic feature in the Septuagint does not necessarily mean it was unconventional, but could simply result from the incomplete evidence for

---

114. Similarly, he states, "The lexicographer is … *not entitled* to make direct inferences from the Septuagint text" (2004b, 151, emphasis added). See also Pietersma's (2008, 12) slightly different formulation.

115. See the example in Boyd-Taylor (2008, 206–9). Dorival (2016, 298) seems to misunderstand Boyd-Taylor's position when he summarizes it: "Il est nécessaire et suffisant de connaître le sens des mots hébreux pour connaître le sens des mots grecs correspondants. En conséquence, un mot grec donné n'a pas forcément la signification qu'il a habituellement en grec, mais celle du mot hébreu qui lui correspond." Contrast Muraoka (2008, 227–28). Then again, some may notice how critics of the interlinear paradigm tend to find themselves accused of simply misunderstanding it.

116. He points out that "much of our current understanding of the biblical text" is founded upon the history of interpretation of the Septuagint and other versions, illustrating this possibility with an example drawn from Boyd-Taylor (2004b). Cf. Muraoka (1984, 442).

postclassical Greek at our disposal (230).[117] Therefore, the best approach to Septuagint lexicography is in the first instance to treat the text as an independent and comprehensible Greek document of Hellenistic Judaism (Muraoka 2009, viii; 2008, 229).[118]

Thus, following the spirit of Deissmann, Thackeray, and Lee with regard to the language of the Septuagint, *GELS* represents a major theoretical departure from the entire history of Septuagint lexicography. The same can be said of his practical approach insofar as Muraoka chose to use definitions to describe lexical meaning, rather than the gloss method that has otherwise dominated (2009, xii; see also n. 26). Muraoka determined word meaning by evaluating its use in context and setting it within syntagmatic and paradigmatic relations to other lexemes (2009, x–xi; 2004, 88). The influence of the source text on the language of the Septuagint is not denied, but in Muraoka's view this is too often exaggerated in lexical semantics (1995; 2004, 85; 2008, 224).[119] Moreover, to Muraoka (2008, 228–29) the ordinarily high degree of formal equivalency in syntagmatic alignment of source and target text does not primarily raise questions about semantics, but style.[120] In terms of the evidentiary value of the Septuagint for Greek, then, Muraoka (2008, 230–31) returns the burden of proof to the Hebrew-priority view by stating that "it is up to those who dismiss linguistic features attested in the LXX but not prior to it or contemporaneous with it to demonstrate that they could not have been part of the contemporary language system."[121]

---

117. This argument is correct in principle but exposes the lexicographer to the risk of attributing unattested meanings to Greek words that are tentative at best and erroneous at worst (e.g., *west* for θάλασσα in *GELS*). In this sense, Muraoka's method is certainly not without problems.

118. In Muraoka's (2008, 226) evaluation, the competency of the translators in both source and target languages was "probably uneven," but he leans toward an assumption of proficiency. Cf. Muraoka (1993b, viii–ix).

119. See his 2005 discussion of several "lexical Hebraisms." Muraoka (2008, 223) also points out that the so-called quantitative equivalence/identity central to the interlinear paradigm "is nowhere in the LXX consistently and systematically maintained, even disregarding elements such as grammatical morphemes or function words."

120. He questions the significance of differences in frequency of usage for a given lexeme, noting that surviving documentary evidence is conditioned by geography and climate as well as internal factors like genre and culture (233).

121. Specifically referring to Boyd-Taylor (2004b, 153). See also Muraoka (2016, xxxviii) and the response by Pietersma (2008).

The Way Forward

The most important issues for the discipline of Septuagint lexicography have always been present: the best method to represent linguistic meaning; the significance of the word-for-word translation style typical of the corpus; and the nature of postclassical Greek and its relationship to the language of the Septuagint. Particularly relevant to the last point, what has not remained constant over time is the available primary evidence for postclassical Greek, most conspicuously the nonliterary evidence.

The developments in how each of the key issues above have been handled highlight numerous inadequacies in the current state of Septuagint lexicography. The prevailing approach to representing lexical meaning from Kircher's earliest attempt in 1607 through LEH in 2003 has been the problematic gloss method. In contrast, this study takes the alternative approach of using definitions to describe lexical meaning, providing sample lexicon entries for several words discussed in chapters 3 and 5. Moreover, that the Hebrew-priority view is still so prevalent within Septuagint scholarship bespeaks its long history. Again, aspects of that view stretch back to Kircher and his dependents. Notably, it is the very word-for-word translation style typical of the corpus that makes producing a Septuagint concordance possible at a superficial textual level, but problematic on a linguistic level. In contrast, this study is concerned less with comparing Greek and Hebrew texts and focuses on understanding the language of the Septuagint as part of postclassical Greek in general.

The history of Septuagint lexicography and its place within scholarship of the Greek language identify the Greek-priority view as the way forward. Muraoka's lexicon represents an important first step in this regard and also in view of his decision to use definitions instead of glosses (Lee 2004a, 130; 2016, 104). Yet he unfortunately made little attempt to incorporate postclassical literature or documentary evidence (Muraoka 2009, ix; see also Aitken 2014b, 10–11).[122] Therefore, the task of sifting and evaluating postclassical evidence to further support and nuance accurate definitions

---

122. On a related note, although it represents an important step in lexical analysis for the Septuagint corpus, the *HTLS* is not only very selective in its coverage, but it also continues the gloss method and (at least in vol. 1) gives outsized attention to classical evidence. As useful as that evidence might be, it must be accompanied by equally or even more thorough investigation of contemporary evidence for postclassical Greek, as is done throughout this study.

is of unrivaled importance for Septuagint lexicography if the discipline is to make headway. All agree that this evidence in particular preserves the variety of language with which the Septuagint was translated, especially as attested in documentary sources. Of course, I do not pretend that the Septuagint contains perfectly conventional Greek at every point. But complete understanding of linguistic conventions in postclassical Greek itself is far from in hand. The key to understanding Septuagint vocabulary, then, is to stop assuming the Greek was always intended to represent the meaning of the Hebrew (even if it ordinarily does) and to start assuming it represents the meaning found in contemporary sources (Muraoka 2008, 229). Comparing the language of the Septuagint to those sources yields valuable results, such as insight into the register and social context of the translation as well as an enriched understanding of Greek lexical semantics. It is to that end that this study is directed by considering the significance of lexical choice in the revision of Greek Judges that is demonstrably free from Hebrew influence.

3
"Who Shall Go Up First?"
ΠΑΡΑΤΑΞΙΣ and ΠΑΡΑΤΑΣΣΩ

> La razón por la que el grupo 1 parece haberse sentido obligado a apartarse de la traducción usual de LXX en Jueces no es fácil de precisar. En todo caso hay que indicar que ha elegido para ello un verbo cuya significación primera y clásica no coincida plenamente con la de la raíz hebrea, pero que in la época helenística había adquirido ya connotaciones muy similares.
> —Targarona Borrás, "Historia del Texto Griego del Libro de los Jueces"

> In the case of frequently used polysemic lexemes one would like to know which meanings known to Classical Greek or Hellenistic, non-Septuagintal Greek are also used in the LXX or not used, and in the latter case one would be tempted to set out investigating why it is so.
> —Takamitsu Muraoka, "Recent Discussions on the Septuagint Lexicography"

The narrative of the book of Judges is an account of Israel's ongoing conquest of Canaan following the death of Joshua (Judg 1:1). In the wake of Joshua's passing, Israel was pitched into a tumultuous period under a number of military leaders and tribal heroes—the so-called judges (שפטים)—until the rise of Samuel and the establishment of the Israelite monarchy (1 Sam 7:3–8:22; Gertz et al. 2012, 360–61). The incomplete possession of the land of Canaan noted in Judg 1:1–3:6 precipitates a variety of military conflicts detailed throughout the rest of the book, not only between Israel and people groups native to Canaan but, ultimately, even among Israelite tribes themselves (Judg 20). On a practical level, the narrative provided repeated opportunities to translate the vocabulary associated with these military conflicts. As some of the most frequently occurring content words in Judges that simultaneously have a rich cultural background, this Greek *battle* vocabulary provides an ideal candidate for lexical analysis.

The words used throughout Judg[LXX] for concepts associated with battle differ distinctly in the OG translation (AII group) versus the later revision (B group). While the difference is evident in the double-text of Rahlfs-Hanhart, it is more accurately analyzed within these textual groups. On the one hand, the OG translator preferred πόλεμος and πολεμέω as the nominal and verb to translate מלחמה and לחם, respectively. On the other hand, the revised Greek text instead has substituted παράταξις and παρατάσσω for the OG lexical choices in almost every instance.[1] The striking consistency in the revision of Greek vocabulary betrays some kind of motivation, but clearly that motivation was not the underlying Hebrew vocabulary. Most Greek lexicons are of little help for explaining this lexical replacement—and indeed could create confusion—since postclassical sources are so poorly incorporated. Fresh examination of the Greek sources, however, sheds light upon the meaning of παράταξις and παρατάσσω in particular and their use in Greek Judges.

The analysis below will proceed in three sections. The first demonstrates that the differing trends in the *battle* vocabulary in Greek Judges fall decisively into textual groups that stand in historical relationship to one another. After identifying the weakness of contemporary lexicons with respect to παράταξις and παρατάσσω, I move in the second section into a fresh lexical analysis to show their (otherwise underdocumented) semantic development in the postclassical period. My analysis suggests that the words παράταξις and παρατάσσω not only underwent semantic change in the Hellenistic period, but also that they became conventional primarily within more formal and educated varieties of postclassical Greek. The final section in this chapter discusses selected texts in Judg[LXX] in light of the lexical analysis. I suggest that Greek stylistic concerns for the target text within its social context helped motivate the revision of Judg[OG]. The conclusions presented here demonstrate the importance of contemporary Greek sources for understanding the language of the Septuagint and representing it lexicographically, as well as the evidentiary value of Septuagint vocabulary as postclassical Greek. In my discussion I refer occasionally to the sample entries for παράταξις and παρατάσσω provided in the appendix.

---

1. Noted without further comment by Fernández Marcos (2012, 167). Cf. Harlé and Roqueplo (1999, 53–54).

3. "Who Shall Go Up First?" ΠΑΡΑΤΑΞΙΣ and ΠΑΡΑΤΑΣΣΩ

The Textual History of *Battle* Vocabulary in Judg[LXX]

As mentioned in chapter 1, the A and B texts of Judg[LXX] presented in Rahlfs-Hanhart provide a rough starting point for discerning the OG and revised text of Judg[LXX], respectively. Differences in Greek *battle* vocabulary are immediately evident, as shown in table 3.1.

Table 3.1. Judg[LXX] battle vocabulary in Rahlfs-Hanhart

	A text	B text
πόλεμος	14	3
πολεμέω	31	7
παράταξις	1	17
παρατάσσω	6	24

Generally speaking, while the A text preserves πόλεμος and πολεμέω, the B text instead preserves παράταξις and παρατάσσω. When these Greek texts are examined against the Hebrew text (MT) it becomes clear that these differences in Greek vocabulary attestation are associated with the same Hebrew vocabulary. That is, what πόλεμος and πολεμέω align with in the A text are (almost) the same Hebrew words as those that align with παράταξις and παρατάσσω in the B text. There are some differences, which can be represented as in table 3.2:

Table 3.2. The underlying Hebrew *battle* vocabulary[2]

	A text		B text	
מלחמה (20×)	πόλεμος	14×	πόλεμος	3×
	παράταξις	—	παράταξις	16×
לחם (31×)	πολεμέω	31×	πολεμέω	6×
	παρατάσσω	1×	παρατάσσω	24×
ערך (5×)	παρατάσσω	5×	παρατάσσω	—

---

2. לחם: 1:1, 3, 5, 8, 9; 5:19 (2×), 20 (2×); 8:1; 9:17, 38, 39, 45, 52; 10:9, 18; 11:4, 5, 6, 8, 9, 12, 20, 25 (2×), 27, 32; 12:1, 3, 4. Note that 5:8 is excluded due to a textual variant discussed below; מלחמה: 3:1, 2, 10; 8:13; 18:11, 16, 17; 20:14, 17, 18, 20 (2×), 22, 23, 28, 34, 39 (2×), 42; 21:22; ערך: 20:20, 22 (2×), 30, 33.

As shown, in the A text almost every instance of לחם corresponds with πολεμέω, whereas in the B text it is almost always aligned with παρατάσσω.³ Likewise, in the A text every instance of מלחמה corresponds with πόλεμος, whereas in the B text it is almost always aligned instead with παράταξις.⁴ Despite the fact that the texts in Rahlfs-Hanhart are eclectic and do not represent any particular stage of the textual history of Judg^LXX, the obvious differences between them in the *battle* vocabulary serve as a prompt for further investigation.⁵ Indeed, many of the exceptions to the trends in the A and B texts shown above are explained after examining the vocabulary in the textual groups of Judg^LXX.

The textual evidence for Judg^LXX bears out the fact that one set of words was replaced with another through a concerted effort at a later period in the textual history of the book in Greek. The trends that appear in Rahlfs-Hanhart are even more pronounced when the readings for the *battle* vocabulary are separated into textual groups. On the one hand, the AII group of witnesses that best represent the OG translation attests πόλεμος and πολεμέω with striking consistency. On the other hand, the B group of witnesses that represent Judg^Rv attests παράταξις and παρατάσσω with similar consistency. Table 3.3 presents the OG translation of לחם and its revision, with bold text indicating lexical substitution in the later stage.

Table 3.3. The *battle* verbs in Judg^LXX

לחם	Judg^OG	Judg^Rv
1:1	πολεμέω	πολεμέω
1:3	**πολεμέω**	**παρατάσσω**
1:5	**πολεμέω**	**παρατάσσω**
1:8	πολεμέω	πολεμέω

---

3. Exceptions occur at 9:52 and 10:9, where ἐκπολεμέω appears in the A text, and at 1:1, 8, 9; 5:19; and 11:25 (twice), where πολεμέω is in the B text. At 5:19, παρατάσσω renders לחם in the A text, but this is a textual variant (see further below).

4. Exceptions occur at 3:1, 2, and 10, where πόλεμος appears in the B text, and at 18:11, 16, and 17, where πολεμικός is used in the A text. Also, παράταξις appears in Judg^A 6:26, but it is used outside a military context and has a different sense.

5. Also, because these texts are eclectic, it is not strictly correct to speak of how they "translate" or "render" their Hebrew source(s). Accordingly, in this and subsequent chapters I have chosen to use the language of "alignment" or "correspondence" when speaking of the relationship of Judg^A or Judg^B with MT.

3. "Who Shall Go Up First?" ΠΑΡΑΤΑΞΙΣ and ΠΑΡΑΤΑΣΣΩ

1:9	πολεμέω	πολεμέω
5:8[6]	—	πολεμέω
5:19	πολεμέω	παρατάσσω
	παρατάσσω	πολεμέω
5:20	πολεμέω	παρατάσσω
	πολεμέω	παρατάσσω
8:1	πολεμέω	παρατάσσω
9:17	πολεμέω	παρατάσσω
9:38	πολεμέω	παρατάσσω
9:39	πολεμέω	παρατάσσω
9:45	πολεμέω	παρατάσσω
9:52	πολεμέω	παρατάσσω
10:9	πολεμέω	παρατάσσω
10:18	πολεμέω	παρατάσσω
11:4	πολεμέω	παρατάσσω
11:5	πολεμέω	παρατάσσω
11:6	πολεμέω	παρατάσσω
11:8	πολεμέω	παρατάσσω
11:9	πολεμέω	παρατάσσω
11:12	πολεμέω	παρατάσσω
11:20	πολεμέω	παρατάσσω
11:25	πολεμέω	πολεμέω
	πολεμέω	πολεμέω
11:27	πολεμέω	παρατάσσω
11:32	πολεμέω	παρατάσσω
12:1	πολεμέω	παρατάσσω
12:3	πολεμέω	παρατάσσω
12:4	πολεμέω	παρατάσσω

---

6. The Masoretes pointed לחם as לָחֶם. The OG likely read ἡρέτισαν θεοὺς καινοὺς ὡς ἄρτους κρίθινον, taking the first consonant of שערים as a שׂ and reading שְׂעֹרִים ("barley;" Tov 2015, 122). This Greek reading was later revised to understand לחם as a verb, as in Judg[B], which reads ἐπολέμησαν. See Fernández Marcos (2011, 56*–57*), Lindars (1995, 239–41), and LaMontagne (2013, 46). I have not included this instance of לחם in my total for the occurrences of the verb.

As shown, in most cases the OG translator chose πολεμέω to represent לחם (thirty out of thirty-one instances), which satisfactorily conveys the meaning of the Hebrew.⁷ Yet at a subsequent point in the textual transmission of Judg^LXX, the OG vocabulary choice was almost universally revised to παρατάσσω (twenty-five out of thirty-one instances).⁸

Consider these two examples of this lexical replacement in context:

(1) Judges 1:5
BHQ

וימצאו את־אדני בזק בבזק <u>וילחמו</u> בו ויכו את־הכנעני ואת־הפרזי

Then they found Adoni-Bezek in Bezek, and <u>they fought</u> with him, and they defeated the Canaanites and the Perizzites.

Judg^OG

καὶ εὗρον τὸν Ἀδωνιβεζεκ ἐν Βεζεκ καὶ <u>ἐπολέμησαν</u> ἐν αὐτῷ καὶ ἐπάταξαν τὸν Χαναναῖον καὶ τὸν Φερεζαῖον

And they found Adonibezek in Bezek and <u>fought</u> with him, and they defeated the Canaanites and the Perizzites.

Judg^Rv

καὶ κατέλαβον τὸν Ἀδωνιβεζεκ ἐν τῇ Βεζεκ καὶ <u>παρετάξαντο</u> πρὸς αὐτὸν καὶ ἔκοψαν τὸν Χαναναῖον καὶ τὸν Φερεζαῖον

And they overtook Adonibezek in Bezek and <u>παρετάξαντο</u> against him, and they destroyed the Canaanites and the Perizzites.

(2) Judges 8:1
BHQ

מה־הדבר הזה עשית לנו לבלתי קראות לנו כי הלכת <u>להלחם</u> במדין ויריבון אתו בחזקה

---

7. Excluding לחם in 5:8 due to the variant discussed above. Also, πολεμέω appears in the OG text in 5:13 (cf. Judg^A 5:14), although לחם does not appear there in the text of *BHQ*. It is possible that Judg^OG read κύριος ἐπολέμει μοι ἐν δυνατοῖς in 5:13, which in later transmission was transposed to 5:14 as a double reading of לי (ירד) יהוה ירד בגברים (Tov 1978, 226–27; LaMontagne 2013, 48–49). Owing to the uncertainty of this variant in the highly complex textual history of the Song of Deborah (Judg 5), I have not included this instance of πολεμέω in my analysis.

8. Throughout, all ancient language translations are my own unless otherwise noted. All ancient text is given first with a translation provided underneath. Within my translations, I generally leave the word in question untranslated (and underlined) to allow for fuller semantic discussion unobstructed by a single translation gloss.

What is this thing you did to us, to not call for us when you went to fight against Midian?" And they contended with him fiercely.

Judg^OG
Τί τὸ ῥῆμα τοῦτο ὃ ἐποίησας ἡμῖν τοῦ μὴ καλέσαι ἡμᾶς, ὅτε ἐξεπορεύου πολεμῆσαι ἐν τῇ Μαδιαμ; καὶ ἐκρίνοντο μετ' αὐτοῦ κραταιῶς.
"What is thing that you did to us, to not summon us when going out to fight against Midian?" And they contested with them vehemently.

Judg^Rv
Τί τὸ ῥῆμα τοῦτο ἐποίησας ἡμῖν τοῦ μὴ καλέσαι ἡμᾶς, ὅτε ἐπορεύθης παρατάξασθαι ἐν Μαδιαμ; καὶ διελέξαντο πρὸς αὐτὸν ἰσχυρῶς.
"Why have you done this thing to us, to not summon us when going παρατάξασθαι with Midian?" And they disputed them harshly.

The witnesses that support the readings of the words under examination vary, but in each case the designated Judg^OG reading is supported by at least the glnw cursives from the AII group, if not the entire group. Likewise, each Judg^Rv reading above is supported primarily by witnesses within the B group. In most instances, the OG reading is retained in the AI and AIII groups and the change appears only in most or all of the B group witnesses. Put differently, the textual evidence for each reading indicates that the vocabulary choices represented in table 3.3 originated in the OG translation and were revised specifically in the B group.[9]

A similar phenomenon occurs in the translation of מלחמה as well and its later revision, as shown in table 3.4. Again, bolded text indicates lexical substitution in the revision.

---

9. I did not find any variants where the revised vocabulary was supported by a majority A group set of witnesses (i.e., AI or AIII). However, even if, hypothetically, a given reading labeled Judg^Rv above originated in the AI or AIII groups chronologically, it was retained in the B group, which demonstrates that it was considered a satisfactory reading. Notice that Judg^Rv does not attest a revision to παρατάσσω at every instance of לחם (e.g., 1:1, 8, 9), but this may have been motivated by a semantic distinction between *war* and *battle* in those contexts. It is not my aim to explain every case of language change in Greek Judges but rather to help understand salient examples within the context of postclassical Greek.

Table 3.4. The *battle* nominals in Judg^LXX

מלחמה	Judg^OG	Judg^Rv
3:1	πόλεμος	πόλεμος
3:2	πόλεμος	πόλεμος
3:10	πόλεμος	πόλεμος
8:13[10]	πόλεμος	παράταξις
18:11	πολεμικός	παράταξις
18:16	πολεμικός	παράταξις
18:17[11]	πολεμικός	—
20:14	πολεμέω	παράταξις
20:17	πολεμιστής	παράταξις
20:18	πολεμέω	παράταξις
20:20[12]	πόλεμος[13]	παράταξις
20:22	πόλεμος	παράταξις
20:23	πόλεμος	παράταξις
20:28	πόλεμος	παράταξις
20:34	πόλεμος	παράταξις
20:39	πόλεμος	παράταξις
	πόλεμος	παράταξις
20:42	πόλεμος	παράταξις
21:22	πόλεμος	παράταξις

---

10. παράταξις appears twice in this verse only in Vaticanus (B) and the cursives iru: ἀπὸ ἐπάνωθεν τῆς παρατάξεως Αρες. However, the other B group cursives efjoqsz + a2 omit the reading, which suggests that it originated in Biru, perhaps due to parablepsis between מלחמה and מלמעלה. See Burney (1970, 232) and Boling (1975, 156) for alternative suggestions arising from possible exegetical treatment in the versions of the lexical items חרם or ההרים, read for חרס in the verse. Cf. Soggin (1987, 135) and Fernández Marcos (2011, 73*).

11. The Hebrew text from באו to המלחמה at the end of 18:17 is missing in most of the B group (Bdmoqsz + rua2) but is preserved in many other witnesses including Judg^OG. However, the B group cursives irsuza2 attest this text as an insertion in 18:18 following τὸ γλυπτόν, and πολεμικός is retained, unlike 18:11, 16 (see Fernández Marcos 2011, 51, 103*).

12. Here מלחמה appears twice, but in the second instance is part of a minus in the B group, and therefore it is not replaced.

13. It is possible that Judg^OG omitted εἰς πόλεμον, as it is missing in OL.

3. "Who Shall Go Up First?" ΠΑΡΑΤΑΞΙΣ and ΠΑΡΑΤΑΣΣΩ

Just as in table 3.3, the vocabulary trends in table 3.4 show how in every case the OG translator rendered מלחמה with πόλεμος or another word from the same lexical root (nineteen instances).[14] Yet again, at a subsequent point in the textual transmission of Judg^{LXX}, the OG vocabulary choice was consistently revised to παράταξις (fifteen out of nineteen instances) in the B group. Consider the following two examples:

(3) Judges 20:20
BHQ

ויצא איש ישראל <u>למלחמה</u> עם־בנימן

And the men of Israel went out <u>to battle</u> with Benjamin

Judg^{OG}
καὶ ἐξῆλθεν πᾶς ἀνὴρ Ισραηλ εἰς <u>πόλεμον</u> μετὰ Βενιαμιν
And every man of Israel went out for <u>battle</u> with Benjamin

Judg^{Rv}
καὶ ἐξῆλθεν πᾶς ἀνὴρ Ισραηλ εἰς <u>παράταξιν</u> πρὸς Βενιαμιν
And every man of Israel went out for <u>παράταξιν</u> against Benjamin

(4) Judges 21:22
BHQ

חננו אותם כי לא לקחנו איש אשתו <u>במלחמה</u>

"Grant them to us freely since we did not take a wife for each man <u>in battle</u>"

Judg^{OG}
ἐλεήσατε αὐτούς ὅτι ἔλαβον γυναῖκα ἕκαστος αὐτῶν ἐν τῷ <u>πολέμῳ</u>
"Show them mercy, for they each obtained their wife in the <u>battle</u>"

Judg^{Rv}
ἐλεήσατε αὐτοῖς ὅτι οὐκ ἔλαβεν ἀνὴρ γυναῖκα αὐτοῦ ἐν τῇ <u>παρατάξει</u>
"Show mercy to them, for each man did not obtain his wife in the <u>παρατάξει</u>"

---

14. On which, see πόλεμος in Beekes (2010, 1218–19). I omit from this total the second occurrence of מלחמה in 20:20 due to the textual variant. Also, in both Judg 20:28 and 21:22 there is a significant plus preserved only in Judg^{OG}, discussed in Satterthwaite (1991), but in neither case is the *battle* vocabulary revision affected.

Much like the vocabulary selection for לחם, the witnesses that support the readings for these Greek *battle* nominals in table 3.4 vary. But the OG readings are supported by the glnw cursives at least, often attested in the entire AII group. Sometimes Judg^{OG} uses words other than πόλεμος from the same lexical root. For example, πολεμικός (18:11, 16, 17), πολεμιστής (20:17), and even the verb form πολεμέω (20:14, 18). Nevertheless in almost all such cases the OG rendering is replaced with παράταξις in the B group revision, which is grammatically possible in each of the clauses. Also, in three verses πόλεμος is retained in Judg^{Rv} (3:1, 2, 10), as was πολεμέω in several places noted above (1:1, 8, 9).

Finally, the lexical item ערך also merits analysis (table 3.5). The way ערך is rendered in the OG and adjusted in later revision illuminates the semantic distinction that apparently underlies and motivates the revision of the Greek *battle* vocabulary already examined.

Table 3.5. Semantic distinction of ערך

ערך	Judg^{OG}	Judg^{Rv}
20:20	παρατάσσω	συνάπτω
22:22	παρατάσσω	συνάπτω
	παρατάσσω	συνάπτω
20:30	παρατάσσω	συνάπτω
20:33	παρατάσσω	συνάπτω

Table 3.5 shows the few instances in which the OG translator himself used παρατάσσω. Yet the OG translator never used this word for translating לחם but only for ערך: "set in order, set in battle array" (*CDCH*, s.v. "ערך"). This choice stands in contrast to that taken in Judg^{Rv}, where παρατάσσω is used exclusively to render לחם. In other words, the OG translation and its later revision prefer to use παρατάσσω in different ways: the former for ערך and the latter for לחם. So, in the process of revision a second and subtle semantic distinction became necessary. Wherever παρατάσσω was already present in the OG text it was replaced in the revised text with a different word, namely, συνάπτω "join together" (*GELS*, s.v. "συνάπτω"). Making the same observation, Judit Targarona Borrás notes that

> Apenas pueden quedar dudas, por tanto, acerca de la intención recensional del grupo 1 en estos cinco pasajes. Si buscamos razones para ello, tal vez puedan encontrarse en su interés por la homogeneidad de la

traducción, y en el hecho de emplear παρατάσσειν para traducir sistemáticamente la raíz לחם.... Consecuente con sus principios, este grupo no parece aceptar fácilmente que un mismo verbo griego traduzca sistemáticamente dos raíces hebreas distintas. (1983b, 1239)

It is important not to construe the notion of "homogeneidad"—lexical consistency in translation—as somehow simplistic. In order to change OG πολεμέω and πόλεμος to παρατάσσω and παράταξις in the revised text consistently, the change from OG παρατάσσω to συνάπτω also became necessary. Such consistency represents an intentional stylistic choice for the Greek target text (both OG and revised) that required semantic nuance within the target language to achieve.

Summary of Translation and Revision Activity

To summarize the trends of *battle* vocabulary preferences in the textual history of Judg[LXX], the OG translator typically chose πολεμέω and πόλεμος to convey respectively the notions of (1) the act of engaging in military combat (לחם) and (2) the battle event (מלחמה). But in the revised text represented by the B group those OG words were systematically changed to παρατάσσω and παράταξις for the same two concepts. However, wherever παρατάσσω was already present in the OG text (five times) it was *not* retained in Judg[Rv] but was *also* replaced, this time with συνάπτω. The decision to use συνάπτω was apparently made to preserve the distinction between the concept of *organizing* for military combat (ערך) from that of *engaging* in military combat (לחם) as expressed by παρατάσσω. It is the latter concept for which παρατάσσω is used throughout Judg[Rv], suggesting that careful and intentional semantic distinctions between *battle* vocabulary were made in the revised text. Consider the following example:

(5) Judges 20:22
BHQ

ויספו לערך מלחמה במקום אשר־ערכו שם ביום הראשון

They again <u>organized for battle</u> in the same place where <u>they had gotten organized</u> on the first day.

Judg[OG]
καὶ προσέθεντο <u>παρατάξασθαι πόλεμον</u> ἐν τῷ τόπῳ ᾧ <u>παρετάξαντο</u> ἐκεῖ ἐν τῇ ἡμέρᾳ τῇ πρώτῃ

And they continued to <u>παρατάξασθαι πόλεμον</u> in the place where they <u>παρετάξαντο</u> there on the first day.

Judg^{Rv}
καὶ προσέθηκαν <u>συνάψαι παράταξιν</u> ἐν τῷ τόπῳ ὅπου <u>συνῆψαν</u> ἐν τῇ ἡμέρᾳ τῇ πρώτῃ
And they went on <u>to join παράταξιν</u> in the place where they had <u>joined</u> on the first day.

Although לחם is not present in this verse, it is a clear illustration of the vocabulary trends discussed above. In the OG text παρατάσσω is used to refer to action *prior* to the πόλεμος battle event, whereas in the revision that action is expressed by συνάπτω and the battle is a παράταξις. Furthermore, though not shown in (5) because לחם is absent, in Judg^{Rv} παρατάσσω is used instead of πολεμέω to refer to the act of engaging in military combat. Although contemporary lexicons do not give the impression that the *battle* vocabulary used in the revised text was conventional within postclassical Greek, the following analysis of sources from that period shows that in fact they were.

The Question of Semantics and Style in Judg^{LXX}

The examples given above in (1) through (5) demonstrate that the word pairs πολεμέω/παρατάσσω and πόλεμος/παράταξις were at some point considered interchangeable. That phenomenon alone should prompt fresh semantic analysis. Judged according to the information provided in most contemporary Greek lexicons, the decision to insert παρατάσσω and παράταξις in place of πολεμέω and πόλεμος appears unconventional at best. The selections from major lexicons in table 3.6 sufficiently represent the state of discussion:

Table 3.6. ΠΑΡΑΤΑΣΣΩ and ΠΑΡΑΤΑΞΙΣ in current lexicons

	παρατάσσω	παράταξις
LSJ	place *or* post side by side, draw up in battle-order,… stand side-by-side in battle	martialing, line of battle … *in the previous* battles (Plb.1.40.1)
LEH	to set up the army in array against, to organise an army in battle formation against … to set in order	marshalling, line of battle, battle array … place of battle

GELS	to draw up in battle-order … mid. to do battle	battle-line … battle … act of posting side by side
MGS	to place beside *or* close to,… to line up, dispose in battle order … to draw up for battle … arrange oneself for battle … to oppose, decline, refuse	lining up (*of troops*), disposition in battle order … drawn-up troop, rank … battle (*regular, in order*) POL. 1.40.1

The range of meanings suggested for these words are hardly interchangeable with those of πολεμέω and πόλεμος, as the replacements in Judg^Rv would suggest.[15] But, as discussed in chapter 2, because most lexicons largely ignore attestations in postclassical literature—and almost completely ignore nonliterary evidence in papyri and inscriptions—they fail to represent sufficiently the semantic development of παρατάσσω and παράταξις in the Hellenistic period. As I demonstrate at length below, παρατάσσω and παράταξις undergo parallel semantic change beginning in the third century BCE whereby they come to be used to refer to concepts similar to those of πολεμέω and πόλεμος. Once this is recognized, it becomes obvious that not only were παρατάσσω and παράταξις possible candidates for lexical substitution, but they were also used in both Judg^OG and Judg^Rv according to contemporary conventions in Greek.

The choice to revise *battle* vocabulary also betrays stylistic concerns. In the revised text there are no significant syntagmatic changes in grammar made to accommodate the insertion of παρατάσσω or παράταξις. Rather, the change is paradigmatic, while the revised syntax remains largely the same as the OG translation.[16] This maintenance of Greek syntax in Judg^Rv highlights two important points about the *battle* vocabulary. First, that the substitution of παρατάσσω and παράταξις as replacements for πολεμέω and πόλεμος was semantically possible at the time of the revision. Second, that the revision was not merely motivated by a desire to more consistently

---

15. The notable exception being *GELS*. Only one text is ever cited for "battle" as a gloss for παράταξις, namely, Polybius, *Hist.* 1.40.1, giving the impression it is an uncommon sense. But that is clearly not the case in postclassical Greek, as I show below. The author-specific lexicons discussed below are a notable exception to the trends shown here, but these are rarely consulted.

16. Some minor changes do appear, such as the addition or deletion of the definite article, relative pronoun, or particle. While these affect the semantics of the Greek text in some way, the general word-for-word translation approach to the Hebrew text apparent in the OG translation is largely preserved and sometimes made more exact.

align the Greek target text to a Hebrew exemplar in syntax, but also by a preference for different vocabulary. The revision therefore appears to have arisen from the communicative goals of those who produced it as a Greek text for their Hellenistic Jewish readership. The thoroughgoing persistence with which πολεμέω and πόλεμος were changed to παρατάσσω and παράταξις indicates the changes were motivated by stylistic concerns and not prompted by the Hebrew. The possible explanations for this stylistic preference can be explored only after the semantic analysis of παρατάσσω and παράταξις below.

Lexical Semantic Analysis

The lexical semantic analysis provided here of the words παρατάσσω and παράταξις does not aim to present and discuss every attestation but rather focuses on the most salient examples of their development. Analysis begins with the verb παρατάσσω since it is attested in earlier sources than the nominal, suggesting that παράταξις was a deverbal form.[17] Since the semantic changes apparent for each of these two words follow very similar trajectories, the bulk of analysis will fall upon παράταξις, which is also more frequently attested in postclassical sources. Nevertheless, to demonstrate the similarity between them, brief observations upon the semantic development of παρατάσσω are also provided at the end of each section.

Classical Evidence

The verb παρατάσσω occurs 193 times prior to the end of the fourth century BCE, appearing most often in the writing of Thucydides (fifth century), Xenophon (fifth/fourth century), and Demosthenes (fourth century).[18] Wherever it occurs in these sources, παρατάσσω is used to portray the activity of entities physically arranging themselves or being arranged side by side. The prototypical concept associated with the word thus appears

---

17. Note that παρατάσσω is itself a compound verb from τάσσω, "place in order" (Beekes 2010, 1454–55), which will not be investigated here. In my analysis of lexical evidence I have accounted for the Attic spelling -ττ- (e.g., παρατάττω) but employ -σσ- throughout.

18. Sixth century: 5×; fifth century: 83×; fourth century: 105×. Searches performed using *TLG*.

to be *arrange side-by-side*.[19] Different senses arise as the word is used in different contexts. For example, παρατάσσω sometimes refers simply to physical location (1 in the sample entry):

(6) Isocrates, *Aeginet*. 19.38
Αἱρεθεὶς γὰρ ἄρχειν αὐτοκράτωρ ἐμὲ καὶ γραμματέα προσείλετο καὶ τῶν χρημάτων ταμίαν ἁπάντων κατέστησεν, καὶ ὅτ' ἠμέλλομεν κινδυνεύειν, αὐτὸς αὑτῷ με <u>παρετάξατο</u>.
For when he was elected to lead as dictator, he both chose me as secretary and appointed me accountant over all funds, and when we were about to engage in combat, he <u>positioned</u> me next to him.

In other contexts the sense is one of value-based appraisal (2 in the sample entry):

(7) Isocrates, *Bus*. 11.7
Πότερα γὰρ τοῖς περὶ Αἰόλου λεγομένοις αὐτὸν <u>παρατάξωμεν</u>;
For can we <u>compare</u> him to what is said about Aeolus?

The majority of classical attestations of παρατάσσω appear in a context of military conflict—a very prominent topic among ancient Greek historians—to refer to troop organization in preparation for formally engaging in battle. Used in this way the meaning of the verb can be defined as follows: *organize a group into side-by-side battle formation facing an enemy* (3 in the sample entry). This sense of the word and its later semantic develop-

---

19. Johnson (1987) developed the idea that human embodied experience gives rise to "preconceptual" image schemas, such as CONTAINER, PATH, or FORCE. These schemas provide the foundation for the concepts that are associated with lexical forms (i.e., words), whose specific meaning emerges as they are used in different contexts, often called semantic frames. Frame semantics was developed by Charles Fillmore (1982, 1985) to describe how language is "used to perspectivize an underlying conceptualization of the world" (Geeraerts 2010, 225). A provisional list of image schemas is provided in Evans and Green (2006, 190), to which SIDE-BY-SIDE could be added as a means of combining the LEFT-AND-RIGHT and COLLECTION schemas. In this schema, trajectors undergo motion from an initial, disbursed position towards their terminal position in a forward-facing line, which becomes the landmark. On landmark (LM) and trajector (TR), see Evans and Green (2006, 178–91). Note that in the SIDE-BY-SIDE image schema the LM does not necessarily exist in physical space but is constituted once the TRs move (or are moved) into organized position. Note that a minimum of two TRs is necessary for the schema, as in (6), but there is no upper limit.

ment in the Hellenistic period must be understood against relevant cultural background information. At the center of Greek military strategy for land combat was the hoplite (ὁπλίτης), who engaged in prearranged and decorous battles between highly organized but slow-moving phalanxes of heavy infantry in open space (see Hanson 2000, 202; Pritchett 1985, 1–93).[20] This form of engagement was deeply embedded in Greek culture and was understood in the classical era as the normal way to resolve conflict—even entire wars—among the Greek city-states from as early as the late eighth century through the late fourth century BCE.[21] Hoplite battle was conducted according to an established set of rules.[22] According to Thucydides, strictly maintaining order (τάξις) in battle was the best strategy and could mean the difference between victory and defeat (*Hist.* 7.23.3; 7.36.6; 8.105.2). Similarly, Herodotus maintained that rigorous organized discipline was the distinguishing mark of Greek strategy (*Hist.* 8.86; Lendon 1999, 282).

The use of the verb παρατάσσω to refer to the tactical organization of Greek hoplites prior to battle is readily illustrated. This sense appears as early as Thucydides in the fifth century:

(8) Thucydides, *Hist.* 7.3.1
Οἱ δὲ Ἀθηναῖοι αἰφνιδίως τοῦ τε Γυλίππου καὶ τῶν Συρακοσίων σφίσιν ἐπιόντων ἐθορυβήθησαν μὲν τὸ πρῶτον, <u>παρετάξαντο</u> δέ.
Now the Athenians, with Gylippus and the Syracusans suddenly arriving upon them, were initially thrown into confusion, so they <u>organized into battle ranks</u>.

In this text the two military forces come into physical proximity (ἐπιόντων) but do not engage in combat. This is clear in the following line where Gylippus dispatches a messenger to treat with the Athenians from his position in the west. Prior to that action, the physical organization of

---

20. For a description of the scale and tactical organization of these engagements, see Lee (2006, 486).

21. Sheldon (2012, 52) illustrates, however, that "military trickery goes all the way back to the beginnings of Greek warfare" and points out that the idealized picture of the hoplite warfare tradition comes primarily from Thucydides, Demosthenes, and Polybius, as seen below.

22. The rules were, however, continuously evolving. Already in the late fifth century there was a sense that this idealized form of warfare was disintegrating, something for which Demosthenes criticized Philip II of Macedonia in the second half of the fourth century (Hanson 2000, 204–6).

3. "Who Shall Go Up First?" ΠΑΡΑΤΑΞΙΣ and ΠΑΡΑΤΑΣΣΩ

the Athenian troops before the Syracusans occurred to resolve the confusion prompted by their unexpected arrival. Disciplined organization of troops facilitates victory. The Athenians refuse the treaty, however, so both sides ready themselves for battle (ἀντιπαρεσκευάζοντο ἀλλήλοις ὡς ἐς μάχην; 7.3.2). But Gylippus and his troops cannot organize properly (οὐ ῥαδίως ξυντασσομένους) owing to difficult terrain at Epipolae, and thus they retreat to more open ground (εὐρυχωρίαν; 7.3.3). The following day Gylippus again organizes the Syracusans into battle formation opposite their Athenian enemy (παρέταξε; 7.3.4).

The same sense of παρατάσσω appears throughout classical sources. It is prevalent within Thucydides.[23] It also occurs in Isocrates.[24] Xenophon uses παρατάσσω in his historical works more than any classical author (forty-three followed by Thucydides at nineteen times), always with the same sense.[25] By the fifth century this use of παρατάσσω in a military context had become conventional enough that it could take another prefix to modify its meaning.[26] An example appears in Xenophon's use of ἀντιπαρατάσσομαι alongside παρατάσσω:

(9) Xenophon, *Hell.* 3.4.22–23
οἱ δ' αὖ Πέρσαι ὡς εἶδον τὴν βοήθειαν, ἠθροίσθησαν καὶ <u>ἀντιπαρετάξαντο</u> παμπλήθεσι τῶν ἱππέων τάξεσιν. ἔνθα δὴ ὁ Ἀγησίλαος γιγνώσκων ὅτι τοῖς μὲν πολεμίοις οὔπω παρείη τὸ πεζόν, αὐτῷ δὲ οὐδὲν ἀπείη τῶν παρεσκευασμένων, καιρὸν ἡγήσατο μάχην συνάψαι, εἰ δύναιτο. σφαγιασάμενος οὖν τὴν μὲν φάλαγγα εὐθὺς ἦγεν ἐπὶ τοὺς <u>παρατεταγμένους</u> ἱππέας

Now on the other hand when the Persians saw this support [sent by Agesilaus], they gathered together and <u>formed into opposing ranks</u> with a large number of units of cavalrymen. At which point Agesilaus, recognizing that the enemy infantry was not yet present, while none of his prepared troops were lacking, believed it the time to join in battle, if

---

23. *Hist.* 1.29.5; 1.52.2; 4.32.4; 4.43.3; 4.73.1; 4.96.3; 5.59.2; 5.65.1; 5.72.4; 7.34.2; 7.69.3; 7.78.3; 7.79.1.

24. *Archid.* 6.80, 99; *Plat.* 14.61; *Panath.* 12.92; *Paneg.* 4.96.

25. See, e.g., *Hell.* 1.1.7; 1.5.15; 1.6.29; 2.1.23; 2.4.34; 3.2.15 (2×); 3.4.13; 4.3.5; 4.3.21; 4.4.9; 4.5.14; 4.6.11; 5.4.51; 5.4.54; 6.2.20; 6.5.52; 7.1.15; 7.1.29; 7.4.29; 7.4.30; 7.5.22; *Cyr.* 3.3.43; 3.3.48; 4.2.27; 5.3.5; 6.4.12; *Anab.* 1.10.10; 4.3.3; 4.3.5; 4.6.25; 4.8.3; 5.2.13.

26. A process called delexification, by which the semantic value of linguistic constituents become less compositional, so that the sequence (word or phrase) becomes more idiomatic (Cruse 2011, 91–93).

possible. Thus, after making a sacrifice, he immediately led the phalanx against the cavalry that <u>had been formed into ranks</u>.[27]

Note in (9) also the use of συνάπτω (line 4) in a way similar to that in Judg[Rv] exemplified in (5) above.

Like the verb, so also does the nominal παράταξις mostly occur in contexts of military conflict in classical sources, although it is less frequent overall (ten times).[28] Still, it is used in some instances in a way that anticipates—and perhaps prompts—its semantic development in the Hellenistic period. Similar to the verb from which it likely derives, the prototypical concept associated with παράταξις appears to be *side-by-side arrangement*.[29] So, when used in a context of military conflict, the meaning of the nominal παράταξις can be defined as follows: *physical formation of troops side by side for battle* (1 in the sample entry).

This sense of παράταξις is bound up with the same cultural background information about hoplite warfare as that of the verb. The earliest attestation of the word reflects this meaning and appears in Thucydides:

(10) Thucydides, *Hist.* 5.11.2
καὶ τοὺς νεκροὺς τοῖς Ἀθηναίοις ἀπέδοσαν. ἀπέθανον δὲ Ἀθηναίων μὲν περὶ ἑξακοσίους, τῶν δ' ἐναντίων ἑπτά, διὰ τὸ μὴ ἐκ <u>παρατάξεως</u>, ἀπὸ δὲ τοιαύτης ξυντυχίας καὶ προεκφοβήσεως τὴν μάχην μᾶλλον γενέσθαι.
And they returned the dead to the Athenians. Now about six hundred Athenians died, but seven of the other side, because the battle did not

---

27. Cf. *Anab.* 4.8.9; 5.2.13; Thucydides, *Hist.* 7.5.1. Xenophon uses ἀντιπαρατάσσομαι nine times (*Hell.* 1.3.5; 3.4.22; 4.3.12; 5.2.41; 7.4.24; 7.5.23; *Anab.* 4.8.9; *Ages.* 1.30; 2.6), but the lexical item appears as early as Thucydides (six times: *Hist.* 1.48.3; 1.63.2; 5.9.4; 6.98.3; 7.5.2; 7.37.3). We also find συμπαρατάσσομαι a few times in Isocrates (*Panath.* 180), Xenophon (*Hell.* 3.5.22), and Demosthenes (*Meg.* 7; *Cor.* 216). Much later, in the mid-second century CE Cassius Dio employs προπαρατάσσω (*Hist.* 49.8.5). All of these words appear in a military context and are used to perspectivize the activity of παρατάσσω.

28. Thucydides, *Hist.* 5.11.2; Isocrates, *Hel. enc.* 53.5; Demosthenes, *3 Philip.* 49.3; Aeschines, *Ctes.* 1.2, 88.4, 151.8; Aeneas, *Pol.* 1.2.5, 15.8.2; Dinarchus, *Demosth.* 82.6; Theophrastus, *Caus. plant.* 1.6.1.

29. The concept associated with this word is thus also the SIDE-BY-SIDE image schema. In the postclassical period, παράταξις occasionally appears in different semantic frames as well, as discussed below. But the concepts prompted by the word are always underpinned by the same image schema.

come about from organized rank, but rather from a kind of panicked incident as previously.

Here Thucydides describes the funeral of Brasidas at Amphipolis after his death in battle with the Athenians. In a cunning and unexpected move explained to his army in advance (5.9), Brasidas had thrown the Athenian army into confusion and divided it near Eion (5.10.5–8). Heavy Athenian losses followed, which is attributed in this example to the surprise engagement not unfolding ἐκ παρατάξεως.[30] The tactical organization of troops that was lacking on the Athenian side is portrayed as a property of the battle (μάχη) using a prepositional phrase.[31] Within the context of classical Greek warfare, a fighting force has a far better chance to prevail to the extent that παράταξις is originally and consistently present for battle.

Certain attestations of the nominal παράταξις suggest its meaning was developing even in the classical period. A possible shift in sense is attested first in a text from Isocrates. In describing the intention of the gods for their own children to become involved in the events surrounding Helen of Troy, he writes:

(11) Isocrates, *Hel. enc.* 53.6
Καὶ τί δεῖ θαυμάζειν ἃ περὶ τῶν παίδων διενοήθησαν; Αὐτοὶ γὰρ πολὺ μείζω καὶ δεινοτέραν ἐποιήσαντο παράταξιν τῆς πρὸς Γίγαντας αὐτοῖς γενομένης· πρὸς μὲν γὰρ ἐκείνους μετ' ἀλλήλων ἐμαχέσαντο, περὶ δὲ ταύτης πρὸς σφᾶς αὐτοὺς ἐπολέμησαν.
And why should what they intended for their children be surprising? For they themselves waged a greater and more dangerous formation than the one by them against the Giants. For against them [the Giants] they fought along with one another, yet for her [Helen] they warred against themselves.

The context in (11) invites a pragmatic inference for the word παράταξις, which I have attempted to reflect with the ambiguous translation "formation."[32] In this text the meaning of παράταξις is constrained by

---

30. Thucydides considered this evidence of the general decline of the hoplite warfare tradition (cf. 5.41).
31. The use of ἐκ here appears to be to be an example of manner (Smyth 1920, 378; Jannaris 1897, §1568).
32. Invited inferencing theory, developed in Traugott and Dasher (2002) and

its grammatical context, in which the main verb ἐποιήσαντο allows different conceptualizations. On the one hand, the gods may have "made/formed" themselves into παράταξις for battle with the Giants—which the Athenians did not in (10)—or they may have "done" παράταξις with the Giants. The former pertains to the tactical strategy of one side, the latter to a battle characterized by such tactical strategies in general. The latter construal may be reinforced by the contrast set up in the following sentence, which describes how the gods fought together side by side (μετ' ἀλλήλων ἐμαχέσαντο) in the παράταξις, not against each other.

The semantic development of παράταξις to refer to a type of battle by metonymy (whole for part) is clearer in a text from Demosthenes and sets the stage for a sense of the word that is much more frequently attested in postclassical sources.[33] As he laments the fading era of traditional hoplite warfare and the professionalization of the Greek military, Demosthenes writes:

(12) Demosthenes, *3 Philip.* 9.49
νυνὶ δ' ὁρᾶτε μὲν δήπου τὰ πλεῖστα τοὺς προδότας ἀπολωλεκότας, οὐδὲν δ' ἐκ <u>παρατάξεως</u> οὐδὲ μάχης γιγνόμενον·
So now presumably you see that deserters[34] have ruined most things, yet no such thing came about from <u>organized battle</u> or combat.

Brinton and Traugott (2005), is a cognitive and usage-based account of diachronic semantic change. See also Geeraerts (2010, 229–39) and Evans and Green (2006, 721–28). An invited inference is novel meaning of a word prompted in context and constructed using encyclopedic background knowledge (Traugott and Dasher 2002, 16–17). This occurs due to what Langacker (1991, 189–201) calls "active zone analysis," where the most salient conceptual profile of a lexical item can shift and thus prompt online meaning construction.

33. The metonymical construal of παράταξις is structured by a different (but related) image schema than the sense in (10), one that I will call ENGAGEMENT. Like the SIDE-BY-SIDE image schema, ENGAGEMENT is a fusion of space and unity/multiplicity categories as given in Evans and Green (2006, 190), in this case bringing CONTACT and MERGING into a single schema. In this schema, two forward-facing and side-by-side groups of entities join together. This schema is acquired by embodied experience in, for example, the simple act of joining together one's hands with intertwined fingers. Notice that the ENGAGEMENT image schema still entails an organized side-by-side formation for παράταξις, although that concept characterizes the entire event rather than simply the tactical formation of one fighting side. The formation conceptualized is that of the entire battle.

34. The sense of προδότη here seems to be one who switches allegiance during battle.

The use of παράταξις alongside μάχη shows that Demosthenes construes them in a similar way. Similar use of the word also appears in the mid-fourth century (Aeschines, *Ctes.* 151; Aeneas, *Pol.* 1.3), which has not escaped the notice of classicists.[35] This use in classical sources suggests the beginnings of a sense of παράταξις that can be defined as follows: *battle between opposing forces in side-by-side formations* (2 in the sample entry).

Again, some historical background provides a possible explanation for why classical authors occasionally used παράταξις in this sense. Despite the traditional precedents for Greek military engagement as described above, the circumstances of the Peloponnesian War precipitated changes in the rules of engagement. Victor Hanson states that "warfare itself had transmogrified beyond hoplite battle and its protocols that had tended to limit most fighting to a particular political, cultural and social context" (2000, 204). As light-infantry, ambush, siege, and skirmish became increasingly common in the fourth century, the word παράταξις became more useful for specifying the older style of battle involving the organization and maintenance of side-by-side formations (see Sheldon 2012, 102–26; Wheeler 2007, 188). Since this more traditional kind of military engagement was no longer the norm, it could no longer be referred to in general terms (e.g., μάχη). Thus some classical authors began to use παράταξις to specify one particular concept of military engagement among diversifying possibilities.[36] Nevertheless, it appears that in military contexts the conventional meaning of παράταξις in the classical period was to refer to the tactical organization of one fighting force in a battle as in (10).[37] It is not until the Hellenistic period that the new meaning of παράταξις, as well as παρατάσσω, fully develops and enters common use.

---

35. E.g., Pritchett (1985, 45 n. 144) notes that μάχη and παράταξις (among other lexical items) referred to distinct concepts in the classical historians.

36. Although Pritchett (1974, 156) maintains that there was no term in Greek for the concept *surprise attack*, he elsewhere provides a thorough survey of the various terminology related to hoplite warfare (1985, 1–93).

37. E.g., Aeschines, *Ctes.* 88; Aeneas, *Pol.* 15.8. A (new) conventional meaning of a lexical item only arises with continued use (Evans and Green 2006, 721). Such semantic development is a product of entrenchment, or the cognitive routinization of a particular construal of a linguistic item by means of increasingly frequent use in a community (Evans 2007, 73).

Postclassical Evidence

Although in the classical period παράταξις appears just ten times, most frequently in Aeschines (three times), it is attested much more frequently in Hellenistic sources. Of course, frequency statistics must always be handled with caution due to the uneven amounts of extant sources from different centuries. Nevertheless, it is noteworthy that attestations of παράταξις peak around the turn of the era in literary sources (table 3.7).[38]

Table 3.7. Postclassical attestations of ΠΑΡΑΤΑΞΙΣ

Third–second century BCE	
Polybius	53
Poseidonius	8
Total	61
First century BCE	
Diodorus Siculus	113
Dionysius of Halicarnassus	32
Asclepiodotus	2
Philodemus	2
Total	149
First century CE	
Josephus	43
Plutarch	42
Onasander	9
Lucanus Annaeus	3
Arrianus	3
Philo	2
Strabo	2
Total	104
Second century CE	
Cassius Dio	21
Polyaenus	14
Aelianus Tacticus	5
Appianus	5
Lucianus	5

---

38. This table is not meant to be exhaustive but is focused on the more prolific writers in order to reflect the broad trends of usage.

Aelius Aristides		4
Dio Cocceianus of Prusa		2
Marcus Aurelius		2
Epictetus		1
	Total	**63**

Attestations of a given linguistic feature do not fully represent the language as it was used—an inevitable drawback of corpus-based linguistic analysis. However, the increased frequency of παράταξις in postclassical sources very likely corresponds with more common use of the word in the language in general, which often corresponds with semantic change (Bybee 2015, 195). Regardless, use of παράταξις is clearly a much more common feature of postclassical Greek composition, at least in literary varieties of the language.

To save space, I use the following abbreviated fashion of referring to the senses of παράταξις and παρατάσσω discussed above. On the one hand, the use of παρατάσσω present in classical sources is called the *form for battle* sense (3 in the sample entry). On the other hand, the more common classical use of παράταξις will be called the *battle formation* sense (1 in the sample entry), and the newer use possible in (11) and present in (12) will be called the *battle event* sense (2 in the sample entry).

Literary Sources

It is within postclassical literature that the semantic development of παράταξις and παρατάσσω is most noticeable. Between these sources and the attestations of παράταξις in inscriptions it becomes clear that the newer meaning of the word was mostly confined to more educated writers communicating in a more formal variety of the language. In order to show how the use of παράταξις and παρατάσσω developed semantically through the early Roman period (and remained unchanged), the following discussion proceeds chronologically. As mentioned above, some attention is given to the verb but the focus falls upon the nominal.

Looking to the evidence in the second and first centuries BCE, the two major Hellenistic authors to use παράταξις with significant frequency prior to the turn of the era are Polybius and Diodorus Siculus.[39] As an aid

---

39. I have excluded the third century here, as there are no relevant literary authors in that period.

for fresh analysis of these words I have consulted—but not relied upon—lexicons pertaining to each author.[40] The nominal παράταξις is attested fifty-three times in Polybius's *Histories*. In eighteen of those uses παράταξις has the *battle formation* sense that was conventional in classical sources.[41] In thirty-five other texts, however, Polybius uses παράταξις with its new *battle event* sense.[42] The following four examples are representative of this semantic development:

(13) Polybius, *Hist.* 1.27.5
Ἄννων ὁ περὶ τὸν Ἀκράγαντα λειφθεὶς τῇ <u>παρατάξει</u>·
Hanno was the one who was defeated in <u>ordered battle</u> at Agrigentum.

(14) Polybius, *Hist.* 12.17.1
μνησθησόμεθα μιᾶς <u>παρατάξεως</u>, ἣν ἅμα μὲν οἵαν ἐπιφανεστάτην εἶναι συμβέβηκεν, ἅμα δὲ τοῖς καιροῖς οὐ μακρὰν ἀπηρτῆσθαι
I will mention one <u>ordered battle</u>, which together with being one of the most remarkable ever joined, is at once not too far distant in time.

(15) Polybius, *Hist.* 16.18.2
ἐξηγούμενος γὰρ ὁ προειρημένος συγγραφεὺς τήν τε Γάζης πολιορκίαν καὶ τὴν γενομένην <u>παράταξιν</u> Ἀντιόχου πρὸς Σκόπαν ἐν Κοίλῃ Συρίᾳ περὶ τὸ Πάνιον
This same one [Zeno], in his explanation of the siege of Gaza and Antiochus's <u>ordered battle</u> with Scopas in Coele-Syria, at Panium.

(16) Polybius, *Hist.* 30.4.2
οἱ γὰρ Ῥόδιοι κομισάμενοι τὴν ἀπόκρισιν, ἣν οἱ περὶ τὸν Ἀγέπολιν ἔλαβον εὐθέως μετὰ τὴν <u>παράταξιν</u>, καὶ θεωροῦντες ἐκ ταύτης τὴν πρὸς αὐτοὺς ὀργὴν

---

40. Namely, Mauersberger et al. (1998–2006) for Polybius and McDougall (1983c) for Diodorus Siculus.

41. See the citations in Mauersberger (1998, 119–21) and the definitions "Aufstellung zur Schlacht" (three times; §1), and "Schlachtlinie, -reihe, -ordnung" (fifteen times; §2.a). Note that §1 contains five citations but combines the two senses.

42. See Mauersberger (1998, 119–21) and the definitions "Konfrontation, Begegnung mit dem Feind" (twice; §1), "förmliche, regelrechte, ordentliche, offene (Feld)schlacht" (twenty-three times; §2.c), and "übh. [überhaupt = in general] Schlacht" (eight times; §2.b). I would also include *Hist.* 3.32.9 and 29.12.9, which Mauersberger defines as "Schlacht(beschreibung, -schilderung)" but which presuppose the *battle event* sense of παράταξις (§3).

For when the Rhodians got the decision, which those of the Agesipolis received immediately following the <u>ordered battle</u>, and saw the rage against them from it [the Senate].

The text in (13) refers to an event in *Hist.* 1.19 in which Hanno ventured decisive action against the Romans and the two forces moved into open space. The Roman army prevailed after they manage to turn (τρέπω) the Carthaginian line, a battle that in (13) Polybius refers to as a whole as a παράταξις. In (14) Polybius describes Callisthenes's report of an organized battle between Alexander and Darius near the River Pinarus in Cilicia (Ἀλέξανδρον σπουδάζειν κατὰ τὴν τάξιν, ἵνα κατὰ τὸν Δαρεῖον αὐτὸν ποιήσηται τὴν μάχην; 12.22) and discusses formations at some length (12.18–22). Although Polybius mostly critiques Callisthenes for his vagueness and inconsistency, he nevertheless refers again in (14) to the entire engagement as a παράταξις. Similarly, in (15) Polybius critiques Zeno's account of the battle of Panium between Antiochus and Scopas (16.18–20). In his discussion of the problems in Zeno's description of the army formations Polybius assumes that the goal of the engagement was the meeting of the two enemy lines (16.18.10), again referring in (15) to the whole event at the outset as a παράταξις. Finally, in (16) Polybius describes events after the famous battle between Andriscus and the Roman army at Pydna. In this battle, again referred to in (16) as a παράταξις, the Macedonian line was somehow disrupted and subsequently the Romans were able to divide, surround, and defeat them (29.17; Lazenby 1996).

About a century later Diodorus Siculus also used παράταξις with its newer sense just like Polybius. The nominal παράταξις is attested 113 times in what survives of his forty-book *Histories* chronicling Greece from pre-Trojan times through the conquest of Britain. The portions that remain attest παράταξις more than any other extant work by a single author. Tellingly, in his entry for the word, J. Iain McDougall provides only a single gloss: "battle" (1983b, 45–6).[43] Diodorus's near exclusive use of παράταξις with the newer *battle event* sense suggests that it had become its conventional meaning by the first century BCE. Four examples are representative of his use:

---

43. He cites 113 instances, while *TLG* gives the number 142, which is inflated by inclusion of the morphologically identical verb form παρατάξεις.

(17) Diodorus Siculus, *Hist.* 1.18.5
οὐ γὰρ πολεμικὸν εἶναι τὸν Ὄσιριν οὐδὲ <u>παρατάξεις</u> συνίστασθαι καὶ κινδύνους
For Osiris was not warlike and did not organize <u>ordered battles</u> or engagements.

(18) Diodorus Siculus, *Hist.* 2.25
καὶ τὸ μὲν πρῶτον γενομένης ἐν τῷ πεδίῳ <u>παρατάξεως</u> ἐλείφθησαν οἵ τ ἣν ἀπόστασιν ποιησάμενοι, καὶ πολλοὺς ἀποβαλόντες συνεδιώχθησαν εἰς ὄρος.... γενομένης οὖν τρίτης <u>παρατάξεως</u> πάλιν ὁ βασιλεὺς ἐνίκησε
And at first, when an <u>ordered battle</u> took place in the field those that were in revolt survived, and taking heavy losses they were pursued to a mountain.... Thus, when a third <u>ordered battle</u> took place again the king was victorious.

(19) Diodorus Siculus, *Hist.* 11.35
τῇ δ' ὑστεραίᾳ παρασκευαζομένων αὐτῶν τὰ πρὸς τὴν <u>παράταξιν</u>, προσέπεσε φήμη ὅτι νενικήκασιν οἱ Ἕλληνες τοὺς Πέρσας κατὰ τὰς Πλαταιάς.... κατὰ γὰρ τὴν αὐτὴν ἡμέραν ἐφάνησαν αἱ παρατάξεις γεγενημέναι
Now the following day, as they were preparing themselves for the <u>ordered battle</u>, a report came that the Greeks had defeated the Persians at Platea.... For the <u>ordered battles</u> that occurred unfolded on the same day.

(20) Diodorus Siculus, *Hist.* 16.35.5
γενομένης δὲ <u>παρατάξεως</u> ἰσχυρᾶς καὶ τῶν Θετταλῶν ἱππέων τῷ πλήθει καὶ ταῖς ἀρεταῖς διαφερόντων ἐνίκησεν ὁ Φίλιππος.
Now a fierce <u>ordered battle</u> took place and, the Thessalonian cavalry being greater in number and valor, Philip won.

In (17) Diodorus discusses an Egyptian account of Osiris's arrival among the Satyr people in Ethiopia. Osiris was welcomed gladly and so, says Diodorus, he did not need to organize his army for either a παράταξις or any other dangerous venture (κίνδυνος) to subdue them but merely left soldiers behind to collect tribute (1.18.6). The text in (18) is Diodorus's account of a rebellion against the Assyrian king Sardanapalus, the first aspect of which was a παράταξις on open ground (2.25.1). After a second battle (μάχη; 2.25.3) where more rebels died they retreated further into the mountains only to be finally defeated in another παράταξις (2.25.6). In (19) Diodorus writes of report by the Greek commander Leotychides of victory in Platea, which he announced to his troops before engaging the Persians in a παράταξις at Mycale (11.35.1). After a Greek victory, however, Diodorus states that in fact both παρατάξεις took place on the same day and Leotychides had bluffed to rally his troops (11.25.2–3). Finally, in (20) Diodorus discusses the engagement between Philip II of Macedon and the Phocian commander Onomarchus who was supporting Lycophron in Thessaly. Philip gained the support of the Thessalians and marshaled twenty thousand soldiers and three thousand cavalrymen for a fierce παράταξις in which he was victorious (16.35.4; cf. 16.38.1).

To recap postclassical Greek sources prior to the turn of the era, the texts in (13) through (20) demonstrate that the *battle event* sense of παράταξις was used frequently within Greek literary writing in the Hellenistic period. After his thorough survey of both the Greek historians and early poets, W. Kendrick Pritchett similarly concludes that παράταξις referred to the concept of a "pitched battle between hoplite phalanxes" (1985, 44–45).[44] Polybius uses the word that way predominantly, suggesting the new sense had become conventional by at least the mid-second century BCE.[45] Although Diodorus Siculus uses the *battle event* sense of παράταξις almost exclusively, the older *battle formation* sense also remains in use in the writing of his near contemporary Dionysius of Halicarnassus (first century BCE) as well as in the earlier work of Polybius.[46] In early postclassical Greek therefore παράταξις has two fully established senses. Also of note is that attestations of the word παράταξις increase markedly in this period compared with classical sources.

Turning now to evidence attested in the first and second centuries CE, the most significant evidence for παράταξις pertains to three authors. First, the first-century CE Jewish historian Flavius Josephus, whose extensive

---

44. Hanson even suggests the gloss "drawn-ups" (2000, 221). Sabin, van Wees, and Whitby suggest "'an organized formation', i.e., a set-piece, open battle" (2007, 539).

45. Palmer notes that the -σις derivational affix proliferated in postclassical Greek with "verbal abstracts usually denoting the action" (1945 §§2, 25; cf. Mayser 1970 §83, 19).

46. Throughout the work of Dionysius of Halicarnassus the *battle formation* and *battle event* senses appear about equally. For the *battle event* sense, see *Ant. rom.* 2.36.1; 3.34.4; 6.5.4; 6.42.3; 10.37.3. In many occasions, there is ambiguity that allows either sense, as in *Ant. rom.* 3.38.2; 3.41.2; 3.49.3; 4.27.3; 6.75.3; 8.29.5; 10.25.4; 10.37.4. The *battle formation* sense occurs, often in a prepositional phrase with ἐκ, in *Ant. rom.* 2.41.1; 2.50.4; 3.32.5; 3.39.2; 3.50.8; 3.55.4; 3.58.3; 6.5.8; 7.6.2; 9.3.3; 9.55.3; 9.61.3; 12.7.2.

writings were the most widely read ancient work in the medieval period apart from the Bible (Landfester 2009, 353). Second is Plutarch, whose prolific output at the turn of the second century CE included forty-eight biographies known as the *Lives* that are ordered according to their time frame in Greek history and seventy-eight philosophical works known as *Moralia*.[47] Third is the second-century CE Greek historian Cassius Dio, who wrote a history of the Roman Empire from the founding of Rome through 229 CE, of which only a portion survives (Landfester 2009, 143).

The near-contemporaneous writings of Josephus and Plutarch provide an opportune corpus for comparison first, as the former is well-known for his Atticizing tendencies, and both authors employed παράταξις with similar frequency.[48] Josephus uses the word forty-three times and Plutarch forty-two. Just like other postclassical literary authors, they both use the older as well as the newer senses, the latter of which is no longer very new. The *battle formation* sense appears in Josephus a minority of seven times and in Plutarch a majority of nineteen.[49] The *battle event* sense appears in Josephus a majority of thirty-four occurrences and in Plutarch a minority eleven times.[50] Some examples of the ongoing use of the *battle event* sense by Josephus include:

---

47. Landfester (2009, 514). All chapter, section, and line numbers for Plutarch are given according the Loeb Classical Library editions.

48. On Atticism, Horsley states that "in Josephus we have good-quality *koine* which betrays some considerable evidence of Atticism … [and] he may be appropriately associated with the Atticising reaction which began in the first century" (1989, 33–34). Plutarch, however, while writing during the Second Sophistic, cannot be considered a sophist, and even his early rhetorical works are insufficient evidence that he ever intended to be one, despite his considerable learning (Bowersock 1985, 665). On Atticism, see Caragounis (2014, 1:196–203), Kazazis (2007), and Horrocks (2014, 99–100).

49. Josephus: *Ant*. 6.172.2; 7.12.4; 7.308.2; 7.390.7; 8.412.3; *J.W.* 3.88.3. Plutarch: *Thes.* 32.4.7; *Rom.* 19.2.3; *Tim.* 27.7.1; *Arist.* 17.8.2; *Aem.* 17.2.1; 17.5.3; 17.6.2; 20.7.2; *Phil.* 6.1.8; *Flam.* 5.4.10; *Comp. Lys.* 4.4.1; *Mar.* 25.7.1; *Pomp.* 69.4.1; *Ant.* 39.3.1; 65.4.2; *Quaest. conv.* 1.10.3. (628e1); 2.5.2 (639e8); *Marc.* 12.2.6; *Pel.* 15.5.1.

50. Josephus: *Ant.* 6.180.3; 12.311.2; 18.87.4; *Life* 341.5; 358.1; 397.4; *J.W.* 1.45.2; 1.95.3; 1.191.3; 1.336.1; 1.341.1; 1.342.2; 2.471.1; 2.581.2; 3.21.2; 3.75.2 (2×); 3.105.1; 3.107.1; 3.282.1; 3.305.2; 4.36.3; 4.231.4; 4.288.4; 5.25.2; 5.487.3; 5.489.3; 6.2.4; 6.47.2; 6.78.1; 6.79.3; 6.128.2; 6.246.1; 7.250.1. A further three instances are ambiguous: *J.W.* 1.102.3; 2.583.2; 6.243.3. The use in *J.W.* 2.464.4 is uncertain but seems closer to the *battle event* sense. Plutarch: *Fab.* 14.1.4; *Comp. Per.* 2.1.4; *Marc.* 8.5.9; *Pomp.* 65.1.3; *Alex.* 1.2.5; *Phoc.* 26.1.2; *Cat. Min.* 53.4.4; *Ag. Cleom.* 15.1.2; *Demetr.* 35.1.6; *Alex. fort.* 11 (332d10); *An seni* 6 (787b7). There are also numerous ambiguous instances where

3. "Who Shall Go Up First?" ΠΑΡΑΤΑΞΙΣ and ΠΑΡΑΤΑΣΣΩ

(21) Josephus, *J.W.* 3.75.2
οὔτε γὰρ ἀταξία διασκίδνησιν αὐτοὺς ἀπὸ τῆς ἐν ἔθει συντάξεως ... καὶ οὐκ ἂν ἁμάρτοι τις εἰπὼν τὰς μὲν μελέτας αὐτῶν χωρὶς αἵματος <u>παρατάξεις</u>, τὰς <u>παρατάξεις</u> δὲ μεθ' αἵματος μελέτας.
For no disorder scatters them from habitual formation.... Indeed, one would not be mistaken saying that their exercises are <u>battles</u> without blood, and the <u>battles</u> bloody exercises.

The idea of strict order and formation involved in the exercises (μελέαι) in (21) and their corresponding employment in battle is clear. The particular conceptualization of battle with which the word παράταξις is associated is still strategically and regularly ordered, even if during Josephus's period in history hoplite warfare is no longer practiced as such. Other examples are similar:

(22) Josephus, *Ant.* 12.311.2
ὡς οὖν ταῦθ' οὕτως ἔχοντα ἔμαθον οἱ σὺν Γοργίᾳ καὶ τοὺς μετὰ Ἰούδου πρὸς <u>παράταξιν</u> ἑτοίμους κατενόησαν, καὶ αὐτοὶ δείσαντες εἰς φυγὴν ἐτράπησαν.
So when those with Georgias learned that things were this way,[51] and realized that those with Judas were ready for <u>battle</u>, they also became alarmed and turned around to retreat.

(23) Josephus, *J.W.* 6.80.1
τοῖς δ' ἔμπροσθεν γινομένοις ἢ τοῦ θνήσκειν ἢ τοῦ κτείνειν ἀνάγκη παρῆν οὐκ οὔσης ἀναφυγῆς.... πλεονεκτούντων δὲ τῶν Ἰουδαίων τοῖς θυμοῖς τὴν Ῥωμαίων ἐμπειρίαν καὶ κλινομένης καθάπαν ἤδη τῆς <u>παρατάξεως</u>
Now for those who were in front the need arose to either die or kill, there was no retreat.... And the Jews were gaining the advantage by fury over the experience of the Romans, and the <u>battle</u> was turning overall.[52]

---

either sense is possible: *Cam.* 29.5.1; *Tim.* 34.1.2; *Pel.* 2.5.9, 17.6.1; *Aem.* 4.3.1, 28.9.4; *Ages.* 27.3.4; *Pomp.* 21.2.6, 67.6.9; *Comp. Ages.* 3.1.4.

51. That is, their camp had been routed by Judas's men; see 310.3–4. Cf. 1 Macc 4:14b–22, where Georgias's men see "the army of Judas in the field ready for battle" (τὴν Ιουδου παρεμβολὴν ἐν τῷ πεδίῳ ἑτοίμην εἰς παράταξιν, 4:21).

52. Thackeray (1989, 399) translates this passage, "At length, Jewish fury prevailing over Roman skill, the whole line began to waver." Notice that this translation of παράταξις brings out both the *battle event* sense and the *battle formation* sense by speaking of a single "line" of action between both fighting forces, the entirety of which constitutes the battle itself (similar to the ENGAGEMENT image schema). It is possible that because the *battle event* sense of παράταξις developed as a metonymical construal

Examples of the *battle event* sense in Plutarch include:

(24) Plutarch, *Phoc.* 26.1.2
Ὀλίγῳ δ' ὕστερον χρόνῳ Κρατεροῦ διαβάντος ἐξ Ἀσίας μετὰ πολλῆς δυνάμεως, καὶ γενομένης πάλιν ἐν Κραννῶνι <u>παρατάξεως</u>
But a little while later Craterus crossed through from Asia with a large army, and again a <u>battle</u> came about at Crannon.

(25) Plutarch, *An seni* 6 (787b7)
οὐδὲ γὰρ αἱ στρατεῖαι <u>παρατάξεις</u> ἀεὶ καὶ μάχας καὶ πολιορκίας ἔχουσιν, ἀλλὰ καὶ θυσίας ἔστιν ὅτε καὶ συνουσίας διὰ μέσου καὶ σχολὴν ἄφθονον ἐν παιδιαῖς καὶ φλυαρίαις δέχονται.
For war campaigns do not forever consist of <u>battles</u> and combats and sieges, but there are also times when they permit sacrifices and gatherings in between, and considerable leisure for pastimes and amusements.

Notice in (25) how παράταξις is clearly distinguished from other kinds of military engagements in the context, specifically combat (μάχη) and siege (πολιορκία). A similar distinction also occurs in the next two examples from Plutarch:

(26) Plutarch, *Ag. Cleom.* 15.1.2
Συμμείξας δὲ τῷ Ἀράτῳ περὶ Κόρινθον ὁ Ἆγις ἔτι βουλευομένῳ περὶ μάχης καὶ <u>παρατάξεως</u> πρὸς τοὺς πολεμίους, ἐπεδείξατο καὶ προθυμίαν πολλὴν καὶ τόλμαν οὐ νεανικὴν οὐδ' ἀλόγιστον.
Now when Aratus joined with Agis near Corinth, he was still deliberating about combat and <u>battle</u> against the enemies, displaying both great eagerness and boldness, neither impetuous nor unthinking.

(27) Plutarch, *Alex.* 1.2.5
οὔτε γὰρ ἱστορίας γράφομεν, ἀλλὰ βίους, οὔτε ταῖς ἐπιφανεστάταις πράξεσι πάντως ἔνεστι δήλωσις ἀρετῆς ἢ κακίας, ἀλλὰ πρᾶγμα βραχὺ πολλάκις καὶ ῥῆμα καὶ παιδιά τις ἔμφασιν ἤθους ἐποίησε μᾶλλον ἢ μάχαι μυριόνεκροι καὶ <u>παρατάξεις</u> αἱ μέγισται καὶ πολιορκίαι πόλεων.
For I am not writing *Histories*, but *Lives*; not always among the most distinguished deeds is an explanation of virtue or vice present, but often minor actions and words and amusements make a greater impression

---

of the *battle formation* sense, the idea of prevailing and succumbing in battle were metaphorically mapped to spatial rotation and linear bending (cf. κλίνω). Thus, the conceptual metaphor might be BATTLE RESOLUTION IS MANIPULATION OF A LINE.

3. "Who Shall Go Up First?" ΠΑΡΑΤΑΞΙΣ and ΠΑΡΑΤΑΣΣΩ

than battles where tens of thousands die or the greatest battles or sieges of cities.

Soon after Plutarch's active period, twenty-one attestations of παράταξις appear in the writing of Cassius Dio.[53] This total is about half of that found in each of the previous two authors, and Cassius Dio uses the *battle event* sense in only seven instances.[54] Some examples show the same kind of contrast between various kinds of military engagements:

(28) Cassius Dio, *Hist.* 18.58.1.1
καὶ διέτριψαν συχνὰς ἡμέρας, ἐς μὲν παράταξιν μὴ συνιόντες, ἀκροβολισμοῖς δέ τισι καὶ πείραις τῶν τε ψιλῶν καὶ τῶν ἱππέων χρώμενοι.
And they delayed many days, not joining into battle, but attacking in some skirmishes and raids of both light-armed troops and cavalry.

(29) Cassius Dio, *Hist.* 55.30.2.3
αἰσθόμενος δὲ τῆς προσόδου αὐτῶν ὁ Βάτων ἀπήντησε τῷ Μεσσαλίνῳ, καίπερ μηδέπω καλῶς ἔχων, καὶ ἐπικρατέστερος αὐτοῦ ἐν παρατάξει γενόμενος ἔπειτ' ἐξ ἐνέδρας ἐνικήθη.
And when he noticed their approach Bato went out to meet Messallinus, although not yet feeling well, and while proving superior to him in battle he was then defeated by ambush.

In another eleven instances Cassius Dio employs the word with its *battle formation* sense.[55] The small sample size of these data discourages drawing firm conclusions. However, the voluminous military history of Cassius Dio suggests an overall decline in use of παράταξις for such topics in the second century CE. It seems also to indicate that with the decline in frequency of παράταξις the *battle event* sense also declined relative to the older *battle formation* sense, if only slightly. Philip Sabin (2000, 2) states that, while "the symmetrical confrontations more characteristic of the hoplite era" continued to some degree, the form of combat significantly

---

53. I have disregarded a possible occurrence in *Hist.* 74.12.1.3 due to the more likely variant reading πρᾶξιν.
54. *Hist.* 9.40.31.2; 15 p. 138 line 10 (Zonaras 9, 1); 15 p. 138 line 20 (Zonaras 9, 1); 18.58.1.1; 36.49.3.4; 55.30.2.3, 56.38.1.5.
55. *Hist.* 14.57.6a.47; 14.57.14.28; 14.57.25.44; 16.57.48.127; 40.40.6.4; 47.37.5.3; 47.47.3.2; 48.25.3.2; 59.10.1.4; 69.12.3.1; 77.13.2.3. There are also three ambiguous uses that could be read as either sense: *Hist.* 47.41.3.4; 54.34.7.3; 71.4.2.3.

changed in the Roman period. For παράταξις to fall out of use would not be unexpected as the era of Greek hoplite warfare with which it was so closely associated came to a close.

Along similar lines, another semantic development of παράταξις appears after the turn of the era. A new sense appears for the first time in Josephus:

(30) Josephus, *J.W.* 5.4.25
συνέβη γοῦν τὰ μὲν περὶ τὸ ἱερὸν πάντα συμφλεγῆναι καὶ μεταίχμιον ἐρημίας γενέσθαι <u>παρατάξεως</u> οἰκείας τὴν πόλιν
So it happened that everything around the temple was burnt to cinders and the city became a desolate no-man's-land from civil <u>conflict</u>.

In (30) Josephus writes of the Roman siege of Jerusalem and the internal factions such that the city was engulfed in violence (5.4.1). In this context παράταξις is completely detached from the trappings of Greek warfare and used instead to refer to Jewish civil conflict in general (παρατάξεως οἰκείας). This new sense of the word could be defined as *physical conflict between parties* (3 in the sample entry). It is an extension of the *battle event* sense but with no association with the cultural background of hoplite battle tactics. The same sense occurs elsewhere:

(31) Josephus, *Life* 358.2
μήθ᾽ ὅσα κατ᾽ ἐμαυτὸν ἔπραξα πολιορκούμενος δυνηθεὶς πυθέσθαι· πάντες γὰρ οἱ ἀπαγγείλαντες ἂν διεφθάρησαν ἐπὶ τῆς <u>παρατάξεως</u> ἐκείνης.
nor were you able to learn what I had accomplished myself in besieging; for all possible informants were killed in that <u>conflict</u>.

In the context of (31) Josephus is discussing the Roman siege (πολιορκία) of Yodfat, a military event that is clearly no ordered Greek battle. He critiques Justus's erroneous account knowing that he had no access to eyewitness reports. Yet Josephus himself was present at what he calls "that conflict" (παρατάξεως ἐκείνης). This new sense of παράταξις is not often attested, but its appearance corroborates the possibility that the *battle event* sense was declining in the Roman period.[56]

---

56. In a spurious (and likely late) text attributed to Demosthenes (*Leoch.* 3.5) this new sense of παράταξις is used metaphorically in a judicial context to refer to an "opposing party." Also notable is the appearance in the late second century CE of the word βρογχοπαράταξις in Athenaeus (*Deipn.* 7.53), which in the context refers to an "eating contest."

To recap postclassical Greek sources after the turn of the era, the examples in (21) through (31) demonstrate that the *battle event* sense of παράταξις continued to be used in Greek literary writing through the early second century. Josephus uses the word that way more frequently than the older *battle formation* sense. Although he is known for Atticizing, his use of the *battle event* sense was not likely motivated by pseudoclassical aspirations since παράταξις is not frequently attested in classical sources. Yet the fact that he favors the *battle event* sense indicates this meaning had become so conventional in the language and literary tradition that Josephus considered it an educated use of Greek. If so, that could have been what led Josephus to use the word that far more frequently than his non-Atticizing contemporary Plutarch. In view of the even less frequent use of παράταξις in Cassius Dio and its occasional use to refer to physical conflict in general, it seems correct to conclude that the *battle event* sense was declining.

Before moving to analysis of the nonliterary evidence, some observations are necessary on the development of the verb παρατάσσω in postclassical Greek. As discussed above, when used in a military context, the verb refers to the organization of troops into side-by-side tactical formation in front of an enemy for battle. This *form for battle* sense continues to be used at least through the end of the second century CE. Within Polybius's corpus παρατάσσω appears forty-eight times, thirty-six of which attest the classical *form for battle* sense (e.g., *Hist.* 3.108.7; 11.1.2; 12.20.7).[57] However, in twelve instances Polybius also suggests the use of παρατάσσω in a new way that is parallel to the nominal's *battle event* sense. Though it goes on to become prevalent in later literature, this sense of the verb appears first in Polybius and can be defined as follows: *engage in battle between opposing forces in side-by-side formations* (4 in the sample entry). I will call this the *engage in battle* sense.[58] In many cases in Polybius the context is ambiguous as to which of the two senses of παρατάσσω is intended,

---

57. *TLG* lists fifty-seven uses, but this is due to confusion with noun forms, e.g., παρατάξει(ς) (3.32.9; 6.26.11, etc.). See the citations in Mauersberger (1998, 121–22), wherein he gives the definitions "e. Schlachtordnung, -linie, -reihe auf-, her-stellen, bilden" (twice; §I.1), "sich in Schlachto., -l., -r., bzw. Zur Sch., zum K[ampf]. aufstellen, formieren" (twenty-two times; §II.1), and "in Schlacto. usw. aufgestellt sein, kampfbereit (da)stehen" (twelve times; §III).

58. Again see the citations in Mauersberger (1998, 121–22) and the definitions "j-n (dem Gegner gegenüber [τινί] in Schlacht., -l, -r., bzw. zur Schlacht, zum Kampf aufstellen" (six times; §I.2) and "j-m e. Schlacht liefern, gegen j-n kämpfen" (six times; §II.2).

which, even if unintentional, likely helped give rise to the new meaning. For example:

(32) Polybius, *Hist.* 2.20.2
ἀθροισθέντες δὲ περὶ τὴν Ὀάδμονα προσαγορευομένην λίμνην <u>παρετάξαντο</u> Ῥωμαίοις.
Then those gathered together near the lake called Vadimonis (<u>formed for battle with/engaged in battle with</u>?) the Romans.

(33) Polybius, *Hist.* 2.19.5
μετὰ δὲ ταῦτα πάλιν ἔτει τετάρτῳ συμφρονήσαντες ἅμα Σαυνῖται καὶ Γαλάται <u>παρετάξαντο</u> Ῥωμαίοις ἐν τῇ Καμερτίων χώρᾳ καὶ πολλοὺς αὐτῶν ἐν τῷ κινδύνῳ διέφθειραν.
So again after four years when the Gauls and Samnites conspired together they (<u>formed for battle with/engaged in battle with</u>?) the Romans in the region of Camerinum and slew many of them in the action.

The use of the verb in this way appears at first to have been elliptical.

The verb παρατάσσω appears fifty-nine times in the work of Diodorus Siculus, somewhat more than in Polybius. McDougall (1983b, 46) apparently does not recognize the *engage in battle* sense of the word.[59] Although the older *form for battle* sense remains present, in my analysis there are twenty-three instances where the new *engage in battle* sense appears in Diodorus's corpus. For example:

(34) Diodorus Siculus, *Hist.* 2.1.10
ὁ δὲ ταύτης βασιλεὺς Φάρνος <u>παραταξάμενος</u> ἀξιολόγῳ δυνάμει καὶ λειφθείς, τῶν τε στρατιωτῶν τοὺς πλείους ἀπέβαλε καὶ αὐτὸς μετὰ τέκνων ἑπτὰ καὶ γυναικὸς αἰχμάλωτος ληφθεὶς ἀνεσταυρώθη
And the king of this country, Pharnus, after <u>engaging in battle</u> with a remarkable force and being defeated, lost both the majority of soldiers and he, taken captive with seven children and wife, was crucified.

(35) Diodorus Siculus, *Hist.* 19.72.7
οὗτοι δὲ τὰς δυνάμεις παραλαβόντες <u>παρετάξαντο</u> πρὸς τοὺς Σαμνίτας περὶ τὰς καλουμένας Λαυστόλας καὶ πολλοὺς τῶν στρατιωτῶν ἀπέβαλον.

---

59. He gives the following: "to draw up in battle order" (I), "to draw oneself up in battle order" (III), but also "to pit against" (II), for which he provides only one citation (*Hist.* 11.11.3) that is a clear instance of the value comparison sense seen in (2) above.

3. "Who Shall Go Up First?" ΠΑΡΑΤΑΞΙΣ and ΠΑΡΑΤΑΣΣΩ 97

Then these men, taking charge of the forces, <u>engaged in battle</u> against Samnites near the place called Laustolae and lost many of the soldiers.

In these examples παρατάσσω refers to an event where combat is engaged.[60] Thus the verb appears to have developed a second sense by some time in the first century BCE.

In the extant writings of Plutarch and Josephus, παρατάσσω appears sixty-six and thirty-four times, respectively. Josephus uses the two senses of the verb with almost equal frequency, although he uses παρατάσσω in other new ways as well.[61] By contrast, Plutarch uses the *engage in battle* sense only five times:[62]

(36) Josephus, *Ant.* 5.2
στρατεύσαντος γὰρ ἐπ' αὐτοὺς Χουσαρσάθου τοῦ τῶν Ἀσσυρίων βασιλέως, πολλούς τε τῶν <u>παραταξαμένων</u> ἀπώλεσαν καὶ πολιορκούμενοι κατὰ κράτος ἡρέθησαν
For after Chusarathus, king of the Assyrians, marched upon them, they lost many <u>engaging in battle</u> and when besieged they were captured by force.

(37) Plutarch, *Caes.* 15.3
πόλεις μὲν ὑπὲρ ὀκτακοσίας κατὰ κράτος εἷλεν, ἔθνη δὲ ἐχειρώσατο τριακόσια, μυριάσι δὲ <u>παραταξάμενος</u> κατὰ μέρος τριακοσίαις, ἑκατὸν μὲν ἐν χερσὶ διέφθειρεν, ἄλλας δὲ τοσαύτας ἐζώγρησεν.
He forcefully seized over eight hundred cities, conquered three hundred nations, and <u>engaging in battle</u> with three million men in turn, he slaughtered a million in hand-to-hand fighting and the same number of others he took captive.

---

60. See also *Hist.* 11.6.1; 11.82.3; 12.43.5; 12.45.2; 12.50.5; 12.52.2; 13.63.4; 13.88.2; 14.27.3; 14.34.5; 14.68.5; 14.69.2; 14.91.3; 14.109.7; 15.31.3; 17.30.2; 17.39.4; 17.48.4; 18.12.4; 19.50.7; 19.104.4. A few ambiguous uses occur at 11.53.4; 12.42.6; 13.75.3; 14.113.4; 19.89.2.
61. *Form for battle*: *Ant.* 6.26.3; 6.174.5; 7.11.5; 7.123.2; 7.138.5; 7.236.1; 7.310.3; 8.364.2; 8.382.6; 9.12.3; 12.426.2; *J.W.* 1.381.4; 4.433.5; 5.312.1; 6.19.1; 6.170.2. *Engage in battle*: *Ant.* 5.180.4; 10.221.2; 18.48.5; *Ag. Ap.* 1.136.2; 1.151.2; *J.W.* 1.265.3; 3.154.1; 3.475.2; 4.219.1; 4.514.3; 4.642.1; 7.83.3.
62. *Luc.* 28.7.7; 31.7.5; *Alex.* 12.3.6; *Caes.* 15.3.8; *Art.* 8.2.3, the last of which may be ambiguous.

In at least one instance Plutarch uses the verb to refer to nonmilitary physical confrontation (*Mulier. virt.* 8 [247c3]), similar to and roughly contemporaneous with the new sense of παράταξις by Josephus in (30) and (31) above.[63] But the significant majority of attestations of παρατάσσω in Plutarch are clearly the *form for battle* sense (fifty times).[64]

In the surviving work of Cassius Dio there are seventeen attestations of παρατάσσω. However, the *engage in battle* sense does not appear at all among them. Rather, the *form for battle* sense is most frequently used, appearing fourteen times.[65] Cassius also uses παρατάσσω to describe military formations in new contexts, such as naval battle (e.g., *Hist.* 48.473.5), and in various other ways.

This brief examination shows that the development of the verb παρατάσσω clearly parallels that of the nominal. Beginning in the work of Polybius in the second century but most clearly in the first century BCE through the first century CE, the verb developed the *engage in battle* sense. This meaning was associated with the same culturally situated Greek military practices and may have developed out of ambiguous or perhaps intentionally elliptical use of the word. The new *engage in battle* sense of the verb does not appear to have become as common as the new *battle event* sense of the nominal. But like παράταξις—and most likely for similar

---

63. This sense is metaphorically extended in an ethical context to mean "resist" (*Tu. san.* 5 [124b1]). Elsewhere Plutarch uses this sense of παρατάσσω metaphorically in a judicial context to mean "oppose" (*Cat. Min.* 28.5.4), much like the fragmentary text attributed to Demosthenes mentioned above (*Leoch.* 3.5), which supports seeing this use of the nominal as a late interpolation or spurious reading. I consider these uses of παρατάσσω to be metaphorical because the action they portray is nonphysical (e.g., legal opposition, or resistance to moral temptation), but it is expressed in physical terms. This occurs by means of conceptually mapping two mental spaces, such that the more abstract (law, morality) is integrated with embodied experience (physical conflict).

64. *Publ.* 9.1.4; *Cam.* 34.5.7; 37.3.9; 41.3.5; *Fab.* 3.1.12; *Marc.* 24.1.4; 24.5.2; 24.5.7; 25.3.4; 28.3.3; *Phil.* 6.1.3; 10.1.6; *Pyrrh.* 17.1.3; *Mar.* 26.1.4; 27.6.4; *Sull.* 16.2.2; 17.3.7; 21.2.1; *Comp. Lys.* 5.1.6; *Cim.* 12.7.5; *Nic.* 16.4.2; 19.2.4; *Crass.* 11.6.3; 23.3.5; *Eum.* 5.3.1; *Ages.* 16.2.3; 18.1.2; 32.2.1; *Pomp.* 19.4.2; 35.2.4; *Alex.* 16.1.2; 33.4.1; 62.1.5; *Caes.* 18.2.6; 42.2.9; 44.1.4; *Phoc.* 16.6.3; 25.2.2; *Ag. Cleom.* 27.2.6; *Demetr.* 29.2.1; *Ant.* 49.2.2; 63.1.3; 65.2.5; *Dion* 39.4.5; 46.3.2; *Oth.* 11.2.6; *Quaest. rom.* 78 (282e1); *Alex. fort.* 10 (341e10); *Glor. Ath.* 3 (347b5); *Praec. ger.* 6 (803b9).

65. *Hist.* 38.33.3.4; 38.48.3.4; 38.48.4.2; 43.6.4.1; 47.42.2.1; 48.36.2.3; 48.40.4.3; 48.473.5; 59.25.2.1; 62.4.3.6; 5 p. 242 line 18 (Zonaras 7, 26); 11 p. 436 line 23 (Zonaras 8, 14); 15 p. 140 lines 24, 25 (Zonaras 9, 1).

3. "Who Shall Go Up First?" ΠΑΡΑΤΑΞΙΣ and ΠΑΡΑΤΑΣΣΩ

reasons—the newer sense of παρατάσσω seems to have been fading from use in the late first and early second century CE, judging by its low attestation in Plutarch and absence from Cassius Dio in favor of the *form for battle* sense. Josephus's use of παρατάσσω with the *engage in battle* sense demonstrates that he felt it was literary Greek, just as he did with the *battle event* sense of the nominal παράταξις. Such an impression could have arisen from the presence of the *engage in battle* sense of παρατάσσω in earlier Hellenistic literature, which in itself could have motivated Josephus's use in his own work.

Moving now to survey the extant papyri and inscriptions dated to the same period of postclassical Greek, we encounter important evidence for understanding παράταξις and παρατάσσω and their use in Judg[LXX]. The words appear numerous times in epigraphical sources in particular, where the nominal is mostly used with its *battle event* sense and the verb is typically semantically ambiguous in military contexts. On the other hand, the near total absence of these words from papyri is striking. From the third century BCE through the second century CE there are, in fact, no attestations of παράταξις. There are only two possible attestations in papyri of παρατάσσω. One is too badly damaged to rely on.[66] The second occurs in a third-century BCE Egyptian tax lease and is editorially reconstructed (*BGU* 6.1243 [TM 7320]). If the reading παρα|[τεταγ]μένου is correct (lines 9–10), it refers to the contractual "arrangement" between parties that is under discussion. I will pursue this point in more detail below since caution is needed to avoid argumentation from silence. But the fact that παράταξις and παρατάσσω are virtually unattested in papyri suggests these words were not in common use outside of more educated and formal settings, such as the literary works where they are quite prevalent.

All reliable nonliterary attestations of παράταξις and παρατάσσω appear in inscriptions. To begin with the nominal, there are seven occurrences up through the early third century CE, five of which occur before the turn of the era.[67] In most cases the *battle event* sense is obvious. In a few texts where there is some uncertainty—owing to lacunae or terseness—there are also reasons to favor understanding the word in the same way.

---

66. P.Heid. 6.376 [TM 3073], verso (220 BCE).
67. I include in this number one fourth-century BCE inscription in (38).

(38) IG 2.1614, lines 16–24 (353–352 BCE)
πηδάλια ΙΙ δό[κιμα],| κλιμακίδες, | κοντοὶ ΙΙΙ δό[κιμοι], | κεραῖαι μεγά[λαι]·
| [Π]αράταξις, | Ἱεροκ[λ]έους [ἔργον]· | ταύτηι [παράκειται]· | ταρρὸς —
—, | πηδά[λια —]
2 usable paddles, ladders, 3 useable poles, large yardarms. Battle(line?),
the work of Hierocles. This was at hand: a set of oars — — , paddles.[68]

The mid-fourth-century inscription partially presented in (38) is an account of the inventories of three-oared galleys (τριήρης), which are traditionally called "triremes." According to Shear (1995, 186), these Athenian-style ships had names that were "generally abstractions with positive connotations," such as Εὐετηρία ("Prosperity," line 3) or Νικήφορος ("Victorious, line 110). Here παράταξις is listed as the name given to a particular trireme built by Hierocles (line 21). In such a terse context it is difficult to determine beyond doubt the intended sense of the word. As the name of a ship, however, the *battle event* sense seems likelier as the more abstract notion than the *battle formation* sense, though the latter cannot be ruled out.[69] The ambiguity here matches that of the word seen in (11) above around the same time and also in Athens.

(39) IPriene 117, lines 16–19 (297 BCE)
ὅπως ἂν το[ῦ] τε γενομένο[υ ἡμῖν ὑπὲρ τῆς αὐτονομίας καὶ] | ἐλευθερίας
ἀγῶνος καὶ τῆς παρατά[ξεως — τῆς] | [θ' ἡ]μέρας ὑπάρχηι κατ' ἐνιαυτὸν
ἀεὶ τ[οῖς τε ἐνδημοῦσι τῶμ] | πολιτῶν καὶ τοῖς παραγινομένοις τ[ῶν ξένων
ὑπόμνημα]
so that what happened to you for the sake of both freedom and liberty from conflict and from battle—is for nine days each year perpetually, for both the native citizen and for those who have come from foreign places, a memorial.

The text in (39) is part of an early-third-century Ionian inscription containing two decrees, one of which regards the inauguration of a new festival to cel-

---

68. On κεραία, see Shear (1995), who also says that the τάρρος is "clearly the complete set of oars assigned to a ship" (193), while the πηδάλια "were assigned to a ship when she was still under construction" (223).

69. Note that, regardless of which sense παράταξις was understood, the use of the word as the proper name of a ship does not necessarily imply that it was associated with naval warfare per se as a tactical formation.

ebrate the regained state of freedom of Priene from a tyrant. In this inscription παράταξις is partially fragmentary but may be reliably restored. In the context of the military conflict necessary to regain freedom and given the grammatical coordination with ἀγών ("conflict"'), the *battle event* sense of παράταξις is clear.

(40) ILindos 2.160, lines 1–9 (ca. 190 BCE)
[ὁ δᾶμος ὁ Ῥοδί]ων | [καὶ τοὶ σύμμ]αχοι | [νικάσαντες τοὺς πολε]μίους ἔν τε τᾶι | [περὶ Δαίδαλ]α <u>παρατάξει</u> | [καὶ τᾶι τῶν φρουρίων κ]αταλάμψει | [Ἁλίωι καὶ Ἀθαναίαι Λι]νδίαι καὶ Διὶ Πολιεῖ.
The Rhodian district and allies, after conquering the enemies in both the <u>ordered battle</u> near Daidala and that of the fortresses, will seize Helios and Athena Lindia and Zeus Polieus.

In the text of (40) another clear instance of the *battle event* sense is attested, this time in the early second century. The two παρατάξεις—the one explicitly said to have occurred near Daidala and the one implied near the fortresses—are presented as the military means by which Pamphilidas (Παμφιλίδας, lines 10, 11; cf. Polybius, *Hist.* 21.10.5) conquered his enemies and seized three cities. This episode is also reported by Livy (first to second century CE), who describes thirteen Rhodian ships sailing to guard their city against a Syrian fleet and joining forces with the Rhodian fleet over which Pamphilidas was commander. Together these forces overcame the blockade of Daedala and several other fortresses of Peraea in armed engagements on land (*Hist.* 37.22).[70]

(41) IG 4.1.28, lines 1–5 (146 BCE)
οἵδε ἀπέθανον ἐν τᾶι <u>παρατάξει</u> ἐπὶ τοῦ Ἰσ|θμοῦ· | Δυμᾶνες· | Πολυκλῆς Γοργάσου | Πυθόδωρος Λαχάρεος
These men died in the <u>ordered battle</u> on the Isthmus: From Duman: Polykles of Gorgas, Pythodoros Lachares.

This example in (41) comes from a mid-second-century casualty list inscription found in Epidauros, which lists fifty-three citizens in four tribal groups along with over one hundred others. Writing in the same period,

---

70. Bresson (1999, 124 n. 95) ties this inscription with Livy's account but contests Blinkenberg's reconstruction of line 4, [ποτὶ Ἀντίοχον βασιλέ]α παρατάξει, which would imply the fighting was the sea battle of Myonnessos. He states that "the restoration is obviously wrong" and instead provides the reading adopted here.

Polybius employs a very similar phrase: μέχρι τῆς Ἀχαιῶν καὶ Ῥωμαίων περὶ τὸν Ἰσθμὸν παρατάξεως, "until the battle of the Achaeans and the Romans at the isthmus" (*Hist.* 3.32.3; Pritchett 1985, 234–35). Both these examples, then, corroborate the *battle event* sense of παράταξις in more formal contexts of use.

A late second-century BCE inscription provides another attestation of the word παράταξις but precious little context:

(42) SEG 52.736, lines 1–2 (cf. IosPE 1.353)
[— — — — — — — — — — — — — — νικάσαν]τες παρατάξει Σκύθας καὶ Σα[ρμά]|[τας] ...
— — — — — — — — — — — — — —
conquering (in battle?) Skythes and Sarmatas

Assuming the reconstruction is correct, the dative form of παράταξις could permit either the *battle event* ("in battle") or the *battle formation* ("by ordered rank") senses. The ostensive accusative form of the fully-preserved personal name Σκύθας suggests the former, but there is not enough text to determine the meaning.[71]

(43) *OGIS* 2.654, lines 10–12 (29 BCE)
[Γ]άϊος Κορνήλιος, Γναίου υἱὸς, Γάλλ[ος ἱππεὺ]ς Ῥωμαίων, μετὰ τὴν κατάλυσιν τῶν | ἐν Αἰγύπτωι βασιλέων πρῶτος ὑπὸ Καίσ[αρος ἐπὶ] τῆς Αἰγύπτου κατασταθείς, τὴν Θηβαΐδα [ἀ]|ποστᾶσαν ἐν πεντεκαίδεκα ἡμέραις δὶς [ἐν παρ]ατάξει κατὰ κράτος νικήσας
Gaius Cornelius Gallus, son of Gnaios, cavalryman of the Romans, after the defeat of the kings in Egypt appointed as prefect by Caesar over Egypt; mightily conquering the revolting Thebaid in battle twice in fifteen days

The late first-century text in (43) is part of the so-called Gallus Inscription, a Latin-Greek-hieroglyphic trilingual monument celebrating the accomplishments of Gaius Cornelius as the newly appointed prefect of Egypt (Thompson and Koenen 1984, 131–32).[72] The use of παράταξις in a prepositional construction with ἐν differentiates the *battle event* sense prompted here from the *battle formation*. The Latin portion of this honor-

---

71. It is even possible that ΠΑΡΑΤΑΞΕΙ here is a verb form, though it seems unlikely.
72. There is extensive bibliography on the so-called Gallus Inscription, e.g, Hoffmann, Minas-Nerpel, and Pfeiffer (2009).

ary decree, although fragmentary, is intact enough here to lend support to the *battle sense* of παράταξις: [bis a]cie victor, "twice winning the battle" (line 3).

A final example dates to just after the second century CE but is worth considering since it attests the *battle event* sense.

(44) IScM 2.106, lines 1–8 (238–244 CE)
ἀγαθῆι τύχηι· | Πόπλ(ιον) Αἴλ(ιον) Ἀμμώνιον τὸν κράτισ|τον ἐπίτροπον τοῦ Σεβ(αστοῦ), πράξαν|τὰ τὴν ἐπαρχείαν πιστῶς, ἔπαρχον | χώρτης Ἐσπάνων, τριβοῦνον | χώρτης α' Γερμάνων, ἡγησάμενον | στρατιωτικοῦ ἐν <u>παρατάξει</u> Ἀρ|μενιακῆ
Regarding a brave act: Publius Aelius Hammonius the powerful procurator of Sebastus, faithfully carrying out his office, commander of the cohort of the Spaniards, tribune of the first cohort of Germans, commander of the soldiers in the <u>battle</u> in Armenia

There is little question in the context that the *battle event* sense of παράταξις is used. So despite the decline of this sense in postclassical literature, (44) shows that even in the early third century CE it was still in use for official purposes.

Moving on to attestations of the verb παρατάσσω in epigraphical sources, a brief overview must suffice. Aside from the papyri mentioned above, when searching between the fourth century BCE and the second century CE the word is attested ten times and all before the turn of the era.[73] In seven of those sources παρατάσσω is used in the context of military conflict.[74]

In one case the verb clearly has the *form for battle* sense:

---

73. See IG 5.2.6, face A. col. II line 28 (fourth century BCE); SEG 45.764, lines 12–13 (345 BCE or 207/206 BCE; TM 127389); IG 4.1.128, line 71 (ca. 280 BCE); GDI 2.1867, line 4 (176 BCE); IPergamon 1.165, line 2 (167–159 BCE); twice in SIG 700, lines 13, 28 (118 BCE); SEG 42.695, col. II lines 7–8 (ca. 110 BCE); TAM 2.1.265, line 5 (early first century BCE); SEG 4.246, line 7 (first century BCE). IAphMcCabe 435, lines 27–28, may read παρέταξε, but it is too damaged to be reliable and dates to the Roman imperial period.

74. Three attestations (IG 4.1.128; IG 5.266; GDI 2.1867) occur in the context of administrative, logistical, or economic organization (i.e., "to set in order," "to arrange"), much like the BGU 6.1243 papyrus mentioned above. A late fifth-century BCE attestation (SEG 30.43) occurs in the context of value comparison as in (7) above.

(45) *SIG* 700, lines 10–14
> ἐν δὲ τῶι παρόντι καιρῶι καὶ τοῦ τῶν Γαλα|τῶν ἔθνους συναχθέντος καὶ ἐπιστρατεύσαντος εἰς τοὺς κα|τὰ Ἄργος τόπους στρατοπέδωι μείζονι, ἐφ' οὓς καὶ ἐκπορευθέν|[τ]ος Σέξτου Πομπηΐου τοῦ στρατηγοῦ καὶ <u>παραταξαμένου</u> μετὰ | [τ]ῶν ἰδίων στρατιωτῶν
> And in the present time, when the Gallic nation gathered and made war upon those lands toward Argos with a large army, against whom Sextus Pompeius the praetor marched out and <u>formed for battle</u> with his own soldiers.

The example in (45) is drawn from a second-century BCE honorific decree for Marcus Annius, who had repelled certain invasions in Macedonia, establishing yearly athletic games in celebration of his accomplishments. Sextus Pompeius died in the battle for which he organized his forces (line 13), a clear use of the *form for battle* sense, given the following phrase μετὰ ἰδίων στρατιωτῶν. Later, Marcus engaged the enemy himself and routed them. A second instance of παρατάσσω occurs a few lines down in the same inscription describing Marcus's ensuing actions:

(46) *SIG* 700, lines 26–29
> ἐκπορευθεὶς με|θ' ὧν εἶχεν ἐν τῆι παρεμβολῆι στρατιωτῶν καὶ οὐθένα κίνδυνον οὐδὲ κακ[ο]|παθίαν ὑποστειλάμενος, <u>παρετάξατο</u> καὶ ἐνίκησεν τοὺς πολεμίους μά|χηι
> he went out with those soldiers he had in the camp and, refraining from no danger or distress, (<u>engaged in/formed for battle</u>?) and defeated the enemy in combat.

The context in (46) gives rise to ambiguity in the sense of παρατάσσω, which permits either the *form for battle* or *engage in battle* senses here. But this use of the verb illustrates a pattern that appears in three of the other four epigraphical sources where it is attested in a military context. That pattern is the combination of παρατάσσω and νικάω to describe a two-stage process by which a victory occurred.[75] It appears that these inscriptions

---

75. IPergamon 1.165; SEG 45.764; TAM 2.1.265. In SEG 42.695 νικάω does not appear but rather τρέπω, though the ambiguity remains (for translation, see Bagnall and Derow 2004, 102). A similar case of ambiguity appears in the fourth and final source, SEG 4.246, where the verb is preserved in full but the surrounding text is damaged. It may read "[having received reinforc]ement without an[y] co[wardice] they (engaged in/formed for) battle [against the Parthians]" (lines 5–6).

in their formality preserve a slightly more expansive statement of military activity, namely, battle action (παρατάσσω) and its outcome (νικάω). Owing to the semantic ambiguity this kind of fuller statement could be condensed simply to παρατάσσω, as in the more elliptical expression of the literary authors discussed above.[76]

Summary

The literary and nonliterary sources surveyed in this chapter provide important evidence for understanding the use of παράταξις and παρατάσσω in postclassical Greek. After fewer than a dozen instances in classical sources, παράταξις is attested far more frequently in the third century BCE through the second century CE. In postclassical literary works the word appears most in the writing of Greek military historians such as Polybius, Diodorus Siculus, and Cassius Dio. Here παράταξις appears almost exclusively in military contexts and by the second century BCE often with a new meaning to refer to a battle between opposing forces in side-by-side formations, which I have referred to as the *battle event* sense (2 in the sample entry). This sense is also prevalent in the relevant epigraphical evidence as early as the fourth century BCE and as late as the third century CE. Even as the new sense became conventional, however, the older sense referring to the physical formation of troops side by side for battle remained in use (1 in the sample entry). Considering its use to describe hoplite-style military battle between the second century BCE and first century CE, using these two senses of παράταξις relies upon cultural background knowledge that is distinctly Greek in detail. As an Atticizing author, Josephus's use of the *battle event* sense indicates he considered it an educated use of the word, likely owing to its Hellenistic literary pedigree. But non-Atticizing authors such as Plutarch and Cassius Dio use παράταξις and its *battle event* sense much less frequently in the late first and second century CE, suggesting it was falling out of use as the cultural knowledge of Greek warfare faded away and new practices emerged.[77]

---

76. For similar instances of παρατάσσω and νικάω in literary works, see Diodorus Siculus, *Hist.* 19.67.2; Plutarch, *Art.* 20.3.3.

77. On Roman battle tactics, see Polybius, *Hist.* 15.15.7–10; and Hays (2003, xvi). Ash (2007, 440) points out that Tacitus (first to second century CE) devotes considerable space to why the traditional Greek hoplite battle was not possible in many Roman military conflicts (e.g., *Ann.* 3.73.3; 12.39.2; 12.55.2; 15.3.1), whether due to an unwill-

The development of the verb παρατάσσω follows a similar trajectory. Its older sense referring to organizing soldiers into side-by-side battle formation remains present throughout the period surveyed (3 in the sample entry). But, beginning in Polybius and most clearly in the first century BCE through first century CE, the verb developed a new sense to refer to engaging in battle between forces in side-by-side arrangements, which I have called the *engage in battle* sense (4 in the sample entry). This newer meaning was associated with the same culturally situated Greek military practices and may have arisen from semantic ambiguity when the word was used to refer to an entire event. While epigraphical sources tend to use παρατάσσω and νικάω together—the ambiguity nevertheless remaining—the literary authors often use only παρατάσσω to refer to actual engagement in combat, not just formation. As with the nominal παράταξις the new sense of the verb seems to have been declining by the second century CE, such that in Cassius Dio it does not appear at all.

Along with these trends, the use of παράταξις in postclassical sources strongly suggests it was part of a more educated variety of Greek, particularly the *battle event* sense. The use of the word throughout literary works is the first such indication. But the nonliterary evidence provides important support. Although epigraphical evidence is nonliterary in genre, often the language used is more formal and educated in nature owing to its public and official purpose.[78] To the extent that the inscriptions examined here are intact enough for analysis, this official function appears in each source where παράταξις appears, which consist of honorary inscriptions (44), dedications (40, 42, 43), memorials (41), and decrees (39).[79] It would therefore be a mistake to conclude that the appearance of παράταξις and its *battle event* sense in postclassical inscriptions implies that the word (or sense) was, on that basis, common in lower register varieties of the language. The less-formal and less-educated varieties of postclassical Greek are far better represented in general by the papyrological evidence. In those sources,

---

ing enemy (*Ann.* 4.49.1; 12.28.1; 12.32.1; 13.37.2; 15.5.3), a swift attack (*Hist.* 4.33), or other distractions of war (*Ann.* 11.20.2; 11.20.3; 13.53.2–3).

78. Speaking of papyri, Aitken (2014c, 188) issues a similar caution against confusing genre with linguistic register. Cf. Lee (2016, 102).

79. The same can be said for most inscriptions in which παρατάσσω appears, which are royal letters and dedications (SEG 45.764; *SIG* 700) and honorary decrees (IPergamon 1.165; TAM 2.1.265; SEG 42.695). The exception is the accounts of naval activity in (38).

however, there are no extant attestations of παράταξις at all. Of course, that absence may be merely an accident of history. However, the words πόλεμος and μάχη do appear around a dozen times in papyri in the same era (third century BCE to second century CE), which suggests that these words were more conventionally used to refer to concepts similar to the *battle event* sense of παράταξις.[80] With this in mind, the absence from papyrological evidence of παράταξις and its *battle event* sense also supports the idea that it was not common in the vocabulary of lower-register varieties of Greek. The evidence shows rather that, until its decline from use overall, παράταξις (and its *battle event* sense) was conventional mainly within educated language of authors communicating in more formal composition, such as military historians, public officials, and Atticizing authors such as Josephus.

Conclusions

The Greek-Priority View and Septuagint Lexicography

Study of the *battle* vocabulary in Greek Judges affirms the importance of a Greek-oriented approach to Septuagint lexicography. I began this chapter by pointing to a clear case of disagreement over the best vocabulary for translating לחם and מלחמה in Judges into Greek. The OG translator preferred πολεμέω and πόλεμος, but these words were later revised with near perfect consistency to παρατάσσω and παράταξις (tables 3.3 and 3.4). Turning to several major Greek lexicons provides no help in understanding why the latter two words would be considered a suitable replacement for the former. It might be tempting to halt investigation at that point and conclude that Judg[Rv] used παρατάσσω and παράταξις unconventionally either in error (owing to incompetence in Greek conventions) or deliberately

---

80. Πόλεμος: P.Grenf. 1.42, line 4 (TM 266; second century BCE); P.Lond. 6.1912, line 74 (TM 16850; first century CE); P.Oxy. 22.2339, lines 8–9 (TM 25937; first century CE); SB 16.12589, line 11 (TM 26738; second century CE); O.Krok. 1.94, line 6 (TM 88691; second century CE). Μάχη: Chrest.Wilck. 1.2.11a, line 16 (TM 362; second century BCE.); P.Tebt. 1.138 (TM 3773; second century BCE); P.Tebt. 1.44, line 15 (TM 3680; second century BCE); SB 14.12084, line 14 (TM 24945; first century CE); O.Did. 460, line 5 (TM 145021; second century CE); P.Iand. 6.111, line 5 (TM 17337; first to second century CE); P.Princ. 3.164, line 9 (TM 24134; second century CE); O.Did. 136, line 5 (TM 144702; early third century CE). Most of these attestations refer to physical conflict, but there are also instances that refer to nonphysical conflict (P.Tebt. 1.44; P.Princ. 3.164; SB 14.12084, 16.12589).

(owing to disregard for Greek conventions). But contemporary lexicons include little if any of the postclassical evidence necessary to reach such conclusions. In this connection, the lexical analysis above demonstrated how παρατάσσω and παράταξις developed semantically in the early Hellenistic period such that their use in Judg[Rv] is in fact conventional as Greek and suitably represents the meaning of the Hebrew words involved. In light of the above analysis the lexical replacement in the revised Greek text no longer seems semantically odd. The suitability of παρατάσσω and παράταξις in examples (1) through (5) provided above is now clear, just like the following examples in which the use of these words is perfectly comprehensible as postclassical Greek:

(47) Judges 20:14
    BHQ
    ויאספו בני־בנימן מן־הערים הגבעתה לצאת <u>למלחמה</u> עם־בני ישראל
    And the sons of Benjamin gathered together from the cities toward Gibeah to go out <u>for battle</u> with the sons of Israel.

    Judg[OG]
    καὶ συνήχθησαν οἱ υἱοὶ Βενιαμιν ἐκ τῶν πόλεων αὐτῶν εἰς Γαβαα τοῦ ἐξελθεῖν καὶ <u>πολεμῆσαι</u> μετὰ υἱῶν Ισραηλ
    And the sons of Benjamin gathered together out of their cities toward Gibeah to go out and <u>to fight</u> with the sons of Israel.

    Judg[Rv]
    καὶ συνήχθησαν οἱ υἱοὶ Βενιαμιν ἀπὸ τῶν πόλεων αὐτῶν εἰς Γαβαα ἐξελθεῖν εἰς <u>παράταξιν</u> πρὸς υἱοὺς Ισραηλ
    And the sons of Benjamin gathered together from their cities toward Gibeah to go out to <u>battle</u> against the sons of Israel.

(48) Judges 11:8b
    BHQ
    לכן עתה שבנו אליך והלכת עמנו <u>ונלחמת</u> בבני עמון
    For this reason we have now turned to you, so you may go with us and <u>fight</u> with the sons of Ammon.

    Judg[OG]
    Οὐχ οὕτως· νῦν ἤλθομεν πρὸς σέ, καὶ συμπορεύσῃ ἡμῖν καὶ <u>πολεμήσωμεν</u> ἐν τοῖς υἱοῖς Αμμων
    Not so. Now we came to you, so you might go with us and so <u>we might fight</u> with the sons of Ammon.

Judg^{Rv}
Διὰ τοῦτο νῦν ἐπεστρέψαμεν πρὸς σέ, καὶ πορεύσῃ μεθ' ἡμῶν καὶ <u>παρατάξῃ</u> πρὸς τοὺς υἱοὺς Αμμων
For this reason now we turned to you, and you will go with us and <u>you will fight</u> against the sons of Ammon

It is worth emphasizing at this point a major implication for study of the language of the Septuagint: the words παρατάσσω and παράταξις are not semantically odd for the contexts in which they appear in Judg^{LXX} *if*, as a prerequisite to making such a judgment, the relevant contemporary Greek sources are examined first. It is the Greek-oriented view of the language of the Septuagint that promoted the analysis necessary for an accurate understanding of these words and their use. In the process of coming to that understanding, moreover, the shortcomings of current lexicons have been further exposed. That exposure highlights the need for renewed lexicographical study of postclassical Greek in tandem with study of the Septuagint lest inaccurate judgments are made about the corpus owing to insufficient or inaccurate lexical data.[81] In my attempt to meet that need the whole range of postclassical evidence—literary and nonliterary sources—has proven to be of vital importance. The time has come for this evidence and its social context to inform Septuagint lexicography.

Battle Vocabulary and Greek Judges

This study of the *battle* vocabulary in Greek Judges also has implications for the translation and revision history of the book itself. The decision to replace certain words in the OG version with παρατάσσω and παράταξις in Judg^{Rv} arose from concerns within the social context of the revised text to communicate in Greek. The revision—at the level of lexical replacement—was not motivated merely by a desire to more accurately represent the Hebrew. That may have happened at certain points, but in the case of *battle* vocabulary the OG translator had already adequately translated the

---

81. This is precisely what van der Meer (2006, 70, citing Hollenberg 1876, 5–6) does when he claims the use of παρατάσσω to translate לחם in Josh 24:9 was due to the translator's desire to "adjust the text of Joshua" toward the Greek Pentateuch. Presuming the *form for battle* sense that seems oddly matched to the Hebrew, van der Meer postulates that, "after all, Balak did not really come to a fight with Israel, which made a literal rendering of the Hebrew verb by πολεμέω inappropriate." But this interpretation is entirely mistaken once the *engage in battle* sense of παρατάσσω is recognized.

meaning of the Hebrew by using πολεμέω and πόλεμος. Their later replacement with παρατάσσω and παράταξις does that job just as well, though in a different way. Why make such a change?

It is important to note that we have no reason to think that anything about the use of πολεμέω or πόλεμος in Judg^OG was problematic, semantically speaking. That is not why they were changed. Rather, the decision to substitute παρατάσσω and παράταξις in Judg^Rv appears to have been motivated by stylistic concerns, namely, a desire to introduce elements of a higher register of the language. As I have suggested along the way, in light of the genre, purpose, and linguistic features of the texts in which παρατάσσω and παράταξις most frequently appear, these words were typical of more educated and formal varieties of Greek. The concern to introduce new vocabulary in place of πολεμέω or πόλεμος arose from the social context of the revision and is distinctly Greek-oriented. Nevertheless, that was not the only concern underlying the revision of Judg^OG. The examples in (47) and (48) above also demonstrate that closer adherence to the word order of a Hebrew exemplar like MT was a motivating concern for Judg^Rv as well. In (47) the OG rendering τοῦ ἐξελθεῖν καὶ πολεμῆσαι μετὰ is revised to ἐξελθεῖν εἰς παράταξιν, the latter of which more closely represents the Hebrew לצאת למלחמה in word order. Likewise, in (48) the OG renderings οὐχ οὕτως and συνπορεύσῃ ἡμῖν are revised to διὰ τοῦτο and πορεύσῃ μεθ' ἡμῶν, the latter of which more closely represent the Hebrew לכן and והלכת עמנו in word order. The language and purpose of the text of Judg^Rv is multifaceted. The revision occurred in part to bring the text closer to a Hebrew *Vorlage* in word order. But it did so in a way that simultaneously introduced aspects of an educated variety of Greek that were unprompted by the source text. To succeed in both of these goals at once requires considerable skill and subtlety, and implies a Jewish readership for the revised text that would have recognized and appreciated both achievements.

Septuagint Vocabulary and Greek Lexicography

Once vocabulary choice in the Septuagint is established as free from source text influence, it can and should inform Greek lexicography as a discipline. Even as a Greek-priority approach to the language of the Septuagint facilitates more nuanced and accurate understanding, that knowledge in turn ought to inform study of postclassical Greek. In this connection, lexicons would do well to note aspects of chronology and register, for example, that help evaluate developments more carefully. The insufficient presentation of the meaning and development of παρατάσσω and παράταξις in current Greek lexicons is symptomatic of their shortcomings for the postclassical phase of the language in particular. Reference works like these that omit the most relevant data cannot serve as a firm basis upon which to evaluate the language of the Septuagint. Notably, Muraoka does the best insofar as the *battle event* and *engage in battle* senses of the words are clearly recognized, although no external support is provided. Yet Muraoka's recognition—proven correct in this chapter—itself demonstrates the potential of the Septuagint corpus to provide valuable evidence for lexicography of postclassical Greek.

4

"For So the Young Men Used to Do": ΠΑΙΔΑΡΙΟΝ, ΠΑΙΔΙΟΝ, ΝΕΑΝΙΣΚΟΣ, and ΝΕΑΝΙΑΣ

> It is wrong to start from the assumption that the LXX Greek, being translational Greek, must necessarily deviate from the "normal" contemporary Greek.
> —Muraoka, "Recent Discussions on the Septuagint Lexicography"

> Few concepts in the contemporary study of style have proven more productive than that of choice.
> —Silva, "Describing Meaning in the LXX Lexicon"

Many individuals participated in the military and political events discussed throughout the Hebrew narrative of Judges. As would be expected, males were a ubiquitous part of this activity, although certainly not exclusively so (e.g., Judg 4–5). Just as with the *battle* vocabulary examined in the previous chapter, the narrative of Judges in Hebrew presented many opportunities to translate the vocabulary associated with these males into Greek. As some of the most frequently occurring content words in the book, this Greek vocabulary is another excellent candidate for lexical analysis. It also presents unique challenges and opportunities insofar as the terminology used to categorize individuals according to their stage of life was associated not only with their perceived age but also with social status that was embedded within the Greek cultural context.

Again, like the *battle* vocabulary, the Greek words used throughout Judg[LXX] to categorize males differ distinctly in the OG translation (AII group) compared with the later revision (B group). These differences show up in the two texts presented in Rahlfs-Hanhart but are more pronounced when the readings for each instance are broken into textual groups. On the one hand, the OG translator almost exclusively prefers παιδάριον to refer to the males in the Judges narratives. On the other hand, in the revised Greek text παιδάριον sometimes remains where it is but elsewhere it is changed to any of the words παιδίον, νεανίσκος, or νεανίας (noted by Fernández Marcos 2012, 168; cf. Harlé and Roqueplo 1999, 54).[1] This revision is not as pervasive as that seen in the *battle* vocabulary. But the distinct trends in lexical choices in the two historical phases of Greek Judges again imply some kind of motivation. Once more, the underlying Hebrew vocabulary cannot have motivated the change. And once more, contemporary Greek lexicons do not provide enough information from the relevant postclassical sources to understand what semantic difference exists between the words involved. But examining this *young male* vocabulary specifically within nonliterary sources helps illuminate its meaning within the ancient cultural context and suggests reasons for its use in the revised text of Greek Judges.

This chapter examines the lexical data in three sections. The first lays out the trends in Greek *young male* vocabulary within textual groups in order to describe the chronological changes that took place in the history of Judg^{LXX}. Then, after showing the problems inherent to the gloss method of lexicography in relation to Greek *young male* vocabulary, I proceed in the second section to analyze the use and meaning of the words in postclassical sources. This analysis is not exhaustive or aimed at producing sample lexical entries as in the last chapter. Rather, I focus the discussion upon select examples drawn from nonliterary evidence that demonstrate how the lexical selection in Judg^{Rv} adheres to linguistic conventions typical of Ptolemaic Egypt in particular. Most of the *young male* vocabulary used in the revised text of Greek Judges is clearly tied to the kind of individual it describes in the narrative context of the book. In the third and final section of this chapter I discuss how the Greek-priority view, which seeks to understand the corpus first in light of contemporary sources, can inform Septuagint lexicography. The documentary evidence provides valuable insight into the meaning and use of the *young male* vocabulary that in turn helps to identify the stylistic concern underlying Judg^{Rv} to introduce greater semantic nuance in Greek. These conclusions also demonstrate once more the value of the Septuagint as a corpus of postclassical Greek to the broader discipline of Greek lexicography.

---

1. Finding the right term to refer to this vocabulary is difficult. Though it may be too general, I have chosen to use the terminology of *young male* vocabulary.

The Textual History of *Young Male* Vocabulary in Judg^{LXX}

The two texts in Rahlfs-Hanhart hint at a disagreement in the textual history of Greek Judges over what *young male* vocabulary to use and where. The differences between the A and B texts are summarized in table 4.1:

Table 4.1. Judg^{LXX} *young male* vocabulary in Rahlfs-Hanhart

	A text	B text
παιδάριον	22	9
παιδίον	—	3
νεανίσκος	2	4
νεανίας	—	7

Except for two instances among the *young male* vocabulary (14:10; 20:15), Judg^A attests παιδάριον to refer to young males in the narrative, while Judg^B exhibits greater lexical diversity for the same purpose.[2] Notably, when this Greek vocabulary is aligned with the Hebrew text (MT), it is associated with almost all twenty-three instances of a single word in Judges: נער.[3] The word נער has a broad semantic range in the Hebrew Bible and is typically translated into English using "boy, lad, youth," "young man," and even "servant, attendant," depending on context.[4] This range of glosses itself provides a clue to the disagreement in Greek translation equivalents within the evidence for Judg^{LXX} and prompts further investigation.

Dividing the textual support for each of these *young male* words in Judg^{LXX} into groups provides a firmer basis for historical and lexical investigation. The evidence for Judg^{OG} and Judg^{Rv} confirms the trends seen above. The OG translator preferred παιδάριον overall, but that word choice was frequently replaced with one of several other words in the later revised text of Greek Judges. As shown in table 4.2, just over half of the instances

---

2. 7:10, 11; 8:14, 20; 9:54 (twice); 13:5, 7, 8, 12, 24; 16:26; 17:7, 11, 12; 18:3, 15; 19:3, 9, 11, 13, 19.

3. The second instance of נער in 8:20 instead corresponds with νεώτερος, which will not be examined. Also note that in 17:12 where נער appears there is a minus in the B text. The word ילד is not attested in Judges, and the six instances of עבד in the book are not examined here owing to the different Greek vocabulary involved.

4. *CDCH*, s.v. "נער." After analysis, Eng (2011, 80) suggests that נער has "two general meanings" that relate to age and social function: "boy" and "servant," respectively.

of OG παιδάριον were changed in the B group. Instances of lexical substitution in the Greek renderings of נער in Judges are denoted using bold text.

Table 4.2. The *young male* vocabulary in Judg^LXX

נער	Judg^OG	Judg^Rv
7:10	παιδάριον	παιδάριον
7:11	παιδάριον	παιδάριον
8:14	παιδάριον	παιδάριον
8:20 (2×)	παιδάριον	παιδάριον
	νεώτερος	νεώτερος
9:54 (2×)	παιδάριον	παιδάριον
	παιδάριον	παιδάριον
13:5	παιδάριον	παιδάριον
13:7	παιδάριον	παιδάριον
13:8	**παιδάριον**	**παιδάριον : παιδίον**
13:12	**παιδάριον**	**παιδάριον : παιδίον**
13:24	**παιδίον**	**παιδάριον**
16:26	παιδάριον	**νεανίας : νεανίσκος**
17:7	παιδάριον	**νεανίας : νεανίσκος**
17:11	παιδάριον	**νεανίας**
17:12	παιδάριον	—[5]
18:3	παιδάριον	**νεανίσκος : παιδίον**
18:15	παιδάριον	**νεανίσκος**
19:3	παιδάριον	**νεανίας**
19:9	παιδάριον	**νεανίας**
19:11	παιδάριον	**νεανίας**
19:13	παιδάριον	**νεανίας**
19:19	παιδάριον	**νεανίσκος : νεανίας**

---

5. While the OG read καὶ ἐγενήθη αὐτῷ τὸ παιδάριον εἰς ἱερέα (Zglnow + dptv and OL), the majority of the B group of witnesses omit τὸ παιδάριον (Befjmqsz + imrua₂). While there are no extant variants in *BHQ*, perhaps τὸ παιδάριον was omitted to revise toward a Hebrew exemplar without הנער or because it was judged redundant.

4. "For So the Young Men Used to Do"

In almost every case the OG translator used παιδάριον to render נער, the exceptions being 8:20 (twice) and 13:24. Notably, in the first eight occurrences of παιδάριον in Judg^OG there are no variant readings. That is, the word παιδάριον was apparently retained in Judg^Rv in those places. But revision occurs in every instance thereafter. As is also indicated in table 4.2, the B group is internally divided over readings to varying degrees in several instances, indicated using a colon (:) in the table. This disagreement occurs in six texts: 13:8, 12; 16:26; 17:7; 18:3; 19:19. In four of those texts (13:12; 17:7; 18:3; 19:19) only one or two witnesses attest the alternative reading(s).[6] However, in two cases (13:8; 16:26) the manuscript support in the B group is more evenly split.[7] The upshot of these data is that, while the OG translation almost universally preferred παιδάριον (twenty-one times), the B group uses a variety of *young male* vocabulary with the following frequency: παιδάριον (eleven times), νεανίας (seven times), νεανίσκος (four times), and παιδίον (once).

The following are examples of lexical revision of *young male* vocabulary in context. They are provided in order of increasing disagreement between Judg^OG and Judg^Rv—starting with none—as well as disagreement internal to the latter among the B group evidence:

(1) Judges 8:20b
     BHQ

     ולא־שלף הַנַעַר חרבו כי ירא כי עודנו נַעַר
     But the youth did not draw his sword since he was afraid since he was still a youth

     Judg^OG
     καὶ οὐκ ἐσπάσατο τὸ παιδάριον τὴν μάχαιραν αὐτοῦ διότι ἐφοβήθη ἦν γὰρ νεώτερος
     But the παιδάριον did not withdraw his dagger because he was afraid, for he was younger

     Judg^Rv
     καὶ οὐκ ἔσπασεν τὸ παιδάριον τὴν ρομφαίαν αὐτοῦ ὅτι ἐφοβήθη ὅτι ἔτι νεώτερος ἦν

---

6. The less-attested B group reading is in gray font in table 4.2 and is respectively supported by Bq, su, c, and m.

7. dfmqsirua₂ vs. Bejqz in the former and Befjsz vs. diqrua₂ in the latter.

But the παιδάριον did not draw his sword since he was afraid, for he was still younger

(2) Judges 17:7
BHQ

ויהי־נער מבית לחם יהודה ממשפחת יהודה

Now there was a youth from Bethlehem of Judah, from the family of Judah

Judg^OG
καὶ ἦν παιδάριον ἐκ Βηθλεεμ δήμου Ιουδα ἐκ τῆς συγγενείας Ιουδα
Now there was a παιδάριον from Bethlehem from Judah, from the family of Judah

Judg^Rv
καὶ ἐγενήθη νεανίας ἐκ Βηθλεεμ δήμου Ιουδα (Judg^Rv)[8]
Now there happened to be a νεανίας from Bethlehem from Judah

(3) Judges 16.26
BHQ

ויאמר שמשון אל־הנער המחזיק בידו

And Samson said to the youth who was holding his hand

Judg^OG
καὶ εἶπεν Σαμψων πρὸς τὸ παιδάριον τὸ χειραγωγοῦν αὐτόν
And Samson said to the παιδάριον who was leading him by the hand

Judg^Rv
καὶ εἶπεν Σαμψων πρός ...
    τὸν νεανίαν τὸν κρατοῦντα τὴν χεῖρα αὐτοῦ (Befjsz)
    τὸν νεανίσκον τὸν κρατοῦντα τὴν χεῖρα αὐτοῦ (diqrua2)
And Samson said to ...
    the νεανίαν holding his hand
    the νεανίσκον holding his hand

(4) Judges 19:19
BHQ

וגם לחם ויין יש־לי ולאמתך ולנער עם־עבדיך

---

8. Fernández Marcos (2011, 100*) argues that יהודה ממשפחת was omitted in the B group through homoioteleuton. Variant readings here include νεανίσκος su : νεάνις a2.

and there is also bread and wine for me and your female servant and for the <u>youth</u> with <u>your servants</u>

Judg^{OG}
καί γε ἄρτος καὶ οἶνος ὑπάρχει μοι καὶ τῇ δούλῃ σου καὶ τῷ <u>παιδαρίῳ</u> καὶ τοῖς <u>παισίν</u> σου
and there is also bread and wine for me and for your female servant and for the <u>παιδαρίῳ</u> and for your <u>servants</u>

Judg^{Rv}
καὶ ἄρτοι καὶ οἶνός ἐστιν ἐμοὶ …
    καὶ τῷ <u>νεανίσκῳ</u> μετὰ τῶν <u>παιδίων</u> σου (Bda₂)
    καὶ τῷ <u>νεανίσκῳ</u> μετὰ τῶν <u>παίδων</u> σου (efjqs)
    καὶ τῷ <u>νεανίσκῳ</u> τοῖς <u>δούλοις</u> σου (iru)
    καὶ τῷ <u>παιδαρίῳ</u> μετὰ τῶν <u>παίδων</u> σου (z)
    καὶ τῷ <u>νεανίᾳ</u> τοῖς <u>δούλοις</u> σου (m)
and there are loaves and wine for me…
    and for the <u>νεανίσκῳ</u> with your <u>παιδίων</u>
    and for the <u>νεανίσκῳ</u> with your <u>παίδων</u>
    and for the <u>νεανίσκῳ</u> with your <u>δούλοις</u>
    and for the <u>παιδαρίῳ</u> with your <u>παίδων</u>
    and for the <u>νεανίᾳ</u> with your <u>δούλοις</u>

In the example in (1), though there are various differences otherwise, both Judg^{OG} and Judg^{Rv} agree upon παιδάριον (and νεώτερος) as a suitable word for the context.[9] However, in (2) Judg^{Rv} employs νεανίας to replace παιδάριον with some divergence among two cursives within the B group as noted above. The example in (3) shows how the B group is elsewhere split fairly evenly between νεανίας and νεανίσκος as a replacement for παιδάριον. And (4) demonstrates the remarkable disagreement among the witnesses to Judg^{Rv} corresponding to the translation of נער and עבד in a single phrase.

A closer look at the use of νεανίσκος in Judg^{LXX} is necessary here as a precursor to later analysis. The word not only appears in Judg^{Rv} as a replacement for παιδάριον in four places (table 4.2), but it is also used twice in Judg^{OG} as follows:

---

9. νεώτερος also appears with no variants at 1:13; 3:9; 9:5; and 15:2 corresponding with MT קטן. At 18:3 OG reads παιδαρίου τοῦ νεωτέρου, which Fernández Marcos (2011, 50) suggests is a double reading of נער.

(5) Judges 14:10
BHQ

ויעש שם שמשון משתה¹⁰ כי כן יעשו הַבַּחוּרִים

And there Samson prepared a feast, for so the <u>young men</u> used to do

Judg^{OG}

καὶ ἐποίησεν ἐκεῖ Σαμψων δοχὴν ἡμέρας ἑπτά, ὅτι οὕτως ἐποίουν οἱ <u>νεανίσκοι</u>

And there Samson held entertainment for seven days, for so the <u>νεανίσκοι</u> would do

Judg^{Rv}

καὶ ἐποίησεν ἐκεῖ Σαμψων πότον ζ΄ ἡμέρας, ὅτι οὕτως ποιοῦσιν οἱ <u>νεανίσκοι</u>

And there Samson threw a drinking party for seven days, because the <u>νεανίσκοι</u> do so

(6) Judges 20:15
BHQ

לבד מישבי הגבעה התפקדו שבע מאות איש בָּחוּר

aside from the inhabitants of Gibeah, who assembled seven hundred chosen men

Judg^{OG}

χωρὶς τῶν κατοικούντων τὴν Γαβαα, οὗτοι δὲ ἐπεσκέπησαν ἑπτακόσιοι ἄνδρες, <u>νεανίσκοι</u> ἐκλεκτοί

apart from those inhabiting Gibeah, and these were numbered seven hundred men, chosen <u>νεανίσκοι</u>

Judg^{Rv}

ἐκτὸς τῶν οἰκούντων τὴν Γαβαα, οἳ ἐπεσκέπησαν ἑπτακόσιοι ἄνδρες ἐκλεκτοί

except for those living in Gibeah, who were numbered seven hundred chosen men

In the first instance in (5) the OG translator uses νεανίσκος to translate the nominal בחור, "young man" (*CDCH*, s.v. "בחור"), and this is retained in Judg^{Rv}. However, in the text of (6), בחור is apparently rendered twice in Judg^{OG}, first as a nominal (νεανίσκοι) and again as an adjective (ἐκλεκτοί;

---

10. Fernández Marcos (2011, 92*) considers משתה an "assimilation to the context" (with Burney 1970, 360–61), but Boling (1975, 231) considers it original.

reading the *qal* passive participle of בחר I, "choose, elect"; *CDCH*, s.v. "בחר").[11] In the revised text of this verse in Greek Judges, however, νεανίσκοι is absent, and only the adjective ἐκλεκτοί remains.

Summary of Translation and Revision Activity

Some noteworthy features of this translation and revision activity in Judg[LXX] emerge, even though the textual evidence is not as straightforward as that of the *battle* vocabulary in the previous chapter. The clearest trend is the preference in the OG translation for παιδάριον to refer to *young males*. This prevailing choice is particularly striking given the diversity of contexts where the word is used in the narrative of Judges. But this stereotyping approach to translation should not be written off as simplistic or mechanistic. For in addition to the alternative νεώτερος (8:20) and παιδίον (13:24) the OG translator also used νεανίσκος in the two texts in (5) and (6).[12] Again, the apparent motivation for using νεανίσκος in the OG translation was the source text, namely, the word בחור. So, although the OG translator preferred παιδάριον as standard translation for נער, he also made a semantic distinction insofar as he chose to use νεανίσκος to translate two instances of בחור. As I show below, the latter is a suitable choice for the narrative contexts judging by the use of νεανίσκος in nonliterary Greek sources. The picture of standard translation equivalency in Judg[OG] is therefore not an example of "Hebrew interference" in Greek usage but rather an example of the source text presenting narrative contexts where, as it happens, conventional use in both Hebrew *and* Greek would call for two different words. The use of νεανίσκος in Judg[OG] thus represents a carefully nuanced choice that satisfied multiple goals for his target text: source-text consistency and target-text style.

The prevailing use of παιδάριον within Judg[OG] fell under scrutiny at a later point. Three aspects of the related revisional activity stand out. First, the *young male* vocabulary is not revised universally, at least not in the same way as the *battle* vocabulary. In about half of its twenty-one instances in the OG text, παιδάριον was left in place in Judg[Rv], while the rest were replaced. Second, the revision of the OG *young male* vocabulary, where it occurred,

---

11. See Fernández Marcos (2011, 13*) for discussion of the uncertain textual situation in 20:15b–16. It is possible that the doublet in (6) could have arisen only in the AII group if OL support is deemed indispensable here.

12. The text in (6) is discussed further below.

was not consistent. That is, rather than using a standard word to replace the OG vocabulary, there are several words used in Judg^Rv. Third, there is some disagreement among the textual evidence for the *young male* vocabulary within the B group that represents the revised text of Greek Judges. Unlike the revision of the *battle* vocabulary—where the B group attested παράταξις and παρατάσσω with much more unanimity—for the *young male* vocabulary there are several alternative readings internal to the group. It is not often clear what led to the disagreement internal to the B group over particular readings for revised *young male* vocabulary. It could have been a product of inner-Greek transmission after the revision occurred. In any case, it is not my goal to explain every translation choice and its revision (or lack thereof). In fact, if anything the variation among the B group witnesses highlights the choice of *young male* vocabulary as semantically motivated yet free from Hebraizing influence. It points to interpretive differences within the textual history of Judg^Rv as a Greek text that were part of, and subject to, the ongoing changes in the broader language.[13] In this connection, the occasional lack of consensus in the B group reinforces the aim of this chapter, which is to evaluate the meaning and use of the relevant words within contemporary sources to demonstrate how doing so is prerequisite to understanding correctly why they were employed in different ways and different contexts in the Septuagint corpus.

The Question of Semantics in Judg^LXX

Since the *young male* vocabulary words were considered interchangeable within Judg^LXX, it is reasonable to assume they were considered semantically similar to some degree. The same phenomenon became apparent with the revision of *battle* vocabulary examined in the last chapter. In that case the current lexicons could not explain the revision because they lack the information to show the semantic *similarity* of the vocabulary involved. For the *young male* vocabulary, the same problem exists with current lexicons but for the opposite reason. In this case they cannot explain the revision because they lack the information to show the semantic *distinctions* between the vocabulary involved. To demonstrate the shortcomings

---

13. The vocabulary diversity in Judg^Rv may also be associated with the B² group discussed in Cañas Reíllo (2020b, 180).

in this respect, table 4.3 presents a selection of glosses from the entries for the *young male* vocabulary in several current lexicons.

Table 4.3. Select lexicon entries for *young male* vocabulary

	παιδίον	παιδάριον	νεανίας	νεανίσκος
MGS	baby, child *male or female* up to seven years old, little slave	little boy, baby, baby girl, little girl, young slave	young man, servant	young man, boy, adolescent, young servant, page
LSJ	little *or* young child (up to 7 years), child, young slave	little boy, child, *pl.* young children, young slave	young man, youth	youth, young man, servant
BDAG	very young child, infant, child	child, youth, young slave	youth, young man	youth, young man, servant
DGF	petit enfant (garçon *ou* fille) au-dessous de sept ans, jeune serviteur, petit esclave	jeune enfant, homme en enfance, jeune esclave	jeune homme	de jeune homme
PGL	child	little boy, babe (in the sense of one who is humble)	young man	young man, slave
GELS	young child (including teenagers)	young male child, young male (of working age)	young man	young man, lad
LEH	young child, infant	little boy, child, young man, servant	young man, servant, *pl.* children, youth	young man, boy, young (cultic) servant

The information provided in Greek lexicons does little to distinguish the meaning of one word from another.[14] In part this descriptive failure

---

14. The only specific information provided pertains to the age range of a παιδίον and conflicts in LSJ and *DGF* versus *GELS*.

is unavoidable owing to the limitations of the gloss method of lexicographical description. With this approach, the lexicons can do little else than provide a few English translation equivalents in slightly different but overlapping arrangements. In fact, the glosses above—almost thirty in total—are for the most part only different ways of phrasing just a few ideas, which can be visualized as in table 4.4.

Table 4.4. Categories of *young male* vocabulary glosses

	παιδίον	παιδάριον	νεανίας	νεανίσκος
Infant[15]	4	4	—	—
Child[16]	9	10	1	
Servant[17]	4	5	2	6
Youth[18]	—	5	10	13

There is some room for interpretation here, but the result is fairly clear. In reality, there are only four basic ideas involved: "infant," "child," "servant," and "youth." Judging by the most frequent glosses, it would even be fair to conclude that both παιδίον and παιδάριον usually mean essentially the same thing ("child") and both νεανίας and νεανίσκος usually mean essentially the same thing ("youth"). Of course, precisely what the English words "child" and "youth" mean, and how they differ, are distinct but inseparable questions, ones the gloss method cannot answer. These problems in themselves might prompt the Greek lexicographer to mount a fresh examination of this vocabulary in an attempt to provide an actual description of its lexical meaning.[19]

---

15. Including "babe," "baby," "baby girl," "infant," "young infant," and "very young child."

16. Including "child," "children, pl.," "little boy," "little girl," "little child," "young male child," "young child," and "young children, pl."

17. Including "slave," "little slave," "young slave," "servant," "young servant," and "page."

18. Including "boy," "young male," "youth," "young man," "lad," "adolescent," and the nebulous suggestion "man in childhood."

19. The glosses also appear to be unhelpfully influenced by the assumption that diminutive morphology must always be reflected in lexical semantics, which is incorrect (Cruse 2011, 345–46). For examples of semantic analysis of diminutives, see Jurafsky (1996), Santibáñez Sáenz (1999), and Matisoff (1991).

The unhelpful generalization in current lexicons reflected in table 4.4 goes to show how difficult it is in practice to describe the meaning of such vocabulary. The disagreement in the textual evidence of Greek Judges certainly shows that there must have been semantic differences among the *young male* words. But what were those differences and how are they best detected? Postclassical Greek, like most languages, had no shortage of words to refer to people in terms of categories for age or physical maturity. Yet scholars generally agree that there was no universal system in Greek for this kind of terminology (Forbes 1933, 2; Golden 1990, 12–16). The absence of such a system was not for lack of trying. Several surviving literary sources preserve attempts by ancient authors to explain numerical age ranges and features typical of life stages, which were known as the ἡλικίαι.[20] Yet such accounts are of little lexicographical value owing to their artificial prescriptiveness and because they often attempt to harmonize the ἡλικίαι with various structures the Greeks found, for example, in numerology, astrology, and biology (Leinieks 1996, 199–203; Garland 1990, 2–8; Thompson 2011, 194). In any case, few in the ancient world would have known their precise birthdate or actual numerical age.[21] The meaning of words like the *young male* vocabulary was associated instead with perceived age and culturally bound judgments about the "physical appearance, mental attitude, circumstances, and intention" of the individual being described (Parkin 2010, 102). These judgments were also informed by the individual's position in society, for instance, "in the order of the family, in the resulting distribution of economic resources, and in the distribution of power within the political system" (Timmer 2013, 174; see also Garland 1990, 13).

Accordingly, social context is essential for understanding the *young male* vocabulary in Greek contemporary to the Septuagint corpus.[22] Only

---

20. E.g., Xenophon, *Cyr.* 1.2.4, 1.5.4, 8.7.6; Aristotle, *Ath. pol.* 42.1-2; Plutarch, *Lyc.* 21; *Inst. Lac.* 14–15 (238a–b); *Se ipsum* 15 (544e); Philo, *Opif.* 105; Aristophanes of Byzantium, Περὶ ὀνομασίας ἡλικιῶν 37–66.

21. Even if they did, there are significant complexities involved with determining the accuracy of age when it is explicitly mentioned in ancient sources. See Parkin (2003, 26–35).

22. E.g., ancient Greek artwork literally illustrates how slavery was socially analogous to "a state of permanent childhood" in that "when a slave iconography develops it involves small size and youth as marks of lower status" (Lewis 2002, 83). Similarly, the fact that "boys, slaves, and pathics" were all addressed as παῖς indicates "how closely their social identities were conflated" (Garland 1990, 106).

after its meaning is understood from the relevant evidence can its use in the Septuagint be properly understood. The lexicons are once again unhelpful guides and fresh analysis is necessary. In this connection, the nonliterary papyri and inscriptions from Egypt are of paramount importance and will receive the bulk of attention in the analysis below, although literary sources will play a supporting role. It is, as stated above, the nonliterary evidence that preserves the variety of postclassical Greek closest to that of the Septuagint corpus. Moreover, it was composed in a social context most likely the same as that of Judg^{Rv}. The approach taken in this chapter for lexical analysis therefore differs from that in the previous chapter, since tracing diachronic semantic change is not of primary interest here. But a challenge to the more synchronic approach in this chapter is the uneven attestation of the *young male* vocabulary in postclassical sources. That is, in some cases one of the more frequently attested words in Greek Judges is very sparsely attested in external evidence, or vice versa. For example, νεανίας is the second most frequent of *young male* vocabulary in Judg^{LXX} (seven times) but is attested fewer than twenty times in nonliterary evidence overall between the third century BCE and second century CE, the majority of which date to after the turn of the era. Conversely, παιδίον is the least common in Judg^{LXX} (once) but is well attested in Greek sources. In view of this challenge, the analysis below focuses primarily upon the two *young male* words that are best attested in both Judg^{LXX} and in external evidence, namely, παιδάριον and νεανίσκος. In order to illustrate the meaning and use of the *young male* vocabulary most clearly, the discussion below integrates analysis of contemporary Greek with examples from Greek Judges.

Illustrating Judg^{Rv} with Postclassical Nonliterary Greek

Within this section, the first subsection addresses those instances where παιδάριον was left in place and not revised in Judg^{Rv}, while the second subsection addresses the remaining instances that were in fact replaced.[23]

---

23. Parts of this section are used and developed in Ross (2020a), particularly with respect to παιδάριον and νεανίσκος.

ΠΑΙΔΑΡΙΟΝ (with Comments on ΠΑΙΔΙΟΝ)

The word παιδάριον is attested thirty-two times in Judg^LXX overall, twenty-one instances in Judg^OG and eleven in Judg^Rv. As the best attested word among the *young male* vocabulary under analysis and one of the best attested in external Greek sources, it makes a natural starting point and will therefore receive most of the focus here. However, I will also briefly comment on the word παιδίον given its singular use in Judg^OG and the fact that it appears in some B group witnesses where otherwise παιδάριον was left in place. To begin this discussion, table 4.5 provides a synopsis of the attestation of παιδάριον.[24]

Table 4.5. ΠΑΙΔΑΡΙΟΝ in Greek sources

Century	BCE					CE	
	Fifth	Fourth	Third	Second	First	First	Second
Literature	14	31	7	7	1	62	81
Papyri	—	—	100	39	14	15	44
Inscriptions	—	—	1	73	16	7	9
Total	14	31	108	119	31	84	134

It bears repeating that care is necessary when evaluating frequency of attestation in extant Greek sources.[25] Not only may results differ depending on the database used, but totals may also disagree depending on what is considered a valid attestation. With this in mind, table 4.5 above indicates that in literary sources παιδάριον is more frequent in the classical period than the following few centuries, until after the turn of the era where attestations increase significantly (as do extant sources). This word is an excellent case study for the value of papyri and inscriptions for postclassical Greek lexicography and the related task of Septuagint lexicography. On its own, the literature of third through first century BCE provides only fifteen attestations of παιδάριον. But in that same period the nonliterary evidence preserves an additional 485 attestations. In both

---

24. On the use of παιδάριον and παιδίον in the Septuagint, see Simpson (1976, 94–104, and 105–14, respectively).

25. Particularly in view of the relative increase of diminutive forms in postclassical Greek (Robertson 1923, 72).

the third and second century BCE παιδάριον appears over 100 times in papyri and inscriptions combined.[26] From the perspective of frequency of attestation, it is certainly significant that the other important corpus for attestations of παιδάριον is the Septuagint, where an additional 234 attestations appear. That both the nonliterary evidence and the Septuagint attest παιδάριον with such frequency—in stark contrast to contemporary literary sources—is an eloquent fact, indicating that both corpora contain a very similar variety of postclassical Greek.

More important than the frequency of its attestation is understanding the linguistic and social contexts in which παιδάριον is used in surviving sources. Analyzing the word within these contexts as a point of departure helps to clarify its use within Judg[Rv]. There are at least two senses attested in nonliterary evidence for παιδάριον, and these appear to account for the cases in Greek Judges where παιδάριον was left unrevised. One sense refers to individuals primarily in terms of their relatively younger age and lower position within the family structure (i.e., *child*), and another refers to individuals primarily in terms of their lesser skill-level and lower status within the socioeconomic structure (i.e., *member of staff*).[27]

Children in the Family Structure

To begin with the former, judging from the glosses typically provided in lexicons for παιδάριον, shown in tables 4.3 and 4.4, it is unsurprising to find the word often used in a context of family relations to refer to a biological child. Accordingly, for comparison I will also present select evidence for παιδίον here as well. An illustrative case study for these two words emerges from several papyri from the third century BCE. The general situation is described in P.Col. 4.83 (TM 1796), a petition by Antipatros, whose wife Simon had borrowed seventy drachmas from a creditor named Nikon at an exorbitant rate of interest. After about ten months had passed, Nikon offered an interest-free repayment plan on the original amount (Bagnall and Derow 2004, 212). Ultimately, in order to recoup his losses, Nikon detained Theodosius, whom Antipatros calls the παιδίον of his wife Simon three times in this letter (lines 10, 12, 16). Antipatros also states that Theodosius is a free person (τὸν ἐλεύθερον; line 16; Scholl 1983, 10). Then in

---

26. In addition to those inscriptions included in the totals, there are a further eighteen where παιδάριον appears in undated sources.

27. These two senses correspond in general terms to those in LSJ for παιδάριον.

two separate papyri pertaining to the same incident Theodosius is called a παιδάριον:

(7) *SB* 3.6762 (TM 1852), lines 4–5
Νίκων δὲ ὁ κρινόμενος πρὸς Ἀντίπατρον οὐκ ἔφατο εἰληφέναι τὸ <u>παιδάριον</u> παρ' αὐτῶν οὐδὲ ἔχειν αὐτὸ | παρευρέσει οὐδεμιᾶι.
But Nikon, the defendant against Antipatros, did not admit to having taken the <u>παιδάριον</u> from them nor to having him under any pretext.

(8) P.Cair.Zen. 3.59347 (TM 990), lines 4–5
ὡρίζετο Νίκων λέγων μήτε εἰληφέναι παρὰ μηδενὸς τὸ <u>παιδάριον</u> | [-ca.?-] μήτε εἷρξαι μήτε ἔχειν τὸ παι\δά[ριον]/ π[αρ]ευρέσει μηδεμίαι.
Nikon laid it out saying he had neither taken the <u>παιδάριον</u> from anyone … nor confined nor held the <u>παιδάριον</u> under any pretext.

So in these documents Theodosius is discussed primarily in terms of his position within a family structure. He is the child (παιδίον) of Simon and (probably) Antipatros, who, as those responsible for him, take measures for his safe recovery. While Theodosius was legally a free person, it seems likely that he was pledged as security in the original contract, for which reason Nikon detained him after he was unable to collect (Westermann 1955, 50). Theodosius is thus socially and economically dependent upon his parents for his well-being, a status that is distinct from yet related to his lower position within his family structure.

Another relevant example appears in P.Col. 3.6 (TM 1728), a third-century BCE letter in which a concerned mother Simale writes a complaint to Zenon about her son, Herophantos. She writes:

(9) P.Col. 3.6 (TM 1728), lines 1–3
ἀκούσασα ἠνωχλῆσθαί μου τ[ὸ <u>παι</u>|]<u>δάριον</u> καὶ σφοδρότερον, παρεγενόμην πρὸς ὑμᾶς καὶ ἐλθοῦσα ἤθελον ἐντυχεῖν σοι ὑ[πὲρ τῶν] | αὐτῶν τούτων.
Having heard that my <u>παιδάριον</u> had been mistreated and quite badly, I came to you and, after arriving, I wished to petition you about these matters.

A few lines down, Herophantos is twice referred to as a παιδίον as well (lines 4, 8) and then still later again as a παιδάριον (lines 11–12). Evidently a certain Olympichos was so hard on Herophantos that he fell ill (lines 6–9). Although the precise arrangement is unclear, Herophantos was part of the retinue of Apollonius. It had been arranged that in return for his service he would receive a regular allotment of olive oil (see P.Corn. 1.66-69, 137-138), a higher grade of remuneration that indicates the social position of Simale's family (White 1986, 33; *pace* Scholl 1983, 12). But in addition to his mistreatment, Herophantos had not been remunerated for some time (lines 9-11), prompting Simale to request that his salary be sent directly to her (lines 12-13). So just like in the previous example, within a single document the words παιδίον and παιδάριον refer to the same individual owing to their position within a family structure. Although Herophantos may be from a family of higher social standing, he is nevertheless economically dependent upon his employer Apollonius. Again, that status is distinct from yet related to his lower position within his family structure, which is precisely why his mother Simale is entitled to claim his salary (Bagnall and Cribiore 2006, 100).

As the examples in (8) and (9) indicate, the word παιδίον was also used frequently to refer to biological children within a family structure. Unlike παιδάριον, this is the sense of παιδίον that predominates within the postclassical documentary evidence. Dickey (2004, 121) found that, beginning in the third century BCE, the word παῖς is "virtually absent" from papyri except to mean "slave," and it was replaced by παιδίον and τέκνον as the default way to refer to a "child."[28] Reinhold Scholl, Graham McGregor Simpson, and others have also reached similar conclusions, finding that in most cases παιδίον means "child" in the Zenon archive.[29] Notably, Simpson (1976, 108-9) concludes that παιδίον virtually always means "child" in the Septuagint as well.[30]

---

28. On the many instances of formulaic use of παιδίον and τέκνον interchangeably, see Dickey (2004, 124-25); Stanton (1988, 469-71).

29. Scholl (1983, 12-13) lists P.Cair.Zen. 3.59482 (TM 1120); twice in P.Col. 3.6 (TM 1728); three times in P.Col. 4.83 (TM 1796); P.Lond. 7.1976 (TM 1539); *PSI* 5.498 (TM 2125); and P.Cair.Zen. 3.59335 (TM 978), along with several texts he considers ambiguous, namely, *PSI* 4.424 (TM 2107); *PSI* 4.418 (TM 2101); and P.Col. 4.81 (TM 1794). In his discussion, Scholl states "daß παιδίον im Zenonarchiv nicht als Sklaventerminus verwendet" (13). Simpson (1976, 112-13) lists P.Tebt. 3.1.800 (TM 5383); *BGU* 6.1244 (TM 4405); six times in *BGU* 4.1058 (TM 18503); five times in *BGU* 4.1107 (TM 18548); P.Giss. 1.2 (TM 2796); four times in *UPZ* 1.60 (TM 3451); *SB* 5.8850 (TM 6370). He identifies, *pace* Scholl, three texts in which παιδίον may mean "slave," namely, P.Col. 4.81 (TM 1794); P.Ryl. 4.593 (TM 5307); and P.Oxy. 41.2979 (TM 16541), but in each case this judgment is debatable. Shipp (1979, 433) also concludes that "Παιδίον is usually 'infant,' 'young child', plur. 'children' in general."

30. His single exception is Judg[B] 19:19, cited in (4). But here Simpson is apparently unaware of the disagreement among textual witnesses, among which παιδίον is

This evidence is sufficient to address several texts in which παιδάριον and παιδίον appear in Greek Judges. Several of the texts in Judg^Rv where the OG vocabulary choice was left in place in the later revised text deal with a family structure in the narrative context, and this appears to be the reason that παιδάριον sometimes went unrevised. First, as shown in (1) above, the OG use of παιδάριον (as well as νεώτερος) in Judg 8:20 is left in place in the later revision. In the narrative context, Gideon is pursuing justice against the Midianite kings Zebah and Zalmunna for those killed in a battle at Tabor (8:18–21), and he commands his son Jether to execute them (8:20a). Several features in the context draw attention to the family structure, such as the phrases "sons of the king" (בני המלך; 8:18), "my brothers, the sons of my mother" (אחי בני־אמי; 8:19), and "his firstborn" (בכורו; 8:20).

Another context dealing with a family structure occurs in the narrative of Judg 13, particularly the divine messenger's announcement to Samson's mother that she will have a child (הנה־נא את־עקרה ולא ילדת והרית וילדת בן, 13:3) who will be a Nazirite and deliverer of Israel (13:5). It is this context in which the sole instance of παιδίον appears in Judg^OG (13:24) in reference to this coming deliverer. In the other instances, Judg^Rv retains παιδάριον in both 13:5 and 7, while in 13:8 and 12 a few witnesses within the B group instead attest παιδίον (13:8 Bejqz; 13:12 Bq; see table 4.2). The alternative readings in the latter two verses could be the result of harmonization with the OG use of παιδίον in 13:24.[31] Regardless, the OG translation choices (both of παιδάριον and παιδίον) as well as the choices made in Judg^Rv (to leave παιδάριον or substitute it with παιδίον) match the use of these words within contemporary postclassical Greek. As shown in examples (7) through (9), the words παιδάριον and παιδίον were each used in postclassical Greek to refer to children, even used side-by-side to refer to a single individual, just as in Greek Judges. More significantly, within the broader trends in *young male* vocabulary use in Greek Judges, the presence of a family structure in the narrative context seems to explain several instances where the OG use of παιδάριον was left unrevised in Judg^Rv.[32] In these

---

aligned not with נער but עבד and is attested only in Bda₂. This reading may be late, however, since Dickey (2004, 121) suggests that παιδίον eventually referred to slaves well after the turn of the era.

31. Although in 13:24 the OG παιδίον is changed to παιδάριον, suggesting a desire for consistency in this narrative context, which might imply the latter is the older reading in each case.

32. Notably, Simpson (1976, 100) suggests that Theodosius in (8) may have been

texts, no change in vocabulary occurred in the revision because lexical choice suited both the narrative context of Judges and the social context of the revised Greek text, so there was no obvious reason to make changes.[33]

Semiskilled Workers in the Socioeconomic Structure

The second and more common sense of παιδάριον in the nonliterary evidence refers to individuals in terms of their lower position in the socioeconomic structure as a semiskilled worker. It is apparently this sense of παιδάριον that lexicons are identifying when they provide glosses like "slave" or "servant" as shown in tables 4.3 and 4.4. For this use of the word it is necessary to recognize that there is something of a fuzzy boundary here due to overlapping categories. In the Hellenistic Egyptian context younger age and a lower position in the family structure naturally coincided with economic dependence, lesser skill level for labor, and lower social status in general. Consequently, many low-status semiskilled workers were children. However, when such an individual was referred to as a παιδάριον it was not (merely) because of their age or position in a family structure, but also owing to their position in the socioeconomic structure. For example, in P.Cair.Zen. 1.59076 a certain Jew named Toubias writes to Apollonius, stating:

(10) P.Cair.Zen. 1.59076 (TM 731), lines 3–6
ἀπέσταλ|κά σοι ἄγοντα Αἰνέ[αν εὐνοῦχον ἕ]να καὶ παιδά[ρια οἰκε]τικά τε | καὶ τῶν εὐγενῶν τέσσαρα, ὧν [ἐστὶν] ἀπερίτμητα δύο. ὑπογεγράφαμεν | δέ σοι καὶ τὰς εἰκόνας [[αὐ]]τῶν π[αιδαρ]ίων ἵνα εἰδῇις.
I have sent you Aineias bringing one eunuch and four παιδάρια, who are both locals and well built, of whom two are uncircumcised. And we have attached for you also the descriptions of the παιδάρια so you know.[34]

The individuals called παιδάρια in this document are subsequently described physically and said to be between seven and ten years old (lines 8–9). They are not part of Toubias's family structure though they depend

---

a baby, which, if correct, would further clarify the use of παιδάριον in Judg 13 to the infant Samson.

33. Among the seven attestations of παιδάριον in Polybius's *Histories*, at least two are used to refer to children in a family structure (15.30.10; 36.16.11; and possibly 30.29.7).

34. Translation adapted from White (1986, 39–40). Tcherikover and Fuks *(CPJ* 1:126) take οἰκετικός as "house-slave."

upon him for their welfare, for which reason they are at his disposal. It was common for people in this age range to be engaged in paid semi-skilled labor in Hellenistic Egypt. In this connection, many estate accounts record the activities of παιδάρια listed alongside γύναι and ἀνδρεῖοι, all of whom are remunerated for their labor (e.g., P.Cair.Zen. 2.59292, line 56 [TM 936]; P.Mich. 1.49, lines 14, 16 [TM 1949]; P.Cair.Zen. 3.59435, line 6 [TM 1075]; Scholl 1983, 10).[35]

The use of παιδάριον to refer to semiskilled workers becomes clearer when it refers to an individual regardless of their age or position in a family structure. Apparently in such cases it is low position in the socio-economic structure—and all that entails—that conceptually grounds the meaning of the word. For example, P.Cair.Zen. 3.59509 is a letter from Somoelis, a Jewish granary guard (φύλαξ) from Philadelphia, to Zenon to report on his agricultural work and other logistical matters.[36] Though the crops he has produced are too abundant to fit in his single granary, he is being paid just one and a half *artabas* of grain. Speaking of this remuneration, Somoelis tells Zenon (see *CPJ* 1:138–40):

(11) P.Cair.Zen. 3.59509 (TM 1147), lines 12–14
οὐχ ἱκανὸν οὖν | [ἐστ]ιν οὐδὲ τὰ <u>παιδάρια</u> [διαβό]σκειν, εἰ μὴ αὐτός τι προσεργάζο|[μαι].
However, it is not enough even to feed the <u>παιδάρια</u> unless I can earn something extra.

A similar use of the word occurs in a letter from Petobastis the pigeon-keeper to Zenon in P.Cair.Zen. 3.59498, who writes of a similar predicament:

---

35. Indeed many, if not most, laborers in the Hellenistic period were remunerated in some way, making impossible a simplistic labeling system of "slave" or "nonslave" status. In her examination of slavery and nonslavery in the Zenon archive Bieżuńska-Małowist (1974, 16; see also 62–63) states that "Il est souvent impossible de trancher entre les deux." Thompson (2011, 195) notes that it is more accurate to speak of "varying degrees of unfreedom." Likewise Gardiner (1930, 212) states that "forced labor was part of Egyptian tradition … but forced labor is not slavery."

36. The work of a granary guard was multifaceted and demanding, particularly during harvest. Certain documents even indicate there was a particular tax used to support granary guards (θησαυροφυλακι[τι]κόν). See Bauschatz (2013, 144).

(12) P.Cair.Zen. 3.59498 (TM 1136), lines 2–15
καλῶς | ἂν ποιήσαις, εἰ καί σοι δοκεῖ, | συντάξας δοθῆναί μοι τὸ | ὀψώνιον· στενῶς γὰρ διά|κειμαι· ὀφείλεται δέ μοι τὸ | ὀψώνιον τετραμήνου. | καὶ εἰς τὴν σιτομετρίαν ἔχω | κριθόπυρα ἀχρεῖα· οὐ δυνά|μεθα καταχρήσασθαι. | χρείας παρέχομαι καὶ τὰ <u>παιδά|ριά</u> μου. δέομαι οὖν σου, | εἰ καί σοι δοκεῖ, \συντάξας/ δοθῆναί μοι τὴν | σιτομετρίαν καὶ τὸ ὀψώνιον | εὐκαίρως, ἵνα σοι τὰς χρείας παρέσ|χωμαι.
Would you please, if you are so minded, arrange for wages to be given to me, as I am in a tight fix. Four months of wages are owed to me. And I have lousy barley-wheat for rations; we cannot be depleted. I have needs and so do my παιδάρια. So I request of you, if you are so minded, arrange rations and wages to be given to me promptly, so I can provide for your needs.

Another business arrangement involving παιδάρια appears in a letter from Alcimus to Zenon in P.Cair.Zen. 3.59378, who makes the following request:

(13) P.Cair.Zen. 3.59378 (TM 1021), lines 2–8
καλῶς ποή|σεις τὰ <u>παιδάριά</u> μοι ἀπο|δούς, καθότι διωμολό|γητο ἡμεῖν· τὰ γὰρ ἔργα | μοι ἐνέστηκε. περὶ δὲ | τοῦ ἱματισμοῦ ἐπίκρινον | αὐτὸς ὅσον δεῖ δοθῆναι
Would you please send me the <u>παιδάρια</u>, as we agreed; for my labors have come to a halt. And about the clothing, decide yourself however much is necessary to provide.

Even three centuries later, the word παιδάριον is used with this sense in a first-century CE letter from Egypt, though with a spelling variant. In *BGU* 4.1079, an Alexandrian merchant named Sarapion writes to Herakleides, one of his staff members who evidently made a bad business deal with a certain Ptollarion, suggesting:[37]

(14) *BGU* 4.1079 (TM 9456), lines 13–20
λέγε | αὐτῷ· ἄ|λλο ἐγώ, ἄλλο πάντες, | ἐγὼ <u>παιδάριν</u> εἰμί. παρὰ | τάλαντόν σοι πέπρακα | τὰ φο[ρτ]ία μου· οὐκ οἶδα | τί μ[ε ὁ] πάτρων ποιςει, | πολλοὺς δανιστὰς ἔχο|μεν. μὴ ἵνα ἀναστατώ|σῃς ἡμᾶς
Tell him [Ptollarion], "It is one thing for me, another for everyone else, I am a παιδάρι[ο]ν. I have sold you my merchandise for a talent too little.

---

37. See Tcherikover and Fuks (*CPJ* 2:33–35), who suggest that "Herakleides was a freedman, or at any rate a dependent of another person; the meaning 'slave' is therefore more probable than the rather vague 'child'" (2:35).

I do not know what my patron will do, as we have many creditors. Do not drive us out of business!" (translation adapted from White 1986, 129–30)

The individuals referred to in each of these examples may have been fairly young children by modern standards, but perhaps not. Simpson concludes that, while in earlier Greek the age reference of the word παιδάριον seems to have been more important, in the postclassical period the word was often used to describe an individual's "status as a slave or servant, *irrespective of his age*" (1976, 102–3, emphasis added).[38] These documents preserve business correspondence. Somoelis and Petobastis mention the παιδάρια in (11) and (12) not to move Zenon with the image of hungry children, but because the agricultural labor they provide is essential for operations and they must have the means to pay them for it. These παιδάρια are members of staff whose welfare is to be provided by their employer, as is clear in (13). Yet the example in (14) also indicates that, owing to their lower socioeconomic position, they were exposed to risk that others were not, even as Sarapion himself presumes a mutual concern for the fate of his business (note ἡμᾶς, line 20). These individuals are referred to as παιδάρια owing to the social status of their role as paid but economically dependent semiskilled workers, not their age or position in a family structure.[39]

A survey of other documentary sources in which παιδάριον is used in this sense provides a more detailed picture of the kinds of labor and the employment conditions typically involved. Many examples are available in the Zenon Archive, such as P.Cair.Zen. 3.59406 (TM 1048), in which παιδάρια are involved in animal husbandry. In another case, Apollonius dispatched παιδάρια from his estate specifically to learn that trade for themselves (P.Cair.Zen. 2.59195 [TM 841]; ὅπως μανθάνωσ[ιν], line 8; Bieżuńska-Małowist 1974, 63), the results of which are reported in P.Cair. Zen 3.59406 (TM 1048). In these sources payment is not explicit, but other papyri make it clear that παιδάρια were ordinarily remunerated for

---

38. Similarly, in their revised supplement to LSJ, Glare and Thompson (1996, 235) note that the "*young slave*" sense (II) should be followed by: "perh. sts. without ref. to age."

39. E.g., in a first-century CE tax document, one Kopreus is said to be παιδ(άριον) Ἀντιπά|τρου καὶ ἀδε(λφοῦ), "slave of Antipatros and of *his brother*" (*CPJ* 2.201, lines 1–2), clearly presenting a socioeconomic status rather than a position within a family structure.

their work. Generally speaking, on Apollonius's estate the kind of remuneration—typically food provisions—was determined on the basis of the gender, age, and position of the laborer while the quantity of payment was determined by the type of work (Reekmans 1966). Within this system, there were many παιδάρια who were assigned to farmers for paid labor (P.Lond. 7.2164 [TM 1724]). The work included tasks such as weeding wheat and flax and tending castor trees (παιδάρια τὰ τὸν πυρὸν βοτανίζοντα, lines 1–2; cf. 3, 7), as well as cultivating various crops such as hemp and olives (τοὺς τὴν ἐλαίαν φυτεύον<τας>, lines 7–8; Bieżuńska-Małowist 1974, 62–63). Notably, in P.Cair.Zen. 4.59677 (TM 1305) the παιδάρια employed on Apollonius's ships receive the same payment in both kind and quantity as the ναυτικοί who operate the vessel (similarly P.Cair.Zen 3.59406 [TM 1048]; P.Cair.Zen. 4.59698 [TM 1325]; see Scholl 1983, 10).[40]

There is also evidence that indicates that παιδάρια were ordinarily employed on a semipermanent basis in various capacities. A useful point of contrast with short-term laborers appears in P.Cair.Zen. 2.59176 (TM 822), a long record of daily expenses extending over the course of almost a month. Among those to whom wages were paid we find παιδάρια (lines 84, 89, 90, 119, 149, 154, 163) listed alongside ἐργάται (lines 16, 23, 41, 56, 80, 105, 147, 152, 157, 160, 178, etc.). According to Iza Bieżuńska-Małowist (1974, 63), ἐργάται were "paysans s'engageant de temps à autre comme journaliers." Similarly, the παιδάρια in P.Cair.Zen. 4.59698 (TM 1325) were employed for at least two months (lines 30–34).

In other sources there is evidence of training and education sponsorships, suggesting that longer-term mutually beneficial relationships between παιδάρια and the gift-estate also existed.[41] For example, P.Lond. 7.1941 (TM 2384) records that a παιδάριον called Pyrrhos was a pupil of Heirocles, the "keeper of a palaestra in Alexandria," and was sponsored by Zenon to be educated in Alexandria (cf. P.Cair.Zen. 1.59098 [TM

---

40. There are also παιδάρια serving as ship hands in Polybius, *Hist.* 31.14.11.

41. Evidence for Zenon training individuals of low socioeconomic, or low status in general, for sporting competition includes, e.g., P.Cair.Zen. 2.59296 (TM 940); P.Cair.Zen. 3.59488 (TM 1126); *PSI* 4.364 (TM 2050). On the education of slaves in the Hellenistic and Roman periods, see Forbes (1955), who states that by "apprenticeship methods and by education formal and informal, slaves were constantly being prepared for skilled trades, for business enterprises, for clerical occupations, for some forms of entertainment, and even for the professions of teaching and medicine" (328).

750]; see Clarysse in Pestman et al. 1981, 346).[42] Heirocles reports in P.Cair.Zen. 1.59060 (TM 718) that, in addition to continuing his studies, Pyrrhos is athletically promising and will soon excel the other trainees (σφόδρα ὀλίγου χρόνου πολὺ ὑπερέξει αὐτῶν; line 6). His expectation of prize money (ἐλπίζω σε στεφανωθήσεσθαι) shows that the added expense of gymnastic training for this παιδάριον was meant to profit his benefactor, who in turn was to supply Pyrrhos with clothing, bedding, and honey (lines 9–11; see Heinen 1977, 144; Gardiner 1930; Legras 1999, 25–27).[43] Likewise, in P.Iand. 6.92 there are other παιδάρια under the supervision of Heirocles in the palaestra, but he explains that he is transferring them to Artemidoros, house master of Apollonius (on whom see Pestman et al. 1981, 302 n. 4), since he is suspected of sexual misconduct with trainees (Montserrat 1996, 150–51). Nevertheless, these same παιδάρια are to receive clothing and further training (μαθήματα) to put to use in service of their employer (see Scholl 1983, 11).[44]

Finally, there is evidence that παιδάρια were sometimes associated with military training and activity. P.Cair.Zen. 3.59298 (TM 942) is a letter to Paramonos from one Rhodon regarding certain recent purchases. Rhodon is a ὁπλομάχος (line 10) responsible for teaching the use of arms in the gymnasium (cf. P.Cair.Zen. 3.59488 [TM 1126]; Gardiner 1930, 212; Scholl 1983, 11). In the salutation, Rhodon extends his greeting τοῖς παιδαρίοις (line 1), suggesting they were his former pupils now in service to Paramonos (so Edgar 1928, 1; Scholl 1983, 11).[45] If, as (Scholl 1983, 11) suggests, this is the same Rhodon entitled to corn provisions in P.Cair.Zen. 4.59697 (TM 1324), this may indicate that he was of similar or equal socioeconomic status as the παιδάρια (see Forbes 1955, 356). Additionally, according to the account of Callixenus of Rhodes preserved in Athenaeus, some παιδάρια—along with παῖδες and παιδισκάρια—took part in the Ptolemai(ei)a and Arsinoeia festival, events associated with the

---

42. Gardiner (1930, 212) suggests the palaestra in question is the one mentioned in P.Zen.Pestm. 51 (TM 1882).

43. Based on P.Cair.Zen. 3.59507 (TM 1145), in which he complains of not receiving his allowance from Zenon, Legras concludes that Pyrrhos was a free person. That Rostovtzeff (1922, 172–74) and Scholl (1983, 11) feel Pyrrhos is a slave demonstrates the ambiguity of his low socioeconomic status.

44. On this papyrus, see Rosenberger (1934, 221–22); Dreyer and Mittag (2011, 144 n. 32).

45. See the similar greeting in P.Cair.Zen. 4.59614 (TM 1247).

Hellenistic ruler cult, as discussed in chapter 5 (Dunand 1981). In these processions, παιδάρια were mounted on teams of horses, dressed in Greek tunics (χιτών), hats (πέτασος), and wearing pine garlands (*Deipn.* 200f) to demonstrate that "la jeunesse grecque devra contribuer à la défense militaire du roi et du royaume" (Legras 1999, 232; see 231–33).[46]

Overall, the use of the word παιδάριον in these documents appears to be associated with members of the rural peasant class who worked the land for others in Ptolemaic Egypt like the one that Dorothy Thompson (2011, 198–200) calls the *laoi*.[47] Gardiner (1930, 212) suggests that παιδάρια such as Pyrrhus and those trained by Rhodon may have belonged to a poor working class of soldiers who were customarily given controlled land to cultivate and who would therefore have taken up the kind of labor discussed above. This lower socioeconomic class of Greeks would have had a "variety of statuses" and are known to have looked to local representatives such as Zenon for provision and protection (Thompson 2011, 199). Perhaps this was the case in some of the papyri discussed above, such as Somoelis or Toubias and their παιδάρια in (11) and (12) who worked hard but relied for their well-being upon a patron of higher socioeconomic position.[48]

---

46. Notably, Legras also surmises that the νεανίσκοι, discussed below at (17), were also part of the parade (198–99).

47. Thompson (2011, 199) notes that, while "tied to their home areas with the withdrawal of labour as their best protection, the peasants of Ptolemaic Egypt remained juridically free. Depending for their livelihood on the Nile and on those who controlled the land that they worked, their lives were tough, but these farmers were not slaves in any sense of the word."

48. Although space prevents detailed analysis, the epigraphical evidence for the word παιδάριον corroborates that of the papyri. First, although over one hundred inscriptions attest παιδάριον, only one is from Egypt from the first century BCE (*OGIS* 1.196). The vast majority are from central or northern Greece, with παιδάριον frequently attested at Delphi in the so-called manumission inscriptions (on which see Hopkins 1978, 137 n. 5). There are roughly one thousand such inscriptions recording the manumission of some twelve hundred slaves, dating to the last two centuries BCE. These sources provide a wealth of information about the labor economy and the fiscal and social means by which a greater degree of independence was obtained in the Hellenistic world. A central part of this process was the παραμονή, a "conditional release" by which individuals could purchase formal freedom but remain contractually bound to those they served. It was "a twilight state of juridical freedom combined with slave-like service, a state which overlapped both slavery and freedom" (Hopkins 1978, 133). Finley (1960, 1964) has shown how the manumission inscriptions con-

4. "For So the Young Men Used to Do"

This evidence provides the linguistic and social context to help understand several other texts in which παιδάριον appears in Greek Judges. In particular, against this background it becomes clear that the remaining texts in Judg^{Rv} where the OG vocabulary choice was left unchanged deal with an individual who might have been called a παιδάριον in Hellenistic Egypt. That is, some characters in the narrative of Judges seem to have a socioeconomic status similar to that of a semiskilled worker in Hellenistic Egypt, and this appears to be another reason (in addition to the cases mentioned above) that the word παιδάριον sometimes went unrevised in Judg^{Rv}.

Several such παιδάρια in Greek Judges appear in two separate narrative contexts. First, in Judg 7, Gideon and his troops come to face the Midianites, who are oppressing Israel (cf. 6:1). In 7:10–11, after recognizing Gideon's hesitations, God suggests that he take Purah, who is clearly a servant of some kind, down into the Midianite camp to investigate their numbers (נערו ... הנערך; τὸ παιδάριον σου ... τὸ παιδάριον αὐτοῦ OG). As a religious leader and the commander of Israel's forces (6:33–35), Gideon had various personal staff (cf. 6:27), among whom Purah apparently served as a kind of military aide. Second, a similar context appears in a second text in Judg 9, where Israel enters into conflict with Shechem following the controversial installation of Abimelech as king (9:1–21) and his subsequent slaughter of Jerubaal's seventy sons (9:22–25). In a final confrontation at Thebez (9:50–57), a woman throws a millstone onto Abimelech's head (9:53). Mortally wounded, Abimelech commands his armor bearer to deliver the coup de grâce, which he does (נערו ... הנער נשא כליו; τὸ παιδάριον τὸ αἶρον τὰ σκεύη αὐτου ...

---

firm, like the Ptolemaic papyri, that Hellenistic slavery and freedom did not form a binary, but existed along a spectrum, recently explored in greater detail by Kamen (2013). In his analysis of the manumission inscriptions, Hopkins (1978, 139) found that in 17 percent of cases the individual freed was called a παιδάριον (see also table III.1 on p. 140), who were either "home born" (οἰκογενῆ) or "foreign born" (ἐνδογενῆ). These inscriptions record the transaction in a formulaic way, beginning with (1) the date, (2) a record of sale to the god Pythian Apollo that served as a functional transfer of ownership, (3) the παραμονή, (4) a statement of release, (5) a statement guaranteeing status, and 6) witnesses (Hopkins 1978, 143). Although it is not certain to what degree these Delphic manumission inscriptions are relevant to the Egyptian socioeconomic context, the limbo-like state of these mainland παιδάρια between legal freedom but contractual servitude is consistent with the low socioeconomic status of the semiskilled laborers known from the papyri.

τὸ παιδάριον αὐτοῦ OG). Thus, this unnamed individual is even more explicitly portrayed as a military aide who served at the behest of Abimelech, much like Purah does for Gideon. As discussed above, this is certainly a role suited to a παιδάριον. The associations between παιδάρια and military or athletic training attested in the documentary evidence would have been part of the social context of the translation and revision of Greek Judges in Egypt.

To reinforce this point, *SB* 16.12221 (TM 4069) provides further evidence for the role of individuals of low social status in the Hellenistic Egyptian military. This papyrus records the names of Greek soldiers who were accompanied by a παῖς and a second person. According to Bieżuńska-Małowist (1985, 14), this document attests the use of servants as auxiliary personnel within the early Ptolemaic armies.[49] After exhaustive analysis, Heinz Heinen (1983, 138) likewise concludes that these individuals were "unfreies Hilfspersonal" accompanying their masters on a military expedition (cf. Straus 1983, 125–26). This practice likely came to Ptolemaic Egypt with Greek military immigrants who brought slaves "pas seulement pour leur service personnel mais aussi pour qu'ils transportent les armes et éxecutent certains fonctions auxiliares" (Bieżuńska-Małowist 1985, 14). Such functions would likely include "questions d'intendance: fourniture de vêtements, de nourriture, réquisition de logements, etc." (Straus 1983, 125). So, the Egyptian social context included an established practice of individuals of similar socioeconomic status as a παιδάριον serving in a similar role of military aide, just like Purah in Judg 7:10–11 and the armor-bearer in 9:53. Thus, the use of παιδάριον in these texts well suited the activity of military aides in both the narrative context of Judges and the social context of the revised Greek text, and this seems to explain why in Judg^Rv the word was left unrevised.

In a different kind of narrative context, a third instance in which the OG use of παιδάριον is left unrevised also makes sense against the background of the Egyptian documentary evidence. In Judg 8 Gideon and his troops come to Succoth following a battle with the Midianites, exhausted but still in pursuit of their kings. After being refused quarter there and at Penuel (8: 6–9), Gideon's company engage in a final battle (8:10–12) and turn back to Succoth to exact vengeance for their inhospitality. When they are nearby, they capture an unnamed local (נער;

---

49. Straus (1983) suggests that the names belong to the παῖδες, not the soldiers.

παιδάριον OG), questioning him to extract strategic information about city leadership (8:14). Although the precise location of the narrative is not clear, the region between Succoth and Penuel is a fertile valley at the junction of two rivers.[50] Even if those responsible for producing the texts of Judg[OG] and Judg[Rv] were ignorant of this location—which is more than likely—several geographical features are mentioned in the context, such as the Jordan River near Succoth (8:4), the caravan route for trade (8:11), and the valley implicit in מלמעלה החרס.[51] These narrative features in the context portray just the kind of region that would have been farmed and worked by agricultural laborers like the παιδάρια in Ptolemaic Egypt. In this connection, once again the OG use of παιδάριον suited both the narrative and the social context of Judg[Rv], and so left no reason to replace it in the revised text.[52]

---

50. Seely (1992, 218) suggests this is the area known as Ghor Abu Obeideh. On the difficulties involved with the reading מלמעלה החרס at the end of 8:13, see Fernández Marcos (2011, 73*).

51. That the translator of Judg[OG] understood מלמעלה as a mountainous geographical feature is evident in his choice of ἀνάβασις to render it (Harlé and Roqueplo 1999, 159). But this is revised two ways in the B group. It was omitted in efjsza₂ and revised in Biru to τῆς παρατάξεως, likely reading מלחמה. As discussed in the last chapter, the latter again demonstrates the efforts made in Judg[Rv] to adhere more closely to a Hebrew *Vorlage* while employing a particular variety of Greek.

52. As a final note, it appears that the common feature associating what could be called the *dependent child* and *staff-member* senses of παιδάριον seems to be their shared dependence upon or subservience to someone with higher social status. For the *dependent child* sense, the word is used to refer to a biological child in a context that typically involves some aspect(s) of their greater physical vulnerability, lesser economic independence, and/or lower rank of authority relative to a parent. For the *staff-member* sense, παιδάριον is used to refer to someone who provides semiskilled labor in a mid- to long-term and mutually beneficial relationship with a patron. For both senses, those characterized as either a *dependent child* or *staff-member* were often of younger age in the nature of the case. But age is not semantically part of the word παιδάριον, which instead was associated with culturally bound aspects of relatively lower status within family or socioeconomic structures. It may be that the *staff-member* sense of παιδάριον arose from the *dependent child* sense by metaphorically conceptualizing the dynamics of certain employment arrangements in terms of family relations as they were manifested in the Hellenistic social context. Note also that the *staff-member* sense appears in three of the seven attestations of παιδάριον in Polybius (*Hist.* 15.25.32; 31.14.11), for which Glockmann et al. (1998, 2) suggest "zum Dienstpersonal gehöriger kleinerer Junge" and "Lustknabe."

ΝΕΑΝΙΣΚΟΣ (with Comments on ΝΕΑΝΙΑΣ)

Analyzing νεανίσκος or νεανίας in postclassical Greek sources again provides a picture of the linguistic and social contexts in which they were used. That information in turn can clarify their use within Judg^{Rv}. It is one thing to attempt, as I did above, to explain on the basis of primary evidence why change did *not* occur within the textual history of Greek Judges. It is perhaps more straightforward to address actual lexical change in the revised text. All of the remaining instances of παιδάριον in Judg^{OG} underwent just such a revision, each being replaced either with νεανίσκος or νεανίας in Judg^{Rv}. As shown in table 4.2, νεανίας appears a few more times than νεανίσκος: seven and four attestations, respectively, given how I have handled the textual evidence from the B group. However, because νεανίας is very sparsely attested in the third through first century BCE—only sixteen occurrences in all sources combined—focus falls here upon νεανίσκος, which is much better attested overall (table 4.6).[53]

Table 4.6. ΝΕΑΝΙΣΚΟΣ in Greek sources

Century	BCE					CE	
	Fifth	Fourth	Third	Second	First	First	Second
Literature	45	89	2	67	83	277	473
Papyri	—	—	17	3	1	2	7
Inscriptions	5	3	8	16	1	5	5
Total	50	92	27	86	85	284	485

Again being cautious not to draw too sweeping conclusions from this frequency data, they do show that νεανίσκος was more common in Greek literature than nonliterary sources. But that likely has more to do with the relevance of the word to Greek military matters so often discussed

---

53. Simpson (1976, 65) notes the sparse attestation of νεανίας in papyri specifically, citing only P.Petr 2.4, a third-century BCE papyrus where the word is fragmentary and in a later edition reconstructed as νεα[νίσκοι (portions of which have been republished numerous times; cf. TM 7650, 7651, 7642, 7659, 44593, 7646, 7640, 7658, 7641, 7657). After the first century CE, νεανίας is far better attested, around 110 times in the first and 101 times in the second century in literature, but only ten and five times in papyri or inscriptions, some of which are fragmentary.

by Hellenistic authors than with linguistic register.[54] As discussed below, νεανίσκος is prevalent also among nonliterary sources and is used there with the same meaning and in similar contexts. For that reason, and in light of the importance of documentary sources for showing the specific status of νεανίσκοι in Ptolemaic Egypt, the papyri will continue to receive the most attention here. Numerous Greek sources show that the word νεανίσκος was closely associated with a certain kind of Greek civic training known as the *ephebic* system (from ἐφηβεία). In connection with this widespread and diverse cultural institution, the word νεανίσκος was used in Ptolemaic sources to refer to a particular kind of civic officer, which is supported in both Ptolemaic documentary evidence and literature from other regions that specifically discusses these Egyptian νεανίσκοι.[55]

Greek *Ephebeia* and Ptolemaic Civic Officers

Beginning at least from 370 BCE in Athens, Greek males from among the social elite went through two years of compulsory and highly structured civic and military training known as *ephebeia* (see Aristotle, *Ath pol.* 42.3–5).[56] The *ephebic* system was a Greek cultural system intentionally designed to "integrate young men into the community of

---

54. Note that almost all of the literary attestations of νεανίσκος in third to first centuries BCE occur in Polybius (sixty-seven), Diodorus Siculus (forty-nine), and Dionysius of Halicarnassus (thirty-one). A further twenty-one inscriptions are undated, and there are seven in which νεανίσκος may appear but which are too fragmentary to be reliable.

55. It is worth noting also the differences between νεανίας and νεανίσκος in the Septuagint. On the one hand, νεανίας appears thirty times in the corpus, mostly in the Historical and Deuterocanonical Books (none in the Pentateuch). On the other hand, νεανίσκος occurs more than twice as often, appearing 110 times and more evenly distributed. This difference in usage in the Septuagint coincides with trends in other Greek sources, with νεανίσκος being the more frequently attested of the two words. On the use of νεανίας and νεανίσκος in the Septuagint, see Simpson (1976, 61–65 and 71–76, respectively).

56. The *ephebic* system has been especially well documented and studied by epigraphers, such as Kennell, who has compiled "a register that enumerates every Greek city possessing a system of citizen training" (2006, vii). Starting in Athens, part of *ephebic* training entailed physically categorizing males into distinct spaces in the gymnasium according to ἡλικίαι (Aristotle, *Pol.* 7.1331a37–8). Kennell (2006, ix) notes that in Athens the *ephebic* system was part of "wide-ranging military reforms that radically altered the method of conscription for hoplites."

adults" (Chankowski 2013, 179). During their period of *ephebeia*, males of around eighteen to twenty years old learned to use a bow, javelin, and other elements of hoplite and light-armed battle tactics, patrolled nearby borders, and were eventually examined in order to take an oath of loyalty to the state and its religion (Garland 1990, 183–84; Casey 2013, 421).[57] Previous generations of scholars felt this fourth-century Athenian institution ultimately fell into disrepair. But that theory has been completely overturned by fresh analysis of the Hellenistic *ephebeia* and its key role in "producing citizen warriors and in projecting a particularly powerful vision of Greek civic culture" (Kennell 2013, 217; 2015, 172). By the second century BCE, sources indicate that *ephebic* training was reduced, no longer compulsory, and open to non-Greeks (Garland 1990, 185; Kennell 2015, 174–75). By that point the *ephebic* system had become one of the most widespread Greek institutions, present "in every corner of the Greek world" (Kennell 2006, vii–viii, quotation on xi; Chankowski 2011, 114–234).

In this connection, *ephebeia* was in fact a significant hellenizing influence throughout the ancient Mediterranean region (cf. 2 Macc. 4:9, 12, 14).[58] Almost as soon as the *ephebic* system was formalized in Athens it functioned as an important means of social mobility, which likely drove its success as an institution in the Hellenistic world (see Oliver 2011; Whitehorne 1982). *Ephebeia* offered males an opportunity to join and identify themselves with the Hellenistic elite (Kennell 2015, 173; Chankowski 2011, 250–51). As the system slowly evolved, it became more educationally oriented (see IG 2.1006)—possibly under the influence of Zeno and the Stoics—and later took on localized features (Kennell 2015, 176–78).[59] Most importantly, there is a considerable amount of evidence for *ephebic* training in Ptolemaic Egypt, not only in Alexandria and other major cities but also in the countryside, which was "the economic backbone of the cities"

---

57. While there was no uniform system to delimit the length of time of *ephebeia*, it usually lasted one year—perhaps two—between age seventeen and twenty-one. However, in a society with no birth registers, age was judged visually, and admission into *ephebic* service was granted by physical examination, at which point the male was considered eighteen years old (Chankowski 2013, 179–80).

58. On the Maccabean incident, see Kennell (2005).

59. Casey (2013, 419, 429–33) states that "Zeno helped transform ephebes from military guards at the periphery to trained thinkers who were by no means peripheral to the future glory and fame of Athens" (437).

(Chaniotis 2007, 107; see Whitehorne 1982, 172; Legras 1999, 133–49). The *ephebic* system was just one measure put in place to protect the important revenues, food, and natural resources produced in rural areas from constant threat.[60] The earliest documents for Egyptian *ephebeia* come from Alexandria as early as the third century BCE, where it appears to have taken a form similar to the Athenian model.[61] This evidence therefore establishes that the Greek *ephebic* system, along with its terminology, would certainly have been part of the social context of the Septuagint translators and its later revisers (even if they did not themselves participate in *ephebeia*).

The significance of the Greek *ephebic* system for this study lies in the sociocultural categories it created for young males in civic life and the terms associated with them, among which is the word νεανίσκος. For purposes associated with their gymnastic training, the Hellenistic *ephebic* system progressed young males through three sequential *ephebic* classes based on their age, physicality, and level of training. These were, in order: παῖς, ἔφηβος, and νέος (Skaltsa 2013, 3006; Kennell 2006, viii; Garland 1990, 184, 200; Chankowski 2013, 178). The first distinction and transition between παῖς and ἔφηβος took place when freeborn males in the first stage began formal training in the second as an ἔφηβος.[62] Those who completed that training then joined the highest and final class of νέος, gaining full citizenship with all of the concomitant benefits and duties (Chankowski 2011, 268–69; Kennell 2015, 173). Primary sources indicate that νέος and ἔφηβος were official terms that were "so familiar as to be stereotyped" in the Greek world (Forbes 1933, 20). However, there is some complexity in that the terms νέοι and νεανίσκοι had two distinct but overlapping uses

---

60. Including enemy invasions, brigands, incursions of barbarian ethnic groups, illegal exploitation, raids, civil strife, and so on (Chaniotis 2007, 119–23).

61. See, e.g., IG 12.Sup.646; Fayoum 1.8; SEG 8.694; IG 7.2715-21; Chankowski (2011, 173–78, 229); Kennell (2015, 173, 181–82); Launey (1950, 859 n. 1). Evidence of *ephebeia* in Ptolemais and Naucratis likely appears by at least the late second century BCE (Chankowski 2011, 179–80). The Athenian *ephebic* system remained in place through the late first century BCE (e.g., IG 2.1008, 1028), and it continued to exist in some form until at least the third century CE (Kennell 2006, x–xi).

62. See the epigraphical evidence cited in Kennell (2015, 173). Chankowski (2011, 250) defines the παῖδες as "un groupe organisé institutionnellement, c'est-à-dire des garçons avant l'éphébie qui suivent un programme d'enseignement prévu par la legislation d'une cite." He goes on to state that "l'éducation des *paides* est, du point de vue de la cité, conçue comme une étape préparatoire à l'éducation civique des éphèbes" (253).

throughout almost all Hellenistic sources.⁶³ These words could refer to either the νέοι class itself or to the νέος and ἔφηβος classes as a whole (i.e., the entire gymnasium, excluding the παῖδες; Chankowski 2011, 249, 253).⁶⁴ But those who had entered the highest νέοι/νεανίσκοι class were certainly a distinct group owing to their central role in civic ceremonies and—particularly important in the conflicted Hellenistic period—defense (Kennell 2013, 218).⁶⁵ Their role in the latter is often attested in both inscriptions and the writing of historians such as Polybius.⁶⁶

Aside from the broader issues concerning terminology related to the Hellenistic *ephebeia*, what is of greatest interest here is that the word νεανίσκος was apparently used in a more specific way in Ptolemaic Egypt than elsewhere. Numerous sources from the third century BCE show that the Egyptian νεανίσκοι formed a particular group of males who had completed their *ephebeia* and who served in a particular civic function (Forbes 1933, 61–64). They appear to have formed "a separate class of young soldiers who were charged with police duties and participated in municipal life" (Kennell 2013, 218). The earliest evidence for this specific role of the νεανίσκοι appears in P.Cair.Zen. 2.59153, in which Apollonius ordered that lodging be prepared for them in the course of their movements (Launey 1950, 859).⁶⁷

---

63. Originally shown by Gauthier and Hatzopoulos (1993) in relation to the *ephebeia* at Beroia, but extended with the same results throughout the Hellenistic world by Chankowski (2011, 250; see 249–68), who states that "le vocabulaire des classes d'âge du gymnase accuse, dans le monde grec, une remarquable coherence." Forbes (1933, 60) notes that prior to the Hellenistic period there is no evidence for a civic organization of males known as the νεανίσκοι.

64. Kennell (2013) reached the same conclusion. Thus only the term ἔφηβος was totally exclusive to other *ephebic* classes. Only the *ephebes* had their names engraved on stone after completing their service, indicating the institutionalization of the term (250). Syracuse was an exception, where, under Hieron II, the ἔφηβοι were called νεανίσκοι, perhaps to distinguish themselves from the Athenian model (Chankowski 2011, 232, 262).

65. Chankowski (2011, 383–432) and D'Amore (2007a, 166–71) discuss their role in the Greek civic reception ceremony called ἀπάντησις, discussed in detail in the next chapter. See also (19) below as well as examples (7), (39), and (40) in ch. 5.

66. E.g., IDelos 6.1501; Illion 73; Polybius, *Hist.* 4.16.6; 4.34.6; 4.35.1; 4.76.8–9; 5.29.9; 5.30.1; 5.96.7; 8.24.10; 8.27.1; 8.27.4; 8. 27.7; 8.28.1; 8.28.5; 8.30.1; 8.30.3. See Kennell (2013, 218; 2015, 179). Chankowski (2011, 366–78) similarly notes that often in literature the word νεανίσκος simply refers to local soldiers.

67. Legras (1999, 202–3) suggests this lodging situation is similar to the σταθμοί,

4. "For So the Young Men Used to Do" 147

(15) P.Cair.Zen. 2.59153 (TM 801)
Ἀπολλώνιος Ζήνωνι χ[αίρειν. καλῶς] | π[οιή]σεις ἐπιμεληθεὶ[ς ἤδη ἵνα τοῖς] | [νεαν]ίσκοις αἱ οἰκήσε[ι]ς [τὴν ταχίστην] | [συντ]ε[λ]ε[σ]θῶσιν κ[αθάπερ πρότερον] | [ἐγράψ]αμεν. ἔρρωσο.
Apollonius to Zenon, greetings. Would you please see to it that the quarters are prepared immediately for the νεανίσκοις just as I wrote earlier. Take care.

The νεανίσκοι were also granted cleruchic land (Legras 1999, 196–97):

(16) P.Cair.Zen. 2.59254 (TM 899)
Φανίας Ζήνωνι χαίρειν. τοὺς κεκληρουχημένους ἐν τῶι Ἀρ[σινοίτηι] | νομῶι νεανίσκους \διέγνωκα/ πάντας ἀρ[ι]θμήσω καὶ ὁρκιῶ ἐν Φιλαδελφ[είαι]. | καλῶς οὖν ποιήσεις καταλυμάτιόν μοι ἑτοιμάσας· | τῶι γὰρ σωματίωι ἐτύγχανον ἀσθενῶς διακείμενος, | ἅμα δὲ καί σε ἰδεῖν βούλομαι ὅσον ἐπιδέχεται ⟦πλεῖστ[ον]⟧ | χρόνον. ἔρρωσο.
Phanias to Zenon, greetings. I have determined I will count all the νεανίσκους who were made cleruchs in the Arsinoite nome and administer oaths in Philadelphia. So would you please prepare a small room for me, for I happen to be poorly disposed in body, so at the same time I would like to see you for as long a time as possible. Take care.

The document in (16) was composed by Phanios, a γραμματεὺς τῶν ἱππέων in the Fayum and the author of another document in which the Egyptian νεανίσκοι are entitled to κλῆροι and bound by oath to the king (Launey 1950, 860):

(17) SB 1.5942 (TM 5644), lines 5–7, 11–13
[Φα]νίας Ἀντιπάτρωι χαίρειν. πρότερον μέν σοι ὑποθεὶς τῆς παρὰ Διοτίμου ἐπιστολῆς τὸ ἀντίγραφον ἔγραψα ἐπιμεληθῆναι ἱππέ[ων] | ὅσοις καταμεμέτρηται γῆ δυναμένη σπείρεσθαι εἰς τ[ὸ] ε καὶ λ (ἔτος) [ὡς] πᾶσα σπαρῆι κ[α]ὶ δυνηθῶσιν οἱ ἐν τῆι ἐπιστατείαι ν[εανίσκοι] | ἀπὸ τῶν γενομένων καρπῶν χορηγηθέντες καταβαίνειν πρὸς τὸν βασιλέα ἔφιπποι καὶ τοῖς ἄλλοις \ἀναγκαίοις/ κατεσκευασμένοι.... ἔστι γὰρ ἀναγκαῖον ἕκαστον τῶν νεανίσκων γινώσκεσθαι πῶς τι ἀπαλλάσσει καὶ ὑμῖν προσῆκον τοῖς ἡγεμονίας αὐτοὺς | ἀξιοῦσιν τὰς τοιαύτας χρείας παρέχεσθαι ἕως

---

housing assigned to cleruchs in the name of the king and to moving troops. The third-century BCE papyrus PSI 4.360 (TM 2047) seems to confirm the existence at least in the Arsinoite of quarters dedicated τοῖς νεανίσκοις (lines 14–15; Legras 1999, 202). Launey (1950, 860 n. 4) thinks this uncertain, however.

ἂν καταστῆι τ[ὰ] περὶ τὴν κληρουχίαν, ἵνα συμπεπονηκότες δικαίως προεδρί|ας τυγχάνητε.[68]

Phanias to Antipatros, greetings. First, enclosed for you is a copy I wrote of a letter by Diotimos to oversee the cavalry, to whom land is allotted that is able to be sown from year 35, so all is sown and the <u>νεανίσκοι</u> in charge are able, having been supplied from the crops produced, to go down to the king by horse, and are fully equipped with whatever else they need.... For it is essential that each of the <u>νεανίσκοι</u> know how he is doing, and it is fitting that you, who are judged worthy of the rank of officer, should perform functions of this nature until everything concerning the clerouchy is totally settled, so that, having labored together, you too may rightly receive a position of honor (translation partly based on Lesquier 1919, 362–63).[69]

Some insight into the regulatory and policing activity of νεανίσκοι in third-century Egypt appears in P.Cair.Zen. 1.59018, which records the interaction of a νεανίσκος and an influential Jew named Jeddous, likely a komarch in Palestine (Tcherikover 1937, 51). In the letter, a certain Alexander writes to collect a debt owed to Zenon by Jeddous and thus sends Zenon's agent Stranton along with a νεανίσκος to intervene. Alexander writes:

(18) P.Cair.Zen. 1.59018 (TM 678), lines 4–9
ἐγὼ μὲν [ο]ῦν | [ἄρρωστ]ος ἐτύγχανον ἐ\κ/ φαρμακείας ὤν, συναπέστειλα [δὲ Στ]ράτωνι | [παρ' ἡ]μῶν <u>νεανίσκον</u> καὶ ἐπιστολὴν ἔγρ[α]ψα πρὸς Ἰεδδοῦν. Παραγενόμενοι | [οὖν εἶπ]όν μοι μηθένα λόγον πεποιῆσθαι τῶι ἐπιστο[λίωι μου], αὐτοῖς δὲ | [χεῖρας] προσενεγκεῖν καὶ ἐγβαλ[εῖ]ν ἐκ τῆς κώμης. γέγραφα οὖν σοι. | ἔρρωσο.

Now I happened to be unwell as a result of taking some medicine, so I sent a <u>νεανίσκος</u> with Straton, and I wrote a letter to Jeddous. When they returned they told me that he [Jeddous] had taken no account of my letter, but had laid hands on them and thrown them out of the village. So I am writing to you. Take care.[70]

---

68. The word νεανίσκοι in line 6 is editorially but confidently restored owing to its presence in line 11 (see Lesquier 1911, 359–75; Launey 1950, 860 n. 3; Legras 1999, 197 n. 7).

69. See Legras (1999, 197–98), who suggests on the basis of P.Ryl. 4.562 (TM 2418) that the expression καταβαίνειν πρὸς τὸν βασιλέα in (17) implies that the νεανίσκοι were on their way to Alexandria for the Ptolemai(ei)a festival.

70. Translation adapted from Kloppenborg (2006, 365). In light of the other Ptolemaic evidence, it is highly doubtful that νεανίσκος should be understood to mean "servant" here, although this judgment is crystallized in both LSJ and MGS, where

4. "For So the Young Men Used to Do" 149

So this particular νεανίσκος in (18) was sent from Egypt by a Ptolemaic official to collect a debt from a powerful figure like Jeddous.[71]

Another third-century text preserves an account of the ceremonial role of νεανίσκοι at the civic reception of Ptolemy III Euergetes at Antioch in the late third century BCE, who was received by various civic officials, including:

(19) P.Petr. 3.74a (TM 7530), col. 3, lines 19–23[72]
[οἵ τε] σατράπαι καὶ οἱ ἄλλοι ἡγε|μόν[ες καὶ οἱ στρατιῶ]ται καὶ οἱ ἱερεῖς καὶ αἱ | συναρχίαι | καὶ [πάντες οἱ ἀπ]ὸ τοῦ γυμνασίου νεανίσκοι καὶ ἄλλος | ὄχ[λος | ἐστεφ]ανωμένος
The satraps and other leaders, and the soldiers and the priests and the magistrates, and all the νεανίσκοι from the gymnasium, and a surrounding crowd besides.

Some later sources are also relevant, such as a mid-second-century BCE papyrus in which the νεανίσκοι appear to be part of an authorized administrative commission associated with the gymnasium (Launey 1950, 859).

(20) *BGU* 6.1256 (TM 4543), lines 24–29
ἀξιῶ μὴ ὑπερ|ιδεῖν με ἀγνωμονούμενον | ἀλλὰ ἐπανενέγκαι ἐπί τε τὸν | γυμνασίαρχον καὶ [ἐ]πὶ τοὺς | ἐκ τοῦ ἐν τῆι Φιλαδελφείαι | γυμνασίου νεανίσκους
I request that you not allow me to be unfairly treated but to refer my case to the gymnasiarch and to the νεανίσκους of the gymnasium in Philadelphia.[73]

---

this papyrus is cited as support for such a meaning. Legras (1999, 207) rightly notes that the distance and danger involved in the journey makes its logical that Straton "soit accompagné par un jeune homme entraîné physiquement et militairement qui puisse lui servir autant de compagnon que de 'garde du corps.'" Simpson (1976, 76) notes that a later edition of this papyrus (*SB* 3.6710) reconstructs [παρ' ἡ]μῶν νεανίσκον as [τῶν ἐ]μῶν νεανίσκον, but this seems to assume the "servant" meaning.

71. Legras (1999, 206–7) argues that P.Cair.Zen. 1.59018 in (18) provides evidence that the νεανίσκοι received training to prepare them for their future role in the royal administration.

72. See Launey (1950, 859 n. 5) and Chankowski (2011, 422–23). This text is also discussed in (40) in ch. 5.

73. Translation adapted from Hunt (1934, 253).

Perhaps the most decisive evidence for the official military role of Egyptian νεανίσκοι comes from a late second-century BCE papyrus in which the officer Porteis, the "captain of recruits" (lines 1–2), writes to Patet in gratitude for his involvement in the Hermonthis games (lines 7–8; Legras 1999, 204). These νεανίσκοι are said to be part of a special unit called a σημεῖον:

(21) P.Grenf. 1.30 (TM 164), lines 1–4
Πόρτεις ἡγεμὼν τῶν ἐν προχειρισ|μῶι καὶ οἱ [ἐκ] τοῦ σημείου <u>νεανίσκοι</u> |
Πατῆτι [καὶ] Παχράτηι καὶ τοῖς ἄλλοις | [στ]ρ[α]τιώται[ς] πᾶσι χαίρειν
Porteis, captain of the recruits and the <u>νεανίσκοι</u> of the standard, to Patet and Pachrate and the other soldiers, many greetings.

Moreover, these νεανίσκοι are also related to a society of royal supporters and soldiers (φιλοβασιλισταῖς καὶ τοῖς ἄλλοις στρατιώ[ταις]; verso line 2; Launey 1950, 851). There is general consensus among scholars that a σημεῖον was "a specific military unit … [that is] a general designation of rank or status, a kind of military equivalent of οἱ ἐκ τοῦ γυμνασίου" (Daniel 1983, 269).[74]

Other evidence could be provided.[75] In summary, however, as the highest class of trainees to go through the Greek *ephebic* system, the νεανίσκοι

---

74. He also notes that it is possible the lacuna [ἐκ] τοῦ in line 1 could be restored as [ἑαυ]τοῦ, which would render the phrase "captain of … the νεανίσκοι of his own standard." On the σημεῖον, see Lesquier (1911, 103–4); cf. Polybius, *Hist*. 4.64.7.

75. See esp. Legras (1999, 196–216), who even discusses Demotic evidence. Also, Polybius often mentions νεανίσκοι in contexts that makes clear their military training (e.g., *Hist*. 4.16.6; 4.35.1–3; 4.76.8–9; 6.20.1–3; 21.3b) and status as civic officers (5.30.1); cf. Chankowski (2011, 357). In one relevant text, Polybius recounts the fall of the Aetolian general Scopas to Aristomenes (*Hist*. 18.53.1–11). Upon learning of a plot for usurping the power of the Ptolemaic administration, Aristomenes surrounded a house where Scopas was located with soldiers (στρατιῶται) and sends from among them one Ptolemy to extract Scopas with the help of νεανίσκοι (7–11; cf. 5.96.6–8). Mauersberger and Helms (2006, 1671–72) list other relevant texts. Although they provide forty-three citations for "nonmilitary" uses of νεανίσκος, twenty-four are listed as specifically military related, for which the glosses provided include "als Waffenträger," "Rekruten," and "Soldaten." Additionally, SEG 28.1540, a second-century BCE inscription, honors Apollodoros of Berenike for defending the region from bandits (κακοῦργοι, line 8) with his unit of νεανίσκοι (line 9), and thus brought about peace (Chaniotis 2007, 107–8). Finally, there is also a first-century CE inscription concerning soldiers (στρατιῶται) whose commander Nicandros is praised: "he provided

of Egypt were well trained and likely of higher social status.⁷⁶ Next to the *ephebic* system itself, Legras (1999, 196) goes so far as to call the status of being part of the νεανίσκοι "la deuxième institution fondamental de la jeunesse dans l'Égypte des Ptolémées." As seen above, the νεανίσκοι were trained to serve in different capacities as a civic officer. They were taught by a ὁπλομάχος, led by a military ἡγεμών, occasionally called στρατιῶται, formed part of a specialized unit known as a σημεῖον, and were dispatched on various assignments related to the Ptolemaic state. Launey (1950, 861–62) thus concludes that the νεανίσκοι of Egypt formed a class of young soldiers or cadets in charge of police functions, who participate in festivals and processions, and even occasionally in municipal life as officers in training.⁷⁷ Andrzej Chankowski (2011, 357) concludes that "la documentation papyrologique montre à l'évidence que le groupe des *neaniskoi* en Égypte ptolémaïque était une composante de l'armée royale et participait à la vie du gymnase. Il s'agit donc de gens certes adultes, mais pas encore très avancés en âge, disons entre 20 et 30 ans."

The evidence discussed above provides sufficient linguistic and social context to help understand several texts in which νεανίσκος was used in Judg^OG and/or Judg^Rv. To be sure, not every instance of revision in table 4.2 is explicable on these grounds, particularly those where νεανίας occurs, as I discuss below.⁷⁸ But beginning with two texts where νεανίσκος appears in Judg^OG points the way forward for several other texts where it was used to replace OG lexical choice in Judg^Rv.

As shown in (5) and (6) above, in contrast to the usual preference for παιδάριον, the OG translator also used νεανίσκος in two texts: 14:10 and

---

orderly lodging for those νεανίσκοι under his command" (τήν τε τῶν [ὑποτεταγμένων] ἑαυτῶι νεανίσκων ἐνδημίαν εὔτ[ακτ]ον παρέχεται; *OGIS* 2.443, lines 8–9); see Launey (1950, 860) and Motta (2010, 116–18). Additionally, (Robert 1937, 106–8) discusses an Apollonian inscription in which a νεανισκάρχης oversees νεανίσκοι in service as mounted police, originally published by Reinach (1908), who dates it to the second century CE.

76. Forbes (1933, 65–66) notes that some have seen the Egyptian νεανίσκοι as part of the upper level of society. See also Cantarella (1990) and the case study of the family of the νεανίσκοι Nikandros and Myrikon in Legras (1999, 199–202).

77. See also Sacco (1979, 39–49), who treats epigraphical evidence. Simpson (1976, 75–76) does not study the Greek social context but after citing some of the texts provided above concludes that "νεανίσκοι were military recruits of some kind."

78. Speaking specifically about Judg^LXX, Simpson (1976, 63) comments that in some cases it "is not clear why νεανίας should be used."

20:15. In both cases this choice reflects careful attention to the narrative context as well as a desire to represent it in terms familiar to a Ptolemaic Egyptian readership. To address the former, at this point in the book of Judges Samson has decided to marry a Philistine woman (14:1–2). After telling his parents the news, Samson returns with them to her hometown of Timnah, and, as shown in (5), there he "prepared a feast, for so the young men [הבחורים] used to do." The use of νεανίσκος in Judg^OG to represent these individuals well suits the narrative context. First of all, the guests are of course Philistine men and, as friends of the marriageable Samson, are conceivably within the age range typical of the νεανίσκοι in Egypt (i.e., between twenty or thirty years old). Moreover, they are part of the nation against which God had been seeking an occasion for confrontation (14:4), which ultimately leads to several episodes that escalate into military conflict (14:10–20; 15:1–8; 15:9–20). An interesting papyrus adds further support to the idea that νεανίσκος is a subtle and appropriate choice to represent these young, party-going Philistines in 14:10. In the late third or early second century BCE, a certain Apion wrote a letter to his son and one other individual regarding various business matters. Although the text is partly damaged, Apion states in no uncertain terms:

(22) P.Oxy. 3.533 (TM 29373), lines 11–14
τὴν οἰ|κίαν Τ[..].βιου μὴ μισθώσῃς μηδενὶ εἰ μή τι<νι> γυναικὶ μελλούσῃ ἐν αὐτῇ οἰ|κεῖν .[....]ατ[.].ρ[.]τε .[....] γὰρ .[..]ον ἐστὶν τοιαύ[τ] ην οἰκίαν παρα[β]άλλε[ι]ν νεανίσ|κοις ἵ[ν]α μὴ ἔχωμεν στομάχου[ς] μηδὲ φθόνον.
Do not lease the house of T[...].bion to anyone except some woman intending to live in it ... for it is [wrong] to expose this house to νεανίσκοις, so that we may have no vexation or annoyance.[79]

Nothing more is said on the matter. But this document suggests that the νεανίσκοι were associated to some extent with public nuisance—perhaps not so hard to believe in regard to young, empowered, upper-class military men. It does not stretch the imagination to envision Egyptian νεανίσκοι in the habit of throwing drinking parties along the lines of those which the Philistine young men (בחורים) apparently "used to do" (Judg 14:10). That this vocabulary choice was suited to the narrative context from the

---

79. Translation based on Grenfell and Hunt (1903, 272).

perspective of a Ptolemaic Jewish readership is also confirmed by it being retained in Judg^Rv.

Turning now to 20:15 presented in (6), as mentioned above, again the OG translator apparently uses νεανίσκος. This time it appears in a double translation of בחור, first rendered as a nominative (νεανίσκος) and then as an adjective (ἐκλεκτοί), which in effect stand together in grammatical apposition to איש (ἀνήρ). Double readings are always difficult to explain, but this OG rendering appears to have resulted in part from the translator's desire to represent בחור with νεανίσκος just as in (5), a preference that is thrown into relief given his prevailing use of παιδάριον elsewhere to render נער.[80] Yet there is more to it than that. For Judg 20 recounts the story of the outbreak of the Israelite civil war and in 20:15 how Gibeah marshaled seven hundred soldiers for battle. Within this narrative context—and given the OG translator's vocabulary choice in 14:10—the use of νεανίσκος is in fact a skilled and appropriate choice in light of the role typical of the νεανίσκοι in the Ptolemaic Egyptian social context. Notably, although the OG use of νεανίσκος in 14:10 was retained in Judg^Rv, in 20:15 it is absent, perhaps owing to its status as a double translation, a point to which I return below.

These texts help clarify a case of *young male* vocabulary revision that appears later in the Samson story when, as a result of his deception by Delilah (16:1–22), Samson is finally captured by the Philistines. At the ensuing celebration and sacrifice to the Philistine god Dagon (16:23–31), their now-blind prisoner is forced to entertain his captors (16:25). As he does so, Samson speaks to the individual (נער; παιδάριον OG) restraining him, shown in (3) above, asking to feel the pillars of the house (16:26). For unclear reasons, the B group is split here between νεανίας (Befjsz) and νεανίσκος (diqrua₂). The latter choice, however, is entirely appropriate for reasons similar to the two texts discussed immediately above. Considering the significant military efforts undertaken to capture Samson in Judg 14–16, it makes little sense to represent Samson's Philistine guard as a παιδάριον (as in Judg^OG), someone who, according to the analysis above, would have no business guarding such a dangerous and high-value prisoner as Samson. It is much more semantically nuanced to replace παιδάριον with νεανίσκος since a military-trained civic officer is a far more

---

80. This double reading is discussed in Targarona Borrás (1983b, 578–79). See also Talshir (1987) for helpful discussion of doublets in general.

obvious choice for the job. The rationale behind those B group witnesses that attest νεανίας is, however, far less clear, much like most of the remaining texts in which OG *young male* vocabulary was replaced in Judg^Rv, to which I now turn.

Some comments are necessary about the word νεανίας prior to any attempt to understand its use in the revised text of Greek Judges. This task is not easy since, as mentioned above, there is so little evidence from which to derive a detailed understanding of the meaning of the word.[81] Moreover, the evidence that does exist is not very useful for semantic analysis. In his discussion, Simpson (1976, 61) concludes that νεανίας is "basically an age word and in the majority of cases means 'young man.'" This conclusion is certainly plausible considering that the word was sometimes used in classical literature as an adjective modifying, for example, ἀνήρ (Homer, *Od.* 10.278), παῖς (Herodotus, *Hist.* 1.61), or γαμβρός (Pindar, *Ol.* 7.4; Beekes 2010, 1001). Much later in the second century BCE an inscription that is equally unhelpful yet typical reads:

(23) IG 9.1.1.188, lines 25–26
  καὶ εἰς τὸ ἔλαιον τοῖς <u>νεανί|οις</u> στατῆρας δέκα
  and for the oil for the <u>νεανίοις</u>, ten coins

The context here is too terse to ascertain much about the meaning of the word beyond the general gloss "young man." Relatively more evidence is available from the Roman period, particularly among honorary funeral inscriptions, but similar challenges are present. Much of this evidence consists of inscriptions that follow a fairly formulaic introduction that includes the parentage of the individual and their achievements that brought honor to their βουλή and δῆμος. Very frequently the deceased is called a νεανίας and ascribed various admirable qualities, but with little else to help understand why the word was chosen over another. For example:

---

81. E.g., it is absent from Shipp (1979) and Parkin (2010). It is attested in P.Leid. Inst. 83 (TM 78488), but the document is too damaged to provide any context. Similarly, it may appear in P.Oxy. 3.471, line 114, but the editorial reconstruction (ν[εανί] ᾳ[ις) is highly dubious. Along similar lines, although in P.Petr.Kleon 32 (TM 7642), col. 8, line 1, an early edition (P.Petr. 2.4) suggested νεα[νίαι, the latest edition instead suggests νεα[νίσκοι.

(24) *MAMA* 8.414, lines 19–20 (third century CE)
νεανίαν γε|[νόμ]ενον ἀγαθὸν

(25) Iasos 118, lines 2–3 (Roman)
νεανίαν ἑλόμενον τὴν | ἐπ' ἀρετὴν ἄσκησιν

(26) IBubon 14, line 8 (Imperial period)
νεᾳ[νία]ν ἔνδοξον

(27) TAM 2.1.584, lines 3–4 (Imperial period)
νε]ανίαν εὐγενέσ|[τατον] καὶ πανάρετον

(28) LBW 1221, lines 31–32 (third century CE)
νεανία[ν καλὸν κα|ὶ ἀγ]αθὸν διὰ [π]ρογόνων

This sparse lexical evidence can lead only to the general conclusion that νεανίας was a broad term to refer to a young man in postclassical Greek.

With only a less than satisfactory understanding of νεανίας possible from the surviving evidence, explaining its selection in Judg^{Rv} is much more difficult than νεανίσκος. To return briefly to its attestation in part of the B group (Befjsz) at 16:25, it may be that the sheer oddness of a παιδάριον playing the role of Samson's personal guard (as in Judg^{OG}) could have prompted its replacement with a word such as νεανίας, which, based on the available evidence, seems to have had much less specific socioeconomic associations in the Ptolemaic milieu than παιδάριον. This same basic explanation could apply to other texts in which νεανίας replaced παιδάριον in the revised text or in part of the B group. Two such replacements occur in Judg 17, both pertaining to one individual in the household of an Ephraimite called Micah.[82] As shown in (2) above, this individual (נער; παιδάριον OG; 17:7, 11) was a Levite from Bethlehem in Judah (17:7) who had left his home to find work (17:8–9). After the two cross paths, Micah invites the Levite to stay and live with him and his family to serve as a personal priest (17:10–12). In both 17:7 and 11

---

82. As noted in table 4.2, παιδάριον appears in OG 17:12 as well but is absent (and lacks any equivalent) in almost the entire B group (Befjmqsz + imrua₂). It is possible this minus represents a deletion in light of a Hebrew exemplar without הנער, which could have entered MT through Judg^{LXX} as a clarifying gloss.

the majority B group reading is νεανίας.[83] This choice to replace the OG παιδάριον may have been made because, while it is sensible to have a general kind of "young man" in the narrative context, the OG reading was deemed odd since παιδάρια did not serve as priests in the social context of the revised Greek text. That said, however, the OG choice of παιδάριον is also understandable to some degree since Micah provides this Levite with wages, clothing, and provisions just like the patrons of παιδάρια in Egypt (καὶ ἐγὼ δώσω σοι δέκα ἀργυρίου εἰς ἡμέρας καὶ ζεῦγος ἱματίων καὶ τὰ πρὸς τὸ ζῆν σου; 17:10 OG). From this perspective it is understandable why there was disagreement over how best to represent this narrative character for a Greek readership within the textual history of Greek Judges.

Things become less clear in Judg 18, where the same Levite encounters the migrating tribe of Dan (18:1–26). When several Danites take up lodging in Micah's house (18:2), they for some reason recognize the voice of the Levite (הנער הלוי; τοῦ παιδαρίου τοῦ νεωτέρου τοῦ Λευίτου OG; 18:3). Later, as the Danites attempt to take possession of Laish (18: 5–13), they learn of valuables to be plundered in Ephraim (18:14) and come again to the house of Micah and speak again with the same Levite (הנער הלוי; τοῦ παιδαρίου τοῦ Λευίτου OG; 18:15). Once again the OG translator chose παιδάριον to represent this Levite, perhaps for similar reasons as those suggested for 17:7, 11, and 12. But this OG choice is replaced in both Judg[Rv] 18:3 and 15 with νεανίσκος, rather than νεανίας as it was twice in chapter 17. Why use a different word for the same narrative character in the revised text, especially νεανίσκος, which is used so subtly elsewhere? The lexical evidence alone does not seem able to provide a plausible explanation for these cases of revision.

Several more unclear cases of *young male* vocabulary revision appear in Judg 19, which recounts the story of a different Levite in Ephraim who has taken a concubine from Bethlehem (19:1). At four points in the narrative this Levite is said to have a servant (נער[ו]; παιδάριον [αὐτοῦ] OG; 19:3, 9, 10, 13), and in each case the OG παιδάριον is changed to νεανίας. On the one hand, the OG use of παιδάριον is certainly understandable since this individual is clearly in a subordinate service relationship with the Levite (ויאמר הנער אל־אדניו; καὶ εἶπεν τὸ παιδάριον πρὸς τὸν κύριον αὐτου OG; 19:11). But Simpson (1976, 64) rightly notes that the use of νεανίας "leaves some unanswered questions," since in his analysis these are the only exam-

---

83. In 17:7 the su cursives attest νεανίσκος, while a₂ preserves νεᾶνις, which is likely a copyist error.

ples in the Septuagint where νεανίας seems to mean "servant." With so few external attestations of the word, it is impossible either to confirm or deny that νεανίας was conventionally used in this way in postclassical Greek.

As a final note, it is worth considering that the witnesses attesting νεανίας may preserve a later reading than is typical of the B group, which scholars have shown is not always uniform in character. This proposal may be supported by the frequency statistics for the word. While νεανίας is attested under twenty times in the third through first century BCE, in each of the following two centuries after the turn of the era it appears over one hundred times, the vast majority of which are in literary sources. These trends indicate the word may have become more common in the early Roman period and perhaps beyond, which in turn could imply later readings within the B group.

Conclusions

The Greek-Priority View and Septuagint Lexicography

This chapter has involved numerous challenges arising from lexical semantics, textual history, and primary evidence. Some questions have been left unanswered. However, despite these difficulties, the Greek-priority view has significantly improved our understanding of the language of Greek Judges, affirming the importance of this approach for Septuagint lexicography. Once more I began by pointing out another case of vocabulary divergence within the textual history of Greek Judges, this time pertaining (mostly) to the translation of נער. On the one hand, the OG translator used παιδάριον almost exclusively, but on the other hand that choice was at a later point both retained in some places but changed in others in Judg[Rv] (table 4.2). Turning to the major Greek lexicons provided no useful information for discerning possible reasons for the distinctions among and changes to *young male* vocabulary in Greek Judges, since the numerous glosses boil down to only a few broad concepts (tables 4.3 and 4.4). It could be considered reasonable to stop there and draw conclusions about Greek Judges; perhaps that the OG translator was merely stereotyping his word choice without regard to Greek conventions while in Judg[Rv] the more diverse *young male* vocabulary indicates at those points a divergent *Vorlage*. But examining the very postclassical Greek evidence that is largely absent from those lexicons—yet most relevant to the language of the Septuagint—unveils a much more nuanced picture. Moreover, in the analysis of this evidence undertaken here, the Hellenistic social context is of great significance for understanding this *young male* vocabulary and how it was used in Greek Judges. Only by means of looking first to postclassical Greek and the social context of the language community is it possible to understand *young male* vocabulary in enough detail to evaluate its use in the Septuagint. That is the basic premise of the Greek-priority view. Taking this approach indicates that, in most cases, the *young male* vocabulary was used not only according to contemporary conventions in Ptolemaic Egypt, but also with careful attention to the narrative contexts in which the words were deployed.

These findings have important implications for lexicography of the Septuagint. First of all, it is not the case that lexical stereotyping—which appears to have occurred with the use of παιδάριον in Judg^{OG}—implies a translator unskilled in or oblivious to semantic nuance in Greek. The OG use of νεανίσκος prevents such a conclusion. Therefore, the lexicographer must be watchful for stereotyping (which has its own motivations) but cannot for that reason dismiss every instance of a given lexeme stereotyped within a particular translation unit. Conventional word use can and does occur within a lexically stereotyped translation style. The only way to determine whether this happened in any particular case is to examine postclassical Greek sources, as advocated by the Greek-priority view. Second, as shown in the revised text of Greek Judges, lexical diversity in the Septuagint is not only contextually motivated but informed by contemporary conventions in postclassical Greek. This observation supports Muraoka's decision to use context to discern lexical meaning in *GELS* and also demonstrates the urgent need for and promise of further research within the available external evidence to improve his analysis. Third, where word use in the Septuagint is not attested in extant sources for postclassical Greek—as in the case of νεανίας in Judg^{Rv} 19—the lack of evidence should not necessarily be taken to indicate unconventional use. On the contrary, the extent to which Septuagint vocabulary choice adheres to linguistic conventions and displays contextual sensitivity should lead to a preliminary assumption that otherwise unattested senses were nonetheless conventional in the language.

Young Male Vocabulary and Greek Judges

Some of the implications for Septuagint lexicography discussed above arise from features I have pointed out in the OG translation and later revision of Greek Judges. To first address the prevailing OG choice of παιδάριον, although this does appear to be a stereotyping approach to rendering נער, the translator also made a careful semantic distinction in his use of νεανίσκος. This distinction was made not simply because of the different underlying Hebrew lexeme (בחור), although that may have prompted the decision to employ a different word, but also because the choice of νεανίσκος suited the narrative context according to the linguistic conventions and social context of a Ptolemaic Greek readership. Along similar lines, in many—perhaps most—cases, the stereotyped translation of נער with παιδάριον in Judg^{OG} also suits the narrative context with subtlety, a reality that very likely underlay the stereotyping choice of παιδάριον rather than some other word. Moreover, as I argued above, it is precisely because παιδάριον so often suits the context that the OG choice of παιδάριον is frequently left unchanged in Judg^{Rv}.[84] In fact, those texts where the rationale for the revisional vocabulary choice is least clear—especially the use of νεανίας in Judg 17:7, 11 and 19:3, 9, 10, and 13—are those in which it seems leaving OG παιδάριον in place would have been appropriate in the narrative context as well. As indicated in the second epigraph to this chapter, at the very least such cases demonstrate the often-inscrutable phenomenon of stylistic preference.

Overall, the way in which the *young male* vocabulary was handled in Judg^{Rv} indicates that each decision—whether to change a word or not—was motivated by concerns for how the text communicates in Greek. It is admittedly possible to view those instances where παιδάριον was left in place in Judg^{Rv} as the result of stereotyping similar to Judg^{OG}. But evaluating this word in contemporary postclassical Greek sources indicates that, in each of these cases, the narrative context left little reason to make a change according to contemporary usage. Moreover, the vocabulary choice in Judg^{Rv} in fact introduces Greek lexical diversity associated with a single Hebrew word (נער), which entails that the revision was not merely Hebraizing. This is not to say that there was no desire to revise Greek Judges toward a Hebrew exemplar in certain ways. There was. For example, the OG translation at 9:53 is likely to have contained a plus, translating הנער נשא כליו as τὸ παιδάριον <u>αὐτοῦ</u> τὸ αἶρον τὰ σκεύη αὐτοῦ.[85] While παιδάριον is retained in Judg^{Rv} for reasons discussed above, αὐτοῦ is excised, apparently owing to the lack of

---

84. It should also be noted that the B group has been shown in some places to preserve unrevised OG readings, which may have occurred among *young male* vocabulary (Cañas Reíllo 2020b, 179).

85. αὐτοῦ is attested in only part of the AII group, namely, dnptv and OL.

equivalent in Hebrew. Similarly, at 20:15 shown in (6), despite the suitability of νεανίσκος to the narrative context—and its retention in Judg^{Rv} 14:10 on similar grounds—as a double translation of בחור the word is removed in the revision, again apparently to better represent the source text. Nevertheless, the *young male* vocabulary in Greek Judges, just like the *battle* vocabulary, demonstrates that the evident desire to more closely represent a Hebrew source text in certain respects overlapped with a concern to improve the translation in terms of its vocabulary choice as a Greek text for a Ptolemaic Egyptian readership. That is to say, there was more than one animating force behind the revision of Greek Judges: greater conformity with a Hebrew source text *and* comprehensibility and subtlety in Greek. Balancing the complex factors involved to achieve both of these goals at once attests to the considerable skill required for the revision of Greek Judges.

Septuagint Vocabulary and Greek Lexicography

As a final point, the *young male* vocabulary in Greek Judges—both that of the OG translation and its later revision—offers valuable evidence to the broader enterprise of Greek lexicography. First of all, because its selection is demonstrably free from Hebrew influence, the vocabulary examined here offers evidence that should not be ignored by Greek lexicographers. On the contrary, I have shown that the diversity of words introduced in the revised texts was in many cases clearly motivated by and suited to the narrative context. As such, the *young male* vocabulary represents conventional use of postclassical Greek and should be treated as such in lexicographical reference works. That conclusion is perhaps most significant—and most controversial—for the word νεανίας. As I have noted throughout this chapter, understanding the use of νεανίας in Greek Judges is a special challenge since it is so sparsely attested in contemporary sources that no well-developed semantic description is possible. But the Greek-priority view is biased toward the position that Septuagint word use is conventional, at least until convincingly demonstrated otherwise in light of contemporary evidence.[86] In this connection, the subtle and conventional use of *young male* vocabulary in Judg^{Rv} suggests that, even though the use of νεανίας to refer to a servant of some kind in Judg 19 is neither supported nor contradicted by

---

86. This argument is directly counter to that of Pietersma (2015, 167), who worries about context acting as "an alien tyrant" over establishing otherwise unattested lexical meaning. There are certainly reasons for such caution, as shown by Lee (1969).

surviving external sources, its use that way in Judg^Rv itself could in fact constitute such evidence. That is to say, Judg 19 may well provide the only extant attestations of a "servant" sense of the word νεανίας—otherwise in use in the Hellenistic period, but for some reason not preserved—that was employed owing to its suitability to the narrative context.

This chapter has shown the respects in which, not only does in-depth examination of extant postclassical Greek sources repay efforts to better understand the language of the Septuagint, but the language of the Septuagint in turn can contribute to scholarly understanding of postclassical Greek. The two corpora coinhere as a single phase of the language. Once that historical linguistic reality has been recognized it follows that, despite its status as a translation, the language of the Septuagint does not necessarily differ categorically from conventional contemporary Greek and therefore it cannot be cordoned off wholesale from the broader discipline of Greek lexicography.

5
"They Went up to Meet Them": ΑΠΑΝΤΑΩ, ΑΠΑΝΤΗΣΙΣ and ΣΥΝΑΝΤΑΩ, ΣΥΝΑΝΤΗΣΙΣ

> No one would suggest that we are here dealing with ordinary Greek in any of its registers. Septuagint Greek is unique and altogether more peculiar.
> —Rajak, *Translation and Survival*

> For illustration of LXX Greek we normally turn to the Egyptian papyri.
> —Thackeray, *The Septuagint and Jewish Worship*

In this final case study of vocabulary in Greek Judges I discuss words that occur in contexts where individuals or groups meet together for some purpose.[1] I will call the key words involved here the *meeting* vocabulary, of which there are just over a dozen instances total of verbs and nominals. As mentioned in the last chapter, the frequency of the *young male* vocabulary in Judges is tied to the typical involvement of such individuals in the military activity discussed in the *battle* vocabulary chapter. So too in this chapter, the narrative of Judges presents many instances where two or more parties meet together for some purpose. In many cases, the *meeting* vocabulary in these contexts is associated with a military engagement of some kind (e.g., Judg 7:24; 20:25), but not always. Other times the event in view is a nonconfrontational meeting between individuals or groups (e.g., Judg 4:18; 6:35; 11:31). In this connection, the *meeting* vocabulary presents another excellent candidate for investigation owing to its relatively high frequency among content words in Greek Judges and, as I will discuss in chapter 6, because this vocabulary is to some extent associated with topics

---

1. Portions of this chapter draw upon Ross (2018).

from the previous two chapters, namely, developments in Hellenistic warfare and the νεανίσκοι of the *ephebic* system.[2]

The *meeting* vocabulary is conspicuous in Greek Judges because it is another clear case of divergence between AII and B textual groups that respectively represent the OG translation and its later revision. This case study, moreover, presents much more consensus among the B group witnesses than the *young male* vocabulary did. That consensus is at first evident within the A and B text in Rahlfs-Hanhart but emerges more clearly once the readings are stratified into textual groups as before. Doing so demonstrates how, on the one hand, the OG translator prefers ἀπαντάω and ἀπάντησις to refer to *meeting* events. However, in nearly every instance in which these lexical choices appeared they were later replaced in Judg[Rv] with συναντάω and συνάντησις. Just as in the previous two chapters, the striking consistency with which the OG lexical choice was revised at a later point indicates some motivation for doing so, but one that is evidently not associated with the Hebrew source text. Once again, turning to current Greek lexicons does little to help discern what other reasons might have existed to prompt this lexical change in the textual history of Greek Judges. By examining postclassical Greek sources and placing the *meeting* vocabulary within its social context, however, a much clearer picture of its meaning emerges, which in turn indicates the rationale underlying their use in Greek Judges.

This chapter will proceed in the same way as the previous two case studies. The first section shows the lexical divergence in Greek Judges in detail and with examples, starting from Rahlfs-Hanhart as a point of departure. This section also explains how the use of a Greek grammatical construction that was conventional in the postclassical period significantly increased the frequency of *meeting* vocabulary in Greek Judges (and the Septuagint in general). Moreover, it is important to note in this section that the revision of Judg[OG] brings the *meeting* vocabulary of Judg[Rv] into alignment with the use of συνάντησις throughout the Greek Pentateuch. I then move in the second section into a fresh lexical semantic analysis of these words, concentrating on diachronic trends in usage, semantic change, and social context. A key finding of that analysis is that, around the late second century BCE, ἀπάντησις (and ἀπαντάω to

---

2. See, e.g., (7) and (39) below, where the νέοι take part in a formal ἀπάντησις, and likewise the νεανίσκοι in (40).

some extent) became a semitechnical term associated with a particular Greek civil ceremony during which cities would formally receive honored guests or sacred objects. In the third and final section of this chapter I discuss how the OG use of ἀπαντάω and ἀπάντησις appears to have been conditioned by the decline in usage of συναντάω and συνάντησις after the third century BCE. However, the subsequent association of ἀπαντάω and ἀπάντησις with Greek civic reception ceremonies seems to have motivated replacing those words with συναντάω and συνάντησις in Judg^{Rv}, perhaps along with their rarity in the language in general and the precedent of their usage in the Greek Pentateuch. Once again, the changes to Greek *meeting* vocabulary also coincide with clear efforts in Judg^{Rv} to align the Greek text more closely with a Hebrew source text, highlighting once more how the revision process was sophisticated and multifaceted in that it had goals related to both the Hebrew and Greek languages.

The Textual History of *Meeting* Vocabulary in Judg^{LXX}

The distinctions in *meeting* vocabulary between the A and B texts of Judges in Rahlfs-Hanhart are obvious and have not gone unnoticed by others. They can be represented as follows:

Table 5.1. Judg^{LXX} *meeting* vocabulary in Rahlfs-Hanhart

	A text	B text
ἀπάντησις	7	—
ἀπαντάω	3	—
συνάντησις	3	10
συναντάω	—	4

As shown in table 5.1, overall the A text attests ἀπάντησις while the B text attests συνάντησις, with few exceptions. Moreover, there is also a corollary in the verb forms, in that the A text attests ἀπαντάω exclusively while in the B text only συναντάω appears.[3] As in the previous case studies, when these A and B texts of Greek Judges are aligned with the Hebrew text (MT) it becomes apparent that the differences in Greek vocabulary attestation are

---

3. The nominal trends are noted without further comment by Fernández Marcos (2012, 165) and Harlé and Roqueplo (1999, 54), but neither mentions the verb forms.

associated with the same underlying Hebrew vocabulary. That is, what the A text *meeting* vocabulary aligns with in MT is (almost) the same as the B text *meeting* vocabulary, which can be represented as follows:

Table 5.2. The underlying Hebrew *meeting* vocabulary[4]

	A text	B text
קרא II (11×)	ἀπάντησις 7×	ἀπάντησις —
	συνάντησις 3×	συνάντησις 10×
פגע (3×)	ἀπαντάω 3×	ἀπαντάω —
	συναντάω —	συναντάω 3×
נגע	—	συναντάω 1×

As shown in table 5.2, instances of the verb קרא II ("to meet, encounter") correspond with ἀπάντησις in the A text but συνάντησις in the B text (*HALOT*, s.v. "קרא II"). On the other hand, wherever פגע ("to meet, encounter") appears it is represented by ἀπαντάω in the A text but συναντάω in the B text, except for one case where the corresponding verb is נגע ("to touch, reach"; *HALOT*, s.vv. "פגע," "נגע"). The importance of showing the Hebrew correspondences at this stage is to demonstrate that the consistent lexical change in Judg^Rv must primarily be motivated by concerns related to the Greek language, not to the Hebrew source text. Of course, that nominals like ἀπάντησις or συνάντησις would align with a verb like קרא II seems odd at first, though there are clear reasons for it discussed below. In any case, these clear divergences in *meeting* vocabulary between the texts of Greek Judges in Rahlfs-Hanhart overall prompt further investigation.

Again, as in previous chapters, the difference in vocabulary attested in Rahlfs-Hanhart becomes more pronounced when the textual evidence for Judg^LXX is separated into groups, at which point some of the unusual features mentioned above are more easily resolved. As in both preceding case studies, the A and B text respectively preserve the OG and revised text of Greek Judges to a remarkable degree. Additionally, the data in table 5.3 below proves once more how, at some point in the textual history of

---

4. קרא II: 4:18, 22; 6:35; 7:24; 11:31, 34; 14:5; 15:14; 19:3; 20:25, 31. Also, Judg^B attests ὑπάντησις at 11:34, while Judg^A attests ἀπαντήν at 4:22. פגע: 8:21; 15:12; 18:25. נגע: 20:14.

the book, a coherent effort was made to revise the OG version of Judges, a revision that is best represented in the B group of witnesses. For reasons discussed below, table 5.3 presents slightly more context in the reconstructed readings, with lexical substitution indicated in bold text.

Table 5.3. The *meeting* vocabulary in Judg^{LXX}

	Judg^{OG}	Judg^{Rv}
	קרא	
4:18	ἐξέρχομαι … εἰς **ἀπάντησιν** Σισαρα	ἐξέρχομαι … εἰς **συνάντησιν** Σισαρα
4:22	ἐξέρχομαι … εἰς **ἀπάντησιν** αὐτοῦ	ἐξέρχομαι … εἰς **συνάντησιν** αὐτῷ
6:35	ἀναβαίνω εἰς **ἀπάντησιν** αὐτοῦ	ἀναβαίνω εἰς **συνάντησιν** αὐτῷ
7:24	καταβαίνω εἰς συνάντησιν Μαδιάμ	καταβαίνω εἰς συνάντησιν Μαδιάμ
11:31	ἐξέρχομαι … εἰς **ἀπάντησιν** μου	ἐξέρχομαι … εἰς **συνάντησιν** μου
11:34	ἐξέρχομαι εἰς ἀπάντησιν αὐτῷ	ἐξέρχομαι εἰς ἀπάντησιν αὐτοῦ
14:5	ὠρύομαι εἰς **ἀπάντησιν** αὐτοῦ	ὠρύομαι εἰς **συνάντησιν** αὐτοῦ
15:14	ἀλαλάζω εἰς **ἀπάντησιν** αὐτοῦ	ἀλαλάζω … εἰς **συνάντησιν** αὐτοῦ
19:3	εὐφραινόμενος **ἀπήντησεν** αὐτῷ	εὐφραίνω εἰς **συνάντησιν** αὐτοῦ
20:25	ἐξέρχομαι … εἰς **ἀπάντησιν** αὐτῶν	ἐξέρχομαι … εἰς **συνάντησιν** αὐτοῖς
20:31	ἐξέρχομαι … εἰς **ἀπάντησιν** τοῦ λαοῦ	ἐξέρχομαι … εἰς **συνάντησιν** τοῦ λαοῦ
	פגע	
8:21	**ἀπαντάω** ἡμῖν	**συναντάω** ἡμῖν
15:12	**ἀπαντάω** ὑμεῖς ἐν ἐμοί	**συναντάω** ἐν ἐμοὶ ὑμεῖς
18:25	**ἀπαντάω** ἐν ἡμῖν	**συναντάω** ἐν ἡμῖν
	נגע	
20:41	**ἅπτω**	**συναντάω**

As is clear in the table above, with only two exceptions (7:24 and 19:3) Judg^{OG} uses ἀπάντησις to translate each instance of קרא II, which in every case but one (11:34) is changed where necessary in Judg^{Rv} to συνάντησις.[5] Similarly, in the three texts that the OG translator encountered פגע he used ἀπαντάω as its translation, but that verb was always changed at a

---

5. The reason for the exception in Judg^{Rv} 11:34 is not clear, but again the B group is known to occasionally preserve old, unrevised readings, which may be the case here (Cañas Reíllo 2020b, 179).

later point to συναντάω in Judg^Rv. Finally, as shown in more detail below, in 20:41 the OG rendering ἅπτω, itself translating נגע, was also changed in Judg^Rv to συναντάω.

Some examples of the translation and revision of the *meeting* words follow to help frame the ensuing discussion. To begin with the nominals, several straightforward examples are readily available:

(1) Judges 4:18
BHQ

ותצא יעל לקראת סיסרא

And Jael went out <u>to meet</u> Sisera

Judg^OG
καὶ ἐξῆλθεν Ιαηλ εἰς <u>ἀπάντησιν</u> Σισαρα
And Jael went out to Sisera's <u>ἀπάντησιν</u>

Judg^Rv
καὶ ἐξῆλθεν Ιαηλ εἰς <u>συνάντησιν</u> Σισαρα
And Jael went out to Sisera's <u>συνάντησιν</u>

(2) Judges 14:5
BHQ

והנה כפיר אריות שאג לקראתו׃

And behold, a young lion came roaring <u>to meet him</u>.

Judg^OG
καὶ ἰδοὺ σκύμνος λεόντων ὠρυόμενος εἰς <u>ἀπάντησιν</u> αὐτοῦ
And behold, the cub of lions went roaring to his <u>ἀπάντησιν</u>

Judg^Rv
καὶ ἰδοὺ σκύμνος λέοντος ὠρυόμενος εἰς <u>συνάντησιν</u> αὐτοῦ
And behold the cub of a lion went roaring to his <u>συνάντησιν</u>

(3) Judges 20:25
BHQ

ויצא בנימן לקראתם מן־הגבעה ביום השני

And Benjamin went out <u>to meet them</u> from Gibeah on the second day.

Judg^OG
καὶ ἐξῆλθεν Βενιαμιν εἰς <u>ἀπάντησιν</u> αὐτῶν ἐκ τῆς Γαβαα ἐν τῇ ἡμέρᾳ τῇ β΄
And Benjamin went out to their <u>ἀπάντησιν</u> from Gibeah on the second day

Judg^{Rv}
καὶ ἐξῆλθον οἱ υἱοὶ Βενιαμιν εἰς <u>συνάντησιν</u> αὐτοῖς ἀπὸ τῆς Γαβαα ἐν τῇ ἡμέρᾳ τῇ β′
And the sons of Benjamin went out for their <u>συνάντησιν</u> from Gibeah on the second day

In each of the examples in (1) through (3) it is clear how the OG choice of ἀπάντησις was changed in Judg^{Rv} to συνάντησις, typically with few other substantive changes in the grammatical context.

The initial use and later revision of the *meeting* verbs follow similar trends and can be illustrated with a single example:

(4) Judges 15:12
   BHQ

   השבעו לי פן־<u>תפגעון</u> בי אתם: ויאמר להם שמשון
   And Samson said to them, "Swear to me that <u>you will not attack</u> me yourselves."

   Judg^{OG}
   καὶ εἶπεν αὐτοῖς Σαμψων Ὀμόσατέ μοι μὴ ἀποκτεῖναί με ὑμεῖς καὶ παράδοτέ με αὐτοῖς καὶ μήποτε <u>ἀπαντήσητε</u> ὑμεῖς ἐν ἐμοί
   And Samson said to them, "Swear to me to not kill me yourselves and hand me over to them and whether you might <u>ἀπαντάω</u> yourselves against me."

   Judg^{Rv}
   καὶ εἶπεν αὐτοῖς Σαμψων Ὀμόσατέ μοι μὴ ἀποκτεῖναί με ὑμεῖς καὶ παράδοτέ με αὐτοῖς μήποτε <u>συναντήσητε</u> ἐν ἐμοὶ ὑμεῖς.
   And Samson said to them, "Swear to me to not kill me yourselves and hand me over to them whether you might <u>συναντάω</u> against me yourselves."

The example in (4) is characteristic of all three instances in which ἀπαντάω was used in Judg^{OG} to translate פגע but later substituted in Judg^{Rv} with συναντάω, again amid few other grammatical changes.[6] Things happened differently, however, in another text:

---

6. Fernández Marcos (2011, 44) suggests the Greek plus is an assimilation from 15:13. I have included it as part of Judg^{Rv} although it is missing in Bx.

(5) Judges 20:41
BHQ

ויבהל איש בנימן כי ראה כי-נגעה עליו הרעה:
And the men of Benjamin were terrified, for they saw that the disaster <u>was close</u> upon them.

Judg^{OG}
καὶ ἔσπευσεν ἀνὴρ Βενιαμιν καὶ ἐπέστρεψεν καὶ ἴδεν ὅτι <u>ἧπται</u> αὐτοῦ ἡ κακία
And the man Benjamin hurried and saw that the misfortune had <u>overtaken</u> him.

Judg^{Rv}
καὶ ἔσπευσαν ἄνδρες Βενιαμιν ὅτι εἶδον ὅτι <u>συνήντησεν</u> ἐπ' αὐτοὺς ἡ πονηρία
And the men of Benjamin hurried for they saw that the evil <u>συναντάω</u> upon them.

In (5), despite the use of ἅπτω in Judg^{OG} the revised text nevertheless substitutes συναντάω. This change is somewhat unusual in that the context portrays a metaphorical "encounter" between the Benjaminites and their misfortune, not a literal meeting between people, as do all the other relevant texts in table 5.3. Yet it is very likely that the graphical similarity of נגע and פגע, which is known to have led to textual variants elsewhere, was involved in how these texts developed (see Tov 2015, 228; Würthwein 2014, 173). Whether נגע or פגע was attested in the OG *Vorlage* is less relevant here than the fact that whatever Hebrew source text was consulted for the revision of Greek Judges must have either read or looked like פגע. In other words, συναντάω was apparently used to replace the OG ἅπτω in 20:41, since συναντάω was the verb used throughout Judg^{Rv} to render פגע.

Summary of Translation and Revision Activity

The *meeting* vocabulary presents one of the most straightforward cases of translation and revision in Greek Judges. This is not to say that there are no intricacies involved. The next section deals with the more complex textual and linguistic issues related to the *meeting* nominals in particular that raise questions of semantics and style in Greek. At this point, however, the broad trends in *meeting* vocabulary are clear. One the one hand, the OG translator preferred ἀπάντησις and ἀπαντάω—along with a single instance of συνάντησις (7:24)—to refer to the events and actions in the narrative of Judges in which individuals or groups meet together physically for some purpose. However, at some later point in the textual history of Greek Judges, this OG vocabulary choice was for some reason revised using different words for the same purpose. Where necessary, the OG *meeting* vocabulary was systematically substituted in Judg^(Rv) with συνάντησις and συναντάω, even as few other changes were made to the grammatical contexts in which they appeared. So, their use in Judg^(Rv) indicates that συνάντησις and συναντάω were considered in some way equivalent to the OG vocabulary ἀπάντησις and ἀπαντάω, yet for some reason better suited to the goals for the revised text.

What prompted the change? It was not the Hebrew text per se. In both the OG and revised texts, the Greek *meeting* vocabulary was used to render the same Hebrew vocabulary: the nominals ἀπάντησις and συνάντησις for קרא II and the verbs ἀπαντάω and συναντάω for פגע. It is true that the revisional activity in 20:41 presented in (5) suggests that consistency in translation equivalents was a motivating concern for Judg^(Rv). I return to that point below. Nevertheless, the lexical changes in Greek *meeting* vocabulary were certainly not dictated by the Hebrew. They were of course related to the Hebrew source text; otherwise it would not be translation. But, as I demonstrate below, the primary reasons for the lexical changes arose from semantic developments in postclassical Greek and stylistic goals for the revised Greek text of Judges. Appreciating such subtleties can occur only from the perspective of the Greek-priority view, one that seeks to situate the language of the Septuagint within the contemporary Greek lexical evidence and its social context.

Broader Issues Related to the *Meeting* Nominals in Greek Judges

Although the trends in translation and revision are in some respects straightforward, certain more complex textual and linguistic issues related to the use of ἀπάντησις and συνάντησις in Greek Judges require further discussion in some detail. As mentioned above, though at first it seems odd, there are clear reasons why these *meeting* nominals were used to translate קרא II. Those reasons, moreover, relate not only to linguistic conventions within postclassical Greek, but simultaneously to an apparent concern to adhere to a word-for-word translation style in Greek Judges. That translation style is present, moreover, in every instance of the *meeting* nominals

(Judg^OG and Judg^Rv) despite the lexical change that occurred. That is, the lexical change of *meeting* vocabulary occurred within what might be called a grammatically stereotyped translation style. Recognizing these features of Greek Judges paves the way for the discussion below of the semantic changes underway in Greek as well as stylistic concerns for the revised text.

As indicated in (1) through (3)—and as shown in table 5.3—in each case where one of the *meeting* nominals appears in Greek Judges it is part of the same grammatical construction, which I will call the *meeting* construction.[7] That construction can be represented as follows, reading left to right as in Greek:

[Verb of Motion] + εἰς + [Meeting Nominal] + [Semantic Patient]

As shown in (3), for instance, ἐξέρχομαι is the verb of motion modified by the εἰς prepositional phrase, of which the *meeting* nominal ἀπάντησις is an object. The personal pronoun αὐτός modifies the *meeting* nominal and represents the semantic patient semantic in the clause. In the instances of this construction in Greek Judges, the verb of motion is not always explicit (14:5; 15:14; 19:3), and, as indicated with the ellipses in table 5.3, other grammatical elements sometimes intervene in different variations of the construction.[8] Nevertheless, the main elements of the construction and its meaning are consistent throughout Greek Judges.

It should not be too surprising by this point that we find this same Greek *meeting* construction in contemporary postclassical sources, although there are only a few examples. As I discuss in more detail below, the *meeting* nominals are attested only twenty-two times in Greek sources prior to the turn of the era. But among those attestations are several instances of the *meeting* construction. The earliest attestation, and the only

---

7. In using the terminology of a construction, I am adopting an approach common within cognitive linguistics known as construction grammar. From this perspective, there is no principled distinction between lexicon and syntax but rather a continuum (see Croft and Cruse 2004, 225–90; Diessel 2015). A construction places constraints upon word choice and, like an idiom, suppresses the semantic properties of the individual words to some degree in favor of the (possibly noncompositional) meaning of the construction as a whole (Cruse 2011, 81–82, 86–88). Within constructions, however, grammatical variation is possible (Croft 2000, 28–29, 53–54; Taylor 2012, 75–80).

8. This variation includes word order, verbal morphology, and case of the lexical unit in the semantic patient role. See Ross (2018, 387–88) for examples.

one from the classical period, appears in a source attributed to Sophocles (fifth century BCE):

(6) Sophocles, *Trag. frag.* 828.1
ἐγὼ δ' εἰς <u>ἀπάντησιν</u> [τινὸς] σπεύδων ἀπανταχῇ τὸ φῶς καλόν[9]
And I was seeking with all speed to <u>meet</u> [someone] during good light.

There is some doubt as to the originality of this text since it is preserved in only a fragment of a larger work now lost. However, there is good reason to view (6) as a genuine fifth-century reading, for this very passage is cited and attributed to Sophocles by the late ninth-century Byzantine scholar Photius in his lexical entry on ἀπάντησις (*Lex.* 2252).[10] In his lexicographical work, Photius is known to have relied upon much earlier scholarship, in this case perhaps a text as early as Σοφιστικὴ προπαρασκευή (*Praep. soph.* frag. 245), which was composed by the Atticist rhetorician and lexicographer Phrynichus Arabius in the second century CE (Dickey 2007, 96–97).[11]

Whether (6) is regarded as genuine or not, the Greek *meeting* construction appears a few times in the Hellenistic period as well. For instance, it appears twice in the work of Polybius:

(7) Polybius, *Hist.* 5.26.8
παραγενομένου δ' εἰς τὴν Κόρινθον αὐτοῦ, μεγάλην σπουδὴν ἐποιοῦντο καὶ παρώξυνον τοὺς νέους εἰς τὴν <u>ἀπάντησιν</u> οἱ περὶ τὸν Λεόντιον καὶ Πτολεμαῖον καὶ Μεγαλέαν, ὄντες ἡγεμόνες τῶν τε πελταστῶν καὶ τῶν ἄλλων τῶν ἐπιφανεστάτων συστημάτων.
Upon his [Philip of Macedon's] arrival at Corinth, Leontius, Ptolemaeus, and Megaleas—who were commanders of the peltasts and the other distinguished corps—made serious effort and urged the νέοι toward the <u>ἀπάντησιν</u>.

---

9. Here the [ ] brackets indicate a variant reading in Greek. This text is drawn from Pearson (1917).

10. For Photius's sources, see the text by Theodoridis (1982, esp. lxxii–lxxvi). See also Dickey (2007, 101–2) and Pontani (2015, 331–37). Pearson (1917, 49) states that despite the questionable text "there is no reason for refusing to assign εἰς ἀπάντησιν σπεύδειν to Sophocles."

11. Radt (1977, 549) supports Sophoclean authorship on the basis of Codex Zavordensis of Photius, unknown to Pearson, but he excises τινός.

(8) Polybius, *Hist.* 28.19.7
οὗτοι μὲν οὖν ἔπλεον ἀνὰ τὸν ποταμὸν εἰς τὴν <u>ἀπάντησιν</u>
These men thus sailed up river toward the <u>ἀπάντησις</u> [with Antiochus].

Given that Polybius was a "man of his own times, both in his choice of vocabulary ... and in his overall style," the presence of the same *meeting* construction in his corpus as the one used in Greek Judges demonstrates that it was a conventional part of postclassical Greek by at least the second century BCE (Horrocks 2014, 97). The evidence is sparse, but it is there. Moreover, this construction is not only attested within literary sources, but appears also in one papyrus from Egypt in the same century:

(9) P.Tebt. 1.43 (TM 3679), lines 5–9
Ἀσκληπιάδην τινὰ τῶν παρ' Ἀμιν[ίου] | τοῦ ἐπιστάτου τῶν φυλακιτῶν τοῦ αὐτοῦ νομοῦ παραγείνεσθαι | εἰς τὴν κώμ[ην κ]αὶ κατὰ τὸ καθ[ῆκ]ον παρεγενήθημεν εἰς <u>ἀπάντησιν</u> | σὺν τῶι τῆς κώμης κωμάρχωι [καί] τινων τῶν πρεσβυτέρων τῶν | [γ]εωργῶν
Asklepaides, one of the agents of Aminias, overseer of the policemen of the same nome, was to appear in the village and, in accordance with custom, we appeared at the <u>ἀπάντησις</u> together with the *komarch* of the village and some of the elders among the tenant farmers.

The document of which (9) is a part was found in Kerkeosiris, a rural village in the Arsinoite nome, and is a petition to Ptolemy VIII Euergetes II (see Crawford 1971; Tcherikover and Fuks 1957, 1–47). It was written by a certain Menkhes, a village clerk (κωμογραμματεύς) who would have been responsible for everyday matters related to local government administration and business (Lewis 2001, 104–23). Perhaps owing to the identity of its intended recipient, the language of the letter is more educated and formal, but it is not literary like that of Polybius. In this connection, the presence of the Greek *meeting* construction in external sources like examples (6) through (9) demonstrate that it was a conventional part of the Greek language prior and contemporary to the translation of the Septuagint.

The reason this conventional—if not widely attested—Greek *meeting* construction appears so much more frequently by comparison in Greek Judges (eleven times) is because it was consistently used to translate a particular Hebrew construction that always involves קרא II. Compare table 5.3 above with the following table 5.4, in which the corresponding Hebrew text is provided with the main verb left uninflected:

Table 5.4. Hebrew *meeting* vocabulary in Judges (*BHQ*)

	קרא
4:18	יצא ... לקראת סיסרא
4:22	יצא ... לקראתו
6:35	עלה לקראתם
7:24	ירד לקראת מדין
11:31	יצא ... לקראתי
11:34	יצא לקראתו
14:5	שאג לקראתו
15:14	רוע לקראו
19:3	שׂמח לקראתו
20:25	יצא ... לקראתם
20:31	יצא ... לקראת העם
	פגע
8:21	ופגע־בנו
15:12	פן־תפבעון בי אתם
18:25	פן־יפגעו בכם אנשים
	נגע
20:41	ראה כי־נגעה עליו הרעה

As can be seen in table 5.4, along with examples (1) through (3) above, this Hebrew construction also has consistent elements, which can be represented as follows, read right to left as in Hebrew:

[Semantic Patient] + [[12]inf. cons. קרא + prep. ל] + [Verb of Motion]

To look again at Judg 20:25 in (3), יצא is the verb of motion to which קרא II acts as complement. In this case קרא II takes a third-person masculine plural pronominal suffix as the grammatical object representing the semantic patient role, but in other instances of the construction the object

---

12. Though this description of לקראת is etymologically correct, it is somewhat artificial given the grammaticalization of the form as a compound preposition. My argument here makes no etymological claims, however, and my use of construction grammar (see n. 7 above) to describe לקראת accounts for its grammaticalization.

is a morphologically independent nominal (4:18; 7:24; 20:31). The importance of recognizing this consistent Hebrew construction is that it helps to explain the appearance of the *meeting* nominals in Greek Judges. In all eleven instances the Hebrew construction appears in Judges, it is translated using the Greek *meeting* construction with either ἀπάντησις or συνάντησις. Translating in this way permitted close adherence to the syntax of the Hebrew source text—which is typical throughout the Septuagint corpus—given the close similarity of the Hebrew and Greek constructions in both form and meaning. Moreover, as shown in (6) through (9), that adherence to the source-text syntax was intentionally achieved within the linguistic conventions of postclassical Greek.

Yet there was at least one further motivating factor for the use of the *meeting* construction in Greek Judges, namely, imitation of the style of the Greek Pentateuch. As might be expected, the Greek *meeting* construction and its Hebrew counterpart are not confined to the book of Judges. In fact, the Hebrew construction is well attested throughout the Hebrew Bible. In 120 of the 137 total occurrences of the verb קרא II, it is a *qal* infinitive construct with a ל prefix. In almost every case, that form is part of the same Hebrew construction described above that expresses an interpersonal meeting event between the semantic agent and patient in the clause.[13] Ordinarily the verb of motion of involved is יצא, but עלה and הלך are also common, among others. Although not every instance of this Hebrew construction describes an event between human participants (e.g., Exod 14:27; Num 24:1), all occur with animate entities of some kind (see also *DCH*, s.v. "קרא II"). Importantly, wherever this construction appears throughout the Hebrew Bible it is almost always translated in the Septuagint corpus using the Greek *meeting* construction.[14] In this connection, the translation approach in Greek Judges described above is

---

13. Variations to the Hebrew meeting construction, typically without a verb denoting motion per se, include Exod 5:20; 7:15; Num 22:34; Josh 11:20; Judg 14:5; 15:14; 19:3; 1 Sam 10:10; 16:4; 17:21; 21:2; 2 Sam 15:32; 16:1; 1 Kgs 18:7; 2 Kings 10:5; Prov 7:10; Amos 4:12.

14. Exceptions to this trend typically involve the use of a *meeting* verb like ἀπαντάω rather than the full construction (Exod 7:15; Josh 11:20; Prov 7:10; Isa 14:9), the use of an alternative word or phrase when the event is a military engagement (Num 21:23; 1 Sam 4:2; 17:2; 2 Sam 10: 9, 10, 17; 1 Chr 19:10, 11, 17), or confusion with קרא I (Amos 4:12). Other exceptions include Exod 14:27; Num 23:3; 1 Sam 10:10; 16:4; 21:2; 2 Sam 18:6; 2 Kgs 9:17; Job 39:21.

obviously just one part of the method that was used consistently throughout the Septuagint corpus.[15]

It is well acknowledged that, as the first section of the Hebrew Bible rendered into Greek, the Greek Pentateuch influenced the production of subsequent Septuagint books.[16] Because it obtained a degree of authority in the communities in which it was used—as apparent in the attitude of the Letter of Aristeas—its style of translation was replicated (see Tov 1999a; Aejmelaeus 2013, 13; and Aitken 2014a, esp. 134). In this way the Greek Pentateuch must have played a key role in the development of the *meeting* construction translation method. Apart from the exceptions noted above, in all the instances of the Hebrew construction the OG translators of the Pentateuch rendered it using the Greek *meeting* construction (twenty-six times). Moreover, in the course of doing so they always used συνάντησις, just like Judg[Rv].[17] Nevertheless, while subsequent Septuagint translators adopted the same approach insofar as they used the Greek *meeting* construction for the same purpose, they were not consistent with the particular Greek *meeting* nominal they used in that construction. Some translators preferred to render לקראת with εἰς ἀπάντησιν while others preferred εἰς συνάντησιν.[18] In the textual history of Greek Judges, even as the *meeting* construction was chosen—as in the Greek Pentateuch—for its simultaneous adherence to Greek linguistic conventions *and* close representation of Hebrew syntax, the variation between the two prevailing lexical choices within that construction is thrown into relief.

To recap these broader observations, the appearance of the *meeting* nominals ἀπάντησις and συνάντησις in Greek Judges is tied to a method of translation consistent throughout the Septuagint. That method most likely

---

15. A corollary of this method was the attestation in the Septuagint of the Greek *meeting* construction—and therefore ἀπάντησις and συνάντησις—with significantly greater frequency than in contemporary Greek sources. Ross (2018) explains how this relatively greater frequency of the construction in the Septuagint seems to have propagated its use in Greek in general.

16. For linguistic arguments for a third-century date of the Greek Pentateuch, see Lee (1983, 136–44) and Evans (2001, 263–64).

17. The same is true in Greek Joshua (four times).

18. It is only in the Historical Books that ἀπάντησις begins to appear at all in the Septuagint, whether or not it is part of the meeting construction in Greek. Another notable trend is that συνάντησις appears nearly twice as often overall within the Septuagint corpus than ἀπάντησις, used eighty and forty-four times, respectively. Statistics derived from LEH.

developed first in the Greek Pentateuch, whose translators chose a particular Greek construction owing to it being conventional in the language *and* grammatically similar to a frequently occurring Hebrew construction (in which קרא II appears). As that same translation method was imitated by subsequent translators, there was nevertheless lexical variation within the Greek construction itself specifically involving the *meeting* nominals ἀπάντησις and συνάντησις. The appearance of precisely such lexical variation in Greek Judges therefore raises questions about changing semantics and stylistic concerns in Greek.

The Question of Semantics and Style in Judg^LXX

This case study highlights the importance of distinguishing, though not divorcing, lexicon from grammar in analysis of the language of the Septuagint, for it is possible in a translated text to handle these two aspects of language in different ways at the same time. Thus far I have shown how, as the Septuagint was produced, a tradition arose of consistently translating a particular Hebrew grammatical construction with a particular Greek grammatical construction. Since that Greek construction always involved a *meeting* nominal, in that respect all of the instances of the *meeting* nominals in the Septuagint (including Greek Judges) were occasioned by the Hebrew source text. However, it will not do merely to label this particular translation approach "Hebraizing" or a straightforward example of linguistic "interference" since, for one thing, the Greek construction used was conventional within contemporary postclassical Greek. Perhaps more importantly, however, the repeated use of the Greek *meeting* construction is simultaneously characterized by lexical variation: sometimes ἀπάντησις and elsewhere συνάντησις. In effect, what was indeed a standardizing grammatical approach to Hebrew nevertheless permitted—perhaps even necessitated—lexical choice in Greek. Put differently, while the source text influenced Greek grammatical choice, it simultaneously left open Greek lexical choice.

In light of these considerations, the question arises all the more acutely: If not the Hebrew source text, what factors did motivate the use of different *meeting* nominals in Judg^OG and Judg^Rv? This leads to the related question of why ἀπάντησις was not used in the Pentateuch, while ultimately συνάντησις is attested around twice as frequently throughout the Septuagint corpus as a whole. Without providing full citation of the information they provide, suffice it to say that turning to current lexicons leads only to implicit possibilities. In general it is fair to say the lexicons are not wrong in their treatment of this *meeting* vocabulary. However, neither do they provide the level of detail necessary to answer the questions raised in Greek Judges. As in the previous chapters, that is the case in part owing to the relatively few postclassical sources incorporated into the data presented. Another reason for the inadequacy, however, is the fact that lexicons do not typically provide the kind of information most relevant to the present inquiry; namely, discussion of the diachronic trends, semantic change, and social context. These desiderata therefore set the course for the next section.

Lexical Semantic Analysis

To promote clarity in my discussion, I address συναντάω and συνάντησις together first and then move on to ἀπαντάω and ἀπάντησις. I have also chosen to approach the lexical analysis diachronically in each case to draw out the changing trends in usage and semantics.

ΣΥΝΑΝΤΑΩ and ΣΥΝΑΝΤΗΣΙΣ (Judg[Rv])

Classical Evidence

There are four, possibly five, classical texts in which a *meeting* nominal appears, and it is the possible fifth text in which the single classical attestation of συνάντησις appears. It occurs, along with the corresponding *meeting* verb συναντάω, in a play by Euripides (fifth century BCE) within dialogue between Xuthus and Ion:

(10) Euripides, *Ion* 534–535
Ιων ὁ δὲ λόγος τίς ἐστι Φοίβου; Ξο. τὸν <u>συναντήσαντά</u> μοι
Ιων τίνα <u>συνάντησιν</u>; Ξο. δόμων τῶνδ' ἐξιόντι τοῦ θεοῦ
Ιων συμφορᾶς τίνος κυρῆσαι; Ξο. παῖδ' ἐμὸν πεφυκέναι.
Ιων What did Phoebus actually say? Ξο. That <u>the person who met</u> me ...
Ιων What <u>meeting</u>? Ξο. ...as I came out of this temple of the god ...
Ιων Was destined for what? Ξο. ...was my son. (translation based on Lee 1997, 83)

The context in (10) clearly pertains to a physical encounter between people, such that the sense of the nominal might be defined: *event in which one or more individuals meet and interact in person*; and that of the verb: *meet and interact with personally* (1 in the respective sample entries). It has not escaped commentators that this text shares a narrative parallel with that of

Jephthah in Judg 11, one that might be called the "first person you meet" type-scene (Lee 1997, 219). For that reason, it is possible that the wording of these lines in Euripides has come in the course of its transmission to reflect the lexical choice of συναντάω and συνάντησις in Judg[Rv] 11:31, rather than preserving genuine classical attestations.[19]

Since evidence in later centuries is of more relevance to the language of the Septuagint, it is only worth commenting briefly on the trends in usage of the verb συναντάω in the classical period. Excluding the less secure attestations as usual, there are only sixteen occurrences of συναντάω through the end of the fourth century BCE.[20] This attestation is far less frequent than that of ἀπαντάω (see below) by a ratio of around one to ten.

Postclassical Evidence

Table 5.5 presents the relevant statistical data for postclassical evidence for συναντάω and συνάντησις.

Table 5.5. Postclassical frequency of ΣΥΝΑΝΤΗΣΙΣ and ΣΥΝΑΝΤΑΩ

	BCE			CE	
	Third	Second	First	First	Second
συνάντησις					
Literature	0	0	1	1	0
Papyri	1	0	0	0	0
Inscriptions	0	0	0	0	0
Total	1	0	1	1	0
συναντάω					
Literature	1	12	12	23	3
Papyri	34	2	0	1	0
Inscriptions	9	7	0	0	0
Total	44	21	12	24	3

---

19. As this text is almost entirely dependent on a single fifteenth-century manuscript, it may not reflect genuine classical usage. See Lee (1997, 40–41) and the edition by Diggle (1981). The textual history of the Euripides corpus is discussed (in Latin) by Diggle (1984, v–xiv) beginning from the 1494 *editio princeps*.

20. Aesop and Hippocrates have again been excluded.

In postclassical evidence, the verb is more common in literary sources, especially in the first century BCE to the first century CE. It is most concentrated within the historical writing of Polybius (eleven times) and Diodorus Siculus (seven times), but also appears in the composition of later Atticists such as Dionysius of Halicarnassus (*Ant. rom.* 4.66.1.7; 4.67.4.2).[21] The frequency of attestation of the verb in nonliterary sources is quite different, however. In the same time frame, συναντάω appears thirty-seven times in papyri and another sixteen in inscriptions. Out of these fifty-four nonliterary attestations of the verb, the vast majority—forty-four—occur in the third century BCE.[22] As for the nominal συνάντησις, there are just three attestations within this time period in all Greek sources combined.[23] Against these data it is all the more striking that συνάντησις is attested eighty times in the Septuagint. Moreover, as I discuss more below, the concentration of συναντάω and συνάντησις attestations in nonliterary evidence from the third century BCE could help explain the appearance of these words in the Greek Pentateuch.

Some salient examples of the verb συναντάω can illustrate its meaning in the third century BCE, when it is most frequently attested. A letter from Apollonius describing the contents of another letter provides a representative use:

(11) P.Cair.Zen. 2.59203 (TM 848), lines 1–5
Ἀπο[λλώνιο]ς Ζήνωνι [χαίρειν]. ἀπέσταλκά σοι | τὰν[τίγ]ραφα τῆ[ς ἐπιστολῆς τῆς πρὸς τοὺς] | ἐν Ἡφαιστιάδι λα[ο]ὺ[ς παρ' ἡμῶν γεγραμμένης] | σήμε[ρον], ὅπως ἄμα τῆι ἡμέραι <u>συναντήσωσ[ιν]</u> | εἰς Φιλα[δέ]λφειαν καὶ μὴ [ἐ]πέχητα[ι] ὁ Πέτων. | [ἔρρωσο.
Apollonius to Zenon, greetings. I have sent to you a copy of the letter to the people in Hephaistias that was written by us today, in order that they might <u>rendezvous</u> one day in Philadelphia and not inconvenience Peton. Goodbye.[24]

A copy of the letter discussed is then subjoined and reads in part:

---

21. For citations of Diodorus Siculus, see McDougall (1983b, 79). For Polybius, see Collatz, Gützlaf, and Helms (2002, 309–10).

22. MM (602) note that συναντάω "does not seem to appear in Roman times" in nonliterary sources, although since their work it has been found once in the first century CE (*SB* 20.15077 [TM 14929], lines 10–11).

23. I exclude from this total the six occurrences in Philo for reasons discussed below.

24. I am grateful to Dr. Patrick James for suggesting "rendezvous" here.

(12) P.Cair.Zen. 2.59203 (TM 848), lines 7–11
... αὐτοὶ μὲν | διὰ τ[ὸ ἄσχολο]ι̣ εἶναι οὐχ [ἠδυνά]μεθα δ[ι]ακοῦσαι ὑμῶν, | Πέτω[να δὲ] τῶν [χρηματισ]τ̣[ῶ]ν ἀπε[στάλ]|καμεν. [σ]υναντήσα[τε ο]ὖν αὐτῶι ἅμα τῆι | ἡμέραι [εἰς] Φιλαδέλφε[ιαν
On account of our being engaged, we are unable to hear your case, but we have sent Peton the circuit judge. So <u>meet with</u> him one day in Philadelphia.

These examples provide instances of συναντάω used both intransitively (11) and transitively (12) within the same document.[25] The transitive sense here is the same as that of (10) and appears often in the third century BCE (1 in the sample entry). For example:

(13) P.Cair.Zen. 2.59247 (TM 892), lines 1–3
Φιλίσκος Ζήνωνι χαίρειν. μέλλοντί μοι παραγίνεσθαι πρὸς ὑμᾶς ἦλθεν | ἐπιστολὴ <u>συναντῆσαι</u> ⟦Ἀρί̣σ̣τ̣ων̣ι⟧ εἰς Πτολεμαΐδα Ἀρίστωνι \τῶι/ παρὰ | τοῦ βασιλέως ἀναπεπλευκότι ἐπὶ θέαν τοῦ νομοῦ·
Philiskos to Zenon, greetings. When I was about to appear to you a letter came to <u>meet with</u> Ariston in Ptolemais, from the royal court, who had sailed up to see the nome.

(14) P.Col. 4.87 (TM 1800), lines 17–19
ἐὰν τεθῆι ὁ λόγος ἔτι δι[α]φ[ό]ρας διδοὺ[ς] | δυσχερές. ἱερ\οῖς/ ⟦γαρμα⟧ γὰρ | γραμματε\ῦσι/ τουτο̣ δ̣ε | καὶ τ\οῖς/ περὶ Ἀλέξανδρον οὐ <u>συνήντηκα</u>.
If the account is balanced still showing discrepancies, that is unfortunate. For I have not <u>met with</u> these temple scribes nor with those of Alexander.

This sense also appears in third-century BCE inscriptions, for example:

(15) IG 4.1.128, lines 63–64
τῶι τύγα ποστείχοντι <u>συνάντησας</u> σὺν ὅπλοισιν | λαμπόμενος χρυσέοισ', Ἀσκλαπιέ.
You <u>met with</u> the one approaching you, shining with golden armor, O Asclepius.

---

25. Grammatically, the transitive meaning of συναντάω is expressed with an oblique argument such as the dative case or a prepositional phrase, which in semantic terms represent the patient role of the clause.

Further examples of συναντάω used with the same transitive sense (1 in the sample entry) could easily be multiplied in papyri and inscriptions.[26]

As for the intransitive sense of συναντάω seen in (11), it is particularly common in legal contexts like that of P.Cair.Zen. 2.59203 above. This sense of the verb might be defined as follows: *present oneself for an appointed meeting* (2 in the sample entry). As another example of this use:

(16) P.Cair.Zen. 2.59179 (twice) (TM 825), lines 8–12 (see also lines 15–16)
[Ἀπο]λλώνιος Κραταιμένει χαίρειν. ἐπειδὴ οἱ | [συ]νταξάμενοι οὐ συνήντησαν ἐπὶ τὴν [κρίσιν] | [περὶ] τῶν ἀμφιζβητουμένων ἀμπελώνων [κα]λῶς ποιήσεις συντάξας τὰ γενήματα | [δια]τηρῆσαι.
Apollonius to Krataimenes, greetings. Since those who were ordered did not <u>appear</u> at the trial concerning the disputed vineyards you would do well giving orders to guard the crops

Another example of this sense in a third-century BCE inscription proves important for later comparison:

(17) IPros.Pierre 9, lines 3–5
οἱ ἀρχιερεῖς | καὶ προφῆται καὶ οἱ εἰς τὸ ἄδυτον εἰσπορευόμενοι πρὸς τὸν στολισμὸν τῶν θεῶν καὶ πτεροφόραι καὶ ἱερογραμματεῖς καὶ | οἱ ἄλλοι ἱερεῖς οἱ <u>συναντήσαντες</u> ἐκ τῶν κατὰ τὴν χώραν ἱερῶν εἰς τὴν πέμ[π]την τοῦ Δίου, ἐν ἧι ἄγεται τὰ γενέθλια τοῦ | βασιλέως, καὶ εἰς τὴν πέμπτην καὶ εἰκάδα τοῦ αὐτοῦ μηνός, ἐν ἧι παρέλαβεν τὴν β[α]σιλείαν παρὰ τοῦ πατρός, καὶ εἰς τὴν πέμπτην καὶ εἰκάδα τοῦ αὐτοῦ μηνός, ἐν ἧι παρέλαβεν τὴν β[α]σιλείαν παρὰ τοῦ πατρός

---

26. In papyri, e.g., P.Ryl. 4.557 (TM 2413), line 1; P.Cair.Zen. 3.59311 (TM 955), line 4; P.Cair.Zen. 3.59470 (TM 1108, line 8; P.Lille. 1.6 (twice; TM 3213), lines 6, 22; *PSI* 5.502 (TM 2443), line 16; P.Sorb. 3.87 (TM 3219), line 2; P.Petr.Kleon 17 (TM 2492), line 6; *PSI* 6.566 (TM 2180), Brp line 2; P.Cair.Zen. 1.59056 (TM 714), line 3; P.Cair.Zen. 4.59593 (TM 1226), line 8; *PSI* 5.495 (TM 2123), line 13. Also in the second century BCE, e.g., P.Mich. 18.776 (twice; TM 8770), lines 2, 4. In third-century BCE inscriptions, e.g., IG 12.6.1.146, line 18; SEG 37.982, line 12; SEG 29.1136, line b.30. Also in the second century BCE: IG 12.Sup.137, line 28; SEG 49.1111, line 4; *SIG* 2.590, line 43; IMT Skam/NebTäler 197, line 9. Oddly, MGS cites "P.Cair.Zen. 35.10 (III[BCE])" in support of my sense 1 for συναντάω, but this does not appear to be an existing papyrus reference number. See also Polybius, *Hist.* 3.52.3; Diodorus Siculus, *Hist.* 3.65.1; 14.104.1 (which occurs in the context of battle).

The high priests, and the prophets, and those who enter the inner sanctuary for the dressing of the gods, and the feather-carriers, and the sacred scribes, and the other priests who have <u>shown up</u> from the temples throughout the land for the fifth of Dios, on which the king's birthday is celebrated, and on the twenty-fifth of the same month, on which he received the kingship from the father.

Other examples could be provided.[27] In summary, συναντάω appears to have been a common way in the third century BCE and later to refer to an event in which personal communication and interaction between or among parties occurs, used both transitively and intransitively (see also Lee 1983, 84).

Turning now to the nominal, with so few attestations of συνάντησις in the relevant time period, it is worth examining all three. The meaning of this word is uniform within these sources and, if the fifth-century attestation in Euripides cited above in (10) is genuine, consistent with its classical use. For example, Dionysius of Halicarnassus uses συνάντησις in the first century BCE with the same sense of a physical encounter between people:

(18) Dionysius of Halicarnassus, *Ant. rom.* 4.66.1
ἡ δὲ Λουκρητία ... τάχους ἐπιβᾶσα τῆς ἀπήνης εἰς Ῥώμην ᾤχετο ... οὔτε προσαγορεύουσα κατὰ <u>τὰς συναντήσεις</u> οὐδένα τῶν ἀσπαζομένων οὔτ᾽ ἀποκρινομένη τοῖς μαθεῖν βουλομένοις, ὅ τι πέπονθεν
Yet Lucretia ... quickly getting in her carriage, departed for Rome ... neither acknowledging anyone who greeted her in the course of <u>meeting</u> nor answering those wishing to learn what had happened.

The same sense of συνάντησις also occurs in the Homeric lexicon compiled in the first century CE by Apollonius Sophista (on whom see Dickey 2007, 24–25). It appears in his explanation of the lexical item ἀβροτάξομεν in Homer (*Il.* 10.65), where Menelaus asks Agamemnon whether he should wait for Agamemnon to come to him, or go to Agamemnon after having delivered a message to Nestor and others. Apollonius explains, citing Homer:

---

27. E.g., P.Enteux. 65 (TM 3340), lines 4–5; P.Hamb. 1.25 (twice; TM 5129), lines 11–12, 16; P.Hib. 2.203 (TM 5187), lines 17–18; P.Sorb. 3.131 (TM 121876), line 10, all from the third century BCE. In P.Hamb. 1.25, this same sense appears in a middle (lines 11–12) and active (line 16) form, both with πρός. See also Polybius, *Hist.* 1.52.6; 4.67.8; and McDougall (1983a, 79).

(19) Apollonius, *Lex. hom.* 301.3
"ἁβροτάξομεν ἀλλήλοιιν ἐρχομένω· πολλαὶ γὰρ ἀνὰ στρατόν εἰσι κέλευθοι"
ὃ ἡμεῖς λέγομεν διαμφοδήσομεν, ἀπὸ τοῦ ἀποτυχεῖν τὸν βροτὸν τοῦ βροτοῦ κατὰ <u>τὴν συνάντησιν</u>.
"[Lest] we miss one another as we go; for there are many pathways through the camp," Which we say "We missed the right way" because man fails at <u>meeting</u> man.

The same meaning appears again in the sole instance of συνάντησις in documentary evidence, found in a third-century BCE papyrus. The nominal appears on the verso as a description of the letter's contents.

(20) P.Ryl. 4.557 (TM 2413), lines 1–4 and verso
Νουμήνιος Ζ[ήν]ωνι χαίρειν. [πα]ρὰ τὸ γεγραφέ[ναι ἡ]μῖν Ἀπολλώνιον <u>συνα[ντῆσαι</u> αὐτῶι] | εἰς Μέμφιν τῇ[ι] β ἠναγκά[σμε]θα περι[ο]δεύ[ειν] τὸν νομὸν οὐθενὶ | κόσμωι, ὅπ[ως ὅ τι τάχος] | ἕτοιμοι ὦμεν τὸν ἀνάπλ[ουν] ποιεῖσθαι (lines 1-4 recto) ... Ζήνω[νι] | Νουμήνιος περὶ | <u>συναντήσεως</u> τῆς | εἰς Μέμφιν. (ἔτους) κη Δύστρου κ, | ἐμ Μέμφει (verso)
Numenius to Zenon, greetings. Owing to Apollonius having written to us <u>to meet</u> him in Memphis on the second we have been compelled to travel around the nome with no aim, so that we might be ready to make a return sail quickly.... From Numenius concerning the <u>meeting</u> at Memphis. Year 28, Dystrus 20, in Memphis.

Notice here that συνάντησις occurs alongside the verb συναντάω to describe the same event. Thus, in all instances where the lexical item is attested—from the third century BCE through the first century CE—συνάντησις refers to a meeting between persons during which there is communication and amicable social interaction. Before moving on to the next section, I should note that συνάντησις also appears six times in Philo, but in every case it occurs within an explicit citation of the Greek Pentateuch (*Det.* 30; 126; *Post.* 132; *Deo* 145; *Migr.* 79; *Somn.* 1.71).

ΑΠΑΝΤΑΩ and ΑΠΑΝΤΗΣΙΣ (Judg^OG)

Classical Evidence

As mentioned above, there are only four attestations of ἀπάντησις in the classical period.[28] Three of these occur in Aristotle where the word is used

---

28. Most attestations of ἀπάντησις in the classical corpus appear in collections or

in contexts dealing with logic and argumentation. The sense in these texts could be defined: *act of responding in argument or dialogue* (1 in the sample entry). Conceptually, we might think of this sense of ἀπάντησις as metaphorically "meeting" the argument or comment of an interlocutor with a cogent reply. For example:

(21) Aristotle, *Soph. elench.* 176a.23 (cf. *Metaph.* 1009a.20; *Phys.* 208a.8)
ἃς δή φαμεν ἐνίοτε μᾶλλον δεῖν φέρειν ἢ τὰς ἀληθεῖς ἐν τοῖς ἀγωνιστικοῖς λόγοις καὶ τῇ πρὸς τὸ διττὸν <u>ἀπαντήσει</u>
Now these [pseudo-refutations] we say it is sometimes necessary to bring to bear rather than the true [refutations] in competitive arguments and for <u>responding</u> to ambiguity.

However, ἀπάντησις appears also in Epicurus (fourth century BCE) in a different sense more relevant to Greek Judges:

(22) Epicurus, *Ep. Her.* 46.8
καὶ μὴν καὶ ἡ διὰ τοῦ κενοῦ φορὰ κατὰ μηδεμίαν <u>ἀπάντησιν</u> τῶν ἀντικοψάντων γινομένη πᾶν μῆκος περιληπτὸν ἐν ἀπερινοήτῳ χρόνῳ συντελεῖ
Moreover, the motion [of atoms] through empty space proceeding toward no <u>encounter</u> at all with resistance covers any conceivable distance in an indefinitely short time.

The text in (22) demonstrates that in the classical period ἀπάντησις was also used in contexts related to physical interaction, though perhaps of a more general nature than συνάντησις as seen in (10) (see the commentary by Salem 1993, 42–43; cf. Rist 1972, 46–52). This sense of ἀπάντησις can be defined: *event in which one entity physically encounters another* (2 in the sample entry). It is this sense, rather than the one seen in (21), that appears most frequently among the attestations of ἀπάντησις in the postclassical period.

Again, only a few words must suffice for the trends in the use of the verb ἀπαντάω in the classical period. Prior to the third century BCE the verb is attested about 191 times, most frequently in the work of Xenophon (37×), Aristotle (37×), and Demosthenes (20×).[29] More commentary is given in the summary below directly contrasting the two verbs and two nominals among this *meeting* vocabulary.

---

scholia that date to the Hellenistic period or later, such as Aesop or Hippocrates, and that are therefore not likely to be original.

29. Also Plato (19×) and Thucydides (18×).

Postclassical Evidence

Table 5.6 presents the relevant statistical data for postclassical evidence for ἀπαντάω and ἀπάντησις.

Table 5.6. Postclassical frequency of ΑΠΑΝΤΗΣΙΣ and ΑΠΑΝΤΑΩ

	BCE			CE	
	Third	Second	First	First	Second
ἀπάντησις					
Literature	0	26	10	25	0
Papyri	0	2	0	0	0
Inscriptions	0	4	4	0	0
Total	**0**	**32**	**14**	**25**	**0**
ἀπαντάω					
Literature	0	85	151	400	59
Papyri	10	35	6	0	2
Inscriptions	8	19	3	0	4
Total	**18**	**139**	**160**	**400**	**65**

As was the case with συναντάω, the verb is more common in literary sources, especially in the first century BCE to the first century CE. Out of all of its occurrences, 70 percent of attestations of ἀπαντάω appear in the writings of just four authors: Polybius (83×), Diodorus Siculus (117×), Plutarch (260×), and Josephus (89×).[30] That ἀπαντάω does not appear in any reliable third-century BCE source almost certainly has more to do with the state of the evidence in that period than with actual trends in language use. Among nonliterary sources, ἀπαντάω is best attested in the second and first century BCE, which is also the case for the nominal ἀπάντησις. Although ἀπάντησις is better attested than συνάντησις, the former nevertheless appears only ten times in nonliterary sources, and only in the second century BCE through first century CE in any Greek source. Clearly ἀπαντάω and ἀπάντησις are far better attested than συναντάω and

---

30. For citations of Diodorus Siculus, see McDougall (1983a, 139–40), who gives seventeen fewer than a search in *TLG*. For Polybius, see Mauersberger et al. (2000, 150–51). Significant attestation also appears in Appian (59×) and Philo (46×).

συνάντησις in postclassical Greek, such that the use of the former in Judg[OG] is consistent with their predominance in the language in general.

In the postclassical period both ἀπαντάω and ἀπάντησις became semi-technical terms. By this I mean that each word had what might be called general meanings as well as specialized ones. For the most part, the general meanings of ἀπαντάω and ἀπάντησις attest the ongoing use of senses that appeared in the classical period, although new meanings appear as well.

First, the verb continues to be used transitively to refer to a meeting event between one or more persons (1 in the sample entry; e.g., Polybius, *Hist.* 8.27.4; Diodorus Siculus, *Hist.* 2.1.8). In papyri, however, when this sense occurs the event in view ordinarily has negative connotations of hostility or aggression. For example:

(23) *SB* 16.12468 (TM 4127), lines 2–6, 10–17 (third century BCE)
ἐμοῦ ἀνα|φέρρντος ἀρτίδια ἐφ' ὄνου| εἰς Κροκοδείλων Πόλιν συνε|χομένωι τινι ἐν τῆι φυλα|κῆι ... <u>ἀπαντήσας</u> μοι Ἀθῶρις ὁ φυλακίτης | τοῦ Φρεμιθιείου ἀφείλε|τό μου τὴν ὄνον ἐπισε|σαγμένην
As I was bringing up food by donkey to Krokodiolopolis for someone detained in the prison ... Hathoris, the prison guard, son of Phremithieios, <u>after confronting</u> me, stripped my laden donkey.

(24) P.Ryl. 2.68 (TM 5286), lines 4–14 (first century CE)
τοῦ β| <u>ἀπαντησας</u>[31] μοι Τετ[εαρ|μ]ᾶις Θοτνάχθιος Ἑ[ρμοπολί]|τιδος ἐπὶ τοῦ δρ[όμου τοῦ] | Ἑρμοῦ κατὰ τὸ ἐντ[αῦθα(?) δικα]|ϛτήριον κα[ὶ ἐμπεσοῦσα] | ἐξ ἀντιλο[γ]ίας ἔ[πληξέν] | με ταῖς αὐτῆς χερσὶν [πλη]|γαῖς πλεί[στα]ις εἰς τυχὸν |τοῦ σώμα[τό]ς μου ἐγ γαστρ[ὶ] | ἐχουσαν[32] π[ε]\ν/ τάμηνον
In the second year Teteharmais, daughter of Thotnachthes of Hermopolis, <u>after confronting</u> me in the square of Hermes near the court there(?) and falling on me owing to a dispute, hit me with many blows with her hands at whim about my body, and I was five months pregnant.

The meaning in (23) and (24) is therefore best considered a subsense and could be defined as follows: *confront one or more individuals in person with aggression* (1a in sample entry).[33]

---

31. Read: ἀπαντήσασ<α>.
32. Read: ἐχούσης.
33. See also P.Enteux. 25 (TM 3300), line 7; and, perhaps, P.Yale 1.42 (TM 6206), line 21.

Among the general meanings of ἀπαντάω, it is somewhat more common to find intransitive uses that appear in judicial contexts, similar to συναντάω.³⁴ When used this way, the event is a formal proceeding of some kind, a sense that could be defined: *appear for official legal purposes* (2a in the sample entry). A quintessential example of this sense occurs several times in P.Tor.Choach 12, a late second-century BCE papyrus recording a complete property trial in Egypt.³⁵

(25) P.Tor.Choach 12 (TM 3563), col. 2, lines 29–31; col. 3, lines 4–5
καὶ διὰ τῶν παρὰ Δημητρίου παραγγελέντος αὐτοῖς ἔρχεσθαι | ἐπὶ τὸ κριτήριον μέχρι τοῦ τὰ καθ' ἡμᾶς διεξαχθῆναι, οἱ δ' ἐκτοπίσαντες | οὐκ ἀπήντησαν ... καὶ παραγγελέντος | αὐτοῖς ἀπαντᾶν ἐπὶ τὸ κριτήριον, φυγοδικοῦντες οὐκ ἀπήντησαν
And when they were ordered by the agents of Demetrios to come before the tribunal until our affairs should be settled, they stayed away and did not <u>appear</u> ... and when they were ordered to <u>appear</u> before the tribunal, they became fugitives from justice and did not <u>appear</u>.

Similarly:

(26) P.Hamb. 4.238 (twice) (TM 43304), lines 32–34, 37–41 (second century BCE)
Σωγέν[ε]ι· παραγ[γεῖλαι] τῷ Λεοντίσκῳ | παραχρῆμα ἀπ[αντᾶν] πρὸ<ς> ἡμᾶς. | ἐὰν δὲ στραγεύηται, μὴ ἐπιτρέψῃς ... ἐκόμισεν | ἡμεῖν Φιλίνα Ἀργαίου Μακέτα κατὰ | Λεοντίσκου τοῦ ἑαυτῆς υἱοῦ ὑπόμνη|μα παρὰ σοῦ κεχρηματισμένον ἔχον | ὑπογραφ[ὴ]ν παραγγεῖλα[ι] αὐτῶι ἀπαν|τᾶν πρὸ[ς σ]ὲ παραχρῆμα
To Sogenes: Instruct Leontiskos <u>to appear</u> to us immediately. And if he delays, do not permit it.... Philina, daughter of Argaios the Macedonian, brought us a petition against Leontiskos her own son bearing a decision authorized by you to instruct him <u>to appear</u> to you immediately.

Often the locale of the judicial meeting event is specified as the "tribunal" (κριτήριον; e.g., P.Tarich. 1 [3×; TM 316241], line 8, second century BCE;

---

34. Some such uses appear outside of a judicial context, however, which I have listed under sense 2 in the sample entry. E.g., P.Tebt. 1.61 (TM 2622), frag. B, line 410; P.Tebt. 4.1113 (TM 3708), lines 421–422.
35. See Bagnall and Derow (2004, 218–25), whose translation is adapted in (25).

BGU 8.1776 [TM 4857], lines 8–9, first century BCE). Other examples of this sense could be provided.³⁶

A third general sense of ἀπαντάω appears as part of an epistolary greeting formula, especially in the second century BCE. For example:

(27) P.Tebt. 3.755 (TM 7842), lines 1–6
Ἡλιόδωρος Ἐπιδώρωι | χαίρειν. εἰ ἔρρωσαι | καὶ τἄλλά³⁷ σοι κατὰ λόγον | <u>ἀπαντᾶι</u>, εὖ ἐϲτιν, | καὶ καυτὸς³⁸ δὲ μετρίως | ἐπανάγω.
Heliodorus to Epidorus, greetings. If you are well and everything <u>meets</u> you agreeably, it is good, and I myself am getting on fine.

This sense could be defined: *meet one's expectations* (3 in the sample entry).³⁹

The nominal ἀπάντησις also has three general meanings within postclassical sources. First, the word develops a subsense that appears in contexts of human social interaction (2a in the sample entry), which is a more specific sense than that seen in (22).⁴⁰ For example:

(28) Diodorus Siculus, *Hist.* 5.59.4
γνωσθείσης δὲ τῆς πράξεως, ὁ [μὲν] Ἀλθαιμένης οὐ δυνάμενος φέρειν τὸ μέγεθος τῆς συμφορᾶς τὰς μὲν <u>ἀπαντήσεις</u> καὶ ὁμιλίας τῶν ἀνθρώπων περιέκαμπτε, διδοὺς δ᾽ ἑαυτὸν εἰς τὰς ἐρημίας ἤλατο μόνος καὶ διὰ τὴν λύπην ἐτελεύτησεν·
Then realizing the result, Althaemenes, unable to bear the magnitude of the misfortune, avoided both the <u>interaction</u> and company of men, and giving himself over to desolate places he roamed around alone and died due to grief.

---

36. See P.Grenf. 1.13 (TM 249), line 5; P.Polit.Iud. 20 (twice; TM 44636), lines 4, 5; P.Polit.Iud. 19 (TM 44635), line 3; P.Polit.Iud. 4 (TM 44620), line 28; P.Tor.Choach. 11bis (TM 3562), line 29; P.Tebt. 1.14 (twice; TM 3650), lines 5, 15; *BGU* 8.1757 (TM 8295), line 5; *BGU* 8.1827 (TM 4906), line 23; P.Tebt. 1.27 (TM 3663), line 108; *UPZ* 1.118 (TM 3510), line 15. P.Hamb. 4.238 (twice; TM 43304), lines 32–34, 37–41. According to MM (s.v. "ἀπαντάω"), the "verb is very common of 'attendance' before a magistrate" (listing some inscriptions as well).

37. Read: τὰ ἄλλα.

38. Read: αὐτὸς.

39. Similarly *UPZ* 1.59 (TM 3450), line 3; *UPZ* 1.60 (TM 3451), line 2; *UPZ* 1.68 (TM 3459), line 2; *UPZ* 1.69 (TM 3460), line 2. See also MM, s.v. "ἀπαντάω."

40. Sense 2 in the sample entry also appears in postclassical Greek. E.g., Plutarch uses ἀπάντησις to describe the "meeting" of sun and earth in a lunar eclipse (*Dion* 24.1; *Superst.* 8 [169b]) and once of the "meeting" of ants on the move (*Soll. an.* 11 [967f]).

5. "They Went up to Meet Them"   191

The sense, which also appeared in (8) and (9) above, seems to be essentially synonymous with that of συνάντησις seen above in (18) and (19). It occurs throughout postclassical sources.⁴¹

Second, ἀπάντησις was sometimes used to refer to physical confrontations in contexts of conflict, another subsense that might be defined: *hostile confrontation between one or more individuals* (2b in the sample entry). For example:

(29) Polybius, *Hist.* 38.16.11
Παράδοξος αὐτῷ ἐφάνη ἡ <u>ἀπάντησις</u> τῶν πολεμίων. ἀλλά μοι δοκεῖ κατὰ τὴν παροιμίαν κενὰ κενοὶ λογίζονται.
The <u>confrontation</u> of the enemies seemed unexpected to him [Critolaus]. But I think as the proverb says, "Empty heads think empty thoughts."

Similarly in Plutarch in the first century CE:

(30) Plutarch, *Pyrrh.* 16.1
Τούτους ἀναλαβὼν ὁ Πύρρος ἐβάδιζεν εἰς Τάραντα. καὶ τοῦ Κινέου προαγαγόντος εἰς <u>ἀπάντησιν</u>, ὡς ᾔσθετο, τοὺς στρατιώτας
Taking along these [forces], Pyrrhus set out for Tarentum. And Cineas led the soldiers on to <u>confrontation</u> when he noticed.

Note also in (30) the appearance of the Greek *meeting* construction discussed above. The same thing occurs in Philo:

(31) Philo, *Deus* 166
φησὶ γάρ· οὐ διελεύσῃ δι' ἐμοῦ· εἰ δὲ μή γε, ἐν πολέμῳ ἐξελεύσομαί σοι εἰς <u>ἀπάντησιν</u>.
For he (Edom) says, "You will not pass through me. Otherwise I will come out against you in war for a <u>confrontation</u>."

---

41. See Polybius, *Hist.* 5.26.8; 16.22.2; 20.11.9; 21.33.2; 26.1.9; Diodorus Siculus, *Hist.* 4.11.2; 18.59.3; Josephus, *Ant.* 7.276; Plutarch, *Num.* 10.3; *Cor.* 30.4; *Ti. C. Gracch.* 21.5; *Cic.* 44.7; *Ant.* 35.6; *Adul. amic.* 21 [62c]). Sometimes the meeting occurs between human and deity (Diodorus Siculus, *Hist.* 4.24.6; BGU 14.2418 [TM 4014], lines 5–6). In certain contexts ἀπάντησις refers to a meeting that is more explicitly political in nature (Polybius, *Hist.* 31.32.3). It is possible given the broader context that in (9) the nominal refers to a meeting for official legal purposes in a similar way to the verb ἀπαντάω. See Lewis (2001, 116–17).

This sense also appears throughout postclassical literature outside the meeting construction.[42]

In addition to the general uses of ἀπαντάω and ἀπάντησις, there were specialized meanings as well. These general and specific meanings are related to one another and arose from specific cultural practices in the Hellenistic era. Broadly speaking, the Mediterranean world conquered by Alexander became heir to the Greek concept of divinity, which focused upon a willingness to listen and respond to the needs of humanity. It was this metaphysical attitude that allowed rulers to attain a status worthy of divine honor, insofar as they too were capable of offering protection to a weaker party. For this reason, certain Hellenistic rulers were given honorary titles such as ἐπιφανής ("renowned") or even σωτήρ ("savior") by those who gratefully received their benefactions, a practice that was wrapped up with the Hellenistic ruler cult.[43] Although having classical roots, the beginnings of the Hellenistic ruler cult is most clearly associated with certain Macedonian kings, most conspicuously Alexander himself, who, like the Ptolemies and Seleucids after him, assimilated the Egyptian practice of claiming divine ancestry (Chaniotis 2006, 434–35; Stewart 1993, 229–43; Rice 1983, 26–27). Ritual sacrifices, processions, and athletic or musical competitions were integral to any festival (πανήγυρις) held in honor of and (often) named after a given royal, also typically scheduled in perpetuity on that person's birthday or a similarly significant anniversary (Chaniotis 2006, 438). The festival in honor of Ptolemy I Soter, for example, occurred every four years and became known as the Ptolemai(ei)a (SEG 28.60, lines 55–56; Athenaeus, *Deipn.* 5; see Thompson 2000; Rice 1983, esp. 26–36; Stewart 1993, 252–60). The reciprocal benefits of receiving royal patronage on the one side and accepting the public portrayal of supreme power on the other incentivized both the intentional presentation of weakness and expression of lavishness on the parts of a Hellenistic city and ruler,

---

42. See also Polybius, *Hist.* 3.95.5; 8.3.6; 11.26.5; 11.27.3; 18.30.10; 38.11.4; Diodorus Siculus, *Hist.* 11.4.1; 17.13.2; cf. Josephus, *Ant.* 11.326; Plutarch, *Ant.* 40.3. Note that in *Hist.* 11.26.5, Polybius uses ἀπάντησις alongside ἀπαντάω to refer to the same event. Additionally, in postclassical literature ἀπάντησις continues, as in (21), to be used to refer to a verbal "response" (1 in the sample entry). E.g., Polybius, *Hist.* 5.63.8; 12.7.4; 28.17.4; Plutarch, *Dem.* 11.5; *Garr.* 17 (511a); *Praec. ger.* 7, 8, 14 (803c, 804a, 810e). This appears also in OGIS 2.737, line 24, on which see Thompson (1984, 1070–71).

43. Chaniotis (2006, 432–33) states, "The godlike royals receive godlike honours, but are not gods; their mortality makes all the difference." See also Shipley (2000, 156).

respectively (Chaniotis 2006, 440). Particularly in Ptolemaic Egypt, this kind of ceremony recognizing mutually beneficial relationships developed between various civic communities and philanthropic dignitaries (not necessarily royals), which continued into the early Roman period (Chaniotis 2006, 442–43).[44]

It was in association with such public ceremonies that a kind of formal civic reception developed in the Hellenistic world. Often when a dignitary visited a city the citizens were invited to celebrate their arrival by proceeding out to meet him or her, an event that inaugurated the πανήγυρις. This civic reception became known officially as an *apantesis*, linking the lexical item ἀπάντησις with this concept and its Greek cultural background (3 in the sample entry; Bouchon 2011, 58–59; Chankowski 2005, 198–202).[45] Notably, the portrayal of the *apantesis* ceremony in literary evidence differs slightly from documentary sources in that it is more idealized in the former. For example, in *Hist.* 16.25–26, Polybius provides the paradigmatic literary description of an *apantesis* ceremony in his report of the arrival of Attalus I at Athens in 200 BCE (Robert 1984, 482; Perrin-Saminadayar 2004, 359):[46]

(32) Polybius, *Hist.* 16.25.3–4
ὁ δὲ τῶν Ἀθηναίων δῆμος γνοὺς τὴν παρουσίαν αὐτοῦ μεγαλομερῶς ἐψηφίσατο περὶ τῆς <u>ἀπαντήσεως</u> καὶ τῆς ὅλης ἀποδοχῆς τοῦ βασιλέως.
Then the people of Athens, recognizing his pending arrival, magnificently supported his <u>civic reception</u> and the general welcoming of the king.

---

44. See Perrin-Saminadayar (2004, 360–64), who also states that "le protocole par lequel ils [royals] étaient officiellement accueillis était le même que celui par lequel Athènes honorait ses autres amis et alliés" (375). On similar maritime ceremonies in the late Hellenistic and Roman period, see Haensch (2009). On the place of queens in the *apantesis* ceremony, see Savalli-Lestrade (2003).

45. The seminal discussion of evidence is in Robert (1984, 1985), which will not be rehearsed here. See also Perrin-Saminadayar (2004), who examines the Athenian *apantesis* protocol and concludes that the reception ceremony was followed by carefully supervised hospitality known as *apodoche* (ἀποδοχή). Pont (2009) also argues that *apantesis* was a means of confirming the status of the welcoming city.

46. The latter argues that Polybius's account is a reconstruction "à partir d'un cérémonial royal bien connu en vigueur dans les monarchies hellénistiques…. elle s'appuie sur des éléments concrets d'un protocole qu'on retrouve à Athènes pour d'autres souverains, mais pas uniquement pour des souverains."

Soon arriving, King Attalus finds a willing ally in Rome against Philip of Macedon. Attalus then proceeds in state with many Athenian officials and is joyfully greeted along the way. Polybius describes the event as follows:

(33) Polybius, *Hist.* 16.25.5-7
> οὐ γὰρ μόνον οἱ τὰς ἀρχὰς ἔχοντες μετὰ τῶν ἱππέων, ἀλλὰ καὶ πάντες οἱ πολῖται μετὰ τῶν τέκνων καὶ γυναικῶν <u>ἀπήντων</u> αὐτοῖς. ὡς δὲ συνέμιξαν, τοιαύτη παρὰ τῶν πολλῶν ἐγένετο κατὰ τὴν <u>ἀπάντησιν</u> φιλανθρωπία πρός τε Ῥωμαίους καὶ ἔτι μᾶλλον πρὸς τὸν Ἄτταλον ὥσθ᾽ ὑπερβολὴν μὴ καταλιπεῖν.
>
> For not only the magistrates with cavalry, but also all the citizens with their children and wives <u>formally received</u> them. And as they joined them, there was at the <u>civic reception</u> such demonstration of goodwill from the crowds for both the Romans and the more for Attalus that nothing could have outstripped it in extravagance.

Notice the presence of the verb ἀπαντάω as well in (33), which was often used in these contexts to describe the activity of the citizens in greeting a dignitary in the *apantesis* ceremony (4 in the sample entry). On many occasions elsewhere in the *Histories*, Polybius describes a formal reception that he calls an ἀπάντησις. These occur between the Boeotian magistrates and Antiochus (20.7.3-7), between Ptolemaic representatives and Antiochus in Egypt (28.19.6-7), between Attalus and the Romans (30.1.1-6), between Antiochus and Tiberias Gracchus (30.27.1-4; cf. 30.30.7-8), as well as between the Roman senate and Eumenes (21.18.1-6). In the last of these Polybius writes:

(34) Polybius, *Hist.* 21.18.3
> ἅπαντας μὲν οὖν τοὺς παραγενομένους ἐπεδέχετο φιλανθρώπως ἡ σύγκλητος, μεγαλομερέστατα δὲ καὶ κατὰ τὴν <u>ἀπάντησιν</u> καὶ τὰς τῶν ξενίων παροχὰς Εὐμένη τὸν βασιλέα, μετὰ δὲ τοῦτον τοὺς Ῥοδίους.
>
> Thus the senate welcomed all those arriving with goodwill, and especially magnificently, both in the manner of the <u>civic reception</u> and the provisions of hospitality, Eumenes the king, and after him the Rhodians.

Similar formal civic receptions of a visiting dignitary occur in many postclassical literary works. Much the same scenario is described by Diodorus Siculus on several occasions.[47] For example, in his account of the arrival at Rome of certain foreign dignitaries he states:

---

47. McDougall (1983a, 140), however, omits several references for ἀπάντησις and

(35) Polybius, *Hist.* 29.22.1
ἀπάντησις γὰρ αὐτοῖς ἐγένετο μεγαλοπρεπὴς καὶ ξένια καὶ τἆλλα φιλάνθρωπα διαφέροντα.
For a magnificent civic reception was undertaken for them and gifts of hospitality and every surpassing courtesy.

When Scipio Africanus and his ambassadors arrived at Alexandria, another reception was held by Ptolemy:

(36) Polybius, *Hist.* 33.28b.1
ὁ δὲ Πτολεμαῖος μετὰ μεγάλης ἀπαντήσεως καὶ παρασκευῆς προσδεξάμενος τοὺς ἄνδρας τάς τε ἑστιάσεις πολυτελεῖς ἐποιεῖτο καὶ τὰ βασίλεια περιάγων ἐπεδείκνυτο καὶ τὴν ἄλλην τὴν βασιλικὴν γάζαν.
Ptolemy, welcoming the men with a great civic reception and preparations, both held costly feasts and, leading them around the palace, also showed the rest of the royal treasury.

Yet a third instance occurs in which Diodorus Siculus uses the word ἀπάντησις twice to describe the formal reception ceremony, this time however with reference to important cultic objects from Pessinus:

(37) Polybius, *Hist.* 34/35.33.2
ἐν μὲν γὰρ τοῖς τῆς Σιβύλλης χρησμοῖς εὑρέθη γεγραμμένον ὅτι δεῖ τοὺς Ῥωμαίους ἱδρύσασθαι νεὼν τῆς μεγάλης μητρὸς τῶν θεῶν, καὶ τῶν μὲν ἱερῶν τὴν καταγωγὴν ἐκ Πεσσινοῦντος τῆς Ἀσίας ποιήσασθαι, τὴν δὲ ἐκδοχὴν αὐτῶν ἐν τῇ Ῥώμῃ γενέσθαι πανδημεὶ τῆς ἀπαντήσεως γινομένης ... καὶ τούτους ἀφηγεῖσθαι τῆς ἀπαντήσεως γενομένης καὶ δέξασθαι τὰ ἱερὰ τῆς θεᾶς.
For in the Sibylline Oracles it was found written that it was necessary for the Romans to found a temple for the great mother of the gods, and they should undertake a retrieval of her sacred objects from Pessinus in Asia, and that there be a reception of them in Rome with the entire populace holding the civic reception ... and that these [men and women] should lead the civic reception when it happened, and receive the sacred items of the goddess.

A similar type of civic reception ceremony that is referred to as an ἀπάντησις also appears in Josephus, *Ant.* 13.101. In an account that involves the Greek

---

provides the single gloss "meeting" for ἀπάντησις, apparently not recognizing the formalized nature of the ceremony being described.

meeting construction, he describes the inhabitants of Ashkelon going out of their city to meet Jonathan after an important victory:[48]

(38) Josephus, *Ant.* 13.101
καὶ καταστρατοπεδεύσαντος ἔξω τῆς πόλεως αὐτοῦ προῆλθον εἰς <u>ἀπάντησιν</u> αὐτῷ οἱ Ἀσκαλωνῖται, ξένια προσφέροντες αὐτῷ καὶ τιμῶντες. ὁ δὲ ἀποδεξάμενος αὐτοὺς τῆς προαιρέσεως ἀνέστρεψεν ἐκεῖθεν εἰς Ἱεροσόλυμα, πολλὴν ἐπαγόμενος λείαν, ἣν ἔλαβεν νικήσας τοὺς πολεμίους.
And when he had set up camp outside the city the Ashkelonians came out for his <u>civic reception</u>, bringing tributes and paying honor to him. So, after gladly receiving their intentions, he returned from there to Jerusalem, bringing along a significant amount of plunder that he had taken after conquering the enemies.

Importantly, many aspects of the idealized descriptions of the Hellenistic *apantesis* typical in literary sources are corroborated in the nonliterary evidence. This material begins to appear after the second half of the second century BCE.[49] The best example, from the second century BCE, records an *apantesis* ceremony held for Attalus III:

(39) *OGIS* 1.332, lines 33–36
<u>ἀπαντῆσαι</u> δὲ αὐτῷ[ι] τού[ς] τε προγεγραμμένους ἱερεῖς καὶ τὰς ἱε|ρείας καὶ τοὺς στρατηγοὺς καὶ τοὺς ἄρχοντας καὶ τοὺς ἱερονίκας ἔχον|τας τοὺς ἀπος(?).ΝΛ[— — —]Ν[— — —]ους καὶ τὸν [γυ]μνασίαρχον μετὰ τῶν | ἐφήβων καὶ τ[ῶ]ν νέ[ων]
Then the above-mentioned priests and the priestesses will go out <u>to formally receive</u> him, also with the generals and the commanders and the victors in the sacred games [with their victory wreaths], the gymnasiarch with the ephebes and the νέοι.[50]

As in (33) above, the text in (39) attests the specialized sense of the verb ἀπαντάω. Note also the similarity in the list of attending celebrants in (39)

---

48. Also see *Ant.* 11.8.4–5; 12.138–144. A variation of the construction but in a similar reception context occurs in Plutarch *Pomp.* 26.1; *Cic.* 33.7; 43.5; *Dion* 13.1; *Arat.* 43.3. Some of these texts are discussed by Robert (1984, 485–86; 1985, 469–70).

49. See Perrin-Saminadayar (2004, 352–59) for a discussion of the differences between literary and nonliterary evidence for *apantesis*.

50. Translation adapted from Klauck (2000, 277). For exhaustive commentary, see Robert (1984, 472–89; 1985, 468–81).

5. "They Went up to Meet Them" 197

to that of the *apantesis* that Polybius describes in (33).[51] Speaking of these two examples in particular, Louis Robert (1984, 483) states that they "nous donnent un tableau complet de l'*apantésis*" (similarly Chankowski 2005, 199–200). On the basis of this and other evidence, Robert (1984, 482) goes so far as to designate the word ἀπάντησις a technical term. Another important source confirming that idea—although dated to the mid-third century and with the verb ἀπαντάω editorially supplied—is the detailed description of the *apantesis* ceremony held for Ptolemy III Euergetes that appears in P.Petr. 2.45, dated to 246 BCE (see Bagnall and Derow 2004, 53–55):

(40) P.Petr. 2.45 (TM 61457), col. 3, lines 19–24

[ἀπήντησαν] γὰρ ἡμῖν ἐκτὸς τῆς πύλης | οἱ [- ca. -] σατράπαι καὶ οἱ ἄλλοι ἡγε|μόν[ες καὶ <οἱ> στρατιῶ]ται καὶ οἱ ἱερεῖς καὶ αἱ συναρχίαι | καὶ [πάντες οἱ ἀπ]ὸ τοῦ γυμνασίου νεανίσκοι καὶ ἄλλος | ὄχ[λος -ca.?- ἐστεφ] ανωμένος καὶ τὰ ἱερὰ πάντα εἰς τὴ[ν] | πρὸ [τῆς πύλης] ὁδὸν ἐξήνεγκαν ...
For the ... satraps and other leaders and the soldiers and the priests and the magistrates and all the νεανίσκοι from the gymnasium and the other ... surrounding crowds <u>formally received</u> us outside the gate and brought out all the holy objects to the road in front of the gate.

Bridgette Le Guen (2006, 346–48) uses the texts in (33), (39), and (40) specifically, along with a few others, as the basis for a synoptic table presenting the stages, procedures, and terminology involved in the Hellenistic civic reception ceremony. She concludes that "l'*apantèsis* est une manifestation polysémique, éminemment politique et religieuse. En atteste la participation des autorités représentatives des différents pouvoirs dans la cité" (348). Among such important city representatives were those associated with the gymnasium: note the presence of the νεανίσκοι at the *apantesis* ceremony in (40).[52] Further evidence along these lines appears in another second-century BCE inscription that describes ἔφηβοι involved in an *apantesis* held for "sacred objects" (τὴν ἀπά[ν]|τησιν τοῖς ἱεροῖς; SEG 15.104, lines 10–11) as in (37) above. A similar civic reception is attested in IG 2.1006 as well:

(41) IG 2.1006, lines 10, 21, 75

<u>ἀπήντησαν</u> δὲ καὶ τοῖς ἱεροῖς καὶ προέπεμψ[α]ν αὐτά (line 10) ... <u>ἀπήντων</u> δὲ διὰ παντὸς τοῖς παραγ[ε]ινομ[ένοις φίλοις] καὶ εὐεργ[έ]ταις Ῥωμαίοις·

---

51. Also notice the presence of the ephebes and the νέοι at this particular event.
52. Also discussed in (19) in ch. 4.

... ἐποιήσατο δ[ὲ καὶ τοὺς] ἐν τοῖς γυμνασ[ίοις δρόμους, τοῖς τε φίλοις καὶ συμ]μάχοις Ῥωμα[ί]οις ποιήσατο τὰς <u>ἀπαντήσεις</u>·
Then they [ἔφηβοι; line 6] both <u>formally received</u> the sacred objects and escorted them.... And were continually <u>formally receiving</u> the arriving Roman friends and benefactors.... And they also held foot-races in the gymnasium, for both friends and Roman allies they held the <u>civic reception</u>.

Other studies have confirmed the involvement of young males in the different stages of *ephebic* training in the *apantesis* ceremony throughout the Mediterranean world, a tradition that was carried into the first century BCE.[53] According to Robert (1984, 486 n. 95), "les éphebes étaient une partie essentielle de la manifestation." Indeed, the practice of formal civic receptions in general continued not only in the Roman era (see, e.g., Cicero, *Att.* 16.11.6) but well beyond.[54] Importantly, however, when moving in the other chronological direction there is no official documentation of a formal *apantesis* ceremony prior to the mid-second century BCE (Perrin-Saminadayar 2004, 360 n. 43).[55] Chankowski (2005, 199) states that "le premier *décret gravé* concernant ce rituel date seulement d'entre 139 et 133." In this connection, it seems that the mid-second-cen-

---

53. E.g., D'Amore (2007b, esp. 340–41), who focuses on the παῖδες, ἔφηβοι, and νέοι in *OGIS* 1.332. First-century BCE evidence includes *SB* 3.6236, line 26; *IG* 5.1.1145, line 26; *IScM* 1.54, line 15; *IG* 2.1029, line 10.

54. The most exhaustive study is that by Chankowski (2011, 383–432), who provides a list of documentary sources in which ἔφηβοι and/or νέοι participated. Civic reception ceremonies for conquering emperors like Trajan are attested in the second through the fourth century CE and beyond, even artistically represented in ancient coinage. Numismatic representations of this ceremony, later known as the *adventus*, "depict the emperor mounted and attended by soldiers and the personification of Felicitas, while the reverse legend identifies the scene as ADVENTVS AVG[VSTVS]" (Harl 1987, 53). This custom spread as far as Roman England and into the Byzantine period, although with various permutations, on which see DesRosiers (2016, 52) and Boytsov (2015, esp. 182–83). See also Ross (2018) for a discussion of ἀπάντησις as a loanword in Latin and even rabbinic Hebrew. Note that the words ὑπαντάω and ὑπάντησις (and even ὑπαπάντησις) are also associated with the same ceremony in the second century BCE, on which see Robert (1984, 482); e.g., *IG* 2.1008, lines 7–8; 1011, lines 7–8. Also *SIG* 2.798, lines 19–24, in the first century BCE. In *IG* 2.1006, cited in (41) above, ὑπαντάω (line 74) is used alongside ἀπάντησις (line 75) in reference to the same event.

55. The earliest papyrological evidence is P.Petr. 2.45, cited in (40), but this constitutes an informal source insofar as it is documentary and not epigraphical.

5. "They Went up to Meet Them" 199

tury BCE is likely the *terminus post quem* for the specialized meaning of ἀπαντάω and ἀπάντησις.[56]

Summary and Comparison

To summarize this analysis of *meeting* vocabulary provided in this section, there are clear distinctions between ἀπαντάω and ἀπάντησις as compared with συναντάω and συνάντησις in three respects: frequency, chronological distribution, and semantics.

In terms of frequency, ἀπαντάω and ἀπάντησις are better attested than συναντάω and συνάντησις from the classical period right through the early Roman period in both literary and nonliterary sources. Table 5.7 summarizes the data within the postclassical period examined here.

Table 5.7. *Meeting* vocabulary frequency

	BCE			CE		
	Third	Second	First	First	Second	**Total**
ἀπαντάω	18	139	160	400	65	**782**
ἀπάντησις	0	32	14	25	0	**71**
συναντάω	44	21	12	24	3	**104**
συνάντησις	1	0	1	1	0	**3**

Although the ratios fluctuate over time, the disparity between the two sets of words is consistent and clear, favoring ἀπαντάω and ἀπάντησις. As shown in tables 5.5 and 5.6 above, within the postclassical period ἀπαντάω and ἀπάντησις are better attested in literary sources by a significant margin: eight and six times more frequently than in documentary evidence for verb and nominal, respectively. In contrast, συναντάω, is slightly better attested in nonliterary sources (fifty-three times to fifty-one times), most of which are papyri (thirty-seven times). Lastly, συνάντησις is barely attested at all (three times).

---

56. On this line of reasoning, the literary evidence for civic receptions that are said to have occurred in the classical period may reflect the retrojection by later authors of ceremonial details only fully codified within the Hellenistic world. This is not to say that a classical version of the civic reception did not exist in preliminary form, only that it became more standardized as it spread throughout the Hellenistic world (Chankowski 2005, 206).

Differences between these sets of *meeting* vocabulary appear also in their chronological distribution. Because attestation of *meeting* vocabulary within postclassical Greek literature is mostly concentrated within the corpora of Polybius and Diodorus Siculus, differences in chronology are difficult to identify in this variety of the language. However, such differences emerge more clearly from the nonliterary evidence. Among those sources συναντάω predominates in the third and early second century BCE, while ἀπαντάω and ἀπάντησις predominate in the second and first century BCE. Particularly in the face of the notable disparity in frequency between the two *meeting* verbs evident in table 5.7, it is significant that, out of all Greek sources, συναντάω is most frequently attested specifically in third-century BCE papyri, constituting almost half of all its occurrences. These data suggest that, at least in nonliterary sources, ἀπαντάω largely replaced συναντάω after the mid-second century BCE.[57]

Such a replacement would certainly have been possible owing to the ways in which the two verbs overlapped semantically. As shown above, ἀπαντάω and ἀπάντησις have a wider range of meanings than συναντάω and συνάντησις (the details of which I will not repeat here). That is somewhat unsurprising given that the former were apparently in more common use in the language in general. Yet as discussed above and shown in the sample entries for these words, senses 1 and 2 of both ἀπαντάω and συναντάω are virtually synonymous. Similarly, sense 2a of ἀπάντησις and sense 1 of συνάντησις are also very close—if not identical—in meaning. These points of semantic overlap permitted the gradual and partial replacement of συναντάω and συνάντησις in the third/second century BCE with ἀπαντάω and ἀπάντησις in the second/first century BCE, at least in nonliterary sources. An excellent example of this replacement is available in comparing the third-century BCE inscription IPros.Pierre 9 presented in (17) with a portion of the second-century BCE Rosetta Stone:

(42) IPros.Pierre 16, lines 6–9 = *OGIS* 1.90A
 οἱ ἀρχιερεῖς καὶ προφῆται καὶ οἱ εἰς τὸ ἄδυτον εἰ<σ>πορευόμενοι πρὸς τὸν στολισμὸν τῶν | θεῶν καὶ πτεροφόραι καὶ ἱερογραμματεῖς καὶ οἱ ἄλλοι

---

57. This is not to say that συναντάω and συνάντησις were completely eclipsed, of course. E.g., Horsley (1982, 98) rightly points out the use of συναντάω with dative in P.Laur. 2.45 (TM 37298), line 3, in the sixth/seventh century CE, stating that the "continuity of usage over a longer period" than that indicated by MM (602) deserves notice.

ἱερεῖς πάντες οἱ <u>ἀπαντήσαντες</u> ἐκ τῶν κατὰ τὴν χώραν ἱερῶν εἰς Μέμφιν τῶι βασιλεῖ πρὸς τὴν πανήγυριν τῆς παραλήψεως τῆς | βασιλείας τῆς Πτολεμαίου αἰωνοβίου

The high priests, and the prophets, and those who enter the inner sanctuary for the dressing of the gods, and the feather-carriers, and the sacred scribes, and the all the other priests from throughout the land <u>who have formally received</u> the king in Memphis for the festival of the royal succession of Ptolemy the ever-living.

Notice the near verbatim parallels between the sources in (17) and (42), most importantly:

οἱ ἄλλοι ἱερεῖς οἱ <u>συναντήσαντες</u> ἐκ τῶν κατὰ τὴν χώραν ἱερῶν (17 line 5)

with:

οἱ ἄλλοι ἱερεῖς πάντες οἱ <u>ἀπαντήσαντες</u> ἐκ τῶν κατὰ τὴν χώραν ἱερῶν (42 line 7)

Both inscriptions are royal decrees written in formal language, and both record the parties attending an important celebration. Consistent with the chronological shift noted above, in the third-century inscription in (17) we find συναντάω, while in the second-century inscription in (42) that word is replaced by ἀπαντάω. There is some semantic difference, however. In (17) the priests "meet together" or "show up" at a certain place for specific purposes (συναντάω sense 2), while in (42) the priests (already together) proceed out to "formally receive" the king in the *apantesis* ceremony (ἀπαντάω sense 4). Virtually all else remains the same in the formulaic expressions in which they appear. Aside from indicating the lexical replacement underway in postclassical Greek *meeting* vocabulary, (42) also contributes to the evidence for the association of ἀπαντάω and ἀπάντησις with the Hellenistic civic reception ceremony that began to formalize around the mid-second century BCE. While these words became specialized terms as a result, however, συναντάω and συνάντησις apparently never had the same associations.[58]

---

58. Diodorus Siculus uses συναντάω twice in similar contexts of public welcome (*Hist.* 3.65.1; 18.28.1). But these uses generally coincide with the senses of the verb already noted. Moreover, they are part of spontaneous events that explicitly involve

Conclusions

The Greek-Priority View and Septuagint Lexicography

The analysis of *meeting* vocabulary undertaken here illustrates once more the importance of approaching the language of the Septuagint with a Greek-priority view. Looking at the trends in usage and developing meaning of these words has contributed important information for evaluating the nuances involved in language change within Greek Judges. At the outset of this chapter, I pointed once more to an example of Greek lexical divergence within the textual history of the book used for translating the Hebrew construction לקראת and the verb פגע. On the one hand, in doing so the OG translator preferred ἀπάντησις and ἀπαντάω while in the revised text these were replaced with συνάντησις and συναντάω.

While most Greek lexicons do a sufficient job indicating how these sets of words overlapped semantically—making the substitution possible—they lack the kind of information most relevant to discerning from actual linguistic evidence the possible motivations for this language change in Greek Judges. Some hints exist. For example, it was almost a century ago that James Moulton and George Milligan, focusing upon the papyri, stated in regard to ἀπάντησις that "the word seems to have been a kind of *t.t.* [technical term] for the official welcome of a newly arrived dignitary" (MM, 53). Despite this important note, it was almost seventy years before this information was absorbed (or independently entered) into wider Greek lexicography, if only to be tucked into the revised supplement to LSJ where the following appears: "*the action of going out to meet* an arrival, esp. as a mark of honour" (Glare and Thompson 1996, 40).

In light of the extensive evidence for this meaning presented above, it is striking that this specialized meaning is not more widely recorded in Greek lexicons, much less better supported with references. This shortcoming demonstrates again the lack of depth in current reference works for postclassical Greek in particular. But it also throws into relief the importance of the nonliterary sources, particularly the epigraphical evidence in this case, to understanding the language in as much

---

disorganized crowds (πανδημεί occurs in both texts), and not a formal ceremony (cf. Luke 9:37).

detail as possible. In the case of the *meeting* vocabulary it is, as shown above, the inscriptions that provide the most evidence for the *apantesis* ceremony as well as the specialized meaning of the verb ἀπαντάω associated with it, which is not presently recognized in Greek lexicons. Yet there are instances in the Septuagint corpus that seem to attest this very meaning (e.g., ἀπαντάω 1 Macc 11:60; Pss. Sol. 8:16; ἀπάντησις 1 Chr 12:18; cf. Matt 25:6).[59] Whatever the significance thereof, it points to the ongoing need for lexicography of the Septuagint to begin to engage with external evidence, especially the nonliterary sources. This approach lends support in this case study to the fact that in both Judg[OG] and Judg[Rv] the *meeting* vocabulary is entirely within the linguistic conventions of postclassical Greek in both semantics and syntax. Moreover, the more detailed understanding of ἀπάντησις and ἀπαντάω that has emerged from examining contemporary sources must inform any judgment regarding how they are used—or avoided—within the Septuagint. Thus, it is the Greek-priority view that places the language of the Septuagint within its historical and linguistic context and, in this case, leads to evidence that helps elucidate the motivations underlying the revised text.

Meeting Vocabulary and Greek Judges

My analysis of the *meeting* vocabulary brings with it implications for understanding how these words were used in Greek Judges. As discussed in this chapter, the appearance of the *meeting* nominals ἀπάντησις and συνάντησις in Greek Judges is associated with translating a recurring Hebrew construction in which קרא II appears. As the earliest translation, the Greek Pentateuch set the precedent for using a Greek construction that was both conventional in the language and closely represented the elements of the Hebrew construction. That approach was followed almost universally in books translated later, including OG Judges. At the same time, however, the nominal ἀπάντησις appears within the Greek *meeting* construction in Judg[OG], in contrast to the use of συνάντησις in the Greek Pentateuch. The best explanation for this particular lexical variation is the predominance of ἀπάντησις in and after the second century BCE (table 5.6). That is,

---

59. Some discussion has occurred in New Testament scholarship regarding whether 1 Thess 4:17 refers to an *apantesis* ceremony. See, e.g., Weima (2014, 333–35); Luckensmeyer (2009, 260–65); Gundry (1996); Cosby (1994); Peterson (1930).

ἀπάντησις was the preferred *meeting* nominal in Judg^OG because it was in more common use by far than συνάντησις (table 5.5). The same thing can be said of the OG choice of ἀπαντάω. Effectively, the evidence indicates that the OG translator simply selected the *meeting* vocabulary that was most familiar within his Greek linguistic context. Moreover, both ἀπάντησις and ἀπαντάω are clearly used in Judg^OG according to broader conventions in the Hellenistic period examined above. The nominal ἀπάντησις refers to a general sense of physical and social interaction (sense 2a: 4:18; 11:31, 34; 19:3) as well as a hostile event (sense 2b: 14:5; 15:14; 20:25, 31). It is with the same sense of hostility that the verb ἀπαντάω is used transitively as well (sense 1a: 8:21; 15:12; 18:25). In this way the use of ἀπάντησις by the OG translator was a choice conditioned by and properly understood within the Greek linguistic environment.[60]

Before looking more closely at the lexical replacement in Judg^Rv, the use of συνάντησις and συναντάω in the Greek Pentateuch deserves comment. In that portion of the Septuagint corpus, the verb ἀπαντάω appears only three times in Genesis (28:11; 33:8; 49:1), and the nominal ἀπάντησις is totally absent. Yet on the other hand, the verb συναντάω is used fifteen times and the nominal συνάντησις twenty-seven. These trends in usage reflect the same trends seen in third-century BCE nonliterary evidence, particularly for συναντάω, which appears more in that period than any other. Similarly, the earliest secure attestation of συνάντησις also occurs in third-century BCE Egypt, as seen in (20), which suggests that the nominal also was in conventional (if infrequently attested) use at that time. These data point to a conclusion similar to that reached for Judg^OG, namely, that συνάντησις and συναντάω were used throughout the Greek Pentateuch—rather than ἀπάντησις and ἀπαντάω—because the former were more common than the latter in their Ptolemaic linguistic context and perhaps felt more suited to the nonliterary variety of Greek they generally employed in their work. Only at a later time were συνάντησις and συναντάω largely overtaken by ἀπάντησις and ἀπαντάω (table 5.7), thus paving the way for the lexical selection in Judg^OG.

---

60. I have shown elsewhere (Ross 2017) that the OG translator was familiar with the Greek Pentateuch—at least with Genesis—which supports the idea that the use of the Greek *meeting* construction in Judg^OG was influenced by the Greek Pentateuch. That familiarity, however, apparently did not prevent the OG translator from updating the *meeting* nominal to suit his own linguistic context at a later time.

Why, then, was the conventional use of ἀπάντησις and ἀπαντάω in Judg^OG so consistently changed to συνάντησις and συναντάω at a later stage in Judg^Rv? After all, the former not only remained in more frequent use throughout the Hellenistic period and beyond, but also continued to be used in ways suitable to the contexts where they appear in Judg^OG. Once again, the conditions of the linguistic context within which the revision occurred is the available best explanation—although not incontrovertible proof—for why one apparently suitable set of *meeting* words was replaced with another. The most significant aspect of those conditions is likely to have been the association of ἀπάντησις and ἀπαντάω with the cultural framework of Greek civic reception ceremonies. As shown above, beginning in the second half of the second century BCE, ἀπάντησις and ἀπαντάω developed a specialized meaning in both literary and nonliterary sources. Accordingly, when preparing to revise the OG text of Judges, the presence of ἀπάντησις and ἀπαντάω there may have seemed poorly suited for the desired goals for Judg^Rv. Since the alternative *meeting* vocabulary συνάντησις and συναντάω were never associated with civic reception ceremonies, however, they present a viable alternative. In light of the lower attestation of συνάντησις and συναντάω in general (and the ostensible replacement of the verb by ἀπαντάω), their use in Judg^Rv also bespeaks a willingness to employ rare words in the revision. For not only is the nominal συνάντησις rare in postclassical sources—attested only three times—but the preposition σύν, which was so common in Classical Greek, is also fading out of use in this period in general.[61] Of course, the significant exception to the rarity of συνάντησις in the postclassical period is its prevalence within the Greek Pentateuch. The preference in the revised text of Greek Judges for rarer words (συνάντησις and συναντάω) and the avoidance of more common ones that served as technical terms (ἀπάντησις and ἀπαντάω) thus appears to have accompanied the desire for the language of Judg^Rv to imitate that of the Greek Pentateuch.[62] In other words, the lexical

---

61. Bortone (2010, 184) points out that σύν was supplanted by μετά in postclassical Greek. See also Abel (1927, 215).

62. This point is supported by the fact that Philo, while using ἀπάντησις a few times, only ever uses συνάντησις in citations of the Greek Pentateuch. The desire to imitate the language of the Greek Pentateuch could help explain the predominance of συνάντησις and συναντάω over ἀπάντησις and ἀπαντάω in the Septuagint as a whole, even though the latter are consistently the more frequently attested in the postclassical Greek generally. Further research both in Greek Judges and elsewhere could clarify this issue.

replacement of *meeting* vocabulary occurred within and was conditioned by the social and linguistic context of the revised text of Greek Judges. It was a consistent textual change that clearly arose from concerns for the target text to communicate effectively in Greek, yet it also preserved aspects of the translation style present in the Greek Pentateuch.

As in the previous two chapters, there are examples of lexical replacement in Judg[Rv] that coincide with a clear concern to more closely represent a Hebrew exemplar. This phenomenon is evident in both word-for-word translation style and the desire for stereotyped translation equivalents. First, in 15:12 presented in (4) above, the OG translation read μήποτε ἀπαντήσητε ὑμεῖς ἐν ἐμοί (so Fernández Marcos 2011, 44). But in Judg[Rv] that rendering is changed to μήποτε συναντήσητε ἐν ἐμοὶ ὑμεῖς, inverting the OG prepositional phrase and pronoun toward a better alignment with the Hebrew word order פן־תפגעון בי אתם. Second, as already discussed, in 20:41 the revised text substitutes συναντάω for the OG rendering ἅπτω, as shown in (5) above, indicating a desire for lexical consistency for a Hebrew text that was read as פגע. Additionally, other elements of the syntax of Judg[Rv] 15:12 more closely reflect the Hebrew (MT), including changing the first καί to ὅτι, the removal of the OG plus καὶ ἐπέστρεψεν, and the use of ἐπί for על. So, while the revised text was meant to more closely conform with a Hebrew *Vorlage* in some ways, the nature and purpose of that conformity nevertheless permitted stylistic aspects within the target language to remain, or even to be introduced, without prompting from the source text. These changes occurred simultaneously to and without conflicting with the efforts discussed above to be sensitive toward Greek linguistic conventions within the Hellenistic social context of the revised text. Adherence to the word-order of the source text within the constraints of linguistic conventions in the target language—which is also what happened in the consistent use of the Greek *meeting* construction—does not constitute interference but reflects a stylistic choice (Lee 2020). The two outcomes are not necessarily in conflict and no doubt require considerable subtlety and skill to achieve.

Septuagint Vocabulary and Greek Lexicography

As a final point, this analysis of *meeting* vocabulary in Greek Judges offers data valuable to the broader lexicographical task for postclassical Greek. Though all the words examined here can inform Greek lexicography, the most important evidence pertains to the *meeting* nominals ἀπάντησις and συνάντησις. I described above how the use of these words in the book is associated with a broader tradition of translating a particular and frequent Hebrew construction with a similar construction that was fully conventional in postclassical Greek. As a result, the *meeting* nominals appear far more frequently in the Septuagint corpus as a whole than in any other source, offering a wealth of lexicographical data as a result. That higher frequency does not, however, mean these attestations should be disregarded as somehow irrelevant or substandard evidence for Greek usage.[63] Instead, precisely because of this consistent approach, the Septuagint translation occasioned the use of *meeting* nominals for which there is limited evidence otherwise. That is especially true of συνάντησις, which is attested eighty times in the Septuagint but only three times elsewhere. To ignore such a wealth of attestations in the lexicographical process of recording semantics in Greek is mistaken.

---

63. This seems to be the implication of the argument made by Boyd-Taylor (2004a), as discussed in ch. 2.

6
General Conclusions

It is manifestly insufficient to examine Κοινή Greek only from the classical side, as our ancestors mostly did; nor can we be discharged from our duty when we have added the monuments of the Hellenistic age.
—Moulton, "New Testament Greek in the Light of Modern Discovery"

The text history of the Greek Judges must include a description of both stages of the language, the Old Greek and the kaige revision [in the B group], without forgetting that the evolution of the Greek language is another element which has strongly influenced the text transmission.
—Fernández Marcos, "The B-Text of Judges"

All lexicography is a slow and (mostly) thankless business. With that in mind, it should be acknowledged that the language of the Septuagint is doubtless better understood now than ever before. New studies and key reference works published in the last decade or still underway represent admirable industry and offer much of value. But the meaningful progress that has occurred cannot be allowed to lull scholarship into contentment in this area. The discipline of Septuagint lexicography remains, despite the emergence of LEH and *GELS*, severely underdeveloped. To this state of affairs the absence of citation to external evidence bears solemn witness. Over its long but sparse history, the discipline of Septuagint lexicography has been characterized by methodological flaws and theoretical disagreements that have inhibited its progress. Using case studies from Greek Judges I have argued, from both the history of scholarship and extensive primary evidence, that the way forward for handling the language of the Septuagint is simple but certainly not easy: a thorough examination of all extant postclassical Greek evidence—especially nonliterary sources—to evaluate the vocabulary of the Septuagint and therefore to understand its language more broadly conceived.

Overview

In chapter 2, I provided an overview of the history of Septuagint lexicography meant to highlight several issues in the current state of the discipline as well as broader scholarly discussion about the language of the Septuagint and its relationship to postclassical Greek. In order to do so, I focused upon the evidentiary basis of the lexical information presented in the reference works and the methods with which it was handled. The entire pre-twentieth century tradition was heavily indebted to Kircher's 1607 concordance. In his efforts to present the meaning of the vocabulary of the Septuagint, Kircher questionably employed the 1550 Basel edition, a diglot whose Latin text presented an early modern translation made in consultation with Vulgate and Hebrew Bible texts. Kircher was also part of the long lexicographical tradition that used glosses, a method now recognized to be ill-suited to accurately describing lexical meaning. Despite later efforts to improve upon and supplement his work in various ways, Kircher's glosses were passed on without recognition that in textual and therefore semantic terms they were, at best, only indirectly linked to the Greek language in general. A clear lineage of lexicographical dependence in this respect is readily demonstrable in reference works stretching over two-hundred years from Kircher to Schleusner. Moreover, the early Septuagint concordance tradition also habituated biblical scholarship to evaluating the language of the Septuagint (syntax and lexicon) primarily, if not exclusively, against its Semitic source text.

While these flaws in method certainly created problems—even if they went long unrecognized—the more serious oversight was the near total absence of any external Greek evidence in Septuagint lexicography. Even once reference works began to appear that were explicitly conceptualized as Septuagint lexicons, such as those of Rosenbach, Biel, and Schleusner, any citation of words in nonbiblical Greek sources was a rare exception. The Septuagint was kept in linguistic isolation. This approach was the result of two distinct but related factors. First, there was the distinct lack of evidence (especially nonliterary) for postclassical Greek until the discovery, publication, and analysis of the papyri beginning in the early twentieth century. Second, even after the papyri had been discovered, there were prevailing attitudes among scholars that the language of the Greek Bible was a degraded form of Attic or, later on, a distinct Jewish dialect. The latter view in particular held sway in the mid-twentieth century and, through the influence of scholars in the SNTS, came to inform

6. General Conclusions

discussions led by Kraft, Tov, and Gehman about Septuagint lexicography in the first fifteen years of the IOSCS.

Scholarship soon came to loggerheads over what kind of language appears in the Septuagint, the ongoing effects of which are still acutely present in the discipline. Yet for the most part it has been an in-house debate. Few outside the septuagintal guild will know that the two broad views involved ultimately led to the production of two Septuagint lexicons, much less that these reference works are in many respects heirs to the same shortcomings in method and evidence as their forebears. On the one hand, LEH subordinates Greek semantics to the Semitic source text by assuming the translators always strove to translate the source text "faithfully" and by using the very lexicons admittedly unsuited for postclassical Greek as a benchmark for determining whether the meaning of Septuagint vocabulary should be semantically "clarified" vis-à-vis the source text. LEH also perpetuates the problematic gloss method. Representing a Greek-priority view, *GELS* on the other hand does well to provide definitions, which are based upon contextual usage in the Septuagint as a corpus. However, while *GELS* rightly attempts to account for the language of the Septuagint without reference to the source text, like LEH, and in fact the entire tradition of Septuagint lexicography, it fails to incorporate virtually any references to external Greek evidence. As a result, although in different ways, both LEH and *GELS* present lexicographical data for Septuagint vocabulary that remains semantically isolated from the broader Greek language of its time.

Chapter 2 therefore set the trajectory for the following three case studies drawn from Greek Judges. In each case study I sought to demonstrate how a Greek-priority view contributes to lexicographical research—chiefly in the form of sample lexical entries with external evidence and definitions—as well as its benefits for understanding the language of the Septuagint in both translation and revision.

In chapter 3 I discussed vocabulary associated with *battle* concepts, in which case the OG choice of πολεμέω and πόλεμος was consistently changed to παρατάσσω and παράταξις. At present the major Greek lexicons do not sufficiently represent the meaning of the latter two words in the postclassical phase of the language, during which time they underwent semantic development that is not widely documented. Analysis of παρατάσσω and παράταξις within postclassical Greek sources demonstrates that these words came to be associated with Greek battle tactics, particularly within the more formal variety of language preserved in literary and epigraphical sources. This analysis provided information indispensable for discerning how and why παρατάσσω and παράταξις were used in Greek Judges. In both the OG and revised texts these words are used in different ways, yet in both cases in conformity with contemporary linguistic conventions. Moreover, based upon the linguistic evidence, the choice to replace the OG battle vocabulary with παρατάσσω and παράταξις in Judg[Rv] reflects a desire to use vocabulary typical of an educated and more formal variety. Investigating the use and meaning of this vocabulary thus shed important light not only the newer senses of the words but also their connection to the ancient social context of the Septuagint.

In chapter 4 I examined vocabulary associated with *young male* concepts, of which the consistent OG use of παιδάριον was both retained and replaced with other options in the revised text, specifically παιδίον, νεανίσκος, or νεανίας. This case study involved more complexity in terms of the textual evidence for Greek Judges insofar as the B group associated with Judg[Rv] less unanimously agreed upon lexical replacement than in other chapters. This chapter also highlighted the shortcomings of the gloss method of lexicography in that such an approach cannot produce meaningful semantic distinctions among lexical items like the *young male* vocabulary. For in the nature of the case, the meaning of that vocabulary is more subtly intertwined at a pragmatic level with the social context in which it was used. In this instance the nonliterary sources in particular provided invaluable lexical and historical evidence for exploring the ways that certain kinds of individuals were categorized with these words in the Ptolemaic Egyptian social context. That information in turn significantly clarified how and why the young male vocabulary was used in Greek Judges. For various reasons, not every example in this case study was fully explicable. Yet the lexical analysis demonstrated that in most cases the lexical choice of the revised text is carefully suited to the narrative context according to contemporary linguistic conventions in Ptolemaic Egypt.

In chapter 5 I considered vocabulary associated with *meeting* concepts, specifically the use of ἀπάντησις and ἀπαντάω in Judg[OG] but συνάντησις and συναντάω in Judg[Rv]. Current lexicons, while for the most part accurately recording the meaning of these words, present only a partial picture of the evidence. Examining postclassical Greek sources demonstrated important fluctuations in the attestation of this vocabulary in nonliterary evidence as well as the association of ἀπάντησις and ἀπαντάω with Hellenistic civil ceremonies as semitechnical terms. These findings had important consequences for understanding how the meeting vocabulary was used in Greek Judges and even in the broader Septuagint corpus. In particular, on the one hand the OG vocabulary ἀπάντησις and ἀπαντάω were used entirely within linguistic conventions. However, on the other hand the lexical choice of συνάντησις and συναντάω in Judg[Rv] reflects, first, its position within a Greek context in which the OG vocabulary was no longer considered suited for translation owing to their semitechnical sense in the language and, second, a preference for translation precedents set in the Greek Pentateuch.

Implications

Understanding Greek Judges

This study has made several contributions to the study of Greek Judges, particularly in relation to its language and complex textual history. At a broad level, the evidence presented here has repeatedly confirmed that the A text is often very close to Judg[OG], and that the A text accordingly represents the older text type compared to the B text.[1] At a more detailed level, there is also some indication of the timeframes in which the OG and revised texts of Greek Judges may have been produced. Most important in this respect are the different chronological trends in lexical attestation seen in the case studies presented here. The best evidence is the *meeting* vocabulary of chapter 5, which discussed the decline of συνάντησις and συναντάω within nonliterary varieties of the language after the third century BCE and the association of ἀπάντησις and ἀπαντάω as specialized terms for Greek civic reception ceremonies beginning in the second half of the second century BCE. These trends suggest that Judg[OG] was produced in the early second century BCE, after συνάντησις and συναντάω (which are preferred in the Greek Pentateuch) had declined but before ἀπάντησις and ἀπαντάω had obtained their specialized meanings.[2] At the same time, the development of those specialized meanings indicates that Judg[Rv] was completed sometime after the mid-second century BCE. Moreover, as noted in chapter 3, παράταξις continued to be used in the *battle event* sense at least through the second century CE and παρατάσσω in the *engage in battle*

---

1. Suggested by Lee (1983, 148).
2. This suggestion agrees with that of Fernández Marcos (2014, 96–97), who argues on the basis of how the OG translator interpreted the figure of Samson that its most likely historical context was that of the Seleucid persecution. Fernández Marcos and Spottorno Díaz-Caro (2011, 14) suggest that Joshua and 1–4 Kingdoms were also translated in this same period.

sense at least through the first century CE. Since it was in the first century BCE that these newer senses of the words are most frequently attested, that century appears to be the most likely timeframe of the revision.[3] The subsequent decline in attestation of the newer senses of παρατάσσω and παράταξις—and of the lexical items themselves—discourages situating the revision after the turn of the era. It is of course unwise to propose firm conclusions and probably impossible to narrow the range of possibility to less than a century. However, external lexical evidence provides one of the more objective criteria for answering questions about textual chronology. This study also provides lexical evidence in chapter 4 in support of the notion that Judg^{Rv} was produced in a Ptolemaic Egyptian context (Cañas Reíllo 2016). Furthermore, the historically and culturally situated associations between hoplite warfare (παρατάσσω/παράταξις), the military life of civic officers (νεανίσκος), and their ceremonial role in Hellenistic reception ceremonies (ἀπαντάω/ἀπάντησις), each discussed throughout this study, suggest that the production of Judg^{Rv} was likely undertaken by one or more individuals acquainted with the details of Ptolemaic military and civic life in Egypt.

More than text-historical issues, however, I have in this study presented linguistic evidence for the nuance and sophistication involved in producing the revised text of Greek Judges. Ever since Thackeray's (1909, 13) classification of Judg^B as a "literal or unintelligent" translation, scholarship has largely followed suit. However, this evaluation looks only at Greek Judges in terms of its relationship to MT. More scholars are beginning to explore the ways in which such an approach creates a false dichotomy between word-for-word correspondence in translation and linguistic skill, semantic nuance, or elements of style in Greek (e.g., Mulroney 2016; Dhont 2018). Aitken (2015) has shown how multiple-causality lies behind even the most notoriously "literal" translation choices such as καί γε. Fernández Marcos (2012, 164) has this same false dichotomy in mind when he surmises that Judg^{Rv} is "not only conditioned by the criterion of a closer approximation to the Hebrew but probably has something to do with the linguistic tastes of the time and the addressees of the target language." This study has proven that suspicion correct and joins other studies in pointing to the need for a more careful approach to describing

---

3. This suggestion also agrees with Fernández Marcos and Spottorno Díaz-Caro (2011, 13–14) regarding the earlier phase of the kaige movement in general.

the motivations for Jewish revision of the Bible in Greek. Traditionally scholarship has emphasized the more obvious tendency to revise toward a Hebrew standard text in syntactical alignment and disparaged the resulting Greek as, for example, "awkward, stilted, and wooden" (Gentry 2016, 218). However, such an approach to revision—apparent beginning in the kaige movement through Aquila and Theodotion—does not preclude other motivations and goals from being part of the process, a process that I have repeatedly shown was multifaceted in Greek Judges. This study thus highlights the need for more nuanced linguistic and cultural analysis of revisional concerns—which often include but are not limited to source-text correspondence—and demonstrates how the Greek-priority approach facilitates such analysis.

Method and Prospects in Septuagint Lexicography

This study also attempts to cast a vision for Septuagint lexicography by pointing out its undeveloped state, demonstrating a working method, and highlighting the interest and value of this kind of research. Lexicography is arduous. Getting a handle upon the relevant evidence for postclassical Greek—both primary and secondary—is particularly challenging for many biblical scholars whose training did not include epigraphy, for example. Whereas gaining access to relevant secondary literature can prove difficult even in the most well-resourced institutions, digital technologies are making accessible the primary evidence in ever more creative and manipulable ways. Almost all of the lexical research in this study was carried out via digital platforms, which seriously improved in various ways over the course of just a few years. In this sense the data gathering will only become easier, even if the data analysis remains challenging. Yet the challenge must be met. As others have pointed out, with the publication of *GELS* the current state of Septuagint lexicography is that of a framework, but much work remains before the building is complete (Lee 2004b, 2004a, 2008, 2010). There are certainly pitfalls inherent to a corpus-based approach to Septuagint lexicography and other methodological challenges besides, as discussed in chapters 1 and 2. Boyd-Taylor (2001, 47) is correct in saying that what is needed is not a lexicon *of* the Septuagint but rather a lexicon *for* the Septuagint, if by that he means a lexicon that describes the meaning of the postclassical Greek vocabulary attested in the Septuagint. Achieving such a goal has no shortcuts, since as yet there is no lexicon for postclassical Greek in general—a simple but crucial fact that most scholars who interact with the language of the Septuagint seem to ignore.

To approach such a lexicographical task for the Septuagint would thus entail facing the distinctly inferior state of the discipline for postclassical Greek as compared with the classical period (or the New Testament corpus). As I have done in this study, each word must be chased down in both literary and nonliterary sources with a diachronic eye to semantic change. It is time-consuming to do so even for lesser-attested words or those already usefully discussed in secondary sources. But all the data are potentially relevant, and this method helps discern variations in meaning over time as well as within different varieties of Greek or contexts of usage. The papyri and inscriptions are of particular importance for reasons well-known among Septuagint scholars, and which were illustrated repeatedly in this study. Septuagint scholarship cannot continue to rely upon lexicons with inferior coverage of postclassical Greek in its analysis of the language of the Septuagint. Nor will simplistic glosses suffice, as lexicographers at large have already recognized. The best path forward is to build upon *GELS*—of course, not without revision or modification—by scouring contemporary Greek sources and beginning to incorporate the mass of external evidence for the language.

Evaluating the Language of the Septuagint

In its most basic articulation, the Greek-priority view holds that the language of the Septuagint can only properly be understood and evaluated with thorough analysis of contemporary linguistic evidence. It does not assume anything about the semantic intentions of the Septuagint translators or revisers except that they intended to communicate in Greek. It therefore does assume that the Septuagint preserves valuable lexicographical evidence because it is a corpus of postclassical Greek in general. This view does not, of course, dismiss the presence of linguistic features in the Septuagint that arose from the word-for-word translation style typical of the corpus and that sometimes depart from postclassical Greek conventions. However, it does not automatically construe the absence of external evidence as evidence of Semitism. Rather, whatever else might be said, this view—recognizing the current limitations in scholarly knowledge of postclassical Greek—construes otherwise unattested linguistic features in the Septuagint as deliberate choices made (perhaps for unclear reasons) by Jews educated in a Hellenistic social context whose first language competency was Greek. In this connection, the Greek-priority view does not universally categorize word-for-word correspondence in source and target texts as examples of Semitism or maintain that such correspondence necessitates an asterisk of qualification about the nature of the language per se. Rather, this view recognizes that even translation that proceeds word-for-word can and often does employ fully conventional Greek, and often displays a remarkable degree of linguistic sophistication and nuance.

The language of the Septuagint must be understood in its historical, social, and linguistic context, lest scholars fail to compare like with like. While there is consensus that the language of the Septuagint is a corpus of postclassical Greek—however that is articulated—that fact is often completely ignored in actual practice. Instead, disciplinary tradition dictates that the source text must receive the bulk of attention, even though that entails anachronistic comparison with MT and relies upon reference works whose insufficient representation of postclassical Greek is widely recognized (or ignored). While it is no doubt necessary to remain aware of how translation style was influenced by the source text in a given portion of the Septuagint (and to consider why that approach might have been taken), understanding that style and the Greek text that resulted from it requires a Greek-priority view. A great quantity of highly relevant linguistic evidence awaits investigation. As a discipline still in its infancy after four hundred years, Septuagint lexicography must begin systematically to incorporate these data. Moreover, Septuagint scholars must recognize that much work remains in the study of postclassical Greek in general. Then we must recognize that, in very important respects, Septuagint scholarship is itself postclassical Greek scholarship and let this set the agenda for future research.

Appendix
Lexicographical Sample Entries

The entries that follow are not meant to exhaustively describe the lexical semantics of a given word. For reasons of space, certain features that might profitably be included in a lexicon entry have been omitted, such as morphology, etymology, statistics, or Greek citations with English translation. Rather, these entries include only definitions—which are meant to state succinctly and unambiguously the lexical meaning(s) of the word—and the relevant references for those senses discussed in this study.[1] References were selected for the clarity with which they demonstrate a given sense but are not exhaustive. Senses within entries are roughly chronologically ordered to give an idea of the semantic development of the word, although senses often overlap synchronically. Each sense is supported, if attested, by evidence from the classical and postclassical periods (labeled appropriately), in both literary and nonliterary sources, up through the second century CE. Subsenses indicate a derivative relationship with the main sense of greater semantic specificity. The (†) symbol indicates that a sense is attested only in the classical or postclassical period, as marked. A greater number of references for a sense indicates higher overall frequency of its attestation respective to others. The criterion for classifying a given source as classical or postclassical was its dating to before the end of the fourth or the beginning of the third century BCE, respectively.

Παρατάσσω
   1. *Physically position immediately nearby.* **CLASS.** Isocrates, *Aeginet.* 19.38; Thucydides, *Hist.* 4.47.3; 5.71.1.
   2. *Compare and evaluate the qualities of entities.* **CLASS.** Isocrates, *Bus.* 11.7; SEG 30.43, line 3 (fifth c. BCE).

---

1. This language for definitions comes from Lee (2010, 130).

3. *Organize a group into side-by-side battle formation facing an enemy.* **CLASS.** Thucydides, *Hist.* 1.29.5; 7.3.1; Isocrates, *Archid.* 6.80; Xenophon, *Hell.* 2.1.23; *Cyr.* 3.3.43; *Anab.* 5.2.13. **POSTCLASS.** Polybius, *Hist.* 3.108.7; 11.1.2; 12.20.7; Diodorus Siculus, *Hist.* 2.26.6; 11.36.3; 19.67.2; Josephus, *Ant.* 6.26.3; 7.123.2; *SIG* 2.700, line 13 (second c. BCE). **LXX** Gen 14:8; Joel 2:5; Ps 27:3; Mal 1:4.
4. *Engage in battle between opposing forces in side-by-side formations.* **POSTCLASS.** (†) Polybius, *Hist.* 2.19.5 (?); Diodorus Siculus, *Hist.* 2.1.10; 19.72.7; Josephus, *Ant.* 5.180.4; *J.W.* 1.265.3; Plutarch, *Caes.* 15.3.8; *Alex.* 12.3.6. **LXX** Judg^B 1:3; 9:38; 11:8; Jdt 1:13; Zech 10:5; 14:3.
5. *Engage in physical confrontation between parties.* **POSTCLASS.** (†) Plutarch, *Mulier. virt.* 8 (247c3).

Παράταξις

1. *Physical formation of troops side by side for battle.* **CLASS.** Thucydides, *Hist.* 5.11.2; Aeschines, *Ctes.* 88; Aeneas, *Pol.* 15.8. **POSTCLASS.** Polybius, *Hist.* 1.41.1; 6.26.11; 7.4.4; Dionysius of Halicarnassus, *Ant. rom.* 2.41.1; 7.6.2; 12.7.2; Josephus, *Ant.* 6.172.2; 8.412.3; *J.W.* 3.88.3; Plutarch, *Thes.* 32.4.7; *Aem.* 17.2.1; *Flam.* 5.4.10; Cassius Dio, *Hist.* 14.57.6a.47; 16.57.48.127; 40.40.6.4. **LXX** Num 31:14, 21.
2. *Battle between opposing forces in side-by-side formations.* **CLASS.** Isocrates, *Hel. enc.* 53.6 (?); Demosthenes, *3 Philip.* 9.49; Aeschines, *Ctes.* 151; Aeneas, *Pol.* 1.3. **POSTCLASS.** Polybius, *Hist.* 1.27.5; 12.17.1; 16.18.2; 30.4.2; Diodorus Siculus, *Hist.* 1.18.5; 2.25.1, 6; 11.35.1, 2; 16.35.5; Dionysius of Halicarnassus, *Ant. rom.* 2.36.1; 6.5.4; 10.37.3; Josephus, *J.W.* 3.75.2; 6.80.1; *Ant.* 12.311.2; Plutarch, *Phoc.* 26.1.2; *Ag. Cleom.* 15.1.2; *An seni* 6 (787b7); Cassius Dio, *Hist.* 18.58.1.1; 55.30.2.3; IPriene 117, line 17 (third c. BCE); ILindos 2.1.160, line 4 (second c. BCE); IG 4.1.28, line 1 (second c. BCE); *OGIS* 2.654, line 12 (first c. BCE). **LXX** Num 31:5, 27, 28; Judg^B 20:14; 1 Par 5:18; Ps 143:1; Zech 14:3; Isa 22:6; 1 Macc 8:20.
3. *Physical conflict between parties.* **POSTCLASS.** (†) Josephus, *J.W.* 5.25.3; *Life* 358.3.

Ἀπάντησις

1. *Act of responding in argument or dialogue.* **CLASS.** Aristotle, *Soph. elench.* 176a.23; *Metaph.* 1009a20; *Phys.* 208a8. **POSTCLASS.** Polybius, *Hist.* 5.63.8; Plutarch, *Dem.* 11.5; *OGIS* 2.737, line 24 (second c. BCE).

2. *Event in which one entity physically encounters another.* **CLASS.** Epicurus, *Ep. Her.* 46.8; Sophocles, *Trag. frag.* 828.1. **POSTCLASS.** Plutarch, *Dion* 24.1; *Superst.* 8 (169b); *Soll. an.* 11 (967f).
   a. *Event in which one or more individuals meet and interact in person.* **POSTCLASS.** (†) Polybius, *Hist.* 5.26.8; 16.22.2; 28.19.7; Diodorus Siculus, *Hist.* 5.59.4.; 18.59.3; Josephus, *Ant.* 7.276; Plutarch, *Num.* 10.3; *BGU* 14.2418, lines 5–6 (second c. BCE); P.Tebt. 1.43, line 7 (second c. BCE). **LXX** 2 Macc 14:30; Sir 19:29; Jer 41:6.
   b. *Hostile confrontation between one or more individuals.* **POSTCLASS.** (†) Polybius, *Hist.* 38.16.11; Diodorus Siculus, *Hist.* 11.4.1; Plutarch, *Pyrrh.* 16.1; Philo, *Deus,* 166. **LXX** Judg^A 14:5; 1 Macc 12:41.
3. *Formal civic reception ceremony for arriving person(s) or object(s) of honor.* **POSTCLASS.** (†) Polybius, *Hist.* 5.26.8; 16.25.4, 6; 21.18.3; Diodorus Siculus, *Hist.* 29.22.1; 33.28b.1; 34/35.33.2; Josephus, *Ant.* 13.101; SEG 15.104, lines 10–11 (second c. BCE); IG 2.1006, line 75 (second c. BCE). **LXX** 1 Chr 12:18.

Ἀπαντάω
1. *Meet and interact with one or more individual in person.* **CLASS.** Herodotus, *Hist.* 8.9; Plato, *Leg.* 893e. **POSTCLASS.** Polybius, *Hist.* 8.27.4; 10.5.4; Diodorus Siculus, *Hist.* 2.1.8; 2.26.2. **LXX** Gen 33:8; 1 Kgdms 10:5; Sir 40:23. **NEW TESTAMENT** Mark 14:13; Luke 17:12.
   a. *Confront one or more individuals in person with aggression.* **CLASS.** Isocrates, *Paneg.* 86.5; Thucydides, *Hist.* 6.34. **POSTCLASS.** Polybius, *Hist.* 3.65.6; 18.3.3; Diodorus Siculus, *Hist.* 13.60.2; 17.12.5; *SB* 16.12468, line 10 (third c. BCE); P.Enteux. 25, line 7 (third c. BCE); P.Ryl. 2.68, line 5 (first c. BCE); SEG 25.563 (third c. BCE); **LXX** Judg^A 15:12; Ruth 2:22 1 Macc 11:68.
2. *Present oneself for an appointed meeting.* **CLASS.** Xenophon, *Hel.* 1.3.13; Thucydides, *Hist.* 7.1.3. **POSTCLASS.** Polybius, *Hist.* 4.23.4; 39.1.5; Diodorus Siculus, *Hist.* 11.26.5; 13.72.5; P.Tebt. 1.61, frag. B, line 410 (second c. BCE); P.Tebt. 4.1113, lines 421–422 (second c. BCE).
   a. *Appear for official legal purposes.* **CLASS.** Plato, *Leg.* 937a; 936e; Demosthenes, *Mid.* 21.90. **POSTCLASS.** P.Tor.Choach 12, col. 3, line 5 (second c. BCE); P.Hamb. 4.238, lines 40–41 (second c. BCE);

3. *Meet one's expectations* (of personal circumstances; epistolary greeting w. κατὰ λόγον). **POSTCLASS.** (†) P.Tebt. 3.755, lines 3–4 (second c. BCE); *UPZ* 1.60, line 2 (second c. BCE); *UPZ* 1.68, line 2 (second c. BCE).
4. *Participate in formal civic reception ceremony for arriving person(s) or object(s) of honor.* **POSTCLASS.** (†) Polybius, *Hist.* 16.25.6; *OGIS* 1.332, line 33 (second c. BCE); P.Petr. 2.45, col. 3, line 19 (mid-third c. BCE); IG 2.1006, lines 10, 21 (second c. BCE); IPros.Pierre 16, lines 7 (second c. BCE); IG 2.1029, line 10 (first c. BCE); **LXX** 1 Macc 11:68; Pss Sol 8:16.

Συνάντησις

1. *Event in which one or more individuals meet and interact in person.* **CLASS.** Euripides, *Ion* 535; **POSTCLASS.** Dionysius of Halicarnassus, *Ant. rom.* 4.66.1; Apollonius Sophista, *Lex. hom.* 301.3; P.Ryl. 4.557 v. **LXX** Gen 14:17; Num 21:33; Judg^B 19:3.

Συναντάω

1. *Meet and interact with personally.* **CLASS.** Euripides, *Ion* 534; Aristophanes, *Ach.* 1187; **POSTCLASS.** Polybius, *Hist.* 3.52.3; Diodorus Siculus, *Hist.* 3.65.1; 14.104.1; P.Cair.Zen. 2.59203, line 13 (third c. BCE); P.Cair.Zen. 2.59247, line 2 (third c. BCE); P.Col. 4.87, line 19 (third c. BCE); IG 4.1.128, line 63 (third c. BCE); P.Ryl. 4.557, line 1 (third c. BCE); **LXX** Gen. 32:1; **NEW TESTAMENT** Luke 9:37; 22:10; Acts 10:25; Heb 7:1, 10.
2. *Present oneself for an appointed meeting.* **POSTCLASS.** (†) Polybius, *Hist.* 1.52.6; 4.67.8; P.Cair.Zen. 2.59203, line 4 (third c. BCE); IPros. Pierre 9, line 5 (third c. BCE); P.Sorb. 3.131, line 10 (third c. BCE); P.Hamb. 1.25, lines 11–12, 16 (third c. BCE).

Bibliography

Abbott, Thomas Kingsmill. 1891. *Essays, Chiefly on the Original Texts of the Old and New Testaments.* London: Longmans, Green.
Abel, F.-M. 1927. *Grammaire du grec biblique: Suivie d'un choix de papyrus.* 2nd ed. Paris: Gabalda.
Abercrombie, John R., William Adler, Robert A. Kraft, and Emanuel Tov, eds. 1986. *Computer Assisted Tools for Septuagint Studies (CATSS): Ruth.* SCS 20. Atlanta: Scholars Press.
Aejmelaeus, Anneli. 2013. "The Septuagint and Oral Translation." Pages 5–13 in *XIV Congress of the IOSCS: Helsinki, 2010.* Edited by Melvin K. H. Peters. SCS 59. Atlanta: Society of Biblical Literature.
———. 2020. "Translation Technique and the Recensions: A Late Review of Ilmari Soisalon-Soininen's Doctoral Thesis on the Text-Forms of Judges." Pages 159–173 in in *The Legacy of Soisalon-Soininen: Towards a Syntax of Septuagint Greek.* Edited by Tuukka Kauhanen and Hanna Vanonen. DSI 13. Göttingen: Vandenhoeck & Ruprecht.
Aitken, James K. 1999. "The Language of the Septuagint: Recent Theories, Future Prospects." *BJGS* 24:24–33.
———. 2014a. "The Language of the Septuagint and Jewish-Greek Identity." Pages 120–34 in *The Jewish-Greek Tradition in Antiquity and the Byzantine Empire.* Edited by James K. Aitken and James Carleton Paget. Cambridge: Cambridge University Press.
———. 2014b. *No Stone Unturned: Greek Inscriptions and Septuagint Vocabulary.* CrStHB 5. Winona Lake, IN: Eisenbrauns.
———. 2014c. "Outlook." Pages 183–94 in *The Reception of Septuagint Words in Jewish-Hellenistic and Christian Literature.* Edited by Eberhard Bons, Ralph Brucker, and Jan Joosten. WUNT 2/367 Tübingen: Mohr Siebeck.
———. 2015. "The Origins of ΚΑΙ ΓΕ." Pages 21–40 in *Biblical Greek in Context: Essays in Honour of John A. L. Lee.* Edited by James K. Aitken and Trevor V. Evans. BTS 22. Leuven: Peeters.

———. 2016. "The Septuagint and Egyptian Translation Methods." Pages 269–93 in *XV Congress of the International Organization for Septuagint and Cognate Studies: Munich, 2013*. Edited by Wolfgang Kraus, Michaël N. van der Meer, and Martin Meiser. SCS 64. Atlanta: SBL Press.

Amit, Yairah. 1999. *The Book of Judges: The Art of Editing*. BibInt 38. Leiden: Brill.

Ash, Rhiannon. 2007. "Tacitus and the Battle of Mons Graupius: A Historiographical Route Map?" Pages 434–40 in *A Companion to Greek and Roman Historiography*. Edited by John Marincola. BCAW. Oxford: Blackwell.

Ausloos, Hans. 2014. "Literary Criticism and Textual Criticism in Judg 6:1–14 in Light of 4QJudg[a]." *OTE* 27:358–76.

———. 2016. "4.1 Textual History of Judges." Pages 277–80 in *Textual History of the Bible: Volume 1B, The Hebrew Bible, Pentateuch, Former and Latter Prophets*. Edited by Armin Lange and Emanuel Tov. Leiden: Brill.

Bagnall, Robert S., and Raffaella Cribiore. 2006. *Women's Letters from Ancient Egypt: 300 BC–AD 800*. Ann Arbor: University of Michigan Press.

Bagnall, Robert S., and Peter Derow, eds. 2004. *The Hellenistic Period: Historical Sources in Translation*. 2nd ed. BSAH. Oxford: Blackwell.

Barthélemy, Dominique. 1963. *Les Devanciers d'Aquila: Première publication intégrale du texte des fragments du Dodécaprophéton*. VTSup 10. Leiden: Brill.

Bauschatz, John. 2013. *Law and Enforcement in Ptolemaic Egypt*. Cambridge: Cambridge University Press.

Beekes, Robert S. P. 2010. *Etymological Dictionary of Greek*. 2 vols. IEED 10. Leiden: Brill.

Bentley, Richard. 1817. *A Dissertation upon the Epistles of Phalaris: With an Answer to the Objections of the Hon. C. Boyle*. London: Auld.

Biber, Douglas, and Susan Conrad. 2009. *Register, Genre and Style*. CTL. Cambridge: Cambridge University Press.

Bickerman, Elias J. 1959. "The Septuagint as a Translation." *PAAJR* 28:1–39.

Biddle, John. 1653. *Ἡ Παλαια Διαθηκη κατα τους Εβδομηκοντα: Vetus Testamentum Græcum, ex versione Septuaginta interpretum*. 4 vols. London: Daniel.

Biel, Johann Christian. 1779–1780. *Novus Thesaurus Philologicus; Sive, Lexicon in LXX. et alios Interpretes et Scriptores Apocryphos Veteris Testamenti; Ex B. autoris MScto edidit ac præfatus est E. H. Mutzenbecher*. 3 vols. The Hague: Bouvink.

Bieżuńska-Małowist, Iza. 1974. *L'esclavage dans l'Egypte gréco-romaine: Vol. 1, Période Ptolémaïque*. Translated by Jerzy Wolf and Janina Kasińska. Archiwum Filologiczne 30. Wrocław: Polska Akademia Nauk.

———. 1985. "L'esclavage dans l'Egypte gréco-romaine: Quelques observations en marge de publications récentes." *BASP* 22:7–14.

Billen, A. V. 1942. "The Hexaplaric Element in the LXX Version of Judges." *JTS* 43:12–19.

Bindseil, Heinrich Ernst. 1867. *Concordantiarum Homericarum specimen cum prolegomenis in quibus praesertim concordantiae biblicae recensentur earumque origo et progressus declarantur* Halle: Hendelius.

Black, Matthew. 1965. "Second Thoughts, IX: The Semitic Element in the New Testament." *ExpTim* 77:20–23.

———. 1970. "The Biblical Languages." Pages 1–11 in *From the Beginnings to Jerome*. Vol. 1 of *The Cambridge History of the Bible*. Edited by Peter R. Ackroyd and C. F. Evans. Cambridge: Cambridge University Press.

Blair, Ann M. 2010. *Too Much to Know: Managing Scholarly Information before the Modern Age*. New Haven: Yale University Press.

Block, Daniel I. 1999. *Judges, Ruth*. NAC. Nashville: Broadman & Holman.

Böckel, Ernst G. A. 1820. *Novæ Clavis in Græcos Interpretes Veteris Testamenti, Scriptoresque Apocryphos, ita adornatæ ut etiam Lexici in Novi Fœderis Libros usum præbere possit, atque Editionis LXX: Interpretum Hexaplaris, Specimina*. Leipzig: Vogel.

Bodine, Walter R. 1980. *The Greek Text of Judges: Recensional Developments*. HSM 23. Chico, CA: Scholars Press.

Boling, Robert G. 1975. *Judges: Introduction, Translation and Commentary*. AB 6A. Garden City, NY: Doubleday.

Bons, Eberhard, Ralph Brucker, and Jan Joosten, eds. 2014. *The Reception of Septuagint Words in Jewish-Hellenistic and Christian Literature*. WUNT 2/367. Tübingen: Mohr Siebeck.

Bons, Eberhard, Jan Joosten, and Regine Hunzkier-Rodewald, eds. 2015. *Biblical Lexicology: Hebrew and Greek; Semantics—Exegesis—Translation*. BZAW 443. Berlin: de Gruyter.

Bortone, Pietro. 2010. *Greek Prepositions: From Antiquity to the Present*. Oxford: Oxford University Press.

Bouchon, Richard 2011. "Réelles présences? Approche matérielle et symbolique des relations entre la Grèce balkanique et les officiels romains, de Mummius Achaïcus à Antoine." Pages 53–74 in *Les gouverneurs et les provinciaux sous la République romaine*. Edited by Nathalie Barrandon and François Kirbihler. Rennes: Presses universitaires de Rennes.

Bowersock, G. W. 1985. "Between Philosophy and Rhetoric: Plutarch." Pages 665–72 in *The Cambridge History of Classical Literature*. Edited by P. E. Easterling and B. M. W. Knox. Cambridge: Cambridge University Press.

Bowman, Alan K., R. A. Coles, N. Gonis, Dirk D. Obbink, and P. J. Parsons, eds. 2007. *Oxyrhynchus: A City and Its Texts*. Graeco-Roman Memoirs 93. London: Egypt Exploration Society.

Boyd-Taylor, Cameron. 2001. "The Evidentiary Value of Septuagintal Usage for Greek Lexicography: Alice's Reply to Humpty Dumpty." *BIOSCS* 34:47–80.

———. 2004a. "Lexicography and Interlanguage: Gaining Our Bearings." *BIOSCS* 37:55–72.

———. 2004b. "Linguistic Register and Septuagintal Lexicography." Pages 149–66 in *Biblical Greek Language and Lexicography: Essays in Honor of Frederick W. Danker*. Edited by Bernard A. Taylor, John A. L. Lee, Peter R. Burton, and Richard E. Whitaker. Grand Rapids: Eerdmans.

———. 2005. "Calque-culations—Loanwords and the Lexicon." *BIOSCS* 38:79–99.

———. 2008. "Who's Afraid of *Verlegenheitsübersetzungen*?" Pages 197–210 in *Translating a Translation: The LXX and Its Modern Translations in the Context of Early Judaism*. Edited by Hans Ausloos, Johann Cook, Florentino García Martínez, Bénédicte Lemmelijn, and Marc Vervenne. BETL 213. Leuven: Peeters.

———. 2011. *Reading between the Lines: The Interlinear Paradigm for Septuagint Studies*. BTS 8. Leuven: Peeters.

Boytsov, Mikhail A. 2015. "The Healing Touch of a Sacred King? Convicts Surrounding a Prince in *adventus* Ceremonies in the Holy Roman Empire during the Fourteenth to Sixteenth Centuries." *German History* 33:177–93.

Bresson, Alain. 1999. "Rhodes and Lycia in Hellenistic Times." Pages 98–131 in *Hellenistic Rhodes: Politics, Culture, and Society*. Edited by Vincent Gabrielsen, Per Bilde, Troels Egngberg-Pedersen, Lise Hannestad, and Jan Zahle. Studies in Hellenistic Civilizations 9. Aarhus: Aarhus University Press.

Bretschneider, Karl Gottlieb. 1805. *Lexici in Interpretes Græcos V. T. maxime scriptores Apocryphos Spicilegia: Post Bielium et Schleusnerum congessit et edidit C. G. Bretschneder.* 8 vols. Leipzig: Sumptibus Lebrecht Crusii.

Brinton, Laurel J., and Elizabeth Closs Traugott. 2005. *Lexicalization and Language Change*. Research Surveys in Linguistics. Cambridge: Cambridge University Press.

Brock, Sebastian P., and John A. L. Lee. 1972. "A Memorandum on the Proposed LXX Lexicon Project." Pages 20–24 in *Septuagintal Lexicography*. Edited by Robert A. Kraft. SCS 1. Missoula, MT: Society of Biblical Literature.

Brooke, Alan E., and Norman McLean. 1897. *The Book of Judges in Greek according to the Text of Codex Alexandrinus*. Cambridge: Cambridge University Press.

———, eds. 1906. *The Old Testament in Greek according to the Text of Codex Vaticanus, Supplemented from Other Uncial Manuscripts, with a Critical Apparatus Containing the Variants of the Chief Ancient Authorities for the Text of the Septuagint: Vol. 1.1 Genesis*. Cambridge: Cambridge University Press.

———, eds. 1917. *The Old Testament in Greek according to the Text of Codex Vaticanus, Supplemented from Other Uncial Manuscripts, with a Critical Apparatus Containing the Variants of the Chief Ancient Authorities for the Text of the Septuagint: Vol. 1 The Octateuch*. Cambridge: Cambridge University Press.

Brylinger, Nikolaus. 1550. *Biblia Graeca et Latina*. 5 vols. Basel: Brylinger.

Bubenik, Vit. 2014. "Koine, Origins of." *EAGLL* 2:277–85.

Büchner, Dirk. 2004. Review of *A Greek-English Lexicon of the Septuagint, Revised Edition*, by Johan Lust, Erik Eynikel, and Katrin Hauspie. *BIOSCS* 37:139–47.

Burney, C. F. 1970. *The Book of Judges with Introduction and Notes*. New York: Ktav.

Bybee, Joan L. 2015. *Language Change*. CTL. Cambridge: Cambridge University Press.

Caird, G. B. 1968. "Towards a Lexicon of the Septuagint, I." *JTS* 19:453–75.

———. 1969. "Towards a Lexicon of the Septuagint, II." *JTS* 20:21–40.

Cañas Reíllo, José Manuel. 2016. "El papiro de Florencia, Bibl. Laur. PSI II 127 (Rahlfs 968): Su lugar en la historia textual del libro griego de Jueces y su relación con las versiones coptas." Pages 43–57 in Τί ἡμῖν καὶ σοί: *Lo que hay entre tú y nosotros; Estudios en honor de María Victoria Spottorno*. Cordoba: UCOPress.

———. 2020a. "Manuscripts and Recensions in LXX-Judges." Pages 544–60 in *Die Septuaginta—Themen, Manuskripte, Wirkungen: 7. Internationale Fachtagung von Septuaginta Deutsch (LXX.D), Wuppertal 19.–22. Juli 2018*. Edited by Eberhard Bons, Michaela Geiger, Frank Ueberschaer, Marcus Sigismund, and Martin Meiser. WUNT 444. Tübingen, Mohr Siebeck.

———. 2020b. "Recensions, Textual Groups, and Vocabulary Differentiation in LXX-Judges," Pages 175–188 in *The Legacy of Soisalon-Soininen: Towards a Syntax of Septuagint Greek*. Edited by Tuukka Kauhanen and Hanna Vanonen. DSI 13. Göttingen: Vandenhoeck & Ruprecht.

Cantarella, Eva. 1990. "*Neaniskoi*: Classi di età e passaggi di 'status' nel diritto ateniese." *Mélanges de l'Ecole française de Rome. Antiquité* 102:37–51.

Caragounis, Chrys C. 2014. "Atticism." *EAGLL* 1:196–203.

Casey, Eric. 2013. "Educating the Youth: The Athenian *Ephebeia* in the Early Hellenistic Era." Pages 418–443 in *The Oxford Handbook of Childhood and Education in the Classical World*. Edited by Judith Evans Grubbs, Tim Parkin, and Roslynne Bell. Oxford: Oxford University Press.

Chalmers, Alexander, ed. 1815. *The General Biographical Dictionary: Containing an Historical and Critical Account of the Lives and Writings of the Most Eminent Persons in Every Nation; Particularly the British and Irish; From the Earliest Accounts to the Present Time. A New Edition, Revised and Enlarged*. Vol. 19 (Jep.–Lan.). London: Nichols.

Chamberlain, Gary A. 2011. *The Greek of the Septuagint: A Supplemental Lexicon*. Peabody, MA: Hendrickson.

Chaniotis, Angelos. 2006. "The Divinity of Hellenistic Rulers." Pages 431–45 in *A Companion to the Hellenistic World*. Edited by Andrew Erskine. BCAW. Oxford: Blackwell.

———. 2007. "Policing the Hellenistic Countryside: Realities and Ideologies." Pages 103–53 in Sécurité collective et ordre public dans les sociétés anciennes: *Sept exposés suivis de discussions*. Edited by Cédric Brélaz and Pierre Ducrey. Geneva: Hardt.

Chankowski, Andrzej S. 2005. "Processions et cérémonies d'accueil: Une image de la cité de la basse époque hellénistique?" Pages 185–206 in *Citoyenneté et participation à la basse époque hellénistique*. Edited by Pierre Fröhlich and Christel Müller. Geneva: Droz.

———. 2011. *L'éphébie hellénistique: Étude d'une institution civique dans les cités grecques des îles de la Mer Égée et de l'Asie Mineure*. Culture et cité 4. Paris: de Boccard.

———. 2013. "Age-class (ephebes, neoi)." Pages 178–80 in *The Encyclopedia of Ancient History*. Edited by Roger S. Bagnall, Kai Brodersen, Craige B. Champion, Andrew Erskine, and Sabine R. Huebner. 12 vols. Oxford: Blackwell.

Christidis, A.-F., ed. 2015a. *A History of Ancient Greek: From the Beginnings to Late Antiquity*. 2 vols. Cambridge: Cambridge University Press.

———. 2015b. "Introduction." Pages 1221–24 in *A History of Ancient Greek: From the Beginnings to Late Antiquity*. Edited by A.-F. Christidis. 2 vols. Cambridge: Cambridge University Press.

Collatz, Christian-Friedrich, Melsene Gützlaf, and Hadwig Helms, eds. 2002. *Polybios-Lexikon, Vol. 3.1: ῥάβδος–τόκος*. Berlin: Akademie.

Colvin, Stephen. 2009. "The Greek *Koine* and the Logic of a Standard Language." Pages 33–45 in *Standard Languages and Language Standards: Greek, Past and Present*. Edited by Alexandra Georgakopoulou and Michael Silk. Farnham: Ashgate.

Considine, John. 2015. "Cutting and Pasting Slips: Early Modern Compilation and Information Management." *Journal of Medieval and Early Modern Studies* 45:487–504.

Conybeare, F. C., and St. George Stock. 1995. *Grammar of Septuagint Greek with Selected Readings, Vocabularies, and Updated Indexes*. Boston: Ginn & Company, 1905. Repr. Peabody, MA: Hendrickson.

Cooper, Charles M. 1941. "Studies in the Greek Text of the Book of Judges: I. The Synonyms of the Alexandrian and Vatican Codices." PhD diss., Dropsie University.

Cosby, Michael R. 1994. "Hellenistic Formal Receptions and Paul's Use of ΑΠΑΝΤΗΣΙΣ in 1 Thess 4:17." *BBR* 4:15–34.

Craster, H. H. E., and Falconer Madan. 1922. *A Summary Catalogue of Western Manuscripts in the Bodleian Library at Oxford, Which Have Not Hitherto Been Catalogued in the Quarto Series: With References to the Oriental and Other Manuscripts; Vol. 2, Part 1; Collections Received before 1660 and Miscellaneous MSS. Acquired during the First Half of the 17th Century; Nos. 1–3490*. Oxford: Clarendon.

Crawford, Dorothy J. 1971. *Kerkeosiris: An Egyptian Village in the Ptolemaic Period*. CCS. Cambridge: Cambridge University Press.

Croft, William. 2000. *Explaining Language Change: An Evolutionary Approach*. LLL. Harlow: Pearson Longman.

Croft, William, and D. A. Cruse. 2004. *Cognitive Linguistics.* CTL. Cambridge: Cambridge University Press.

Cruse, D. A. 2011. *Meaning in Language: An Introduction to Semantics and Pragmatics.* Oxford Textbooks in Linguistics. Oxford: Oxford University Press.

Cuvigny, Hélène. 2009. "The Finds of the Papyri: The Archaeology of Papyrology." Pages 30–58 in *The Oxford Handbook of Papyrology.* Edited by Roger S. Bagnall. Oxford: Oxford University Press.

D'Amore, Lucia. 2007a. "Ginnasio e difesa civica nelle *poleis* d'Asia minore (IV–I Sec. A.C.)." *REA* 109:147–73.

———. 2007b. "Il culto civico dei sovrani e degli evergeti nelle città ellenistiche d'Asia Minore: Il ruolo del ginnasio." Pages 339–46 in *XII Congressus internationalis epigraphiae Graecae et Latinae: Provinciae imperii Romani inscriptionibus descriptae; Barcelona, 3–8 septembris 2002.* Edited by Marc Mayer Olivé, Giulia Baratta, and Alejandra Guzmán Almagro. Barcelona: Universitat Autònoma de Barcelona.

Daniel, R. W. 1983. "The Military [σημεῖον] in P.Amh. II 39." *ZPE* 52:269–71.

Danker, Frederick W., Walter Bauer, William F. Arndt, and F. Wilbur Gingrich. 2000. *Greek-English Lexicon of the New Testament and Other Early Christian Literature.* 3rd ed. Chicago: University of Chicago Press.

Deissmann, Adolf. 1895. *Bibelstudien: Beiträge, zumeist aus den Papyri und Inschriften, zur Geschichte der Sprache, des Schrifttums und der Religion des hellenistischen Judentums und des Urchristentums.* Marburg: Elwert.

———. 1901. *Bible Studies: Contributions Chiefly from Papyri and Inscriptions to the History of the Language, the Literature, and the Religion of Hellenistic Judaism and Primitive Christianity.* Translated by Alexander Grieve. Edinburgh: T&T Clark.

———. 1907–1908. "The Philology of the Greek Bible: Its Present and Future." *The Expositor* 7:506–20.

———. 1908a. *New Light on the New Testament from Records of the Greco-Roman Period.* Translated by Lionel R. M. Strachan. Edinburgh: T&T Clark.

———. 1908b. *The Philology of the Greek Bible: Its Present and Future.* London: Hodder & Stoughton.

———. 1909a. *Licht vom Osten: Das Neue Testament und die neuendeckten Texte der hellenistische-römischen Welt.* Tübingen: Mohr.

―――. 1909b. "Hellenistic Greek." Pages 211–15 in vol. 5 of *The New Schaff-Herzog Encyclopedia of Religious Knowledge*. Edited by Samuel Macauley Jackson. 15 vols. Edinburgh: T&T Clark.

―――. 1910. *Light from the Ancient East: The New Testament Illustrated by Recently Discovered Texts of the Graeco-Roman World with Sixty-Eight Illustrations*. Translated by Lionel R. M. Strachan. London: Hodder & Stoughton.

―――. 1991. "Hellenistic Greek with Special Consideration of the Greek Bible." Pages 39–59 in *The Language of the New Testament: Classic Essays*. Edited by Stanley E. Porter. JSNTSup 60. Sheffield: Sheffield Academic.

Depauw, Mark, and Tom Gheldof. 2014. "Trismegistos: An Interdisciplinary Platform for Ancient World Texts and Related Information." Pages 40–52 in *Theory and Practice of Digital Libraries: TPDL 2013 Selected Workshops*. Edited by Łukasz Bolikowski, Vittore Casarosa, Paula Goodale, Nikos Houssos, Paolo Manghi, and Jochen Schirrwagen. Charm: Springer.

DesRosiers, Nathaniel P. 2016. "Suns, Snakes, and Altars: Competitive Imagery in Constantinian Numismatics." Pages 41–61 in *Religious Competition in the Greco-Roman World*. Edited by Nathaniel P. DesRosiers and Lily C. Vuong. WGRWSup 10. Atlanta: SBL Press.

Dhont, Marieke. 2018. *Style and Context of Old Greek Job*. JSJSup 183. Leiden: Brill.

Dickey, Eleanor. 2004. "Rules without Reasons? Words for Children in Papyrus Letters." Pages 119–30 in *Indo-European Perspectives: Studies in Honour of Anna Morpurgo Davies*. Edited by J. H. W. Penney. Oxford: Oxford University Press.

―――. 2007. *Ancient Greek Scholarship: A Guide to Finding, Reading, and Understanding Scholia, Commentaries, Lexica, and Grammatical Treatises, from Their Beginnings to the Byzantine Period*. Oxford: Oxford University Press.

―――. 2015. "The Sources of Our Knowledge of Ancient Scholarship." Pages 459–514 in *Brill's Companion to Ancient Greek Scholarship*. Edited by Franco Montanari, Stephanos Matthaios, and Antonios Rengakos. Leiden: Brill.

Diessel, H. 2015. "Usage-Based Construction Grammar." Pages 296–321 in *Handbook of Cognitive Linguistics*. Edited by Ewa Dąbrowska and Dagmar Divjak. HSK. Berlin: de Gruyter.

Diggle, James. 1981. *Euripidis Fabulae: Vol. 2, Supplices, Electra, Hercules, Troades, Iphigenia in Tauris, Ion.* OCT. Oxford: Oxford University Press.

———. 1984. *Euripidis Fabulae: Vol. 1, Cyclops, Alcestis, Medea, Hereclidae, Hippolytus, Andromacha, Hecuba.* OCT. Oxford: Oxford University Press.

Dines, Jennifer M. 2004. *The Septuagint.* Understanding the Bible and Its World. London: T&T Clark.

Dionisotti, Anna Carlotta. 1988. "Greek Grammars and Dictionaries in Carolingian Europe." Pages 1–56 in *The Sacred Nectar of the Greeks: The Study of Greek in the West in the Early Middle Ages.* Edited by Michael W. Herren and Shirley Ann Brown. King's College London Medieval Studies 2. London: King's College.

Doble, C. E., ed. 1889. *Remarks and Collections of Thomas Hearne: Vol. 3, May 25, 1710–December 14, 1712.* 11 vols. Oxford: Clarendon.

Dogniez, Cécile. 2016. "4.3 Septuagint." Pages 294–97 in *Textual History of the Bible: Volume 1B The Hebrew Bible, Pentateuch, Former and Latter Prophets.* Edited by Armin Lange and Emanuel Tov. Leiden: Brill.

Dorival, Gilles. 2015. "La lexicographie de la Septante entre Sem et Japhet." Pages 227–41 in *Biblical Lexicology: Hebrew and Greek; Semantics—Exegesis—Translation.* Edited by Romina Vergari, Eberhard Bons, Jan Joosten, and Regine Hunziker-Rodewald. BZAW 443. Berlin: de Gruyter.

———. 2016. "La lexicographie de la Septante." Pages 271–305 in *Die Sprache der Septuaginta/The Language of the Septuagint.* Vol. 3 of *Handbuch zur Septuaginta.* Edited by Eberhard Bons and Jan Joosten. Gütersloh: Gütersloher Verlagshaus.

Dorival, Gilles, Marguerite Harl, and Olivier Munnich. 1988. *La Bible Grecque des Septante: Du judaïsme hellénistique au christianisme ancient.* Initiations au Christianisme Ancien. Paris: Cerf.

Dreyer, Boris, and Peter Franz Mittag. 2011. *Lokale Eliten und hellenistische Könige: Zwischen Kooperation und Konfrontation.* Oikumene 8. Berlin: Antike.

Dunand, Françoise. 1981. "Fête et propagande à Alexandrie sous les Lagides." Pages 13–40 in *La fête, pratique et discours: D'Alexandrie hellénistique à la mission de Besançon.* Centre de recherches d'histoire ancienne 42. Annales littéraires de l'Université de Besançon 262. Paris: Les Belles Lettres.

Edgar, Campbell Cowan, ed. 1928. *Zenon Papyri*. Catalogue général des antiquités égyptiennes du Musée du Caire 3. Cairo: L'Institut français d'archéologie orientale.
Eng, Milton. 2011. *The Days of Our Years: A Lexical Semantic Study of the Life Cycle in Biblical Israel*. LHBOTS 464. New York: T&T Clark.
Erasmus, Desiderius. 1526. *Sacra Biblia ad LXX: Interpretum fidem diligentissime tralata*. Basel: Cratander.
Evans, Trevor V. 2001. *Verbal Syntax in the Greek Pentateuch: Natural Greek Usage and Hebrew Interference*. Oxford: Oxford University Press.
——. 2005. "Approaches to the Language of the Septuagint." *JJS* 56:25–33.
——. 2010. "The Potential of Linguistic Criteria for Dating Septuagint Books." *BIOSCS* 43:5–22.
Evans, Trevor V., and Dirk D. Obbink. 2010. "Introduction." Page 1–12 in *The Language of the Papyri*. Edited by Trevor V. Evans and Dirk D. Obbink. Oxford: Oxford University Press.
Evans, Vyvyan. 2007. *A Glossary of Cognitive Linguistics*. Edinburgh: Edinburgh University Press.
Evans, Vyvyan, and Melanie Green. 2006. *Cognitive Linguistics: An Introduction*. Edinburgh: Edinburgh University Press.
Ewing, Greville. 1827. *A Greek and English Lexicon: Originally a Scripture Lexicon; and Now Adapted to the Greek Classics*. 3rd ed. Glasgow: University Press.
Eynikel, Erik. 1999. "La lexicographie de la Septante: Aspects méthodologiques." *RSR* 73:135–50.
Fernández Marcos, Natalio. 2000. *The Septuagint in Context: Introduction to the Greek Version of the Bible*. Translated by Wilfred G. E. Watson. Leiden: Brill.
——. 2003. "The Hebrew and Greek Texts of Judges." Pages 1–16 in *The Earliest Text of the Hebrew Bible: The Relationship between the Masoretic Text and the Hebrew Base of the Septuagint Reconsidered*. Edited by Adrian Schenker. SCS 52. Atlanta: Society of Biblical Literature.
——. 2006. "The Genuine Text of Judges." Pages 33–45 in *Sôfer Mahîr: Essays in Honour of Adrian Schenker Offered by Editors of Biblia Hebraica Quinta*. Edited by Yohanan P. Goldman, Arie van der Kooij, and Richard D. Weis. VTSup 110. Leiden: Brill.
——. 2010. "Jephthah's Daughter in the Old Greek (Judges 11:29–40)." Pages 478–88 in *Die Septuaginta—Texte, Theologien, Einflüsse: 2. Internationale Fachtagung veranstaltet von Septuaginta Deutsch (LXX.D)*,

Wuppertal 23.–27.7.2008. Edited by Wolfgang Kraus and Martin Karrer. WUNT 252. Tübingen: Mohr Siebeck.

———. 2011. שפטים/*Judges*. BHQ 7. Stuttgart: Deutsche Bibelgesellschaft.

———. 2012. "The B-Text of Judges: *Kaige* Revision and Beyond." Pages 161–70 in *After Qumran: Old and Modern Editions of the Biblical Texts; The Historical Books*. Edited by Hans Ausloos, Bénédicte Lemmelijn, and Julio Trebolle Barrera. BETL 246. Leuven: Peeters.

———. 2014. "The Septuagint Reading of the Samson Cycle." Pages 87–99 in *Samson: Hero or Fool? The Many Faces of Samson*. Edited by Erik Eynikel and Tobias Nicklas. TBN 17. Leiden: Brill.

———. 2016a. "The First Polyglot Bible." Pages 3–18 in *The Text of the Hebrew Bible and Its Editions: Studies in Celebration of the Fifth Centennial of the Complutensian Polyglot*. Edited by Andrés Piquer Otero and Pablo Torijano Morales. Supplements to the Textual History of the Bible 1. Leiden: Brill.

———. 2016b. "Kritai/Iudices/Das Buch der Richter." Pages 188–98 in *Einleitung in die Septuaginta*. Vol. 1 of *Handbuch zur Septuaginta*. Edited by Siegfried Kreuzer. Gütersloh: Gütersloher Verlagshaus.

Fernández Marcos, Natalio, and María Victoria Spottorno Díaz-Caro, eds. 2011. *La Biblia Griega Septuaginta: Vol. 2 Libros Históricos*. Biblioteca de Estudios Bíblicos 128. Salamanca: Sígueme.

Fillmore, Charles J. 1982. "Frame Semantics." Pages 111–37 in *Linguistics in the Morning Calm: Selected Papers from SICOL-1981*. Seoul: Hanshin.

———. 1985. "Frames and the Semantics of Understanding." *Quaderni di Semantica* 6:222–54.

Finley, M. I. 1960. "The Servile Statuses of Ancient Greece." *Revue Internationale des droits de l'antiquite* 7:165–89.

———. 1964. "Between Slavery and Freedom." *Comparative Studies in Society and History* 6:233–49.

Fischer, Johann Friedrich. 1758. *Clavis reliquiarum versionum Graecarum V. T. Specimen*. Leipzig: Fritschia.

Flanders, Judith. 2020. *A Place for Everything: The Curious History of Alphabetical Order*. New York: Basic Books.

Flashar, Martin. 1912. "Exegetische Studien zum LXX-Psalter." *ZAW* 32:81–116, 161–89, 241–68.

Forbes, Clarence A. 1933. *Neoi: A Contribution to the Study of Greek Associations*. Philological Monographs 2. Middletown: American Philological Association.

———. 1955. "The Education and Training of Slaves in Antiquity." *TAPA* 86:321–60.
Fritsch, Charles T. 1969. "Organizational Meeting of IOSCS." *BIOSCS* 2:4–5.
———. 1970a. "The Future of Septuagint Studies: A Brief Survey." *BIOSCS* 3:4–8.
———. 1970b. "Minutes of IOSCS Meeting Wednesday, Nov. 19, 1969, Royal York Hotel, Toronto, Canada." *BIOSCS* 3:3.
———. 1971. "Minutes: Meeting on Monday, Oct. 26, 12:30 P.M. at the Hotel New Yorker." *BIOSCS* 4:5–6.
———. 1973. "IOSCS Meeting September 2–5, 1972 Century Plaza Hotel, Los Angeles." *BIOSCS* 6:3–7.
Gardiner, E. Norman. 1930. "A School in Ptolemaic Egypt." *ClR* 44:211–13.
Garland, Robert. 1990. *The Greek Way of Life: From Conception to Old Age*. London: Duckworth.
Gates, J. E. 1972. "A Note on Lexicographic Resources for Septuagint Studies." Pages 8–10 in *Septuagintal Lexicography*. Edited by Robert A. Kraft. SCS 1. Missoula, MT: Scholars Press.
Gauthier, Philippe, and Militiades B. Hatzopoulos. 1993. *La loi gymnasiarchique de Béroia*. Μελετήματα 16. Athens: de Boccard.
Geeraerts, Dirk. 2010. *Theories of Lexical Semantics*. Oxford Linguistics. Oxford: Oxford University Press.
———. 2015. "Lexical Semantics." Pages 273–95 in *Handbook of Cognitive Linguistics*. Edited by Ewa Dąbrowska and Dagmar Divjak. HSK 39. Berlin: de Gruyter.
Gehman, Henry S. 1951. "The Hebraic Character of Septuagint Greek." *VT* 1:81–90.
———. 1953. "Hebraisms of the Old Greek Version of Genesis." *VT* 3:141–48.
———. 1954. "Ἅγιος in the Septuagint, and Its Relation to the Hebrew Original." *VT* 4:337–48.
———. 1966. "Adventures in Septuagint Lexicography." *Text* 5:125–32.
———. 1974. "Peregrinations in Septuagint Lexicography." Pages 223–40 in *A Light unto My Path: Old Testament Studies in Honor of Jacob M. Myers*. Edited by Howard N. Bream, Ralph D. Heim, and Carey A. Moore. GTS 4. Philadelphia: Temple University Press.
Gentry, Peter J. 2016. "New Ultra-Literal Translation Techniques in Kaige-Theodotion and Aquila." Pages 202–20 in *Die Sprache der Septuaginta/ The Language of the Septuagint*. Vol. 3 of *Handbuch zur Septuaginta*.

Edited by Eberhard Bons and Jan Joosten. Gütersloh: Gütersloher Verlagshaus.

Gerber, Albrecht. 2010. *Deissmann the Philologist*. BZNW 171. Berlin: de Gruyter.

Gertz, Jan Christian, Angelika Berlejung, Konrad Schmid, and Markus Witte. 2012. *T&T Clark Handbook of the Old Testament: An Introduction to the Literature, Religion and History of the Old Testament*. London: T&T Clark.

Gesenius, Wilhelm. 1833. "On the Sources of Hebrew Philology and Lexicography." Translated by Edward Robinson. *Biblical Respository* 3:1–44.

Gibson, R. J., and Constantine R. Campbell. 2017. *Reading Biblical Greek: A Grammar for Students*. Grand Rapids: Zondervan.

Gilbert, John Thomas. 1886. "Boate, de Boot, Bootius, or Botius, Arnold (1600?–1653?)." Pages 283–84 in vol. 5 of *Dictionary of National Biography*. Edited by Leslie Stephen. 66 vols. New York: Macmillan.

Glare, P. G. W., and A. A. Thompson, eds. 1996. *Greek-English Lexicon: Revised Supplement*. Oxford: Clarendon.

Glassius, Salomon. 1623–1636. *Philologiae sacrae qua totius sacrosanctae Veteris et Novi Testamenti, scripturae, tum stylus et literatura, tum sensus et genuinae interpretationis ratio expenditur*. 5 vols. Jenna: Steinmann.

Glockmann, Günter, Hadwig Helms, Christian–Friedrick Collatz, Wolf–Peter Funk, Reinhard Schumacher, and Hannelore Weissenow, eds. 1998. *Polybios-Lexikon*. Vol. 2.1. Berlin: Akademie.

Golden, Mark. 1990. *Childhood in Classical Athens*. Ancient Society and History. Baltimore: Johns Hopkins University Press.

Goshen-Gottstein, M. H. 1976. "Hebrew Biblical Manuscripts: Their History and Their Place in the HUBP Edition." *Bib* 48:243–90.

Gosling, Frank A. 2000. "The Inaccessible Lexicon of J. F. Schleusner." *JNSL* 26.1:19–31.

Greenspoon, Leonard J. 1995. "The IOSCS at 25 Years." Pages 171–181 in *VIII Congress of the International Organization for Septuagint and Cognate Studies, Paris 1992*. Edited by Leonard Greenspoon and Olivier Munnich. SCS 41. Atlanta: Scholars Press.

Grenfell, Bernard P., and Arthur S. Hunt, eds. 1903. *The Oxyrhynchus Papyri Vol. 3: Edited with Translations and Notes*. Graeco-Roman Memoirs 5. London: Egypt Exploration Fund.

Grosse, Jacob. 1640. *Trias Propositionum Theologicarum: Graecum textum et stilum Novi Testamenti a barbaris criminationibus vindicantium, et sententiam criticorum Hellenismum propugnantium rectitudini istius nihil derogare, ostendentium*. Jenna: Wernerus.

Grün, Hugo. 1961. "Zacharias Rosenbach, 1595–1638." Pages 54–65 in vol. 6 of *Nassauische Lebensbilder*. Edited by Rudolf Vaupel, Fritz Adolf Schmidt and Karl Wolf. Nassau: Historische Kommission für Nassau.

Gundry, Robert H. 1996. "A Brief Note on 'Hellenistic Formal Receptions and Paul's Use of ΑΠΑΝΤΗΣΙΣ in 1 Thessalonians 4:17.'" *BBR* 6:39–41.

Gwynn, R. M. 1920. "Notes on the Vocabulary of Ecclesiastes in Greek." *Hermathena* 42:115–22.

Haensch, Rudolf. 2009. "L'entrée par la mer dans l'antiquité." Pages 91–99 in *Les entrées royales et impériales: Histoire, représentations et diffusion d'une cérémonie publique, de l'Orient ancien à Byzance*. Edited by Agnès Bérenger and Éric Perrin-Saminadayar. De l'archéologie à l'histoire. Paris: de Boccard.

Hall, Basil. 1963. "Biblical Scholarship: Editions and Commentaries." Pages 38–93 in *The West from the Reformation to the Present Day*. Vol. 3 of *The Cambridge History of the Bible*. Edited by S. L. Greenslade. Cambridge: Cambridge University Press.

Hamilton, Alistair. 2016. "In Search of the Most Perfect Text: The Early Modern Printed Polyglot Bibles from Alcalá (1510–1520) to Brian Walton (1654–1658)." Pages 138–56 in *From 1450 to 1750*. Vol. 3 of *The New Cambridge History of the Bible*. Edited by Euan Cameron. Cambridge: Cambridge University Press.

Hanson, Ann Ellis. 2015. "Papyri and Efforts by Adults in Egyptian Villages to Write Greek." Pages 10–29 in *Learning Latin and Greek from Antiquity to the Present*. Edited by Elizabeth P. Archibald, William Brockliss, and Jonathan Gnoza. YCS 37. Cambridge: Cambridge University Press.

Hanson, Victor David. 2000. "The Hoplite Battle as Ancient Greek Warfare: When, Where, and Why?" Pages 201–32 in *War and Violence in Ancient Greece*. Edited by Hans van Wees. London: Duckworth; Swansea: Classical Press of Wales.

Harl, Kenneth W. 1987. *Civic Coins and Civic Politics in the Roman East, A.D. 180–275*. Transformation of the Classical Heritage 12. Berkeley: University of California Press.

Harlé, Paul. 1995. "Flavius Josèphe et la Septante des Juges." Pages 129–32 in *Selon les Septante: Hommage à Marguerite Harl*. Edited by Gilles Dorival and Olivier Munnich. Paris Éditions du Cerf.

Harlé, Paul, and Thérèse Roqueplo. 1999. *La Bible d'Alexandrie: Les Juges; Traduction des textes grecs de la Septante, introduction et notes*. BA 7. Paris: Cerf.

Hatch, Edwin. 1889. *Essays in Biblical Greek*. Oxford: Clarendon.

Hatch, Edwin, and Henry A. Redpath. 1897. *A Concordance to the Septuagint and Other Greek Versions of the Old Testament*. 2 vols. Oxford: Clarendon.

———. 1906. *A Concordance to the Septuagint and Other Greek Versions of the Old Testament: Supplement*. Oxford: Clarendon.

Hauspie, Katrin. 2003. "The Contribution of Semantic Flexibility to Septuagint Greek Lexicography." Pages 219–38 in *The Bible through Metaphor and Translation: A Cognitive Semantic Perspective*. Edited by Kurt Feyaerts. RelDis 15. Bern: Lang.

Hays, Gregory. 2003. *Marcus Aurelius: Meditations, A New Translation with an Introduction*. London: Weidenfeld & Nicolson.

Heinen, Heinz. 1977. "Zur Sklaverei in der hellenistischen Welt (II)." *Ancient Society* 8:121–54.

———. 1983. "Zum militärischen Hilfspersonal in P. Med. inv. 69.65." Pages 129–42 in *Egypt and the Hellenistic World: Proceedings of the International Colloquium Leuven 24–26 May 1982*. Edited by Edmond van't Dack, Peter Van Dessel, and Wilfried van Gucht. StHell 27. Leuven: Katholieke Universiteit Leuven.

Helbing, Robert. 1907. *Grammatik der Septuaginta: Laut- und Wortlehre*. Göttingen: Vandenhoeck & Ruprecht.

———. 1928. *Die Kasussyntax der Verba bei den Septuaginta: Bin Beitrag zur Hebraismenfrage und zur Syntax der Κοινή*. Göttingen: Vandenhoeck & Ruprecht.

Hendel, Ronald, and Jan Joosten. 2018. *How Old Is the Hebrew Bible? A Linguistic, Textual, and Historical Study*. New Haven: Yale University Press.

Herren, Michael W. 2015. "Pelasgian Fountains: Learning Greek in the Early Middle Ages." Pages 65–82 in *Learning Latin and Greek from Antiquity to the Present*. Edited by Elizabeth P. Archibald, William Brockliss, and Jonathan Gnoza. YCS 37. Cambridge: Cambridge University Press.

Hess, Richard S. 1997. "The Dead Sea Scrolls and Higher Criticism of the Hebrew Bible: The Case of 4QJudg^a." Pages 122–28 in *The Scrolls and the Scriptures: Qumran Fifty Years After*. Edited by Stanley E. Porter and Craig A. Evans. JSPSup 26. Sheffield: Sheffield Academic.

Hilhorst, A. 1989. Review of *Septuaginta-Vokabular*, by Friedrich Rehkopf. *JSJ* 20:256–57.

Hill, David. 1967. *Greek Words and Hebrew Meanings: Studies in the Semantics of Soteriological Terms*. SNTSMS 5. Cambridge: Cambridge University Press.

Hobhouse, John Cam. 1813. *A Journey through Albania and Other Provinces of Turkey in Europe and Asia, to Constantinople during the Years 1809 and 1810*. 2nd ed. 2 vols. London: Cawthorn.

Hoffmann, Friedhelm, Martina Minas-Nerpel, and Sefan Pfeiffer. 2009. *Die dreisprachige Stele des C. Cornelius Gallus: Übersetzung und Kommentar*. APF.B 9. Berlin: de Gruyter.

Hollenberg, Johannes. 1876. *Der Charakter der alexandrinischen Uebersetzung des Buches Josua und ihr textkritischer Werth*. Moers: Eckner.

Holmes, Robert, and James Parsons. 1798. *Vetus Testamentum Græcum, cum variis Lectionibus*. Vol. 1. Oxford: Clarendon.

Hoogendyk, Isiaiah, David A. deSilva, Randall K. Tan, and Rick Brannan. 2012. *Lexham Analytical Lexicon to the Septuagint: H. B. Swete Edition*. Bellingham: Lexham Press.

Hopkins, Keith. 1978. *Conquerors and Slaves*. Vol. 1 of *Sociological Studies in Roman History*. CCS. Cambridge: Cambridge University Press.

Horne, Thomas Hartwell. 1825. *An Introduction to the Critical Study and Knowledge of the Holy Scriptures*. 4th ed. Philadelphia: Littell.

———. 1833. *A Compendious Introduction to the Study of the Bible: Being an Analysis of an Introduction to the Critical Study and Knowledge of the Holy Scriptures, in Four Volumes, by the Same Author*. 4th ed. London: Cadell.

———. 1836. *An Introduction to the Critical Study and Knowledge of the Holy Scriptures: New Edition from the Seventh London Edition Corrected and Enlarged*. 4th ed. Vol. 1. Philadelphia: Littell.

———. 1839. *A Manual of Biblical Bibliography; Comprising a Catalogue, Methodically Arranged, of the Principal Editions and Versions of the Holy Scriptures; Together with Notices of the Principal Philologers, Critics, and Interpreters of the Bible*. London: Cadell.

Horrocks, Geoffrey. 2014. *Greek: A History of the Language and Its Speakers*. 2nd ed. Oxford: Wiley Blackwell.

Horsley, Greg H. R. 1982. *NewDocs* 2.

———. 1984. "Divergent Views on the Nature of Greek of the Bible." *Bib* 65:393–403.

———. 1989. "The Fiction of 'Jewish Greek.'" *NewDocs* 5:5–40.

———. 2014. "'Christian' Greek." *EAGLL* 1:280–83.

Horsley, G. H. R., and John A. L. Lee. 1994. "A Preliminary Checklist of Abbreviations of Greek Epigraphic Volumes." *Epigraphica: Periodico Internazionale di Epigraphica* 56:129–69.

Howard, George. 1974. "News and Notes." *BIOSCS* 7:4–9.

Hunt, Arthur S., ed. 1934. *Select Papyri: Vol. 2, Public Documents*. LCL. Cambridge: Harvard University Press.

Jackson, Samuel Macauley, ed. 1952. *The New Schaff-Herzog Encyclopedia of Religious Knowledge*. Vol. 3. Grand Rapids: Baker.

Jacob, B. 1890. "Das Buch Esther bei den LXX." *ZAW* 10:241–98.

Jahn, Johann, Samuel H. Turner, and William Rollinson Whittingham. 1827. *An Introduction to the Old Testament: Translated from the Latin and German Works of John Jahn*. New York: Carvill.

Jannaris, Antonius N. 1897. *An Historical Greek Grammar Chiefly of the Attic Dialect as Written and Spoken from Classical Antiquity Down to the Present Time, Founded upon the Ancient Texts, Inscriptions, Papyri and Present Popular Greek*. London: Macmillan.

Janse, Mark. 2007. "The Greek of the New Testament." Pages 646–53 in *A History of Ancient Greek: From the Beginnings to Late Antiquity*. Edited by A.-F. Christidis. 2 vols. Cambridge: Cambridge University Press.

Jebb, John. 1828. *Sacred Literature: Comprising a Review of the Principles of Composition Laid Down by the Late Robert Lowth, D.D., Lord Bishop of London, in His Praelections, and Isaiah; And an Application of the Principles so Reviewed, to the Illustration of the New Testament; In a Series of Critical Observations on the Style and Structure of That Sacred Volume*. London: Cadell.

Jellicoe, Sidney. 1968. *The Septuagint and Modern Study*. Oxford: Clarendon.

———. 1969a. "Coordination Project for Septuagintal and Cognate Studies, Bulletin No. 1. June 1968." *BIOSCS* 2:12–16.

———. 1969b. "Septuagint Studies in the Current Century." *JBL* 88:191–99.

———. 1970. "Editorial." *BIOSCS* 3:2.

———. 1971a. "Abstracts of Papers Delivered at the IOSCS Meeting in New York, October 25, 1970." *BIOSCS* 4:7–10.

———. 1971b. "Editorial." *BIOSCS* 4:2–3.

———. 1972. "Uppsala Papers and Reports." *BIOSCS* 5:6–14.
Johnson, Mark. 1987. *The Body in the Mind: The Bodily Basis of Meaning, Imagination, and Reason*. Chicago: University of Chicago Press.
Jon, François du. 1597. Τῆς Θείας Γραφῆς, παλαιᾶς δηλαδὴ καὶ νέας, ἅπαντα: *Divinæ Scripturæ, nempe Veteris ac Novi Testamenti, omnia*. Frankfort: Wecheli Heredes.
Jones, D. R. 1963. "Appendix I: Aids to the Study of the Bible." Pages 520–35 in *The West from the Reformation to the Present Day*. Vol. 3 of *The Cambridge History of the Bible*. Edited by S. L. Greenslade. 3 vols. Cambridge: Cambridge University Press.
Joosten, Jan, and Eberhard Bons, eds. 2011. *Septuagint Vocabulary: Pre-History, Usage, Reception*. SCS 58. Atlanta: Society of Biblical Literature.
Jung, Joachim. 1640. *Sententiae doctiss. virorum, de Hellenistis et Hellenistica Dialecto*.
Jurafsky, Daniel. 1996. "Universal Tendencies in the Semantics of the Diminutive." *Language* 72:533–78.
Kahle, Paul E. 1959. *The Cairo Geniza*. 2nd ed. New York: Praeger.
Kamen, Deborah. 2013. *Status in Classical Athens*. Princeton: Princeton University Press.
Karrer, Martin. 2012. "The New Leaves of Sinaiticus Judges." Pages 600–617 in *Die Septuaginta—Entstehung, Sprache, Geschichte: 3. Internationale Fachtagung veranstaltet von Septuaginta Deutsch (LXX.D), Wuppertal 22.–25. Juli 2010*. Edited by Siegfried Kreuzer, Martin Meiser, and Marcus Sigismund. WUNT 286. Tübingen: Mohr Siebeck.
Katz, P. 1956. "Septuagintal Studies in the Mid-Century: Their Links with the Past and Their Present Tendencies." Pages 176–208 in *The Background of the New Testament and Its Eschatology: Studies in Honor of C. H. Dodd*. Edited by W. D. Davies and David Daube. Cambridge: Cambridge University Press.
Kazazis, J. N. 2007. "Atticism." Pages 1200–1217 in *A History of Ancient Greek: From the Beginnings to Late Antiquity*. Edited by A.-F. Christidis. 2 vols. Cambridge: Cambridge University Press.
Keenan, James G. 2009. "The History of the Discipline." Pages 59–78 in *The Oxford Handbook of Papyrology*. Edited by Roger S. Bagnall. Oxford: Oxford University Press.
Kennedy, H. A. A. 1895. *Sources of New Testament Greek, or the Influence of the Septuagint on the Vocabulary of the New Testament*. Edinburgh: T&T Clark.

Kennell, Nigel M. 2005. "New Light on 2 Maccabees 4:7–15." *JJS* 56:10–24.

———. 2006. *Ephebeia: A Register of Greek Cities with Citizen Training Systems in the Hellenistic and Roman Periods*. Nikephoros Beihefte: Beiträge zu Sport und Kultur im Altertum 12. Hildesheim: Weidmann.

———. 2013. "Who Were the *Neoi*?" Pages 217–32 in *Epigraphical Approaches to the Post-Classical Polis: Fourth Century BC to Second Century AD*. Edited by Paraskevi Martzavou and Nikolaos Papazarkadas. Oxford Studies in Ancient Documents. Oxford: Oxford University Press.

———. 2015. "The *Ephebeia* in the Hellenistic Period." Pages 172–83 in *A Companion to Ancient Education*. Edited by W. Martin Bloomer. BCAW. Oxford: Wiley Blackwell.

Kircher, Conrad. 1607. *Concordantiae Veteris Testamenti Graecae, Ebraeis Vocibus Respondentes πολύχρηστοι: Simul enim et Lexicon Ebraicolatinum, Ebraicograecum, Graecoebraicum; Genuinam vocabulorum significationem, ex Septuaginta duorum, ut vulgo volunt, interpretum (vel istis, pro tempore, deficientibus, ex Aquilae nonnunquam, vel Symmachi, vel Theodotionis) translatione petitam; Homonymiam ac synonymiam Graecam et Ebraeam: quin et Ebraismorum variorum explanationem Graecam; Graecismorum elocutionem Ebraeam; et sic διασάφησιν Veteris et Novi Testamenti, collatione linguarum utrobique facta, suavissima συμφωνία, lectoribus exhibent*. 2 vols. Frankfurt am Main: Marnium & heredes Aubrii.

Klauck, Hans-Josef. 2000. *The Religious Context of Early Christianity: A Guide to Graeco-Roman Religions*. Translated by Brian McNeil. SNTW. Edinburgh: T&T Clark.

Kloppenborg, John S. 2006. *The Tenants in the Vineyard: Ideology, Economics, and Agrarian Conflict in Jewish Palestine*. WUNT 195. Tübingen: Mohr Siebeck.

Kraft, Robert A. 1969–1970. "Jewish Greek Scriptures and Related Topics." *NTS* 16:384–96.

———. 1970–1971. "Jewish Greek Scriptures and Related Topics, II." *NTS* 17:488–90.

———. 1972a. "Approaches to Translation Greek Lexicography." Pages 30–39 in *Septuagintal Lexicography*. Edited by Robert A. Kraft. SCS 1. Missoula, MT: Scholars Press.

———. 1972b. "The Eisenbeis Experiment and Proposals." Pages 25–29 in *Septuagintal Lexicography*. Edited by Robert A. Kraft. Missoula: University of Montana.

———. 1972c. "Introduction and Reactions." Pages 15–19 in *Septuagintal Lexicography*. Edited by Robert A. Kraft. SCS 1. Missoula, MT: Scholars Press.

———. 1972d. "Prefatory Remarks to the Lexical 'Probes.'" Pages 157–78 in *Septuagintal Lexicography*. Edited by Robert A. Kraft. SCS 1. Missoula, MT: Scholars Press.

———, ed. 1972e. *Septuagintal Lexicography*. SCS 1. Missoula, MT: Scholars Press.

———. 1979. "Lexicon Project: Progress Report." *BIOSCS* 12:14–16.

Kraft, Robert A., and Emanuel Tov. 1981. "Computer Assisted Tools for Septuagint Studies." *BIOSCS* 14:22–40.

———. 1998. "Introductory Essay." HRCS xi–xix.

Kroeger, Paul R. 2018. *Analyzing Meaning: An Introduction to Semantics and Pragmatics*. Textsbooks in Language Sciences 5. Berlin: Language Science Press.

Lagarde, Paul A. de. 1863. *Anmerkungen zur griechischen Übersetzung der Proverbien*. Leipzig: Brockhaus.

———. 1891. *Septuaginta Studien*. Göttingen: Dieterich.

LaMontagne, Nathan. 2013. "The Song of Deborah (Judges 5): Meaning and Poetry in the Septuagint." PhD diss., Catholic University of America.

———. 2016. "Reconsidering the Relationship of A and B in LXX Judges." Pages 49–59 in *XV Congress of the International Organization for Septuagint and Cognate Studies (IOSCS), Munich, 2013*. Edited by Wolfgang Kraus, Michaël N van der Meer, and Martin Meise. SCS 64. Atlanta: Scholars Press.

———. 2019. *The Song of Deborah in the Septuagint*. FAT 2/110. Tübingen: Mohr Siebeck.

Landfester, Manfred, ed. 2009. *Brill's Dictionary of Greek and Latin Authors and Texts*. BNPSup 2. Leiden: Brill.

Langacker, Ronald W. 1991. *Concept, Image, and Symbol: The Cognitive Basis of Grammar*. CLR 1. Berlin: de Gruyter.

———. 2013. *Essentials of Cognitive Grammar*. Oxford: Oxford University Press.

Lange, Armin. 2016. "4.2.1 Ancient Manuscript Evidence." Pages 281–83 in *Textual History of the Bible Textual History of the Bible: Volume 1B The Hebrew Bible, Pentateuch, Former and Latter Prophets*. Edited by Armin Lange and Emanuel Tov. Leiden: Brill.

Lange, Nicholas de. 2007. "Jewish Greek." Pages 638–45 in *A History of Ancient Greek: From the Beginnings to Late Antiquity*. Edited by A.-F. Christidis. 2 vols. Cambridge: Cambridge University Press.

Lanier, Gregory R., and William A. Ross. 2019. *A Book-by-Book Guide to Septuagint Vocabulary*. Peabody, MA: Hendrickson.

Launey, Marcel. 1950. *Recherches sur les armées hellénistiques, Vol. 2*. Paris: de Boccard.

Lazenby, John F. 1996. "Pydna." Page 1281 in *The Oxford Classical Dictionary*. Edited by Simon Hornblower and Antony Spawforth. 3rd ed. Oxford: Oxford University Press.

Le Guen, Bridgette. 2006. "L'accueil d' Athéniôn, messager de Mithridate VI, par les artistes dionysiaques d'Athènes en 88 av. J.-C." Pages 333–63 in *Studi Ellenistici*. Edited by Biagio Virgilio. Vol. 19. Pisa: Giardini.

Le Long, Jacques. 1723. *Bibliotheca Sacra in binos syllabos distincta, quorum prior qui jam tertio auctior prodit, omnes sive textus sacri sive versionum ejusdem quavis lingua expressarum editiones; Nec non praestantiores MSS. codices, cum notis historicis & criticis exhibit; Posterior vero continet omnia eorum opera quovis idiomate conscripta, qui huc usque in sacram Scripturam quidpiam ediderunt simil collecta tum ordine auctorum alphabetico disposita; Tum serie scrorum librorum; Huic coronidis loco subjiciuntur grammaticae et lexica linguarum, praesertim orientalium, quae ad illustrandas sacras paginas aliquid adjumenti conferre possunt*. 2 vols. Paris: Montalant.

Lee, John A. L. 1969. "A Note on Septuagint Material in the Supplement to Liddell and Scott." *Glotta* 47:234–42.

———. 1983. *A Lexical Study of the Septuagint Version of the Pentateuch*, Septuagint and Cognate Studies. SCS 14. Chico, CA: Scholars Press.

———. 1990. "Συνίστημι: A Sample Lexical Entry." Pages 1–15 in *Melbourne Symposium on Septuagint Lexicography*. Edited by Takamitsu Muraoka. SCS 28. Atlanta: Scholars Press.

———. 2003a. *A History of New Testament Lexicography*. SBG 8. New York: Lang.

———. 2003b. "*A Lexical Study* Thirty Years on, with Observations on 'Order' Words in the LXX Pentateuch." Pages 513–24 in *Emanuel: Studies in Hebrew Bible, Septuagint, and Dead Sea Scrolls in Honor of Emanuel Tov*. Edited by Shalom M. Paul, Robert A. Kraft, Lawrence H. Schiffman, and Weston W. Fields. VTSup 94. Leiden: Brill.

Bibliography 245

———. 2004a. Review of *A Greek-English Lexicon of the Septuagint: Chiefly of the Pentateuch and the Twelve Prophets*, by Takamitsu Muraoka. *BIOSCS* 37:127–39.
———. 2004b. "The Present State of Lexicography of Ancient Greek." Pages 66–74 in *Biblical Greek Language and Lexicography: Essays in Honor of Frederick W. Danker*. Edited by Bernard A. Taylor, John A. L. Lee, Peter R. Burton, and Richard E. Whitaker. Grand Rapids: Eerdmans.
———. 2008. "A Lexicographical Database for Greek: Can It Be Far Off? The Case of *amphodon*." Pages 214–20 in *Die Septuaginta—Texte, Kontexte, Lebenswelten: Internationale Fachtagung veranstaltet von Septuaginta Deutsch (LXX.D), Wuppertal 20.–23. Juli 2006*. Edited by Martin Karrer and Wolfgang Kraus. WUNT 219. Tübingen: Mohr Siebeck.
———. 2010. "Releasing Liddell-Scott-Jones from Its Past." Pages 119–38 in *Classical Dictionaries: Past, Present and Future*. Edited by Christopher Stray. London: Duckworth.
———. 2016. "The Vocabulary of the Septuagint and Documentary Evidence." Pages 98–108 in *Die Sprache der Septuaginta/The Language of the Septuagint*. Vol. 3 of *Handbuch zur Septuaginta*. Edited by Eberhard Bons and Jan Joosten. Gütersloh: Gütersloher Verlagshaus.
———. 2018. *The Greek of the Pentateuch: Grinfield Lectures on the Septuagint 2011–2012*. Oxford: Oxford University Press.
———. 2020. "Back to the Question of Greek Idiom." Pages 13–25 in *The Legacy of Soisalon-Soininen: Towards a Syntax of Septuagint Greek*. Edited by Tuukka Kauhanen and Hanna Vanonen. DSI 13. Göttingen: Vandenhoeck & Ruprecht
Lee, John W. I. 2006. "Warfare in the Classical Age." Pages 480–508 in *A Companion to the Classical Greek World*. Edited by Konrad H. Kinzl. BCAW. Oxford: Blackwell.
Lee, K. H. 1997. *Euripides: Ion*. Warminster: Aris & Phillips.
Legras, Bernard. 1999. *Néotês, recherches sur les jeunes Grecs dans l'Égypte ptolémaïque et romaine*. Hautes études du monde gréco-romaine 26. Geneva: Droz.
Leinieks, Valdis. 1996. *The City of Dionysos: A Study of Euripides' Bakchai*. BzA 88. Leipzig: Teubner.
Lendon, J. E. 1999. "The Rhetoric of Combat: Greek Military Theory and Roman Culture in Julius Caesar's Battle Descriptions." *ClAnt* 18:273–329.
Lesquier, Jean. 1911. *Les institutions militaires de l'Égypte sous les Lagides*. Paris: Leroux.

———. 1919. "Le papyrus 7 de Fribourg." *REG* 32.146–150:359–75.
Lewis, Naphtali. 2001. *Greeks in Ptolemaic Egypt: Case Studies in the Social History of the Hellenistic World*. Classics in Papyrology 2. Oakville: American Society of Papyrologists.
Lewis, Sian. 2002. *The Athenian Woman: An Iconographic Handbook*. London: Routledge.
Liddell, Henry George, Robert Scott, and Henry Stuart Jones. 1940. *A Greek-English Lexicon: A New Edition*. 9th ed. 2 vols. Oxford: Oxford University Press.
Liliencron, Rochus von. 1875. "Biel, Johann Christian." Page 623 in vol. 2 of *Allgemeine Deutsche Biographie*. Leipzig: Duncker & Humblot.
Lindars, Barnabas. 1987. "A Commentary on the Greek Judges?" Pages 167–200 in *VI Congress of the International Organization for Septuagint and Cognate Studies. Jerusalem 1986*. Edited by Claude E. Cox. SCS 23. Atlanta: Scholars Press.
———. 1995. *Judges 1–5: A New Translation and Commentary*. Edited by A. D. H. Mayes. Edinburgh: T&T Clark.
Louw, J. P. 1991. "How Do Words Mean—If They Do?" *FNT* 6:125–142.
Luckensmeyer, David. 2009. *The Eschatology of First Thessalonians*. NTOA 71. Göttingen: Vandenhoeck & Ruprecht.
Ludlum, John H. 1957. "The Dual Greek Text of Judges in Codices A and B." PhD diss., Yale University.
Lust, Johan. 1990. "J. F. Schleusner and the Lexicon of the Septuagint." *ZAW* 102:256–62.
———. 1992. "Introduction." Pages i–xv in *A Greek-English Lexicon of the Septuagint*. Edited by Johan Lust, Erik Eynikel and Katrin Hauspie. Stuttgart: Deutsche Bibelgesellschaft.
———. 1993a. "Translation Greek and the Lexicography of the Septuagint." *JSOT* 18:109–20.
———. 1993b. "Two New Lexica of the Septuagint and Related Remarks." *JNSL* 19:95–105.
———. 2001. "Syntax and Translation Greek." *ETL* 77:395–401.
———. 2003. "Introduction." Pages xi–xxiv in *Greek-English Lexicon of the Septuagint*. Edited by Johan Lust, Erik Eynikel and Katrin Hauspie. Rev. ed. Stuttgart: Deutsche Bibelgesellschaft.
Lust, Johan, Erik Eynikel, and Katrin Hauspie. 1992. *A Greek-English Lexicon of the Septuagint*. Vol. 1. Stuttgart: Deutsche Bibelgesellschaft.
———. 1996. *A Greek-English Lexicon of the Septuagint*. Vol. 2. Stuttgart: Deutsch Bibelgesellschaft.

———. 2003. *A Greek-English Lexicon of the Septuagint*. Rev. ed. Stuttgart: Deutsche Bibelgesellschaft.

Mandelbrote, Scott. 2016. "The Old Testament and Its Ancient Versions in Manuscript and Print in the West, from c. 1480 to c. 1780." Pages 82–109 in *From 1450–1750*. Vol. 3 of *The New Cambridge History of the Bible*. Edited by Euan Cameron. Cambridge: Cambridge University Press.

Mangenot, Eugène. 1912. "Concordances de la Bible." Cols. 891b–905a in vol. 2 of *Dictionnaire de la Bible*. Edited by Fulcran Vigouroux. 5 vols. Paris: Letouzey et Ané.

Mant, Richard. 1840. *History of the Church of Ireland, from the Revolution to the Union of the Churches of England and Ireland, January 1, 1801; With a Catalogue of the Archbishops and Bishops, Continued to November, 1840; And a Notice of the Alterations Made in the Hierarchy by the Act of 3 and 4 William IV., Chap. 37*. London: Parker.

Marquis, Galen. 1991. "CATSS-Base: Computer Assisted Tools for Septuagint and Bible Study for All—Transcript of a Demonstration." Pages 165–203 in *VII Congress of the International Organization for Septuagint and Cognate Studies, Leuven, 1989*. Edited by Claude E. Cox. SCS 41. Atlanta: Scholars Press.

Matisoff, James A. 1991. "The Mother of All Morphemes: Augmentatives and Diminutives in Areal and Universal Perspective." Pages 293–349 in *Papers from the First Annual Meeting of the Southeast Asian Linguistics Society*. Edited by Martha Ratliff and Eric Schiller. Tempe: Arizona State University, Program for Southeast Asian Studies.

Matthaios, Stephanos. 2015. "Greek Scholarship in the Imperial Era and Late Antiquity." Pages 184–296 in *Brill's Companion to Ancient Greek Scholarship*. Edited by Franco Montanari, Stephanos Matthaios, and Antonios Rengakos. 2 vols. Leiden: Brill.

Mauersberger, Arno. 1998. *Polybios-Lexikon 2.1: Pankratiastēs–Poieō*. Edited by Günter Glockmann and Hadwig Helms. Berlin: Akademie.

Mauersberger, Arno, Christian-Friedrich Collatz, Melsene Gützlaf, Hadwig Helms, Günter Glockmann, Wolf-Peter Funk, Reinhard Schumacher, Hannelore Weissenow, H. Labuske, B. Schulz, and W. Schwickardi, eds. 1998–2006. *Polybios-Lexikon*. 2nd ed. 3 vols. Berlin: Akademie.

Mauersberger, Arno, Christian-Friedrich Collatz, Hadwig Helms, and Melsene Schäfer, eds. 2000. *Polybios-Lexikon 1.1: Alpha–Gamma*. 2nd ed. Berlin: Akademie.

Mauersberger, Arno, and Hadwig Helms, eds. 2006. *Polybios-Lexikon 1.4: Lambda–Omicron*. 2nd ed. Berlin: Akademie.

Mayser, Edwin. 1970. *Grammatik der Griechischen Papyri Aus der Ptolemäerzeit: Mit Einschluss der Gleichzeitigen Ostraka und der in Ägypten Verfassten Inschriften; Vol. 1 Laut- und Wortlehre, III: Stammbildung*. 2d ed. Berlin: de Gruyter.

McDougall, J. Iain, ed. 1983a. *Lexicon in Diodorum Siculum: Vol. 1: A–K*. Lexika, Indizes, Konkordanzen zur Klassischen Philologie. Hildesheim: Olms.

———, ed. 1983b. *Lexicon in Diodorum Siculum: Vol. 2: Λ–Ω*. Lexika, Indizes, Konkordanzen zur Klassischen Philologie. Hildesheim: Olms.

———, ed. 1983c. *Lexicon in Diodorum Siculum*. 2 vols. Lexika, Indizes, Konkordanzen zur Klassischen Philologie. Hildesheim: Olms.

McKnight, Edgar V. 1965. "Is the New Testament Written in 'Holy Ghost' Greek?" *BT* 16:87–93.

McLean, B. H. 2002. *An Introduction to Greek Epigraphy of the Hellenistic and Roman Periods from Alexander the Great Down to the Reign of Constantine (323 B.C.–A.D. 337)*. Ann Arbor: University of Michigan Press.

Meer, Michaël N. van der. 2006. "Provenance, Profile, and Purpose of the Greek Joshua." Pages 55–80 in *XII Congress of the International Organization for Septuagint and Cognate Studies, Leiden, 2004*. Edited by Melvin K. Peters. SCS 54. Atlanta: Society of Biblical Literature.

———. 2011. "Problems and Perspectives in Septuagint Lexicography: The Case of Non-Compliance (ἀπειθέω)." Pages 65–86 in in *Septuagint Vocabulary: Pre-History, Usage, Reception*. Edited by Jan Joosten and Eberhard Bons. SCS 58. Atlanta: Society of Biblical Literature.

Montalvo, David E. 1977. "The Texts of A and B in the Book of Judges." PhD diss., Dropsie University.

Montana, Fausto. 2015. "Hellenistic Scholarship." Pages 60–183 in *Brill's Companion to Ancient Greek Scholarship*. Edited by Franco Montanari, Stephanos Matthaios, and Antonios Rengakos. Leiden: Brill.

Montanari, Franco, Stephanos Matthaios, and Antonios Rengakos, eds. 2015. *Brill's Companion to Ancient Greek Scholarship*. 2 vols. Leiden: Brill.

Montfaucon, Bernard de. 1714. *Hexaplorum Origenis quae supersunt multis partibus auctoria, quam a Flaminio Nobilio et Joanne Drusio edita fuerint; Ex manuscriptis et ex libris editis eruit et notis illustravit D. Bernardus de Montfaucon, Monachus Benedictinus e congrega-*

tione S. Mauri; Accedunt opuscula quædam Origenis Anecdota, et ad calcem Lexicon Hebaïcum ex Veterum Interpretationibus concinnatum, itemque Lexicon Græcum et alia, quæ præmissus initio laterculus indicabit. 2 vols. Paris: Ludovicum Guerin.

Montserrat, Dominic. 1996. *Sex and Society in Graeco-Roman Egypt.* London: Routledge.

Moore, George F. 1895. *A Critical and Exegetical Commentary on Judges.* ICC. Edinburgh: T&T Clark.

———. 1912. "The Antiochian Recension of the Septuagint." *AJSL* 29:37–62.

Motta, Daniela. 2010. "Gli onori civici ai comandanti: Il caso di Ilio tra guerre piratiche e mitridatiche." ὅρμος: *Ricerche di Storia Antica* NS 2:114–27.

Moulton, James Hope. 1901. "Deissmann's 'Bible Studies.'" *ET* 12:362–63.

———. 1908. *A Grammar of New Testament Greek: 1, Prolegomena.* 3rd ed. Edinburgh: T&T Clark.

———. 1909. "New Testament Greek in the Light of Modern Discovery." Pages 461–505 in *Cambridge Biblical Essays: Essays on Some Biblical Questions of the Day.* Edited by Henry Barclay Swete. London: Macmillan.

———. 1916. *From Egyptian Rubbish-Heaps: Five Popular Lectures on the New Testament.* London: Kelly.

Mulroney, James A. E. 2016. *The Translation Style of Old Greek Habakkuk.* FAT 2/86. Tübingen: Mohr Siebeck.

Muraoka, Takamitsu. 1984. "On Septuagint Lexicography and Patristics." *JTS* 35:441–48.

———. 1987. "Towards a Septuagint Lexicon." Pages 255–76 in *VI Congress of the International Organization for Septuagint and Cognate Studies, Jerusalem 1986.* Edited by Claude E. Cox. SCS 23. Atlanta: Scholars Press.

———. 1990a. "Introduction by the Editor." Pages vii–xiv in *Melbourne Symposium on Septuagint Lexicography.* Edited by Takamitsu Muraoka. SCS 28. Atlanta: Scholars Press.

———, ed. 1990b. *Melbourne Symposium on Septuagint Lexicography.* Edited by Takamitsu Muraoka. SCS 28. Atlanta: Scholars Press.

———. 1990c. "Septugintal Lexicography: Some General Issues." Pages 17–47 in *Melbourne Symposium on Septuagint Lexicography.* Edited by Takamitsu Muraoka. SCS 28. Atlanta: Scholars Press.

———. 1993a. *A Greek-English Lexicon of the Septuagint: (Twelve Prophets)*. Leuven: Peeters.

———. 1993b. "Introduction." Pages vii–xvi in *A Greek-English Lexicon of the Septuagint: (Twelve Prophets)*. Leuven: Peeters.

———. 1995. "The Semantics of the LXX and Its Role in Clarifying Ancient Hebrew Semantics." Pages 19–32 in *Studies in Ancient Hebrew Semantics*. Edited by Takamitsu Muraoka. AbrNSup 4. Leuven: Peeters.

———. 2002. "Introduction." Pages vii–xviii in *A Greek-English Lexicon of the Septuagint: Chiefly of the Pentateuch and the Twelve Prophets*. Leuven: Peeters.

———. 2004. "Septuagintal Lexicography." Pages 85–90 in *Biblical Greek Language and Lexicography: Essays in Honor of Frederick W. Danker*. Edited by Bernard A. Taylor, John A. L. Lee, Peter R. Burton, and Richard E. Whitaker. Grand Rapids: Eerdmans.

———. 2005. "Gleanings of a Septuagint Lexicographer." *BIOSCS* 38:101–8.

———. 2008. "Recent Discussions on the Septuagint Lexicography with Special Reference to the So-called Interlinear Model." Pages 221–35 in *Die Septuaginta—Texte, Kontexte, Lebenswelten: Internationale Fachtagung veranstaltet von Septuaginta Deutsch (LXX.D), Wuppertal 20.–23. Juli 2006*. Edited by Martin Karrer and Wolfgang Kraus. WUNT 219. Tübingen: Mohr Siebeck.

———. 2009. "Introduction." Pages vii–xvii in *A Greek-English Lexicon of the Septuagint*. Leuven: Peeters.

———. 2016. *A Syntax of Septuagint Greek*. Leuven: Peeters.

Murphy, Kelly J. 2017. "Judges in Recent Research." *CurBR* 15:179–213.

Nebrissensis, Ælius Antonius, Demetrius Ducas, Ferdinandus Pincianus, Lopez de Stunica, Alfonsus de Zamora, Paulus Coronellus, and Johannes de Vergera. 1514–1517. *Biblia Sacra Polyglotta, complectentia Vetus Testamentum, Hebraico, Græco, et Latino Idiomate; Novum Testamentum Græcum et Latinum; Et Vocabularium Hebraicum et Chaldaicum Veteris Testamenti, cum Grammaticâ Hebraicâ, nec non Dictionario Græco; Studio, Opera, et Impensis Cardinalis Francisci Ximenes de Cisneros; Industria Arnaldi Gulielmi de Brocario artis impressorie magistri*. 6 vols. Madrid: Complutum/Alcalá de Henares.

Novokhatko, Anna. 2015. "Greek Scholarship from Its Beginnings to Alexandria." Pages 3–59 in *Brill's Companion to Ancient Greek Scholarship*. Edited by Franco Montanari, Stephanos Matthaios, and Antonios Rengakos. Leiden: Brill.

O'Connell, Robert H. 1996. *The Rhetoric of the Book of Judges*. VTSup 63. Leiden: Brill.

Oates, John F., Roger S. Bagnall, Sarah J. Clackson, Alexandra A. O'Brien, Joshua D. Sosin, Terry G. Wilfong, and Klaas A. Worp. 2001. *Checklist of Editions of Greek, Latin, Demotic and Coptic Papyri, Ostraca and Tablets*. 5th ed. BASPSup 9. Oxford: Oxbow.

Olearius, Gottfried. 1713. *Observationes sacrae ad Evangelium Matthae*. Leipzig: Georg.

Oliver, G. J. 2011. "Mobility, Society, and Economy in the Hellenistic Period." Pages 345-67 in *The Economies of Hellenistic Societies, Third to First Centuries BC*. Edited by Zosia H. Archibald, John K. Davies, and Vincent Gabrielsen. Oxford: Oxford University Press.

Ottley, Richard R. 1920. *A Handbook to the Septuagint*. London: Methuen.

Pagani, L. 2015. "Language Correctness (Hellenismos) and Its Criteria." Pages 798-849 in *Brill's Companion to Ancient Greek Scholarship*. Edited by Franco Montanari, Stephanos Matthaios, and Antonios Rengakos. Leiden: Brill.

Pagninus, Samte. 1529. אוצר לשון הקדש: *Hoc est, Thesaurus linguae sanctae; Sic enim inscribere placuit lexicon hoc hebraicum; Quod quem admodum ex thesauro pretiosissima quæque depromere in proclivi est, ita ex hoc uno, non solum vocularum significata, sed et abstrusiores quosque Sacræ Scripturæ sensus, è variis rabinorum commentariis selectos, haurire liceat; Autore reverendo patre Sancte Pagnino Lucensi, idiomatum eruditiorum et parente & antistite*. Lyon: Gryphius.

Palmer, Leonard R. 1945. *A Grammar of the Post-Ptolemaic Papyri, Vol. 1: Accidence and Word-Formation, Part I; The Suffixes*. Publications of the Philological Society. Oxford: Oxford University Press.

Pantelia, Maria. 2014a. "Databases and Dictionaries [Papyrology and Epigraphy included]." *EAGLL* 1:411-13.

———. 2014b. "Lexicography, History of." *EAGLL* 2:348-53.

Parkin, Tim G. 2003. *Old Age in the Roman World: A Cultural and Social History*. Ancient Society and History. Baltimore: Johns Hopkins University Press.

———. 2010. "Life Cycle." Pages 97-114 in vol. 1 of *A Cultural History of Childhood and Family in Antiquity*. Edited by Mary Harlow and Ray Laurence. 6 vols. Oxford: Berg.

Parpulov, Georgi R. 2012. "The Bibles of the Christian East." Pages 309-24 in *From 600-1450*. Vol. 2 in *The New Cambridge History of the Bible*.

Edited by Richard Marsden and E. Ann Matter. Cambridge: Cambridge University Press.

Parsons, Peter J. 2007. *The City of the Sharp-Nosed Fish: Greek Papyri beneath the Egyptian Sand Reveal a Long-Lost World.* London: Weidenfeld & Nicolson.

Pearson, A. C., ed. 1917. *The Fragments of Sophocles: Edited with Additional Notes from the Papers of Sir R. C. Jebb and Dr W. G. Headlam.* 3 vols. Cambridge: Cambridge University Press.

Perrin-Saminadayar, Éric. 2004. "L'accueil officiel des souverains et des princes à Athènes à l'époque hellénistique." *BCH* 128–129:351–75.

Pestman, Pieter Willem, Willy Clarysse, Monika Korver, Michel Muszynski, Annette Schutgens, William John Tait, and Jan Krzysztof Winnicki. 1981. *A Guide to the Zenon Archive (P. L. Bat. 21): Lists and Surveys.* Papyrologica Lugduno-Batava 21A. Leiden: Brill.

Peterson, Erik. 1930. "Die Einholung des Kyrios." *ZST* 7:682–702.

Pfochen, Sebastian. 1629. *Diatribe de linguae graecae N.T. puritate.* Amsterdam: Jansonius.

Pietersma, Albert. 1974. "Minutes of IOSCS Meeting Saturday, November 1, 1975 Palmer House, Chicago, Il. Room 6-b." *BIOSCS* 7:2–4.

———. 1977. "Minutes of IOSCS Meeting October 29, 1976 Breckenridge Hotel, St. Louis, Mo. Room 1." *BIOSCS* 10:1–3.

———. 1978. "Minutes of IOSCS Meeting August 19–20, 1977 Theologicum of the University Room T01." *BIOSCS* 11:1–4.

———. 1979. "Minutes of IOSCS Meeting November 19, 1978 Marriott Hotel (Galvez), New Orleans, Louisiana." *BIOSCS* 12:1–2.

———. 1996. *Translation Manual for "A New English Translation of the Septuagint" (NETS).* Ada: Uncial.

———. 1997. "A New English Translation of the Septuagint." Pages 177–87 in *IX Congress of the International Organization for Septuagint and Cognate Studies, Cambridge, 1995.* Edited by Bernard A. Taylor. SCS 45. Atlanta: Scholars Press.

———. 2000. "A New Paradigm for Addressing Old Questions: The Relevance of the Interlinear Model for the Study of the Septuagint." Pages 337–64 in *Bible and Computer: The Stellenbosch AIBI-6 Conference; Proceedings of the Association Internationale Bible et Informatique "From Alpha to Byte"; University of Stellenbosch, 17–21 July, 2000.* Edited by Johann Cook. Leiden: Brill.

———. 2001. "A New English Translation of the Septuagint." Pages 217–28 in *X Congress of the International Organization for Septuagint and Cog-*

nate Studies, Oslo, 1998. Edited by Bernard A. Taylor. SCS 51. Atlanta: Society of Biblical Literature.

———. 2008. "Response to: T. Muraoka, 'Recent Discussions on the Septuagint Lexicography with Special Reference to the So-Called Interlinear Model,' in *Die Septuaginta—Texte, Kontexte, Lebenswelten*, ed. M. Karrer/W. Kraus, Tübingen: J.C.B. Mohr (Paul Siebeck) 2008 pp. 221–235." https://tinyurl.com/SBL0475A.

———. 2015. "Context Is King in Septuagint Lexicography—Or Is It?" Pages 165–75 in *Biblical Greek in Context: Essays in Honour of John A. L. Lee*. Edited by James K. Aitken and Trevor V. Evans. BTS 22. Leuven: Peeters.

Pietersma, Albert, and Benjamin G. Wright. 2009. "To the Reader of NETS." Pages xiii–xx in *A New English Translation of the Septuagint and the Other Greek Translations Traditionally Included under That Title*. Edited by Albert Pietersma and Benjamin G. Wright. Oxford: Oxford University Press.

Planck, Heinrich Ludwig. 1810. *De vera natura atque indole orationis Graecae Novi Testamenti*. Göttingen: Röwer.

Pont, Anne-Valérie. 2009. "Rituels civiques (*apantēsis* et acclamations) et gouverneurs à l'époque romaine en Asie Mineure." Pages 185–211 in *Ritual Dynamics and Religious Change in the Roman Empire: Proceedings of the Eighth Workshop of the International Network Impact of Empire (Heidelberg, July 5–7, 2007)*. Edited by Oliver Hekster, Sebastian Schmidt-Hofner, and Christian Witschel. Impact of Empire 9. Leiden: Brill.

Pontani, F. 2015. "Scholarship in the Byzantine Empire (529–1453)." Pages 297–455 in *Brill's Companion to Ancient Greek Scholarship*. Edited by Franco Montanari, Stephanos Matthaios, and Antonios Rengakos. Leiden: Brill.

Porter, Stanley E. 2016. "Historical Scholarship on the Language of the Septuagint." Pages 15–38 in *Die Sprache der Septuaginta/The Language of the Septuagint*. Vol. 3 of *Handbuch zur Septuaginta*. Edited by Eberhard Bons and Jan Joosten. Gütersloh: Gütersloher Verlagshaus.

Pretzl, Otto. 1926. "Septuaginta Probleme im Buch der Richter." *Bib* 7:233–69, 353–83.

Pritchett, W. Kendrick. 1974. *The Greek State at War*. Vol. 2. Berkeley: University of California Press.

———. 1985. *The Greek State at War*. Vol. 4. Berkeley: University of California Press.

Rabin, Chaim. 1968. "The Translation Process and the Character of the Septuagint." *Text* 6:1–26.
Radt, Stefan, ed. 1977. *Tragicorum Graecorum fragmenta: Vol. 4, Sophocles*. Göttingen: Vandenhoeck & Ruprecht.
Rahlfs, Alfred. 1914. *Verzeichnis der griechischen Handschriften des Alten Testaments, für das Septuaginta-Unternehmen*. MSU 2. Berlin: Weidmann.
———, ed. 1935. *Septuaginta: Id est Vetus Testamentum graece iuxta LXX interpretes*. Stuttgart: Wurttembergische Bibelanstalt.
———. 2004. *Verzeichnis der griechischen Handschriften des Alten Testaments, Bd, I,1. Die Überlieferung bis zum VIII. Jahrhundert*. Edited by Detlef Fraenkel. SVTG Supplement 1.1. Göttingen: Vandenhoeck & Ruprecht.
Rajak, Tessa. 2009. *Translation and Survival: The Greek Bible and the Jewish Diaspora*. Oxford: Oxford University Press.
Redpath, Henry A. 1896. "Concordances to the Old Testament in Greek." *Expositor* 5.3:69–77.
Reekmans, Tony. 1966. *La sitométrie dans les archives de Zénon*. Papyrologica Bruxellensia 3. Brussels: Fondation épgytologique reine Elisabeth.
Reggiani, Nicola. 2017. *Digital Papyrology I: Methods, Tools, and Trends*. Berlin: de Gruyter.
Rehkopf, Friedrich. 1989. *Septuaginta-Vokabular*. Göttingen: Vandenhoeck & Ruprecht.
Reinach, Théodore. 1908. "Parthenon (en grec)." *BCH* 32:499–513.
Rezetko, Robert. 2013. "The Qumran Scrolls of the Book of Judges: Literary Formation, Textual Criticism, and Historical Linguistics." *JHebS* 13:1–68. DOI: 10.5508/jhs.2013.v13.a2.
Rice, E. E. 1983. *The Grand Procession of Ptolemy Philadelphus*. Oxford Classical and Philosophical Monographs. Oxford: Oxford University Press.
Rife, J. Merle. 1933. "The Mechanics of Translation Greek." *JBL* 52:244–52.
Rist, John M. 1972. *Epicurus: An Introduction*. Cambridge: Cambridge University Press.
Robert, Louis. 1937. *Études anatoliennes: Recherches sur les inscriptions grecques de l'Asie Mineure*. Études orientales publiées par l'Institut français d'archéologie de Stamboul 5. Paris: de Boccard.
———. 1984. "Documents d'Asie Mineure." *BCH* 108:457–532.

———. 1985. "Documents d'Asie Mineure XXXIV–XXXV." *BCH* 109:467–84.
Robertson, A. T. 1923. *A Grammar of the Greek New Testament in Light of Historical Research*. 4th ed. New York: Hodder & Stoughton.
Rofé, Alexander. 2011. "Studying the Biblical Text in the Light of Historico-Literary Criticism: The Reproach of the Prophet in Judg 6:7–10 and 4QJudg^a." Pages 111–123 in *The Dead Sea Scrolls in Context: Integrating the Dead Sea Scrolls in the Study of Ancient Texts, Languages, and Cultures*. Edited by Armin Lange, Emanuel Tov, and Matthias Weigold. VTSup 140. Leiden: Brill.
Rosenbach, Zacharias. 1634. *Lexikon breve in LXX interpretes et libros apocryphos: Methodo omniscientiae Christi adiunctum, ut studiosi universa S. Biblia Graeca in posterum sibi familiarissima reddant*. Herborn: Typis Corvinianis.
Rosenberger, Grete, ed. 1934. *Griechische Privatbriefe*. Papyri Iandanae 6. Leipzig: Teubner.
Ross, William A. 2016. "Lexical Possibilities in Septuagint Research: Revision and Expansion." Pages 341–59 in *XV Congress of the International Organization for Septuagint and Cognate Studies, Munich, 2013*. Edited by Wolfgang Kraus, Michaël N. van der Meer, and Martin Meiser. SCS 64. Atlanta: Scholars Press.
———. 2017. "Style and Familiarity in Judges 19,7 (Old Greek): Establishing Dependence within the Septuagint." *Bib* 98:25–36.
———. 2018. "The Septuagint as a Catalyst for Language Change: A Usage-Based Approach." Pages 383–397 in *Die Septuaginta—Geschichte, Wirkung, Relevanz: 6 Internationale Fachtagung von Septuaginta-Deutsch (LXX.D), Wuppertal 21.–24. Juli 2016*. Edited by Martin Meiser, Michaela Geiger, Siegfried Kreuzer, and Marcus Sigismund. WUNT 405. Tübingen, Mohr Siebeck.
———. 2020a. "Some Aspects of Παιδάριον and Νεανίσκος in Ptolemaic Egypt." Pages 189–205 in *The Legacy of Soisalon-Soininen: Towards a Syntax of Septuagint Greek*. Edited by Tuukka Kauhanen. DSI 13. Göttingen: Vandenhoeck & Ruprecht.
———. 2020b. "The 'Scissors and Paste' Septuagint Concordance in the Bodleian Library (Auct. E 1.2,3)." Pages 886–901 in *Die Septuaginta—Themen, Manuskripte, Wirkungen: 7. Internationale Fachtagung von Septuaginta Deutsch (LXX.D), Wuppertal 19.–22. Juli 2018*. Edited by Eberhard Bons, Michaela Geiger, Frank Ueberschaer, Marcus Sigismund, and Martin Meiser. WUNT 444. Tübingen, Mohr Siebeck.

———. Forthcoming. "Some Problems with Talking about 'Septuagint Greek.'" *JSJ*.
Rostovtzeff, M. I. 1922. *A Large Estate in Egypt in the Third Century B.C.: A Study in Economic History*. Madison: University of Wisconsin.
Sabin, Phiilip. 2000. "The Face of Roman Battle." *JRS* 90:1–17.
Sabin, Philip, Hans van Wees, and Michael Whitby, eds. 2007. *Greece, the Hellenistic World and the Rise of Rome*. Vol. 1 of *The Cambridge History of Greek and Roman Warfare*. Cambridge: Cambridge University Press.
Sacco, Giulia. 1979. "Sui ΝΕΑΝΙΣΚΟΙ dell'età ellenistica." *RFIC* 107:39–49.
Sáenz-Badillos, Angel. 1973. "Tradición griega y texto hebreo del Canto de Débora (Jue 5)." *Sef* 33:245–57.
Sacy, Baron Solvestre de. 1841. *Sciences médicales et arts utiles; Psychologie; Sciences morales; Linguistique; Littérature et beaux-arts; Histoire littéraire*. Vol. 2 of *Bibliothèaue de M. le baron Silvestre de Sacy*. Paris: Duprat.
Salem, Jean. 1993. *Commentaire de la lettre d'Epicure à Hérodote*. Cahiers de philosophie ancienne 9. Brussels: Ousia.
Sanders, James A. 1999. "The Hebrew University Bible and *Biblia Hebraica Quinta*."*JBL* 118:518–26.
Santibáñez Sáenz, Francisco. 1999. "Conceptual Interaction and Spanish Diminutives." *Cuadernos de Investigación Filológica* 25:173–90.
Satterthwaite, Philip E. 1991. "Some Septuagintal Pluses in Judges 20 and 21." *BIOSCS* 24:25–35.
———. 2015. "Judges." Pages 102–17 in *T&T Clark Companion to the Septuagint*. Edited by James K. Aitken. London: Bloomsbury T&T Clark.
Savalli-Lestrade, Ivana. 2003. "La place des reines à la cour et dans le royaume à l'époque hellénistique." Pages 59–76 in *Les femmes antiques entre sphère privée et sphère publique: Actes du Diplôme d'Etudes Avancées, Universités de Lausanne et Neuchâtel, 2000–2002*. Edited by Regula Frei-Stolba, Anne Bielman, and Olivier Bianchi. Echo 2. Bern: Lang.
Schenker, Adrian. 2008a. "From the First Printed Hebrew, Greek and Latin Bibles to the First Polyglot Bible, the Complutensian Polyglot: 1477–1517." Pages 276–91 in *Hebrew Bible/Old Testament: The History of Its Interpretation; 2, From the Renaissance to the Enlightenment*. Edited by Magne Sæbø. Göttingen: Vandenhoeck & Ruprecht.

———. 2008b. "The Polyglot Bibles of Antwerp, Paris and London: 1568–1658." Pages 774–84 in *Hebrew Bible/Old Testament: The History of Its Interpretation; 2, From the Renaissance to the Enlightenment*. Edited by Magne Sæbø. Göttingen: Vandenhoeck & Ruprecht.

Schilling, David. 1886. *Commentarius exegetico-philologicus in hebraismos Novi Testamenti, seu de dictione hebraica Novi Testamenti Graeci*. Malines: Dessain.

Schleusner, Johann Friedrich. 1820–1821. *Novus Thesaurus Philologico-Criticus: Sive, Lexicon in LXX. et reliquos interpretes Græcos; Ac Scriptores Apocryphos Veteris Testamenti; Post Bielium et alios viros doctos congessit et edidit Johannes Friedericus Schleusner*. 5 vols. Leipzig: Weidmann.

———. 1822. *Novus Thesaurus Philologico-Criticus: Sive, lexicon in LXX. et reliquos interpretes Græcos, Ac Scriptores Apocryphos Veteris Testamenti; Post Bielium et alios viros doctos congessit et edidit Johannes Friedericus Schleusner*. 2nd ed. 3 vols. Glasgow: Duncan.

Schmidt, Mauricius, ed. 1858–1868. *Hesychii Alexandrini Lexicon*. 5 vols. Jena: Mauke.

Scholl, Reinhold. 1983. *Sklaverei in den Zenonpapyri: Eine Untersuchung zu den Sklaventermini, zum Sklavenerwerb und zur Sklavenflucht*. Trierer Historische Forschungen 4. Trier: Verlag Trierer Historische Forschungen.

Schreiner, Joseph. 1957. *Septuaginta-Massora des Buches der Richter: Eine textkritische Studie*. AnBib 7. Rome: Pontificio Istituto Biblico.

———. 1961a. "Textformen und Urtext des Deboraliedes in der Septuaginta." *Bib* 42:173–200.

———. 1961b. "Zum B-text des griechischen Canticum Deborae." *Bib* 42:333–58.

Seely, Jo Ann A. 1992. "Succoth." Pages 217–18 in vol. 6 of *The Anchor Bible Dictionary*. Edited by David N. Freedman. 6 vols. New York: Doubleday.

Shear, Julia L. 1995. "Fragments of Naval Inventories from the Athenian Agora." *Hesperia* 64:179–224.

Sheldon, Rose Mary. 2012. *Ambush: Surprise Attack in Ancient Greek Warfare*. London: Frontline.

Shipley, Graham. 2000. *The Greek World after Alexander: 323–30 BC*. Routledge History of the Ancient World. London: Routledge.

Shipp, George P. 1979. *Modern Greek Evidence for the Ancient Greek Vocabulary*. Sydney: Sydney University Press.

Silva, Moisés. 1978. "Describing Meaning in the LXX Lexicon." *BIOSCS* 11:19–26.

———. 1980. "Bilingualism and the Character of Palestinian Greek." *Bib* 61:198–219.

Simcox, W. H. 1889. *The Language of the New Testament.* London: Hodder & Stoughton.

Simpson, Graham McGregor. 1976. "A Semantic Study of Words for Young Person, Servant and Child in the Septuagint and Other Early Koine Greek." MA thesis, University of Sydney.

Sipilä, Seppo. 1999. *Between Literalness and Freedom: Translation Technique in the Septuagint of Joshua and Judges Regarding the Clause Connections Introduced by* ו *and* כי. PFES 75. Helsinki: Finnish Exegetical Society; Göttingen: Vandenhoeck & Ruprecht.

Skaltsa, Stella. 2013. "Gymnasiarchic Law (Beroia)." Pages 3006–7 in *The Encyclopedia of Ancient History.* Edited by Roger S. Bagnall, Kai Brodersen, Craige B. Champion, Andrew Erskine, and Sabine R. Huebner. 12 vols. Oxford: Blackwell.

Smyth, Herbert W. 1920. *Greek Grammar for Colleges.* Revised ed. New York: American Book Company.

Soggin, J. Alberto. 1981. *Judges: A Commentary.* Translated by John Bowden. OTL. Philadelphia: Westminster.

———. 1987. *Le livre des Juges.* Commentaire de l'Ancien Testament 5b. Geneva: Labor et Fides.

Soisalon-Soininen, Ilmari. 1951. *Die Textformen der Septuaginta-Übersetzung des Richterbuches.* AASF 72. Helsinki: Suomalainen Tiedeakatemia.

———. 1987. "Der Gebrauch des *genetivus absolutus* in der Septuaginta." Pages 175–80 in *Studien zur Septuaginta-Syntax: Zu seinem 70. Geburtstag am 4. Juni 1987.* Edited by Anneli Aejmelaeus and Raija Sollamo. AASF 237. Helsinki: Suomalainen Tiedeakatemia.

Sollamo, Raija. 1979. *Renderings of Hebrew Semiprepositions in the Septuagint.* AASF: Dissertationes Humanarum Litterarum 19. Helsinki: Suomalainen Tiedeakatemia.

Stanton, G. R. 1988. "Τέχνον, παῖς and Related Words in Koine Greek." Pages 463–80 *Proceedings of the XVIII International Congress of Papyrology: Athens 25–31 May 1986.* Edited by Basil G. Mandelaras. Athens: Greek Papyrological Society.

Stewart, Andrew F. 1993. *Faces of Power: Alexander's Image and Hellenistic Politics.* HCS 11. Berkeley: University of California Press.

Storr, Gottlob Christian. 1779. *Observationes ad analogiam et syntaxin hebraicam pertinentes*. Tübingen: Heerbrandt.

Straus, Jean A. 1983. "P.Med. Inv. 69.65: Dénombrement de valets d'armes serviles." *ZPE* 50:123–26.

Stray, Christopher, Michael Clarke, and Joshua T. Katz, eds. 2019. *Liddell and Scott: The History, Methodology, and Languages of the World's Leading Lexicon of Ancient Greek*. Oxford: Oxford University Press.

Stuart, Moses, and Edward H. Robinson. 1826. "Lexicography of the New Testament." *North American Review* 23:80–108.

Swete, Henry Barclay. 1887. *The Old Testament in Greek According to the Septuagint: Vol. 1 Genesis–IV Kings*. Cambridge: Cambridge University Press.

———. 1900. *An Introduction to the Old Testament in Greek: With an Appendix Containing the Letter of Aristeas Edited by H. St J. Thackeray*. Cambridge: Cambridge University Press.

———. 1902. *An Introduction to the Old Testament in Greek: With an Appendix Containing the Letter of Aristeas Edited by H. St J. Thackeray*. 2nd ed. Cambridge: Cambridge University Press.

Swinn, S. P. 1990. "ΑΓΑΠΑΝ in the Septuagint." Pages 49–81 in *Melbourne Symposium on Septuagint Lexicography*. Edited by Takamitsu Muraoka. SCS 28. Atlanta: Scholars Press.

Tal, Abraham. 2015. *Genesis*. BHQ 1. Stuttgart: Deutsche Bibelgesellschaft.

Talshir, Zipora. 1987. "Double Translations in the Septuagint." Pages 21–63 in *VI Congress of the International Organization for Septuagint and Cognate Studies. Jerusalem 1986*. Edited by Claude E. Cox. SCS 23. Atlanta: Scholars Press.

Targarona Borrás, Judit. 1983a. "Historia del texto griego del libro de los Jueces." Vol. 1. PhD diss., Universidad Complutense de Madrid.

———. 1983b. "Historia del Texto Griego del Libro de los Jueces." Vol. 2. PhD diss., Universidad Complutense de Madrid.

Taylor, Bernard A. 1994. *The Analytical Lexicon to the Septuagint: A Complete Parsing Guide*. Grand Rapids: Zondervan.

———. 2009. *Analytical Lexicon to the Septuagint: Expanded Edition*. Peabody, MA: Hendrickson.

Taylor, John R. 2003. *Linguistic Categorization*. 3rd ed. Oxford Textbooks in Linguistics. Oxford: Oxford University Press.

———. 2012. *The Mental Corpus: How Language Is Represented in the Mind*. Oxford: Oxford University Press.

Tcherikover, Victor A. 1937. "Palestine Under the Ptolemies." *Mizraim* 4–5:9–90.

Thackeray, Henry St J. 1909. *A Grammar of the Old Testament in Greek According to the Septuagint: Vol. 1 Introduction, Orthography and Accidence.* Cambridge: Cambridge University Press.

———. 1921. *The Septuagint and Jewish Worship: A Study in Origins.* Schweich Lectures. London: Oxford University Press.

———. 1989. *Josephus: The Jewish War, Books 5–7.* LCL. Cambridge: Harvard University Press.

Theodoridis, Christos, ed. 1982. *Photii patriarchae lexicon.* Vol. 1. Berlin: de Gruyter.v

Thiersch, Heinrich Wilhelm Josias. 1841. *De Pentateuchi versione Alexandrina libri tres.* Erlangen: Blaesing.

Thompson, Dorothy J. 1984. "The Idumaeans of Memphis and the Ptolemaic *Politeumata*." Pages 1069–75 in *Atti del XVII Congresso internazionale di papirologia. (Napoli, 19–26 maggio 1983).* 3 vols. Naples: Centro internazionale per lo studio dei papiri ercolanes.

———. 2000. "Philadelphus' Procession: Dynastic Power in a Mediterranean Context." Pages 365–88 in *Politics, Administration and Society in the Hellenistic and Roman World: Proceedings of the International Colloquium, Bertinoro 19–24 July 1997.* Edited by Leon Mooren. StHell 36. Leuven: Peeters.

———. 2011. "Slavery in the Hellenistic World." Pages 194–213 in *The Cambridge World History of Slavery.* Edited by Keith Bradley and Paul Cartledge. Cambridge: Cambridge University Press.

Thompson, Dorothy J., and Ludwig Koenen. 1984. "Gallus as Triptolemos on the Tazza Farnese." *BASP* 21:111–56.

Thumb, Albert. 1901. *Die griechische Sprache im Zeitalter des Hellenismus: Beiträge zur Geschichte und Beurteilung der Κοινή.* Strassbourg: Trübner.

Timmer, Jan. 2013. "Age." Pages 173–78 in *The Encyclopedia of Ancient History.* Edited by Roger S. Bagnall, Kai Brodersen, Craige B. Champion, Andrew Erskine, and Sabine R. Huebner. Oxford: Blackwell.

Tov, Emanuel. 1975. *Lexical and Grammatical Studies on the Language of the Septuagint.* Jerusalem: Hebrew University.

———. 1976. "Some Thoughts on a Lexicon of the LXX." *BIOSCS* 9:14–46.

———. 1978. "The Textual History of the Song of Deborah in the A-Text of the LXX." *VT* 28:224–32.

———. 1983. *A Classified Bibliography of Lexical and Grammatical Studies on the Language of the Septuagint and Its Revisions*. Rev. and enlarged ed. Jerusalem: Academon.

———. 1986. *A Computerized Data Base for Septuagint Studies: The Parallel Aligned Text of the Greek and Hebrew Bible*. CATSS 2. JNSLSup 1. Stellenbosch: University of Stellenbosch.

———. 1990. "Greek Words and Hebrew Meanings." Pages 83–125 in *Melbourne Symposium on Septuagint Lexicography*. Edited by Takamitsu Muraoka. SCS 28. Atlanta: Scholars Press.

———. 1991. "The CATSS Project—A Progress Report." Pages 157–163 in *VII Congress of the International Organization for Septuagint and Cognate Studies: Leuven, 1989*. Edited by Claude E. Cox. SCS 31. Atlanta: Scholars Press.

———. 1999a. "The Impact of the Septuagint Translation of the Torah on the Translation of the Other Books." Pages 183–94 in *The Greek and Hebrew Bible: Collected Essays on the Septuagint*. VTSup 72. Leiden: Brill.

———. 1999b. "Some Thoughts on a Lexicon of the Septuagint." Pages 95–108 in *The Greek and Hebrew Bible: Collected Essays on the Septuagint*. VTSup 72. Leiden: Brill.

———. 2002. "The Biblical Texts from the Judaean Desert—An Overview and Analysis of the Published Texts." Pages 139–66 in *The Bible as Book: The Hebrew Bible and the Judaean Desert Discoveries*. Edited by Edward D. Herbert and Emanuel Tov. London: British Library; New Castle, DE: Oak Knoll.

———. 2010. "Some Academic Memoirs." Pages 1–28 in *Qumran and the Bible: Studying the Jewish and Christian Scriptures in Light of the Dead Sea Scrolls*. Edited by Nóra Dávid and Armin Lange. CBET 57. Leuven: Peeters.

———. 2012. "*Biblia Hebraica Quinta*: Judges." *Sef* 72:483–89.

———. 2015. *The Text-Critical Use of the Septuagint in Biblical Research*. 3rd ed. Winona Lake, IN: Eisenbrauns.

Traugott, Elizabeth Closs, and Richard B. Dasher. 2002. *Regularity in Semantic Change*. CSL 96. Cambridge: Cambridge University Press.

Trebolle Barrera, Julio. 1989. "Textual Variants in 4QJudg[a] and the Textual and Editorial History of the Book of Judges." *RevQ* 14:229–45.

———. 1991. "Édition préliminaire de *4QJugesb*: Contribution des manuscrits qumrâniens des Juges à l'étude textuelle et littéraire du livre." *RevQ* 15:79–100.

———. 1995. "4QJudg^a" Pages 161–64, pl. XXXVI in *Qumran Cave 4.IX: Deuteronomy, Joshua, Judges, Kings*. Edited by Eugene C. Ulrich et al. DJD XIV. Oxford: Clarendon.

———. 2000. "Judges, Book of." Page 455 in vol. 1 of *Encyclopedia of the Dead Sea Scrolls*. Edited by Lawrence H. Schiffman and James C. VanderKam. 2 vols. Oxford: Oxford University Press.

———. 2005. "The Text-Critical Value of the Old Latin and Antiochean Greek Texts in the Books of Judges and Joshua." Pages 401–13 in *Interpreting Translation: Studies on the LXX and Ezekiel in Honour of Johan Lust*. Edited by Florentino García Martínez and Marc Vervenne. BETL 192. Leuven: Peeters.

———. 2008. "A Combined Textual and Literary Criticism Analysis: Editorial Traces in Joshua and Judges." Pages 437–63 in *Florilegium Lovaniense: Studies in Septuagint and Textual Criticism in Honour of Florentino García Martínez*. Edited by Hans Ausloos, Bénédicte Lemmelijn, and Marc Vervenne. BETL 224. Leuven: Peeters.

———. 2016a. "4.2.2 Masoretic Texts and Ancient Texts Close to MT." Pages 284–89 in *Textual History of the Bible: Volume 1B The Hebrew Bible, Pentateuch, Former and Latter Prophets*. Edited by Armin Lange and Emanuel Tov. Leiden: Brill.

———. 2016b. "4.2.3 Other Texts." Pages 289–93 in *Textual History of the Bible: Volume 1B The Hebrew Bible, Pentateuch, Former and Latter Prophets*. Edited by Armin Lange and Emanuel Tov. Leiden: Brill.

Trollope, William. 1842. *A Greek Grammar to the New Testament and to the Common or Hellenic Diction of the Later Greek Writers: Arranged as a Supplement to Dr. Philip Buttmann's "Intermediate or Larger Greek Grammar."* London: Whittaker & Co.

Tromm, Abraham. 1718. *Abrahami Trommii Concordantiae Graecae versionis vulgo dictae LXX interpretum: Cujus voces secundum ordinem elementorum sermonis Græci digestæ recensentur, contra atque in opere Kircheriano factum fuerat; Leguntur hic praeterea voces Graecae pro Hebraicis redditae ab antiquis omnibus Veteris Testamenti interpretibus, quorum nonnisi fragmenta extant, Aquila, Symmacho, Theodotione et aliis; Quorum maximam partem nuper in lucem edidit Domnus Bernardus de Montfaucon*. 2 vols. Amsterdam: Sumptibus Societatis.

Turner, Eric G. 1980a. *Greek Papyri: An Introduction*. Oxford: Clarendon.

Turner, Nigel. 1954–1955. "The 'Testament of Abraham': Problems in Biblical Greek." *NTS* 1:219–23.

———. 1955. "The Unique Character of Biblical Greek." *VT* 5:208–13.

———. 1962. "The Language of the New Testament." Pages 659–62 in *Peake's Commentary on the Bible*. Edited by Matthew Black and H. H. Rowley. London: Nelson.

———. 1963. *A Grammar of New Testament Greek, Vol. 3: Syntax*. Edinburgh: T&T Clark.

———. 1964. "Second Thoughts–VII Papyrus Finds." *ExpTim* 76:44–48.

———. 1965. *Grammatical Insights into the New Testament*. Edinburgh: T&T Clark.

———. 1980b. *Christian Words*. Edinburgh: T&T Clark.

Ulrich, Eugene. 1981. "Septuagint Abstracts." *BIOSCS* 14:41–56.

———. 1985. "News and Notes." *BIOSCS* 18:4–9.

———. 2008. "Deuteronomistically Inspired Scribal Insertions into the Developing Biblical Texts: 4QJudg^a and 4 QJer^a." Pages 489–506 in *Houses Full of Good Things: Essays in Memory of Timo Veijola*. Edited by Juha Pakkala and Marrti Nissinen. PFES 95. Helsinki: Finnish Exegetical Society; Göttingen: Vandenhoeck & Ruprecht.

Vervenne, Marc. 1998. "A Greek-English Lexicon of the Septuagint." *ETL* 74:83–86.

Viteau, Joseph. 1893–1896. *Étude sur le grec du Nouveau Testament comparé avec celui des Septante*. 2 vols. Paris: Bouillion.

Voelz, James W. 1984. "The Language of the New Testament." *ANRW* 25.2:893–977.

Walch, Jo Ern Imm. 1779. *Observationes in Matthaeum ex graecis inscriptionibus*. Jena: Croecker.

Weima, Jeffrey A. D. 2014. *1–2 Thessalonians*. BECNT. Grand Rapids: Baker Academic.

Wellhausen, Julius. 1871. *Der Text der Bücher Samuelis*. Göttingen: Vandenhoeck & Ruprecht.

Westermann, William L. 1955. *The Slave Systems of Greek and Roman Antiquity*. Memoirs of the American Philosophical Society 114. Philadelphia: American Philosophical Society.

Wettstein, J. J. 1751–1752. *Novum Testamentum Graecum editionis receptae: Cum lectionibus variantibus codicum MSS.; Editionum aliarum, versionum et patrum, necnon commentario pleniore ex Scriptoribus veteribus, Hebraeis, Graecis, et Latinis, historiam et vim verborum illustrante*. 2 vols. Amsterdam: Dommeriana.

Wevers, John W. 1972. "On 'Slipping.'" Pages 40–45 in *Septuagintal Lexicography*. Edited by Robert A. Kraft. SCS 1. Missoula, MT: Scholars Press.

———, ed. 1974. *Genesis*. SVTG 1. Göttingen: Vandenhoeck & Ruprecht.
———. 1981. "In Memoriam Henry Snyder Gehman." *BIOSCS* 14:1.
Wheeler, Everett L. 2007. "Battle." Pages 186–247 in *Greece, the Hellenistic World and the Rise of Rome*. Vol. 1 of *The Cambridge History of Greek and Roman Warfare*. Edited by Philip Sabin, Hans van Wees, and Michael Whitby. Cambridge: Cambridge University Press.
White, John L. 1986. *Light from Ancient Letters*. FF. Philadelphia: Fortress.
Whitehorne, J. E. G. 1982. "The Ephebate and the Gymnasial Class in Roman Egypt." *BASP* 19:171–84.
Wiedemeyer, Jäger. 1699. *Nova Literaria Maris Balthici & Septentrionis*. Lübeck: Venator.
Willi, Andreas. 2010. "Register Variation." Pages 297–310 in *A Companion to the Ancient Greek Language*. Edited by Egbert J. Bakker. Oxford: Blackwell.
Winer, G. B. 1822. *Grammatik des neutestamentlichen Sprachidioms als sichere Grundlage der neutestamentlichen Exegese*. Leipzig: Vogel.
———. 1882. *A Treatise on the Grammar of New Testament Greek, Regarded as a Sure Basis for New Testament Exegesis*. Translated by William F. Moulton. 3rd rev. German ed. 9th English ed. Edinburgh: T&T Clark.
Worp, Klaas A. 2014. "Papyrology." *EAGLL* 3:14–17.
Würthwein, Ernst. 1995. *The Text of the Old Testament: An Introduction to the Biblia Hebraica*. Translated by Erroll F. Rhodes. 2nd ed. Grand Rapids: Eerdmans.
———. 2014. *The Text of the Old Testament: An Introduction to the Biblia Hebraica*. Revised and expanded by Alexander A. Fischer. Translated by Erroll F. Rhodes. 3rd ed. Grand Rapids: Eerdmans.
Ziegler, Joseph. 1945. "Der Text der Aldina im Dodekapropheton." *Bib* 26:37–51.

Ancient Sources Index

Hebrew Bible/Old Testament

Genesis
- 28:11 — 204
- 33:8 — 204
- 45:16 — 32–33
- 49:1 — 204

Exodus
- 14:27 — 176

Leviticus
- 25:10 — 32–33

Numbers
- 24:1 — 176

Judges
- 1:1 — 63, 66, 72
- 1:1–3:6 — 63
- 1:3 — 66
- 1:5 — 66, 68
- 1:8 — 66, 72
- 1:9 — 67, 72
- 3:1–2 — 70, 72
- 3:10 — 70, 72
- 4–5 — 113
- 4:18 — 163, 167, 168, 175–76, 204
- 4:22 — 167, 175
- 5:8 — 67
- 5:19–20 — 67
- 6:7–10 — 5
- 6:27–35 — 139
- 6:35 — 163, 167, 175
- 7:10–11 — 116, 139–40
- 7:24 — 163, 167, 175–76
- 8:1 — 67–69
- 8:4–14 — 140–41
- 8:13 — 70
- 8:14 — 116
- 8:18–21 — 131
- 8:20 — 116–17, 121
- 8:21 — 167, 175, 204
- 9:1–57 — 139
- 9:17 — 67
- 9:38 — 67
- 9:39 — 67
- 9:45 — 67
- 9:52 — 67
- 9:53 — 140, 159
- 9:54 — 116
- 10:9 — 67
- 10:18 — 67
- 11:12 — 67
- 11:20 — 67
- 11:25 — 67
- 11:27 — 67
- 11:31 — 163, 167, 175, 180
- 11:31–34 — 204
- 11:32 — 67
- 11:34 — 167, 175
- 11:4–9 — 67
- 11:8 — 67, 108–9
- 12:1 — 67
- 12:3 — 67
- 12:4 — 67
- 13:3–24 — 131
- 13:5 — 116
- 13:7 — 116
- 13:8 — 116–17

Judges (cont.)		21:22	70–71
13:12	116–17		
13:24	116–17, 121	1 Samuel	
14:1–4	152	7:3–8:22	63
14:5	167–68, 172, 175, 204		
14:10	115, 120, 151, 160	1 Chronicles	
14:10–20	152–53	12:18	203
15:1–20	152		
15:12	167, 169, 175, 204, 206	Deuterocanonical Books	
15:14	167, 172, 175, 204		
16:1–31	153	Judith	
16:26	116–18	10:18	33
17:7	116–18		
17:7–11	159	1 Maccabees	
17:7–12	155–56	11:60	203
17:11–12	116		
18:1–26	156	2 Maccabees	
18:11	70, 72	4:9–14	144
18:15	116		
18:16–17	70, 72	Pseudepigrapha	
18:25	167, 175, 204		
18:3	116–17	Letter of Aristeas	177
19	158, 160–61		
19:1–13	156	Psalms of Solomon	
19:3	116, 167, 172, 175, 204	8:16	203
19:3–13	159		
19:9	116	Ancient Jewish Authors	
19:11	116		
19:13	116	Josephus, *Jewish Antiquities*	84, 89–90,
19:19	116–19	98–99, 105, 107, 187	
20:14	70, 108	5.2	97
20:15	115, 120, 152–53, 160	12.311.2	91
20:17	70, 72	13.101	195–96
20:18	70		
20:20	70–71	Josephus, *Jewish War*	
20:22	73–74	3.75.2	91
20:23	70	5.4.25	94
20:25	163, 167–69, 175	6.80.1	91
20:25–31	204		
20:28	70	Josephus, *Life*	
20:31	167, 175–76	358.2	94
20:34	70		
20:39	70	Philo, *De Deo*	
20:41	167–68, 170–71, 175, 206	145	185
20:42	70		

Ancient Sources Index   267

Philo, *Quod deterius potiori insidari soleat*
  30   185

Philo, *Quod Deus sit immutabilis*
  166   191

Philo, *De migratione Abrahami*
  79   185

Philo, *De posteritate Caini*
  132   185

Philo, *De somniis*
  1.71   185

Greco-Roman Authors and Works

Aelianus Tacitus   84

Aelius Aristides   85

Aeneas Tacticus, *Poliorcetica*
  1.3   83

Aeschines, In Ctesiphonem   84
  151   83

Apollonius, *Lexicon Homericum* 181, 184
  301.3   185

Appianus   84

Aquila   28, 47, 215

Aristotle, *Sophistici elenchi* (*Top*. 9)
  176a.23   186

Arrianus   84

Asclepiodotus   84

Athenaeus, *Deipnosophistae*
  5   192

Cassius Dio, *Historiae*   84, 90, 95, 99,
  105–6
  18.58.1.1   93
  48.473.5   98
  55.30.2.3   93

Cicero, *Epistulae ad Atticum*
  16.11.6   198

Demosthenes, *3 Philippica*   76, 186
  9.49   82–83

Dio Cocceianus of Prusa   85

Diodorus Siculus, *Historiae*   37, 84–85,
  87, 105, 181, 187, 195, 200
  1.18.5   88
  2.1.8   188
  2.1.10   96
  2.25   88
  5.59.4   190
  11.25.2–3   89
  11.35   88–89
  16.35.5   88–89
  19.72.7   96

Dionysius of Halicarnassus, *Antiquitates
  romanae*   84, 89
  4.66–67   181, 184

Epictetus   85

Epicurus, *Epistula ad Herodotum*
  46.8   186

Euripides, *Ion*
  534–535   179–80, 184

Euthalius of Rhodes   18–19

Herodotus, *Historiae*   78
  1.61   154

Hesychius   9

Homer, *Ilias*		Plutarch, *Phocion*	
10.65	184	26.1.2	92
Homer, *Odyssea*		Plutarch, *Pyrrhus*	
10.278	154	16.1	191
Isocrates, *Aegineticus* (*Or.* 7)	79	Polyaenus	84
19.38	77		
		Polybius, *Historiae*	37, 84–85, 89, 98,
Isocrates, *Busiris* (*Or.* 11)		105–6, 181, 187, 200	
11.7	77	1.19	87
		1.27.5	86
Isocrates, *Helenae encomium* (*Or.* 10)		2.19.5	96
53.6	81–82	2.20.2	96
		3.32.3	102
Lucanus Annaeus	84	3.108.7	95
		5.26.8	173
Marcus Aurelius	85	8.27.4	188
		11.1.2	95
Onasander	84	12.17.1	86
		12.18–22	87
Philodemus	84	12.20.7	95
		16.18–20	87
Photius, *Patriarchae Lexicon*		16.18.2	86
2252	173	16.25.3–7	193–94
		20.7.3–7	194
Pindar, *Olympionikai*		21.10.5	101
7.4	154	21.18.1–6	194
		28.19.6–7	174, 194
Plutarch, *Agis et Cleomenes*		29.17	87
15.1.2	92	29.22.1	195
		30.1.1–6	194
Plutarch, *Alexander*		30.4.2	86–87
1.2.5	92	30.27.1–4	194
		30.30.7–8	194
Plutarch, *An seni respublica gerenda sit*		33.28	195
6	92	34/35.33.2	195
		37.22	101
Plutarch, *Caesar*		38.16.11	191
15.3	97		
		Poseidonius	84
Plutarch, *Mulierum virtutes*			
8	98	Phrynichus, *Praeparatio sophistica*	
		frag. 245	173

Ancient Sources Index

Sophocles	173	*Inscriptiones Scythiae Minoris*	
Strabo	84	2.106	103
		LBW	
Thucydides, *Historiae*	76, 78	1221	155
5.11.2	80–81		
7.3.1	78–79	*Monumenta Asiae Minoris Antiqua*	
		8.414	155
Xenophon, *Hellenica*	76, 186		
3.4.22–23	79–80	*Orientis graeci inscriptiones selectae*	
		1.332	196
Inscriptions		2.654	102

Sammelbuch griechischer Urkunden aus Aegypten

BGU			
4.1079	134	1.5942	147–48
6.1243	99	16:12221	140
6.1256	149		
8.1776	190	*Supplementum Epigraphicum Graecum*	
		28.60	192
Gallus	102	52.736	102
Iasos		*Sylloge inscriptionum graecarum*	
118	155	2.700	104
IBubon		*Tituli Asiae Minoris*	
14	155	2.1.584	155

Inscriptiones Graecae		Papyri
2.1006	144, 197–98	
2.1614	100	
4.1.28	101	P.Cair.Zen.
4.1.128	182	1.59018 148–49
9.1.1.188	154	1.59076 132
		1.59060 137
ILindos		1.59098 136
2.160	101	2.59153 146–47
		2.59176 136
IPreine		2.59179 183
117	100	2.59195 135
		2.59203 181–82
IPros.Pierre		2.59247 182
9	183	2.59254 147
16	200–201	2.59292 133
		3.59298 137
		3.59347 129

P.Cair.Zen. (cont.)

3.59378	134
3.59406	135, 136
3.59488	137
3.59498	133–34
3.59509	133
4.59677	136
4.59697	137
4.59698	136

P.Col.

3.6	129
4.83	128
4.87	182

P.Corn.

1.66–69	130

P.Grenf.

1.30	150

P.Hamb.

4.238	189

P.Iand.

6.92	137

P.Lond.

7.1941	136
7.2164	136

P.Mich.

1.49	133

P.Oxy.

3.533	152

P.Petr.

3.74a	149

P.Ryl.

2.68	188
4.557	185

P.Tarich.

1	189

P.Tebt.

1.43	174
3.755	190

P.Tor.Choach 12	189

Papiri greci e latini

2.127	11

Sammelbuch griechischer Urkunden aus Aegypten

3.6762	129
16.12468	188

Modern Authors Index

Aejmelaeus, Anneli 177
Aitken, James K. 2, 14, 17, 57, 61, 177, 214
Amit, Yairah 5
Aungier, Ambrose 25–26
Ausloos. Hans 5
Bagnall, Robert S. 128, 130
Barrera, Trebolle 4–5, 8, 11
Barthélemy, Dominique 7
Beekes, Robert S. P. 154
Bentley, Richard 1, 37
Beza, Theodore 35
Biel, Johann Christian 30–34, 210
Bieżuńska-Małowist, Iza 135–36, 140
Billen, A. V. 6
Bindseil, Heinrich Ernst 18
Black, Matthew 44
Block, Daniel 5
Bodine, Walter 7–8
Boot, Arnold de 24–25
Borrás, Judit Targarona 63, 72
Bos, Lambert 29
Bouchon, Richard 193
Bowman, Alan K. 39
Boyd-Taylor, Cameron 57–58, 215
Bretschneider, Karl Gottlieb 33
Brock, Sebastian P. 47–48
Brooke, Alan 10
Bubenik, Vit 13
Bybee, Joan L. 85
Canas Reillo, Jose Manuel 8, 10–11, 214
Casey, Eric 144
Chalmers, Alexander 19
Chamberlain, Gary 54
Chaniotis, Angelos 145, 192–193
Chankowski, Andrzej S. 144–46, 151, 193, 197–98
Clarysse, Willy 137
Conybeare, F. C. 42–43
Cooper, Charles 9
Craster, H. H. E. 24
Crawford, Dorothy J. 174
Cribiore, Raffaella 130
Cruse, D. A. 15
Cuvigny, Hélène 40
Daniel, R. W. 150
Danker, Frederick 54
Deissman, Adolf 2, 12, 17, 32, 40–43, 48, 52, 55, 60
Derow, Peter 128
Dhont, Marieke 214
Diaz-Caro, Spottorno 10
Dickey, Eleanor 130, 173, 184
Dogniez, Cécile 11
Dorival, Gilles 8, 54
Dunand, Françoise 138
Edgar, Campbell Cowan 137
Eisenbeis, Walter 46–47, 49
Euthalius of Rhodes 18
Evans, Trevor V. 2, 40, 53
Ewing, Greville 37, 38
Eynikel, Erik 53, 56
Fernández Marcos, Natalio 4–6, 8, 10–12, 114, 206, 209, 214
Forbes, Clarence A. 125, 137, 145–46
Fritsch, Charles T. 44–45
Fuks, Alexander 174
Gardiner, E. Norman 137–38
Garland, Robert 125, 144–45
Geeraerts, Dirk 15

Gehman, Henry S.	43–46, 211	Le Guen, Bridgette	197
Gerber, Albrecht	40	Le Long, Jacques	18
Gertz, Jan Christian	63	Lee, John A. L.	1–2, 12–13, 22, 47–48, 51–53, 55–57, 60–61, 184, 206, 215
Gesenius, Wilhelm	34, 43		
Glare, P. G. W.	202	Legras, Bernard	137, 145, 147, 150–51
Glassius, Salomon	36	Leinieks, Valdis	125
Golden, Mark	125	Lewis, Naphtali	174
Grenfell, Bernard	39	Liddell, Henry George	57
Grosse, Jacob	36	Lightfoot, J. B.	39
Gwynn, R. M.	40	Lindars, Barnabas	8
Hanhart, Robert	65, 115, 164–67	Ludlum, John	8–9
Hanson, Ann Ellis	14	Lust, Johan	32, 53, 55–57
Hanson, Victor David	78, 83	Madan, Falconer	24
Harl, Marguerite	8	Mant, Richard	26
Harlé, Paul	6, 12, 114	McDougall, J. Iain	87, 96
Hatch, Edwin	37–38	McLean, Norman	10
Hauspie, Katrin	53, 56	Milligan, George	202
Heinen, Heinz	137, 140	Montalvo, David E.	8–9
Hess, Richard	5	Montfaucon, Bernard de	29
Hilhorst, A.	54	Montserrat, Dominic	137
Hill, David	44	Moulton, James H.	39–41, 48, 52, 202, 209
Horne, Thomas Hartwell	19, 37		
Horrocks, Geoffrey	14, 174	Mulroney, James A. E.	214
Hugh of St. Cher	20	Munnich, Olivier	8
Hunt, Arthur	39	Muraoka, Takamitsu	49–53, 56, 58–63, 111, 113, 158
Jackson, Samuel Macauley	29		
Jacob, B.	40	Mutzenbecher, E. H.	30
Janse, Mark	37	Nathan, Mordecai	20
Jellicoe, Sidney	6, 43, 45–46, 48	O'Connell, Robert	5
Jones, Henry Stuart	57	Obbink, Dirk D.	40
Katz, P.	43	Olearius, Gottfried	36
Keenan, James G.	39	Oliver, G. J.	144
Kennell, Nigel M.	144–45	Ottley, Richard R.	6
Kenyon, Frederic George	39	Parkin, Tim G.	125
Kircher, Conrad	19–23, 25–27, 33–34, 38, 61, 210	Perrin-Saminadayar, Eric	193, 198
		Pestman, Pieter Willem	137
Koenen, Ludwig	102	Pfochen, Sebastien	36
Kraft, Robert A.	18, 28, 33, 46–47, 49–50, 54, 211	Pietersma, Albert	49, 57
		Planck, Heinrich Ludwig	37
Kroeger, Paul R.	15	Porter, Stanley E.	37
Lagarde, Paul A. de	6–7	Pretzl, Otto	7
LaMontagne, Nathan	9	Pritchett, W. Kendrick	78, 89, 102
Landfester, Manfred	90	Rahlfs, Alfred	6, 11, 46, 53–54, 65–66, 113, 115, 164–66
Lange, Armin	4		
Launey, Marcel	146–47, 149, 151	Rajak, Tessa	163

Redpath, Henry	19, 24, 28, 38	Toury, Gideon	57
Reekmans, Tony	136	Tov, Emanuel	5, 18, 28, 33, 48–50, 54, 170, 177, 211
Rehkopf, Friedrich	53		
Rezetko, Robert	5	Trollope, William	37–38
Rice, E. E.	192	Tromm, Abraham	28–29, 34
Rist, John M.	186	Turner, Nigel	44
Robert, Louis	193, 197–98	Ulrich, Eugene	5
Robinson, Edward H.	37	Voelz, James W.	37
Rofé, Alexander	5	Walch, Jo Ern Imm	40
Roqueplo, Thérèse	12, 114	Wellhausen, Julius	4
Rosenbach, Zacharias	27–28, 210	Westermann, William L.	129
Sabin, Philip	93	Wettstein, J. J.	36
Saenz-Badillos, Angel	10	Wevers, John W.	47
Salem, Jean	186	Wheeler, Everett L.	83
Saville, Henry	24	White, John L.	130
Schleusner, Johann Friedrich	30–34, 56, 210	Whitehorne, J. E. G.	144–45
Schmidt, Mauricius	9	Wilcken, Ulrich	39
Scholl, Reinhold	128, 130, 133, 136–37	Winer, G. B.	37
Scott, Robert	57	Wright, Benjamin G.	57
Shear, Julia	100	Würthwein, Ernst	170
Sheldon, Rose Mary	83	Ziegler, Joseph	51
Silva, Moise's	51, 113		
Simcox, W. H.	38		
Simpson, Graham McGregor	130, 154, 156		
Soisalon-Soininen, Ilmari	7		
Stephens, Henry	35–36		
Stewart, Andrew F.	192		
Stock, St. George	42–43		
Storr, Gottlob Christian	36		
Straus, Jean A.	140		
Stuart, Moses	37		
Sugdures, George	23		
Swete, Henry Barclay	42		
Targarona Borras, Judit	10		
Taylor, Bernard	54		
Taylor, John R.	15		
Tcherikover, Victor A.	148, 174		
Thackeray, Henry St. John	2, 42–43, 48, 60, 163, 214		
Thompson, A. A.	202		
Thompson, Dorothy J.	102, 125, 138, 192		
Timmer, Jan	125		

www.ingramcontent.com/pod-product-compliance
Lightning Source LLC
Chambersburg PA
CBHW021348300426
44114CB00012B/1125